Biopolitics in Central and Eastern Europe in the 20th Century

The field of biopolitics encompasses issues from health and hygiene, birth rates, fertility and sexuality, life expectancy and demography to eugenics and racial regimes. This book is the first to provide a comprehensive view on these issues for Central and Eastern Europe in the twentieth century.

The cataclysms of imperial collapse, World War(s) and the Holocaust but also the rise of state socialism after 1945 provided extraordinary and distinct conditions for the governing of life and death. The volume collects the latest research and empirical studies from the region to showcase the diversity of biopolitical regimes in their regional and global context – from hunger relief for Hungarian children after the First World War to abortion legislation in communist Poland. It underlines the similarities as well, demonstrating how biopolitical strategies in this area often revolved around the notion of an endangered nation; and how ideological schemes and post-imperial experiences in Eastern Europe further complicate a 'western' understanding of democratic participatory and authoritarian repressive biopolitics.

The new geographical focus invites scholars and students of social and human sciences to reconsider established perspectives on the history of population management and the history of Europe.

Barbara Klich-Kluczewska is an Associate Professor at the Jagiellonian University in Cracow and a cultural historian of twentieth-century Poland. Her fields of research include history of family, history of sexuality and gender, biopolitics and history of experts' knowledge.

Joachim von Puttkamer is Director of the Imre Kertész Kolleg Jena at the Friedrich Schiller University Jena. His research focusses on nationalism and statehood in modern Central and Eastern Europe.

Immo Rebitschek is an Assistant Professor at the Department for Eastern European History at the Friedrich Schiller University Jena. He has published widely on the history of the Soviet procuracy in Stalinist Russia and is currently focussing his research on the history of famines in the late Russian empire.

Routledge Histories of Central and Eastern Europe

The nations of Central and Eastern Europe experienced a time of momentous change in the period following the Second World War. The vast majority were subject to Communism and central planning while events such as the Hungarian uprising and Prague Spring stood out as key watershed moments against a distinct social, cultural and political backcloth. With the fall of the Berlin Wall, German reunification and the break-up of the Soviet Union, changes from the 1990s onwards have also been momentous with countries adjusting to various capitalist realities. The volumes in this series will help shine a light on the experiences of this key geopolitical zone with many lessons to be learned for the future.

Hungary since 1945
Árpád von Klimó, translated by Kevin McAleer

Jewish Culture and Urban Form
A Case Study of Central Poland before the Holocaust
Małgorzata Hanzl

The Mentality of Partisans of the Polish Anti-Communist Underground 1944–1956
Mariusz Mazur

Biopolitics in Central and Eastern Europe in the 20th Century
Fearing for the Nation
Edited by Barbara Klich-Kluczewska, Joachim von Puttkamer and Immo Rebitschek

The Intellectual Foundations of Modern Ukraine
The Nineteenth Century
Andriy Zayarnyuk and Ostap Sereda

For more information about this series, please visit: https://www.routledge.com/Routledge-Histories-of-Central-and-Eastern-Europe/book-series/CEE

Biopolitics in Central and Eastern Europe in the 20th Century

Fearing for the Nation

Edited by
Barbara Klich-Kluczewska, Joachim von Puttkamer and Immo Rebitschek

Routledge
Taylor & Francis Group
LONDON AND NEW YORK

First published 2023
by Routledge
4 Park Square, Milton Park, Abingdon, Oxon OX14 4RN

and by Routledge
605 Third Avenue, New York, NY 10158

Routledge is an imprint of the Taylor & Francis Group, an informa business

British Library Cataloguing-in-Publication Data
A catalogue record for this book is available from the British Library

ISBN: 978-0-367-75123-4 (hbk)
ISBN: 978-0-367-75124-1 (pbk)
ISBN: 978-1-003-16108-0 (ebk)

DOI: 10.4324/9781003161080

Typeset in Sabon
by KnowledgeWorks Global Ltd.

Contents

Figures

Table

Introduction

Joachim von Puttkamer and Immo Rebitschek

Biopolitics has been a rich and fruitful field of research for historians during the last decades. The onset of the SarsCov-2 or 'COVID 19' pandemic not only brought its overriding relevance to the fore, it also shifted primary attention from control over human reproduction and fertility to broader issues. Shaking hands suddenly turned into a serious health risk, and basic hygiene became a matter of life and death. Governments were overrun with keeping up medical care, protecting vulnerable age cohorts, rushing the licensing of new vaccines and preparing for all-encompassing vaccination campaigns. Never before had governments demonstrated their biopower so massively by interfering deeply in everyday life on a global scale. At the same time, one could witness the limits of state capacity in this field and the need to rely on general compliance with rules that it was unable to enforce by administrative means alone. Since 2020, governments have had to strike a new balance between the fear of collapsing health systems and the promise of security. The foundations of modern statehood itself are at stake.

Most chapters of this volume were written during the first phase of the pandemic, but this was not their primary incentive. Instead, they refer to the annual conference of the Imre Kertész Kolleg, held in June 2019, on the topic: 'Fearing for the Nation: Biopolitics in Central and Eastern Europe in the Twentieth Century'. The intention was to bring together current research on various dimensions of biopolitics in twentieth-century Eastern Europe and to situate them in a broader European context. COVID-19 did not alter this premise. The experience of the past two years, however, did encourage us to place additional emphasis on the conceptual multiplicity of 'biopolitics' and the significance of an Eastern European setting.

The field of biopolitics as such encompasses a huge range of issues, from health and hygiene, birth rates, fertility and sexuality, life expectancy and demography, to eugenics and racial regimes (and it is probably not a coincidence that sensitivity for racial discrimination, another major field of biopolitics, has increased enormously precisely during the pandemic).[1] Since Michel Foucault, biopolitics has been deeply rooted in the basic issues of statehood and governmentality stemming from the eighteenth century,

DOI: 10.4324/9781003161080-1

which turned human life into an abstraction, thereby opening its basic features to categorization, optimization, intervention and coercion. The fierce debate and the protests surrounding the Polish abortion law during the pandemic might serve as an example for how these roots have a particular sway in Eastern Europe. The theoretical discourse on biopolitics provided little or no space for these experiences. Foucault and subsequent theorists omitted the question of socialist biopolitics altogether. Either they placed practices and ideas of twentieth-century Eastern Europe in a wider framework of totalitarianism, or they denied any specificity in comparison with Western liberal systems. Even Sergei Prozorov's plea to open the discourse to the 'socialist case' is, in actuality, a reference to the Soviet experience and its inadequate reflection in Western theoretical approaches.[2] The history of twentieth-century East Central and Eastern Europe shows remarkable particularities for each of these countries, thus encouraging a more differentiated look at the area. Research is rich on individual countries in Central and Eastern Europe, but there have been few attempts to bring them into dialogue, let alone to synthesize them.[3] While editors and authors alike are far from essentializing Eastern Europe, several common features stick out which are relevant to the overall topic.

When looking at the experience of East Central and Eastern Europe during the twentieth century, it appears that this area went through particularly virulent and often violent cataclysms. These developments also provided a very distinct set of conditions for the governing of life and death. Countries like Poland, Austria or Hungary shared a post-imperial space that went through social upheaval and a violent reshuffle of imperial borderland communities into nation states both during and after the First World War.[4] Situated at this point in time and space, citizens' bodies – just like language, territory and culture – were contested political objects for a (re)emerging nation (or a resurrected empire). In the biopolitics of Eastern European societies, it was a crucial feature that the primary focus was on the nation rather than the populace. Here, state activity in the field of biopolitics did not simply derive from the urge to secure social welfare and individual well-being. When small and large nations competed on a European scale, sometimes their very survival was at stake.

After 1945, this region bore the marks of another world war but also of the Holocaust. Eastern European governments and communities were re-formulating biological survival as a political antithesis to the past and mandate for the future. New ideological front lines between liberal democracy and state socialism added further tension to these debates. Life and death in state socialism had to fit the grander materialist schemes of class advancement, but it simultaneously left room for (and utilized) nationalist overtones, eugenic rationales, religious dogmatism and individual decision-making. One of the strengths of this volume lies in the fact that the spatial configuration and regional perspectives further complicate the outdated juxtaposition of democratic participatory and authoritarian repressive biopolitics. At the same time, it shows how, in this particular area, the changing nature of bio-power and biopolitics in Foucauldian terms cannot be directly linked to the advance of liberalism and state-sponsored self-regulation in an age of capitalism to the same extent as in the Western World. In the post-imperial setting of Eastern Europe, the establishment of state institutions that not only aimed to regulate individual behaviour but were capable of enforcing this claim, varied enormously, only to rise to an extreme point during the socialist period.

Coming from various, diverse backgrounds, the contributions are far from strictly adhering to a Foucauldian approach, though many of them are more or less explicitly informed by it. This volume, therefore, makes no attempt to propose a conclusive definition of biopolitics. Barbara Klich-Kluczewska elaborates on this issue (and its historiographical setting) to a full extent in her contribution. Rather, this volume seeks to benefit from both a broad and focussed concept of biopolitics, therefore allowing the authors to contribute distinct observations and definitions of their own (grounded in local experiences). Our observations herein are based on a wider Foucauldian understanding of biopolitics, however, the sample has been structured in relation to the particular experience of twentieth-century Eastern Europe. To be clear: we perceive biopolitics as a set of means, practices, ideas and institutions aimed at regulating and managing individual and collective bodies.[5] Within this framework, the chapters of this volume have been sorted according to re-creational aspects in particular and matters of health and population management in general.

Following up on Barbara Klich-Kluczewska's conceptual introduction, part one of the volume focuses on conflicts immediately tied to the issue of reproduction. From contraception to abortion, but also through marriage law and dynastic arrangements, reproductive rights and practices have long been subject to considerable regulation and discussion.[6] Female fertility and (the lack of) female agency take centre stage for the studies in this volume due to the fact that most policing technologies are inherently designed to regulate and interfere with female biology. Societies and governments in twentieth century East Central and Eastern Europe raised, enforced or negotiated their claim on potential life (and women's bodies) for the sake of communal and national survival, a thriving economy, or even racial supremacy. Herwig Czech demonstrates in the opening chapter of this section how notions of racial hygiene began to gain ground in interwar Austria, picking up on discourses on eugenics that date back to the late Habsburg Monarchy. Even though ideas varied widely across the fragmented political landscape, they helped to break ground for the key role which racial hygiene played after 1934. Natalia Aleksiun discusses the centrality of Jewish children to notions of national recovery among Jewish survivors in the immediate aftermath of the Holocaust. Parenthood and reproduction offered hope towards rebuilding the Jewish community in Poland and held out the promise of ultimate triumph over Hitler. Yet, the lack of organizational power and the onset of mass emigration thwarted such attempts. Agata Ignaciuk takes a close look at Catholic marriage preparation guides in state-socialist Poland. She argues that Catholic sexual expertise went hand in hand with sex education programmes that were sponsored by the communist state and its own experts. While positions on contraception and abortion remained irreconcilable, the triad of love–sex–marriage and the understanding of gender roles in a relationship provided common ground on matters of reproduction. Corina Doboş addresses the interlinkages between social categorization and pronatalist policies in socialist Romania during the same period. While the harsh ban on abortions addressed the entire population indistinctively, pronatalist incentives were designed to favour and support the urban working population and thus became instrumental in forging new social hierarchies and shaping a society that was presumed to be loyal to the socialist regime. Ivana Dobrivojević offers a broad overview of policies on family planning and abortion in socialist Yugoslavia. Looking at key policymakers and institutions, she argues that the liberalization of abortion was less the result of socialist modernity and female emancipation, as was being propagated by the authorities, and might rather be seen as the tacit admission that the state held little institutional power to actively regulate reproduction. In the concluding chapter of this section, Wannes Dupont again focuses on the Catholic Church and how it addressed global population growth and attempts to curb it. From the Vatican's point of view, the world was divided in biopolitical matters along the lines of a Protestant north, a communist east, a heterogeneous south and the Catholic sphere, consisting of Southern Europe, Latin America and the Philippines. While the Church outwardly remained firm in rejecting active family planning on a global scale, the chapter also shows fissures behind the scenes that came to divide the Church internally in the long run.

Part two of the book shifts to a wider understanding of biopolitics – beyond the sphere of procreation and reproduction. This segment features population management issues in relation to matters of health, nutrition and hygiene. Naturally, reproduction cannot be detached from these fields, yet this segment focuses more on the bodies in existence and less on the promise of new life. Friederike Kind-Kovács provides a borderline case in that regard. Her chapter inhabits a position between these two poles by addressing issues of preserving young life. Due to mal- and undernourishment, the lives of children and infants in Hungary after the First World War were at stake – and with them, the promise for a future healthy Hungarian nation. Kind-Kovács shows how feeding programs were an important biopolitical technique apparatus present at the social core of the nation at a point when humanitarians from Hungary, but especially from abroad, were in close cooperation over exploring the connection between diet and disease. The notion of food as 'preventive medicine' became a crucial factor in order to save both the Hungarian collective body and the individual bodies of children after the destitutions of the war.

The (re)emerging Polish state faced similar challenges both during and in the aftermath of the First World War. Łukasz Mieszkowski, therefore, focuses on a different biopolitical technology – in the literal sense of the word. Bathing and disinfection trains were used by European armies to combat bacteriological diseases that were spreading throughout European warzones. The case of the Polish disinfection trains shows how these sanitary measures, on the one hand, reflected not just a tactical tool against typhus but a political premise to cleanse the Polish army and the collective body from lice, dirt and other impurities. On the other hand, Mieszkowski shows how this premise had impractical, if not devastating, effects on the soldiers' hygiene and health. The coercive use of bathing and disinfection trains was less an epidemiological advancement than a means to enforce obedience and control over a collective body. Ewelina Szpak's contribution provides insights into disease and population control in Poland after 1945. Just like in 1918, major epidemics caused the new communist state to establish a functioning healthcare system for the rural populace. The 'medicalization and hygienization' of the countryside, however, proved to be an inconsistent and time-consuming project. As the medical infrastructure grew, so did the tensions among the rural population. The lack of resources and the distrust and indifference of the local peasantry towards these initiatives complicated the establishment and functioning of rural medical facilities. It turned out that biopolitical control could not be asserted through coercion alone but could only be reached through negotiation and persuasion. Radka Šustrová and Jakub Rákosník provide a similar case study with their take on communist Czechoslovakia. They examine a complex set of social policies in order to develop a holistic biopolitical perspective on socialist population management. After the war, children, parents, workers and senior citizens were the main targets of a wider socialist biopolitical strategy to foster socialist 'personalities' and an ultimately classless society. Šustrová and Rákosník show how, in this process, class and race served as central categories for a socialist biopolitical regime that targeted deviant social behaviour on the central level but left room for racial discrimination on the ground.

The last two contributions expand the frame of time and space and direct our attention to the longer trajectories of biopolitical disaster management: combating hunger and disease. Immo Rebitschek focuses on the major famines in Russian and Soviet history in order to discuss famine relief as a form of 'imperial biopolitics'. By drawing the focus on hunger relief in multiethnic peripheries, the biopolitical premise to 'let live and induce death' reveals continuities and changes in Russian and Soviet imperial policies. As the autocracy strove to maintain order through preserving life, the new rulers in the Kremlin observed and then seized the opportunity to enforce their will through 'inducing death'. Still, both St. Petersburg and Moscow sought to preserve the 'body of the empire' with little to no regard for the ethnic or national affiliation of their subjects. Malte Thießen approaches the other end of the geographical spectrum by engaging with the history of compulsory vaccination in twentieth-century Germany. His analysis of vaccination policies and debates sheds light on the biopolitical regimes in five different political systems. It reveals how changing (but also recurring) narratives helped to justify compulsory legislation. Vaccination programs were in all systems crucial to the establishment of social order, while the interplay of compulsion and persuasion refers to a complex relationship between state and society – even in authoritarian regimes.

Researching, providing and compiling scientific results in order to put a volume like this together was no easy feat in the midst of a global pandemic. The circumstances for scholarly work were anything but encouraging. Many of us had to meet deadlines in the face of lockdowns, quarantine, human tragedies and the literal threat of disease. We as editors owe gratitude to the authors and to all those who supported this project both from within and outside of the Imre Kertész Kolleg Jena. Gwendolyn Albert, Sarah Swift and Jasper Tilbury reliably produced excellent translations from Czech, German and Polish. Dylan Cram once again spent great time and effort in language- and copy-editing, supported by Laird McNeal and Jaime Hyatt in the final stages. Finally, we owe much to Daniela Gruber, who kept things running smoothly behind the scenes and who only intervened when they threatened to get out of hand. All flaws and errors that might have remained are, of course, our own.

Notes

1 Thomas Lemke, *Biopolitics: An Advanced Introduction*, trans. Eric Frederic Trump (New York and London: New York University Press, 2011).

2 Sergei Prozorov, 'Biopolitics and Socialism: Foucault, Agamben, Esposito', in *The Routledge Handbook of Biopolitics*, eds. Sergei Prozorov and Simona Rentea (London and New York: Routledge, 2020), 94–111.

3 Barbara Klich-Kluczewska provides a detailed account of her contribution to this volume. For more examples, see also Barbara Klich-Kluczewska, *Rodzina, tabu i komunizm w Polsce: 1956–1989* (Kraków: Wydawnictwo Libron, 2015); Marius Turda, ed., *The History of East-Central-European Eugenics: Sources and Commentaries* (London: Bloomsbury Publishing, 2017); Victoria Shmidt, *The Politics of Disability in Interwar and Socialist Czechoslovakia: Segregating in the Name of the Nation* (Amsterdam: Amsterdam University Press, 2019).

4 Mark Biondich, 'Eastern Borderlands and Prospective Shatter Zones: Identity and Conflict in East Central and Southeastern Europe on the Eve of the First World War', in *Legacies of Violence. Eastern Europe's First World War*, eds. Jochen Böhler, Włodzimierz Borodziej and Joachim von Puttkamer (München: Oldenbourg, 2014), S. 50; Jochen Boehler, *Civil War in Central Europe. 1918–1921: The Reconstruction of Poland* (Oxford/New York: Oxford University Press, 2018); Karen Barkey, 'Thinking about Consequences

of Empire', in *After Empire. Multiethnic Societies and Nation-Building. The Soviet Union and the Russian, Ottoman and Habsburg Empires*, eds. dies./ Mark von Hagen (Hrsg.) (Boulder: 1997), S. 104–112.

5 This definition is derived mainly from Marius Turda: Marius Turda, 'Eugenic and Biopolitical Studies in Romania: State-of-the-Art and Future Objectives', *Studia Universitatis Petru Maior. Historia* 9, no 1 (2009): 344.

6 See e.g. Modhumita Roy and Mary Thompson, eds., *The Politics of Reproduction. Adoption, Abortion, and Surrogacy in the Age of Neoliberalism* (Columbus: Ohio State University Press, 2019); Cynthia R. Daniels, *At Women's Expense. State Power and the Politics of Fetal Rights* (Cambridge, MA: Harvard University Press, 1993); Mary E. Fissell, *The Polics of Reproduction in Early Modern England* (New York: Oxford University Press, 2004); Christina Antenhofer and Elena Taddei, Fürstliche Körper und ihre Fortpflanzungsfähigkeit als Politikum: Begutachtungsformen im Kontext dynastischer Heiratspolitik (15.-16. Jahrhundert)', *Österreichische Zeitschrift für Geschichtswissenschaften* 31, no. 3 (2020): 28–53.

1 Is Biopower Something to Be Afraid Of?

Biopolitics as a Research Category in Historiography

Barbara Klich-Kluczewska

Introduction

> [W]hat kinds of research problems and questions legitimate or undermine the choice of history as the dominant and privileged method of creating [knowledge about the past]? Thus, for some it will be, for example, global capitalism, neo-colonialism, biopolitics, poverty, transnationalism, migration, diaspora, hybrid identities, for others global warming, environmental degradation, interspecies relations, and for still others the sacred and religion, democracy, justice, human dignity, human rights (as well as the rights of animals, things, or nature).[1]

According to Ewa Domańska, a historian and theorist of history who in 2013 reviewed the new trends in historiography in the twenty-first century, biopolitics is one of those important social phenomena that will determine the shape of this discipline in the near future.[2] However, somewhat tellingly, she locates biopolitics far away from democracy and human rights, placing it together with poverty on the one hand and neo-colonialism on the other, hence with phenomena that arouse justified social anxiety. Domańska seems to internalize the fears of the historians whose statements she has analyzed, stating that the humanities are looking for new ways to legitimize their research by referring, among others, to the challenges posed by 'a dehumanizing biopolitics and trans-humanizing biotechnological progress'. This statement by an experienced methodologist makes it abundantly clear that the understanding of biopolitics dominant today, and not just in historiography, should be associated not with Foucauldian biopower but with what Thomas Lemke has called 'technocentric biopolitics', that is, 'the collective negotiation of, and agreement on, the social acceptability of what is technologically possible'.[3] This preeminent understanding of biopolitics, which borders on bioethics, is – Domańska argues – the result of the development of genetic and reproductive technologies. Alternatively, this contemporary 'dehumanizing biopolitics' could also be associated with 'ecological biopolitics', which emerged in the 1960s and 1970s as a 'policy of securing and protecting the global natural foundation

DOI: 10.4324/9781003161080-2

of life'.[4] It raises the issue of the consequences of the growing number of people on earth, the critical food situation and hunger, pollution and the shortage of raw materials and energy'.[5] Even if we transfer biopolitics to other, for instance, methodological, contexts where it functions very well today in the broadly understood humanities, we should remember that, despite Michel Foucault's best efforts, biopolitics has become a permanent fixture in a world of imagery giving rise to suspicion; imagery associated with soulless engineering that can sow the seeds of destruction.

Should we, then, be afraid of the category of biopolitics? Are we able to break away from the seemingly permanent negative associations it has in the public imagination? What role does Foucault-inspired biopolitics (even if in some cases it severs the link with him) play in contemporary historiographical research?

In this chapter, whilst being aware of the particular aversion towards biopolitics felt by the public and professionals alike, I would like to draw attention to the pathways along which the methodology of historical research using this uncomfortable and ambiguous notion has developed and is developing. In what contexts do historians most readily employ this category? How should we assess its potential as a future research tool? For not only does biopolitics provoke new questions about the past, but its popularity as a research tool among historians of the modern era continues to grow.

What Is Biopolitics?

> A few years ago biopolitics was known only to a limited number of experts, but it is used today in many different disciplines and discourses. Beyond the limited domain of specialists, it is also attracting increasing interest among the general public. The term is used to discuss political asylum policies, as well as the prevention of AIDS and questions of demographic change. ... Some argue strongly that 'biopolitics' is necessarily bound to rational decision-making and the democratic organization of social life, while others link the term to eugenics and racism. The term figures prominently in texts of the Old Right but is also used by representatives of the New Left. It is used by both critics and advocates of biotechnological progress, by committed Marxists and unapologetic racists.[6]

Starting with Thomas Lemke's well-known but very accurate claim about biopolitics, let us note the equally well-known fact that biopolitics as a paradigm for studying power relations can, and has been, used to analyze both liberal democracies and totalitarian states. It has been particularly applied to analyses of the Third Reich on account of the special role that racial ideology and eugenics played in that system.[7] Therefore, modern democratic states, and authoritarian regimes, have had the potential to use biopolitical mechanisms in their national administration systems. For me, the starting point is the definition of biopolitics proposed by Michel Foucault, namely, that it is a 'specific modern form of exercising power'; 'a constellation in which modern human and natural sciences and the normative concepts that emerge from them structure political action and determine its goals', where human life is subject to constant rational evaluation.[8] This, of course, requires knowledge that makes it possible to manage not only individuals but also collective entities, i.e. populations; such knowledge is offered primarily by statistics and demography, medicine, social sciences and sexology. Knowledge in this area allows for the creation of various strategies to correct errors and develop optimal solutions through the implementation of specific normative, disciplinary or therapeutic solutions.

At this juncture, it is worth mentioning the notion of prerogatives of power, which is crucial to Foucault's conception of biopolitics. Andrey Makarychev and Alexandra Yatsik explain it as follows:

> Michel Foucault conceptualized the crux of biopower as a transition from the right to take life (the sovereign power's prerogative) to the state's investments in administering life, which is the crux of biopower. This shift implies a transfer from disciplining the individual body to disciplining the population as a whole through managing health, hygiene, nutrition, birth, and sexuality. In this sense, biopolitics develops the so-called apparatuses of control aimed at improving, promoting, and managing life, which becomes a matter of government, thus making life no longer a private affair, but a matter of policy.[9]

Analyses of biopolitics have long testified to the impassable boundary between biopolitics practised under democratic conditions as opposed to authoritarian conditions. In terms of the interactions between specific social groups and individuals, (bio)politics in a democracy was, unlike the top-down pressure applied in authoritarian states, more likely to 'live a life of its own' and be subject to change, not always following the path prescribed by technocrats. This brings us to the phenomenon known as participatory biopolitics, which stands in complete contrast to the seemingly unmodifiable (bio)politics favoured by autocratic regimes. Social research on sterilization in the United States and Sweden has painfully shaken this bipolar picture. Detailed historical studies has had a similar impact. As Erik G. Huneke points out in his analysis of family counselling in communist East Germany, studies have shown that authorities at various levels abandoned repressive policies and promoted independent birth control supported by access to contraceptives, sex therapists and family planning advisors. Instead of imposing bans or issuing orders, the advocates of this type of 'soft' biopolitics only had (have) to suggest certain solutions.[10] The theory of the potential negotiability of biopolitics is fundamentally closer to Foucault's conception of it given his belief that 'power' operates not through negative repression but rather through the creation of 'positive effects'. It, therefore, acts as an inspiration and encouragement, offering possibilities and creating role models and desires in the spaces of everyday reality (according to some commentators, biopolitics, in this case, becomes even more dangerous – diffuse, hidden and therefore suspect).

From Eugenics to Negative Biopolitics

One of the most important research fields traditionally associated with the impact of biopolitics on populations is the historiography of eugenics and racism. In principle, the concept of biopolitics itself did not at first radically change the ways in which eugenic phenomena were analyzed in the countries of Western Europe and the United States, and later – after 1989 – in Central, Eastern and Southeastern Europe. It mainly shifted the focus of research away from attempts to reconstruct the world of eugenic movements and towards the tools used by states to exert eugenic impact on populations.[11] Biopolitics also acted as a link for comparative research within European countries and, as such, was used as a kind of metaphor to connect the different cases analyzed in study collections or during conferences. Often it served as a kind of umbrella which made it possible to link the practical impact of eugenics in different disciplines, such as psychiatry or social policy. Finally, biopolitics channelled the interest of scholars towards the question of its relationship with modernity and knowledge.[12] However, it did not do so consistently and was never applied as a means of conceptualizing research. Nevertheless, in time, such attempts were made, and some of them proved very important. It is worth noting here, for example, one analysis relating to the United Kingdom[13] and another relating to Romania.[14] An interesting, in-depth reflection on the interrelationships between eugenics and biopolitics was put forward by Marius Turda, a researcher of Central and Southern European countries in the first half of the twentieth century. Turda writes:

> It must be emphasised that between 1860 and 1960 eugenics became part of a larger biopolitical agenda, which included social hygiene, racial hygiene, public health and family planning as well as racial research on social and ethnic minorities. Often, eugenics served as a vehicle for transmitting a social and political message that transcended political differences and opposing ideological camps. Moreover, eugenics and biopolitics were as diverse ideologically as they were geographically: they were adhered to by professional and political elites across Europe, from West to East, irrespective of their political and cultural context.[15]

Biopolitics is treated here as a much broader concept than eugenics, but it still provides a political context for the term. Biopolitics and eugenics seem to go hand in hand. Turda understands biopolitics itself as: 'an extensive complex of ideas, practices, and institutions focused on the care, regulation, disciplining, improvement, and shaping of individual bodies and the collective "body" of nations'.[16]

For Turda, the introduction of the concept of biopolitics was a consequence of many years of research on eugenics, but in the end, the Romanian case proved most important. In his article 'The Nation as Object: Race, Blood, and Biopolitics in Interwar Romania', which appeared in *Slavic Review* in 2007, Turda developed a theme which Maria Bucur had touched upon a few years earlier. Bucur recalled that in 1926 the Romanian hygienist and eugenicist Ioliou Moldovan had introduced the concept of biopolitics into public discourse in Romania with the publication of his book *Biopolitica*. She described that work as a manifesto which called for Romanian state policy to be based on biological principles, which would ultimately lead to a complete reorganization of politics in the country.[17] Moldovan's biopolitics signified in practice a national mission to do everything possible in order to improve the 'racial quality' of the nation. To describe the latter, Moldovan employed the metaphor of a living organism that was supposed to function in accordance with the laws of biology. A similar approach had been taken six years earlier by Rudolf Kjellén, considered to be the author of the concept of biopolitics and, like Moldovan, an advocate of viewing the state as an organism. For Turda, what was critically important in Romania was that 'the relationship between nation and state was turned into a specific scientific form of knowledge, one based on biology. Biopolitics thus operated through investigations of biological processes regulating the triadic relationship between individual, nation and state'.[18] Thus, according to Moldovan, biopolitics was to become synonymous with the national policy of the Romanian state.

Turda's assumption was that (with a few exceptions) biopolitics had not been given the attention it deserved in studies on Romania (having been overshadowed by the relationship between the nation and religion or by intergenerational conflicts), and that anthropological and serological studies had been unjustly marginalized. As he wrote:

> anthropological and serological definitions of national belonging do not make other debates on the nation less important, but they do indicate that the origins of eugenic programs of biopolitical rejuvenation (...) are to be sought not only in 'critiques of parliamentary democracy and liberal politics' (as Maria Bucur has argued) but more importantly in the attempt to achieve a new national body amid alleged domestic spiritual decline ('modernity's ontological crisis' according to Roger Griffin) and unfavorable international conditions (territorial losses and war).[19]

Historians who followed this path naturally paid special attention to the links between biopolitics and modernity (usually through the medium of fascism). Such links had previously been noticed by Zygmunt Bauman and Roger Griffin, who pointed out that biopolitics should not be treated as an episode independent of the changes in social and political life, but as an integral part of European modernity.[20] Going down this route, some historians and political scientists refused from the outset to use the concept of biopolitics in the context of traditional societies (including the countries of Central and Eastern Europe and Southeastern Europe), restricting its application to 'modern and more homogenous' countries.[21]

Biopolitics as an Alternative to the Totalitarian Paradigm

In recent decades, thanks to Sergei Prozorov, biopolitics has become not only a kind of alternative tool for analyzing totalitarian systems (which has, at least to some extent, influenced the view of European totalitarianisms overall) but also – and this is especially important from a methodological point of view – a tool for criticizing the ways in which biopolitics has been used to date. These two aspects of Prozorov's analysis might constitute the final breakthrough and thus help to sever the hitherto close ties between biopolitics on the one hand and the historiography of eugenics and racial ideology on the other.

Sergei Prozorov is a political scientist at the University of Helsinki whose research focuses on political philosophy and international relations.[22] He has used biopolitics to analyze Stalinism and the system of terror and, to some extent, current state policy in the Russian Federation.

His starting point is the observation that theorists of biopolitics have ignored the Soviet experience, pointing only to some of its similarities with Nazism. In his view, not even Michel Foucault, Giorgio Agamben or Roberto Esposito noticed the differences between the Nazi and the Soviet experience. It is through biopolitics that the essence of the system initiated at the time of the Great Breakthrough (1928–1932) can be revealed. The key question that accompanies all of Prozorov's (largely not empirical, it must be emphasized) research is the question of the coexistence of development plans and plans for the protection of human life, which in practice end in mass death, i.e. the coexistence of biopolitics and thanatopolitics:

> [it] examines the experience of Stalinism as an important case for the study of biopolitics that helps resolve a problem preoccupying scholars from Foucault onward: the proximity of biopolitics to its opposite, the thanatopolitics of the mass production of death. How is it that a mode of power presenting itself in terms of care, augmentation, and intensification of life so frequently end up negating life itself?[23]

Crucial for us is the indication by Prozorov of new pathways for interpreting biopolitics. As mentioned earlier, this essentially involves a rejection of mainstream thinking about the subject. That thinking was mostly employed to study liberal democracies, but lately also – and perhaps even more frequently – to study totalitarianisms and authoritarianisms, mainly

Nazism and eugenics. According to Prozorov, this is a downright distortion of Foucault's basic idea:

> The application of the Foucauldian theory of biopolitics to the twentieth-century experience of totalitarianism has been curiously one-sided. Michel Foucault's original thesis about the historical shift from the negative and repressive power of the sovereign toward the positive and productive power over life has been ceaselessly addressed, restated, and corrected in the context of European fascism and particularly German Nazism. (...) This omission illustrates a wider lack of interest in the phenomenon of Stalinism in contemporary philosophy and political theory, which either subsume it along with Nazism under the vague rubric of totalitarianism or dismiss it as a modern version of traditional Russian despotism.[24]

Prozorov also rejects a feature of biopolitics which is usually considered to be decidedly positive, i.e. its universality for analyzing power relations under conditions of modernity, the latter being determined by such factors as the development of knowledge, rational management, the growth of bureaucracy, etc. In his highly engaging approach, biopolitics is relevant to describing only those systems that assume a complete social transformation: the death of the old life and the birth of the new; the birth of a new individual. This is also, in Prozorov's view, in keeping with Foucault's original assumptions. Importantly, Stalinism, because it envisaged changing an entire population, offered a fundamentally positive transformation in all aspects of human life: hygiene, sexuality, friendship, diet, work, etc.

And here we arrive at what I believe to be the most significant shift in thinking about biopolitics. Prozorov criticizes the reduction of biopolitics to biological life (including medicine and social care), writing, somewhat caustically, that: 'after all, there are only so many ways to clean one's teeth or treat venereal disease, even for a Bolshevik'. Despite the fact that the idea of 'rebuilding life from scratch' remains hugely interesting, it is difficult, from a historical point of view, to accept the statement that:

> Nor can these similarities be traced to the idea of modernity: there is nothing specifically 'modern' about the governance of health, reproductive behavior, physiological processes, or bodily demeanor, which dates back to ancient history and about which we have ample evidence from the political thought of Antiquity. The specificity of biopolitics cannot simply be defined by its object (the biological aspect of human existence) or domain (the medico-social field of intervention). Not every governmental regulation of infectious diseases, sexual deviance, hygienic practices or modes of appearance of its subjects is biopolitical; otherwise, the concept of biopolitics would be so general as to be coextensive with human history as such.[25]

Prozorov thus seems to undermine the thesis, central to Foucault's theory, about the transformation in the mechanisms of exercising power initiated by the Enlightenment and their historical contexts.

From a historical point of view, what is certainly interesting about Prozorov's work is that it opens up new areas hitherto untouched by biopolitical analysis. His ideas will no doubt be invoked by scholars who wish to go beyond the 'negative biopolitics' of the first half of the twentieth century. A broader acceptance of Prozorov's point of view, however, will be hampered by two of his assumptions: first, biopolitics is to be used to describe a unique system that presupposed the complete reconstruction (destruction) of the existing life of the population, and, in Prozorov's view, only the Stalinist system did this. More important, however, is his complete rejection of the biological context of biopower, which will inevitably deprive that concept of uniqueness and perhaps interest.

The Potential Negotiability of Biopolitics: The Tactics of Biopower in the Polish People's Republic

As my previous research on biopolitics in post-war Poland shows, an interesting example of the application of this concept is participatory biopolitics, which was mentioned in the introduction. It also shows, however, that it is necessary to remain cautious when referring to the Foucauldian model or to treat it very flexibly (as Prozorov does, for instance). For in the case of communist Poland, we are dealing not so much with the encouragement of certain activities that fall within the remit of biopolitical impact but – conversely – with intimidation, or rather, with individuals (and thus the whole nation) being kept in a 'state of fear'. A prime example of this type of biopolitics was the policy towards abortion. In both the USSR and Poland, abortion was – officially, at least – viewed in positive terms, but in order to discourage it, the authorities used persuasion rather than coercion. In the USSR in the late 1950s, hundreds of lectures were organized and thousands of posters were printed warning of the dangers of abortion. It was argued that abortion was a medical procedure that could irreversibly deprive a woman and her partner of the chance to experience parenthood. In order to inform the public about the harmfulness of abortion for women's health (haemorrhages, infections, infertility), the Polish Society for Planned Motherhood followed the same path, using not only traditional methods to spread health propaganda (newsletters, handbooks, radio programmes), but also popular culture, such as television series. In this instance, controlling the population by means of 'management through fear' seems to be a halfway solution between 'participatory biopolitics' and management through violence. What is particularly interesting in the case of biopolitics in Poland is the use of linguistic mechanisms borrowed from religious rhetoric.

Furthermore, the example of post-war Poland reveals the special situation of biopolitics after the Second World War, its complexity and heterogeneity. I would like to draw attention to examples of biopolitical phenomena that were typical of the policy of intimidation. These included, firstly, the echoes of eugenics policy that were prevalent in the 1950s and 1960s, and secondly, the efforts to map deviations and pathologies. These examples point to the deep fissures and inconsistencies of biopolitics within the context of a single state and single population, but they nevertheless represent a particular example of participatory biopolitics, which, in my view, was, to some extent, typical of post-war Central and Eastern Europe.

Echoes of Eugenics or 'Resource Optimization'

During the first and last period of Poland's limited anti-natalist policy, i.e. in the 1960s, the idea of controlling the body through discipline and exclusion seemingly came back into favour among physicians and sex therapists or at least became part of official public discourse. Because the broad range of measures aimed at disseminating chemical and mechanical contraceptives among Polish women proved ineffective, there emerged the radical idea of imposing special sanctions on those women who persistently 'resist the use of any reasonable preventative method and instead repeatedly submit themselves to abortion' (according to doctors, the abortions could not be justified). Those sanctions were to include, for instance, an additional fee for carrying out the procedure. At that time, especially in the second half of the 1960s, there were also calls to improve the quality of contraceptives manufactured in Poland, to install automatic contraceptive dispensers, and to import and distribute foreign contraceptives. The tendency to penalize both men and women who neglected the rational regulation of their own fertility was, along with the promotion of contraception, a very characteristic feature of the first, quite important stage in the development of the Planned Parenthood Association (Towarzystwo Rozwoju Rodziny). The motions passed at the Association's First Congress and the detailed motions proposed at its Second Congress revealed a range of ideas for controlling those who, it was felt, should be deprived of the right to reproduce. The sanctions to be applied to them were also considered. In Foucauldian terms, such individuals were to be excluded from the biopolitical body for the socio-economic good of the community. Some of these measures clearly recalled the pre-war eugenics tradition. The Association's activists – mainly gynaecologists and midwives – as well as journalists and directors of state-owned enterprises tried in the mid-1960s to work with patients in order to prevent births in a 'tuberculosis-friendly environment'. Voluntary sterilization and certain forms of forced sterilization were proposed, the latter for 'schizophrenics, imbeciles, and alcoholics, when such persons already have several children'. In addition, the Association confirmed its plan – widely discussed in the press – to introduce compulsory premarital examinations for both future spouses (the plan was eventually scrapped).

Whereas in Poznań, the focus was on the aforementioned community of tuberculosis sufferers, activists in Cracow identified poor mothers with multiple children as the target of their efforts to promote 'rational fertility', thus combining this activity with research on new contraceptives. The project was carried out under the auspices of the Gynaecological Disorders Clinic of the Academy of Medicine in Cracow:

> The [female] patients assigned for these examinations are selected from low-income backgrounds and have numerous children; they cannot bear the costs themselves and will instead participate in scientific experiments. Given the cost of rendering of such services, a separate subsidy for the Clinic will be necessary in order to balance the budget. It is expected that within a half-year period experiments will be carried out on fifty female patients, the value of those experiments being approximately 400 zloty.[26]

From today's perspective, it is difficult to say whether such activities actually promoted the Association as an avant-garde institution specializing in family research or whether, on the contrary, they brought it enemies. Nevertheless, such biopolitical practices disappeared after new pronatalist policies were introduced in the 1970s and 1980s.

Pathologization and the Stigma of Deviance

Most of my own research over the past 10 years has been devoted to those areas of family life which from 1956 onwards, contemporaries and experts referred to as *social pathologies*. The popularity of the term 'pathology' should be sought in the sociological debates of the 1970s and 1980s, in particular, concerning the alleged 'deep crisis of the family'. In those days, sociologists were not predicting the decline of the family. There was talk of a crisis, of course, but in the socialist system, experts regarded the family to be an integral part of the social fabric, while marriage and having children occurred in the natural course of things and were an important aspect of people's sense of personal fulfilment. In any case, until the mid-1980s, Polish sociologists invariably spoke of family values being embedded in the social consciousness of Poles.

However, an in-depth analysis reveals a certain schizophrenia in sociological research on the family. On the one hand, this was connected with the unrealistic glorification of the Polish family as a socialist family – a theme which can be found in many works, especially from the last two decades of the People's Republic. On the other hand, there was a rapid growth in research on phenomena that were described as deviations from social norms or – to use the nomenclature of the time – 'family pathologies'. I call this situation schizophrenic because the conclusions from these two strands of scholarship were rarely juxtaposed. Research on domestic violence, divorce, single mothers and alcoholism, which was increasingly detailed and wide-ranging, focussed strictly on pathological families and did not have a major impact on how the Polish family was perceived as such. This safe separation was bolstered by the fact that it was often lawyers or sociologists of law, rather than sociologists of the family, who studied pathologies. The intensification of research on pathologies and deviance even fuelled the anxiety of some observers and participants of the debate in the 1970s.

Considering all the breakthroughs in discourse on the family that occurred in Poland in the mid-1970s, we can certainly speak of the development of research on divorce and domestic violence. It would seem reasonable to risk the thesis that the debates of the 1970s were a visible manifestation of the policy of individualization of all family members, of equal opportunities, and of the new emancipatory policy towards women and children. But this is not entirely true. Each of those debates was still essentially a debate about the 'pathologies of social life', whose existence in the public space did not transform thinking about individual rights in the 1970s. This lack of individualistic thinking had a huge impact on the way the suffering of excluded people and their social marginalization was perceived. Divorce and single motherhood remained 'pathogenic factors' which – this time using rational knowledge – even reinforced the image of the 'normal healthy family'.

The most important result of this approach, in other words, the strong insistence on the separation of normality from 'pathology', remained a natural constraint on the vibrant and free demographic development of the country.

Conclusion

The concept of "biopolitics" undoubtedly continues to play today an incomparably less important role in historiography than in the case of related disciplines, such as political science or social science. Nevertheless, its presence seems to be more and more noticeable, and its application both in the field of historiosophy and in empirical studies - interesting and promising. From the perspective of research on East-Central European societies in the twentieth century, the increasing presence of biopolitics as a research tool also seems to be evidence of an intensification of searching for new research paths in various comparative contexts. Finally, the permanent coexistence of significantly different models of understanding and applying biopolitics in the processes of analyzing past phenomena is particularly noteworthy.

Notes

1 E. Domańska, 'Wiedza o przeszłości–perspektywy na przyszłość', *Kwartalnik Historyczny* 120, no. 2 (2013): 230–231.
2 This chapter was translated by Jasper Tilbury.

3 Thomas Lemke, *Biopolitics: An Advanced Introduction*, translated by Eric Frederic Trump (New York and London: New York University Press, 2011), 26.
4 Ibid., 23.
5 Ibid., 26.
6 Ibid., 1 (Introduction).
7 Richard F. Wetzell refers the notion of nazi biopolitics "to the complex of ideas, policies, and practices that are concerned with the regulation of bodies, both at the individual level and at the collective level of the national population; a complex that, in the case of the Nazi regime, ranged from public health to eugenic and racial policy, including the Holocaust". See Richard F. Wetzell 'Eugenics, Racial Science, and Nazi Biopolitics: Was There a Genesis of the 'Final Solution' from the Spirit of Science?', in *Beyond the Racial State: Rethinking Nazi Germany*, eds. Devin Pendas, Mark Roseman, and Richard F. Wetzell (Cambridge, New York: Cambridge University Press, 2017), p. 147.
8 Lemke, *Biopolitics*, 33.
9 Andrey Makarychev and Alexandra Yatsyk 'Biopolitics and National Identities: Between Liberalism and Totalization', *Nationalities Papers* 45, no. 1 (2017): 1–7.
10 See Erik G. Huneke, Morality, Law, and the Socialist Sexual Self in the German Democratic Republic, 1945–1972, PhD diss., University of Michigan, Ann Arbor, 2013, https://deepblue.lib.umich.edu/handle/2027.42/97942.
11 Björn M. Felder and Paul J. Weindling eds., *Baltic eugenics: bio-politics, race and nation in interwar Estonia, Latvia and Lithuania 1918-1940* (Amsterdam, New York: Rodopi, 2013); Magdalena Gawin and Kamila Uzarczyk eds., *Eugenika - Biopolityka – Państwo* (Warszawa: Neriton, 2010).
12 For a bibliography of research on eugenics, cf.: Paul J. Weindling, 'The History and Historiography of Eugenics' in *Handbook of the Historiography of Biology. Historiographies of Science*, ed. M.R. Dietrich, M.E. Borrello, and O. Harman (Cham: Springer, 2021); Marius Turda and Paul J. Weindling, 'Eugenics, Race and Nation in Central and Southeast Europe, 1900–1940: A Historiographic Overview', in *Blood and Homeland: Eugenics and Racial Nationalism in Central and Southeast Europe, 1900–1940*, eds. Marius Turda and Paul J. Weindling, NED – New edition, 1, (Budapest: Central European University Press, 2007), 1–20; Maria Bucur, *Eugenics and Modernization in Interwar Romania* (Pittsburgh: University of Pittsburgh Press, 2002).
13 Clare Hanson, 'Biopolitics, Biological Racism and Eugenics', in *Foucault in an Age of Terror*, eds. Stephen Morton and Steven Bygrave (London: Palgrave Macmillan, 2008), 106–117; Edward Ross Dickinson, 'Biopolitics, Fascism, Democracy: Some Reflections on Our Discourse about "Modernity"', *Central European History* 37, no. 1 (2004): 1–48.
14 Marius Turda, 'The Nation as Object: Race, Blood and Biopolitics in Interwar Romania', *Slavic Review* 66, no. 3 (2007): 413–441.
15 Marius Turda, 'Eugenic and Biopolitical Studies in Romania: State-of-the-Art and Future Objectives', *Studia Universitatis Petru Maior. Historia* 9, no. 1 (2009): 344.
16 Ibid.
17 Bucur 2002, 83.
18 Turda 2009, 413.
19 Ibid., 441.
20 For more, see, for instance, Marius Turda, *Modernism and Eugenics* (Basingstoke: Palgrave Macmillan, 2010).
21 Piotr Madajczyk emphasized that in the case of traditional societies, one should speak not of biopolitics but of ethnopolitics. The distinction between these two concepts is unclear, especially as it is argued that biopolitics and

ethnopolitics are based on the same principle: disciplining the individual body and imposing norms on the whole body of the nation. Nevertheless, these two types of 'social engineering' ostensibly differed in their methods. While in biopolitics, it was necessary to strengthen the valuable members of the community and exclude those deemed biologically worthless using negative eugenics, positive eugenics, education and public hygiene, ethnopolitics included homogenizing measures such as ethnic cleansing. See P. Madajczyk, *Marzenie o narodzie doskonałym. Między biopolityką a etnopolityką* (Warszawa: Neriton, 2017).

22 Sergei Prozorov, *The Biopolitics of Stalinism: Ideology and Life in Soviet Socialism* (Edinburgh: Edinburgh University Press, 2016).

23 Sergei Prozorov, 'Foucault and Soviet Biopolitics', *History of the Human Sciences* 27, no. 5 (2014): 6–25.

24 Sergei Prozorov, 'Living Ideas and Dead Bodies: The Biopolitics of Stalinism', *Alternatives: Global, Local, Political* 38, no. 3 (2013): 208.

25 Ibid., 210.

26 The National Archives in Cracow (Archiwum Narodowe w Krakowie), Planned Parenthood Association (Towarzystwo Rozwoju Rodziny) 1435/16, Record 14/65 of 15 November 1965.

Section I

Issues of Reproduction

2 Regenerating the Nation

Eugenics and Racial Hygiene in Early Twentieth-Century Austria

Herwig Czech

Introduction

In Austria, as in other European countries, the First World War was a decisive catalyst for the dissemination and at least partial application of biopolitical ideas and practices in many fields of scholarship, politics and society.[1] This contribution concerns itself with eugenics/racial hygiene as a central (but not the sole) paradigm within the biopolitical field.[2] The Austrian example is striking in several respects. The viability of the rump state constituted by the dismantling of the Habsburg monarchy was debated and interpreted not only in political and economic terms but also with reference to demographic, ethnic and biopolitical concepts. Fears of biological decay crystallized around the city of Vienna with its two million people, the political, economic and intellectual centre of the new republic. At the same time, the city became the location of a large-scale social experiment, 'Red Vienna', that caught the attention of the world. This project and its conscious pursuit of deep social transformation was abruptly ended by the corporatist Austro-Fascist state installed in 1933/34, when the politically polarized landscape that had characterized the republic founded in 1918 was blanketed over by the enforcement of dictatorship. Austria's annexation to Germany in March 1938 marked the beginning of a further phase of radical biopolitical change, now under the banner of National Socialist racial hygiene and the Holocaust.[3]

The Beginnings of a Eugenics Movement in Austria

Racial hygiene ideas were taken up and shared early on in Austria, for example, by the anthropologist Rudolf Pöch (1870–1921) and the hygienist Max von Gruber (1853–1927). Both men belonged to the Zürich circle of the founder of German racial hygiene, Alfred Ploetz (1860–1940), by as early as the late 1890s.[4] The forensic psychiatrist Emil Raimann, an assistant of Julius Wagner-Jauregg for many years, demanded in 1907 that 'persons with constitutional mental illness, but also psychopathic inferiors, should not have children' but he objected to the eugenic castration proposed by figures such as Paul Näcke in Germany.[5] In the State Parliament of Lower Austria, the avoidance of marriages was called for 'of which it

DOI: 10.4324/9781003161080-4

can be foreseen that they will beget a mentally deranged generation that must fall victim to a lifetime of misery and wretchedness'.[6] The economist Michael Hainisch (1858–1940) was also influenced by Ploetz and affirmed his commitment to racial hygiene; as President of Austria from 1920 to 1928, he can be counted (along with Julius Tandler) among the movement's most politically influential exponents.[7]

An early voice in the eugenic discourse in Austria – later to become the most influential voice of all – was that of the hygienist Heinrich Reichel (1876–1943), who is reported to have spoken 'well before the war [...] about public nutrition and the significance of racial hygiene in public lectures and also to have written about them and about issues in medicine and population statistics'.[8] He expressed the view that racial hygiene should be the departure point for social policy as early as 1912 in a report on the International Hygiene Exhibition held the year before in Dresden.[9] The lecture Reichel gave on racial hygiene to the Natural Sciences Association at the University of Vienna (Naturwissenschaftlicher Verein an der Universität Wien) in 1913 is likely to have been among the very first scholarly talks delivered on the subject in Austria. Promoting scientific research into heredity was the most important goal proclaimed by Reichel in this lecture; at this point he did not yet mention any concrete measures.[10]

Several organizations with a specific focus on eugenics emerged before the outbreak of the First World War. An organization with German nationalist leanings was founded in the spring of 1913, the German-Austrian Counselling Service for National Welfare (Deutsch-Österreichische Beratungsstelle für Volkswohlfahrt). In November of the same year, the Sociological Society founded in Vienna in 1907 (by Rudolf Goldscheid, among others) gained a new (albeit short-lived) Section of Social Biology and Eugenics (Sektion für Sozialbiologie und Eugenik). Under its president Julius Tandler, the Section leaned towards social democracy and neo-Lamarckian positions. Eugenics also found a bridgehead in the Arbeiterabstinentenbund (Workers' Abstinence Society), with its leading member Rudolf Wlassak (1865–1930) also coming under the influence of Ploetz.[11]

Elements of eugenic/racial hygiene thinking were thus already present in various fields (including population policy, anthropology, social welfare and public health) before the First World War, but they had not yet taken on hegemonic character. The dominance of Catholicism in Austria was one factor inhibiting their breakthrough. The fragmentation of the political landscape and the obstacles it threw up for coordinated approaches was another. In addition, several intellectual movements competed against the premises of eugenics to some degree – especially Goldscheid's conception of the economics of human beings (Menschenökonomie), which had adherents in socialist circles,[12] and an anti-Malthusianism (see below) that was reflected in a strong focus on quantitative aspects of population policy in biopolitical discourses. The adoption of racial hygiene concepts was additionally impeded by the strong presence of neo-Lamarckian positions in

Austria and a widespread propensity to reject the view advanced by August Weismann, especially of the mechanism for transmitting inherited characteristics being essentially unalterable and not subject to significant influence from external factors.[13]

Although eugenic arguments increasingly gained ground, low birth rates remained the central issue in population policy discourses in Austria up to the end of the 1930s. Leopold Moll, who headed the Reich Institute for Maternity and Infant Care founded in Vienna in 1912 (Reichsanstalt für Mutter- und Säuglingsfürsorge), highlighted two phenomena as 'major and alarming harms to the body of the nation and the state' in 1913: the declining birth rate and the high infant mortality rate. Moll stressed that births in Austria had been declining since 1877, a trend that had been buffered to a degree by increasing life expectancy. Still, more than 20 out of 100 infants (or 200,000 children annually) did not live to see their first birthday. A year before the outbreak of the First World War, he formulated the significance of the question of the birth rate in unmistakeably geopolitical terms: 'Every nation that wishes to gain ascendancy over others must see the life of the child as a public good of its people and strive to preserve it by all means'.[14] Eugenicists like Julius Tandler expressly demarcated their own positions from such views by highlighting the importance they attached to the quality of the population and contrasting this with purely quantitative policy approaches focussed on the birth rate.[15]

Eugenics also had to assert itself on an additional front in Austria: the scientific basis for its postulates did not go uncontested there. In his inaugural lecture in 1902, Julius Wagner-Jauregg subjected the question of the hereditary transmission of mental disorders to a criticism that targeted its weak empirical foundations. Given the small number of comparative studies that existed on the hereditary burden of healthy and mentally disordered individuals, Wagner-Jauregg expressly warned against overestimating the significance of heredity for the emergence of mental disorders. He objected, especially, to the widespread assumption that a homogeneous and heritable 'psychopathic disposition' existed and could allegedly trigger a highly diverse range of mental disorders. It was assumed in some quarters, he criticized, that such a disposition not only explained the transmission of mental disorders from one generation to the next but also susceptibility to neurological disorders, alcoholism and even suicidal tendencies.[16]

Such sceptical attitudes were only replaced by broad calls for state intervention under the influence of the First World War and the fears of counterselective effects it provoked.

'War and Population': The First World War as a Catalyst

Interpretations of the First World War with a focus on population policy emerged and circulated quite early. In Austria, as elsewhere, the war catalyzed a surge in eugenics and related biopolitical discourses. The state sent masses of citizens to their deaths on the battlefield, and this fundamentally altered the relationship between individuals and the authority of the state. Professor Julius Tandler, at this point Dean of the Medical Faculty at the University of Vienna, initiated a discussion of the consequences of the war for population policy in 1916.[17] Tandler was subsequently to become director of the Public Health Office (Volksgesundheitsamt) in 1919/20 and served, as a socialist politician, as Vienna's city councillor in charge of health from 1920 to 1934.

Tandler interpreted the war from a social Darwinist perspective as a 'monumental amalgamation of thousands of facets of the struggle for existence'. He was mainly concerned about its biological consequences. Like numerous other eugenicists, Tandler warned of the danger of a reversal of 'natural selection': 'Not only does the war destroy or harm the group within the population that is most valuable in reproductive terms, but it also affects the most valuable members within this group by selecting on the basis of recruitment'. Tandler concluded that 'precisely the fact that so many unfit individuals, so many minus variants, will succeed in reproducing because of the war means that the threat from the procreation of these minus variants will be greater for the next generation than for the current generation and that this next generation will thus be all the more compelled to prune back these minus variants. Cruel though it may sound, it has to be said that continuously increasing support for these minus variants is wrong from the perspective of the economics of human beings and wrong from the standpoint of racial hygiene'.[18]

Tandler's intervention into the debate is not only interesting because of his subsequent prominence in health and social policy but also because of the numerous further interventions that it provoked, including some from prominent colleagues. One of them was the psychiatrist Erwin Stransky, who was concerned above all with the 'psychopathic inferiors' he feared would be able to reproduce unhindered in the hinterland because they were exempt from military service. As a counter-measure, he proposed that these individuals should be dispatched to the front to perform dangerous tasks: 'Individuals whose reproduction is, at any rate, less desirable, could be exposed [i.e. placed at risk of death] in place of those who are selectively more valuable'.[19] The pathologist Anton Weichselbaum (1845–1920), who had been Rector of the University of Vienna in 1912/13, stressed the importance of increasing the birth rate and combating tuberculosis, venereal diseases and alcoholism as soon as the war was over to prevent harm to the 'vitality of the nation' (*Volkskraft*). He was thinking, above all, of the country's future military strength as he portrayed a grim future scenario in which Russia, where the birth rate was far higher than in Germany and Austria, would have a population of 300 million by the year 2000 that would give it military superiority.[20]

To compensate for the human losses in the war, Tandler called for a comprehensive programme to raise the birth rate and reduce mortality among children and younger adults with the goal of 'rearing as many good elements as possible to reproductive age'.[21] What comes into view here is an unambiguously biopolitical rationale for the modern welfare state structures put in place in the Red Vienna of the interwar years, with Julius Tandler as one of the main instigators – even if the signature projects of Red Vienna, and especially its social housing, were guided more by social hygiene principles than by eugenics.[22]

The degree to which the expansion of youth welfare services from 1917 onwards was driven by biologistic assumptions about heredity and supposed genetic inferiority – and this despite the obvious effects of the war and by extension of environmental influences – is also apparent in an agenda-setting lecture given by Josef Gold, the head of Vienna's youth welfare office, that was published early in 1918 in a journal dedicated to social welfare issues in Vienna, *Blätter für das Wohlfahrts- und Armenwesen der Stadt Wien*.[23] As Gold saw it, 'hereditarily burdened' children represented the gravest problem faced by welfare services: he lamented that their upbringing was the most difficult and cost-intensive and that they were prone to relapse.[24]

In 1916, Gold had still put the need to address falling birth rates centre stage and had seen it as a continuation or complement of the war by population policy means: 'The infant welfare service is tasked with preserving the life force of born children in the first year of life, the point at which it faces the greatest threats, and with avoiding the senseless waste of the strength and wealth of the nation caused by excessive infant mortality by suppressing it to the level of necessary selection, which is approximately eight per cent'.[25] The concept of a eugenically 'optimal' rate of infant mortality was destined to continue playing a role in debates on infant welfare and eugenics for many years; infant welfare services repeatedly had to defend themselves against accusations that they were preserving the lives of 'inferior' children and thus hindering the workings of natural selection.[26]

Biopolitics and the State: Institution-Building in Response to the First World War

From what he saw as an existential biological crisis of the state, Julius Tandler derived the necessity of a dedicated health ministry – a project he suggested to Emperor Karl during an audience in January 1917.[27] A document signed by the Emperor from 1 June 1917 contains his decision to establish a ministry for public health and social welfare 'to counteract losses in the strength of the nation caused by the long war and ensure the bundling of activities undertaken to address this issue by the state, organs of self-government and society'.[28]

A new Ministry of Public Health (Ministerium für Volksgesundheit) was set up via legislation passed on 27 July 1918 and took over the agenda of the health department previously located within the Ministry of the Interior.

Ignaz Kaup (1870–1944), a race hygienist who had studied under Max von Gruber, was the most senior civil servant in the new ministry.[29] Kaup was a member of the Deutsche Gesellschaft für Rassenhygiene (German Society for Racial Hygiene) from an early stage. In 1913, he published a piece in *Archiv für Rassen- und Gesellschaftsbiologie*, the academic mouthpiece of German racial hygiene, on the costs of 'inferior elements' for society and the state. Kaup proposed that parents of children with disabilities should, 'in the interest of eugenics', be compelled to cover the expense entailed in looking after their children and placed in forced labour institutions where appropriate to achieve this purpose.[30]

In April 1919, at a German-Austrian conference on child-raising, Kaup spoke about the nexus between infant mortality and population policy. While his 1913 article had voiced concerns about expenditure made necessary by 'inferiors', his focus now was on population policy strategies that could compensate for the human losses caused by the war as quickly as possible and embarking on a path towards 'national renewal' (*Volkserneuerung*).[31]

The Republic of German-Austria that emerged from the break-up of the Austro-Hungarian Empire after the capitulation of November 1918 had a biopolitical mission inscribed in its constitution: along with areas such as maternal, infant and youth welfare and poverty relief, population policy was explicitly defined as a task of the state in the Austrian constitution of 1920. Fundamental legislative competence in this area rested with the federal state, while the federated states were responsible for implementation and execution.[32] From 1924 on, questions of population policy and eugenics appear on the agenda of the Supreme Medical Council (Oberster Sanitätsrat), the most important body advising the government on public health issues.[33]

Eugenic and racial hygiene content was also starting to become established at universities, for example, in teaching. Eugenics or racial hygiene was not a subject taught in its own right before the First World War, but initial courses at the University of Vienna are documented from 1919 on – at the Faculty of Law. From the summer semester of 1919 on, Heinrich Reichel gave lectures on 'Social Hygiene for Lawyers' (*Volksgesundheitslehre für Juristen*) that were well-attended, according to Ploetz, along with other courses that were similar in content. Starting in the summer semester of 1920, Reichel gave the first lecture expressly dedicated to 'racial hygiene' in Austria (and one of the first in the German-speaking countries).[34] In 1923/24, Reichel became the director of a new department at Vienna University's Hygiene Institute tasked with training public health doctors. This decisively shifted the training of future medical officials, who would be mainstays of the public health system, towards racial hygiene and eugenics.[35] Reichel had already been cooperating with Ilse von Arlt (1876–1960), the director of the School of Welfare in Vienna, since 1912 by giving lectures on hygiene and social hygiene in the context of courses in 'people's care' (*Volkspflege*) for welfare workers.[36] Reichel's work here was able to exert direct influence on social work, a field that was undergoing a process of increasing professionalization.

Heinrich Reichel presented a racial hygiene manifesto in 1922. It was based on a lecture he had given to a committee of experts assembled to discuss questions of racial hygiene at the invitation of the Austrian president, Dr Michael Hainisch. Its publication by the Public Health Office in the Ministry of Social Affairs lent extra gravity to its contents. In addition to legislation prohibiting 'miscegenation' (racial mixing), Reichel called for compulsory medical examinations for prospective marriage partners and the use of mandatory confinement and sterilization to eliminate the transmission of undesirable heritable traits. He also mentioned the possibility of directly killing 'bearers of undesirable heritable traits' as the 'simplest method', albeit without unambiguously advocating it.[37] In the Public Health Office, the introduction of obligatory health screening before marriage – a central demand of eugenicists – had been given consideration as early as 1920. It was envisaged that this would allow the exclusion from marriage of those afflicted with venereal diseases, tuberculosis, mental disorders or possible 'hereditary burdens'. The introduction of such screening was initially deemed impracticable. It was decided that attempts would be made to reach the population through education and guidance to prepare the way for introducing legislation at a later stage.[38] Venereal diseases, tuberculosis and alcoholism were seen as the main 'national plagues' (*Volksseuchen*) and all three were sited at points of intersection between the concerns of individual medical care, social hygiene and eugenics. The increase in sexually transmitted diseases during and after the First World War was a central motivating factor for firming up institutional structures in health care during and after the war. In this area, too, an increase in the significance of concepts from hereditary biology is evident. Up to 1921, the data on prostitution collated annually by the State Office for Social Administration (Staatsamt für Soziale Verwaltung) focused almost exclusively on documenting the social and geographical background of prostitutes. But a table produced in 1922 with details of 277 prostitutes newly registered over the previous year reveals that the authorities were now clearly interested in possible hereditary factors. Financial distress was only acknowledged as a motivation in 56 cases; in the others, a hereditary component was suspected.[39] Later on, police reports on prostitutes regularly contained information on alleged 'hereditary burdens'.[40]

In November 1921, parliamentarians from the Greater German People's Party (Großdeutsche Volkspartei) proposed legislation barring 'persons with heritable or infectious diseases' from marriage but did not succeed in having it passed.[41] In the same year, Vienna's Committee of Medical Experts, the Landessanitätsrat, produced draft legislation mandating medical reports as a prerequisite for marriage. Although it received support from the socialist *Arbeiter-Zeitung*, this initiative was also unsuccessful.[42]

The draft legislation proposed that three commissions be established to deal, respectively, with 'venereal diseases', 'tuberculosis' and 'persons with incurable mental disorders and certain other physical or mental impairments'.[43]

The Austrian version of the hygiene exhibition originally held in the German Hygiene Museum in Dresden was an important crystallization point in the popularization of scientifically rationalized lifestyles. It took place in Vienna's Messepalast (Trade Fair Palace) in 1925 and its long list of prominent champions from public life (headed by Federal President Michael Hainisch) indicates the broad support it attracted from members of the political and academic elite and its quasi-official character. Among other topics, the exhibition offered an overview of hereditary biology and eugenics. It focused especially on 'selection and counterselection, poisoning of the germ, degeneration and regeneration' and 'hygienic foundations of marriage'.[44] Heinrich Reichel's ideas reached the zenith of their popularity with the general public in 1930 in a series of lectures advertised by the Public Health Office and broadcast by the public radio station, Ravag.[45]

Eugenics and Racial Hygiene in the First Republic (1918–1934)

In the period after the First World War and before the Anschluss with National Socialist Germany in 1938, eugenic thinking was already so firmly established in Austria that it was propagated in scholarly and popular discourses, in education, the mainstream media, and by various associations, political parties and other organizations. There were also instances of practical implementation, for instance, the founding in 1922 of Vienna's Marriage Advice Service (Eheberatungsstelle). In the literature, this service is seen as an early institutional crystallization point for the pursuit of eugenics in Vienna and thus as supporting evidence for its biopolitical potency.[46] Both Julius Tandler, the initiator of the municipal Marriage Advice Service, and its director Karl Kautsky Jun. saw its significance in the opportunities it opened up to introduce the population to eugenic ideas and generate increasing acceptance for the principles of 'reproductive hygiene' and 'generative ethics'. As the service was the first of its kind in Europe, they also saw it as a model for other cities to emulate.[47] Counselling was voluntary in principle, but welfare officers were tasked with finding people in their districts with plans to marry and directing them towards the service.[48] Over time, the original eugenic goals of the service receded into the background to some degree, as the sexual counselling also provided proved more popular.[49] A certain amount of disillusionment, at least regarding the eugenic goals of the Marriage Advice Service, is apparent in Kautsky's conclusion eight years after its founding: 'Cases of a purely eugenic kind are relatively rare, partly because the population is only inadequately informed about the significance of hereditary predispositions to illnesses and partly because very few people can supply reliable information about the fates of their forebears'.[50] The Viennese Marriage Advice Service was not to remain one of a kind for long. Within Austria, a similar institution was founded in 1923 in Graz but saw only 38 visitors in the first 2 years of its existence and is lost in obscurity beyond that point.[51] In Germany, over a hundred marriage advice centres joined forces to form an association in 1927. By this point, the idea seems to have established firm roots in the German context.[52]

What role did eugenic thinking play in the activities of the municipal health office in Vienna, one of the most important institutions in the biopolitical field? In a collection of essays published in 1930 as *Einführung in die soziale Hygiene* [An Introduction to Social Hygiene], its director's appraisal of the situation saw eugenic precepts realized only in rudiments and essentially only in connection with the prevention of germ deterioration attributable to toxins, certain infectious diseases and stimulants such as alcohol and nicotine. Eugenic measures in the narrower sense of the concept he saw as a task for the future: 'To prevent the inferior individuals, such as heavy drinkers, criminals, persons with certain mental disorders and persons with severe heritable diseases from procreating, special measures going beyond standard hygiene will be required: marriage advice, sterilization and abortion'.[53]

References to the 'inferiority of the children of drinkers' demonstrate that alcohol abuse was also seen as a central problem in this context. This 'inferiority' allegedly led to both higher child mortality in 'drinker families' and to a large number of 'severe deficiencies' such as 'cases of imbecility, psychosis, psychopathy, epilepsy, alcoholism, moral defects'.[54] As alcoholism was widespread, had manifold social consequences and took a heavy economic toll, it was seen as one of the three main public health problems (with the other two, as mentioned above, being tuberculosis and sexually transmitted diseases). Calls to curb all three phenomena were thus contained in every reform programme with a eugenics agenda. Heinrich Reichel, the leading figure in Austrian eugenics, played a major role in the anti-alcohol movement – an indicator of the significance attributed to alcoholism within eugenics/racial hygiene.[55]

The struggle against abortions (waged by medical means but also with the force of the police and penal law) was one of the most controversial issues in population policy.[56] The Association of Vienna's Social Democratic Doctors (Vereinigung sozialdemokratischer Ärzte Wiens) adopted a resolution on 'interruptions of pregnancy and population policy' in 1924 that aimed to combat the decline in births by eliminating its social and economic root causes. The resolution also called for the introduction of medical, social and eugenic indications for abortion. The doctors advocated a regulation regime that would consider the health and social interests of the affected women, as well as and especially population policy and eugenic concerns, and opted not to base their position on the rights of pregnant women to self-determination.[57] Doctors like Karl Kautsky Jun. expressly rejected the idea of taking 'a woman's right to self-determination over her body' as the departure point for a reform of abortion regulations.[58] The nurse and party theoretician Oda Olberg (1872–1955) went one step further in this regard and demanded 'the ex officio induction of abortus in certain cases'. Doctors in the service of municipalities, the courts and residential institutions would be required to report relevant pregnancies. The consent of women would be required if they were held to be of sound mind, but Olberg argued that 'idiots and the mentally deficient' should in every instance be prevented from carrying pregnancies to term.[59]

Johannes Ude, a professor of theology in Graz, founded the Austrian People's Watch League (Österreichs Völkerwacht. Verein zur Bekämpfung der öffentlichen Unsittlichkeit) in March 1917 as an 'Association for Combating Public Immorality'. Its main aim, as he saw it, was to combat a perceived loosening of Catholic sexual morals – the dire consequences of which he described in the most drastic terms. Ude's reasoning was largely based on religion, but also referred to eugenics, population policy and the economics of human beings.[60]

As in many other countries, a number of organizations were established in Austria with the aim of promoting public awareness of eugenics and racial hygiene, preparing the ground for the implementation of concrete measures. The Viennese Society for Racial Hygiene (Racial Care), founded in Vienna in 1924/1925, is the best known of these. Societies for Racial Hygiene were also founded in Graz and in Upper Austria in 1923, and two other initiatives of no more than local significance also appeared. These associations were all oriented towards the Munich chapter of the German Society for Racial Hygiene. They were racist, anti-Semitic and had pan-German nationalist leanings and later enjoyed close ties with the National Socialist movement in Germany and Austria.[61]

To some extent, the Austrian Society for Population Policy and Welfare (Österreichische Gesellschaft für Bevölkerungspolitik und Fürsorgewesen) founded early on, in 1917, acted as a bridge between different political camps and between biopolitical models that were radical to different degrees. One of its founding members was Rudolf Goldscheid, who has already been mentioned more than once.[62] Wilhelm Hecke was a further leading member and an important nexus with the politically charged interwar population policy discourses that were especially sensitive where they touched on ethnic minorities and their roles.[63]

The Austrian League for National Regeneration and Heredity (Österreichischer Bund für Volksaufartung und Erbkunde) played a role that was similarly above partisan politics. The League was founded in 1928 and its leading members included Julius Tandler, Julius Wagner-Jauregg and Heinrich Reichel.[64] Its draft legislation for eugenic sterilizations was tabled in the Austrian parliament in 1929, but this legislative push was unsuccessful.[65] The social democratic paediatrician Felix Tietze (1883–1960), who was forced into emigration in 1938 on account of his Jewish background, spoke at the general meeting of the League in 1929 on the international discussion since the beginning of the century and early attempts to see proposed measures through to the implementation stage, especially in the United States.[66] He saw only negative measures as genuinely holding out potential for biopolitical intervention: 'In contrast [to positive racial hygiene], negative racial hygiene is highly active. Really eliminating carriers of undesirable heritable traits involves intervening actively'.[67]

Racial hygiene also found a bulwark in (physical) anthropology and racial studies. Apart from the universities, these disciplines had an institutional base at the Museum of Natural History in Vienna, especially.[68] The racialist anthropologist and pan-German nationalist Otto Reche (1879–1966) was highly active during his time at the helm of the Department of Anthropology at the University of Vienna (1924–1927), not least as the founder of the Viennese Society for Racial Hygiene (Wiener Gesellschaft für Rassenpflege) in 1924/1925.[69]

Eugenics and Racial Hygiene under the Austro-Fascist Regime

The sociopolitical experiment of Red Vienna was ended abruptly by the establishment of an Austro-Facist dictatorship in 1933/34. Julius Tandler left Austria after a brief period of imprisonment and died in exile in 1936. The new regime took Catholic doctrine as its guiding compass and racial hygiene discourses were among those not left untouched by this development. Heinrich Reichel, the most prominent advocate for racial hygiene in Austria, had unambiguously advocated for the option of compulsorily sterilizing people with 'certain special kinds of degeneration of the soul' (*bestimmten besonderen Arten seelischer Entartungen*) in 1922.[70] In 1934 – after the introduction of the Law for the Prevention of Hereditarily Diseased Offspring in 1933 in Germany – he treaded with much more caution.

The constitution researcher Julius Bauer voiced strong criticism of the National Socialist sterilization law, which he appraised as unsuitable for reaching the desired eugenic objectives. Bauer took the view that sterilization on eugenic grounds might be appropriate in individual cases but that a policy of coerced sterilization mandated by law and implemented on the scale that was becoming apparent in Germany ought, 'for the time being', to be rejected.[71] The law did, however, also have advocates in Austria who were prepared to speak out publicly in its favour. They included the neurologist Heinrich Kogerer (1887–1958).[72] The Nobel prize holder Julius Wagner-Jauregg, the most renowned Austrian psychiatrist of the first half of the twentieth century, had already called for legislation enabling eugenic sterilization in 1931.[73] He now commented, with an eye to the introduction of forced eugenic sterilization in Nazi Germany, 'that the idea underlying this measure is sound in theory'. Whether the measure would 'prove' itself in practice would, he believed, have to be determined by experience.[74]

The orthopaedist Adolf Lorenz (1854–1946) was even more direct in the views he expressed in 1937. He demanded that all special treatment of children born prematurely, such as the use of incubators, should be abandoned and that children should be left to perish if they were incapable of surviving under standard care: 'But the true paradise that our Earth could be and should be will only come about when all who cannot exercise responsibility – all intellectual cripples with or without a deformity – are interned to protect the current generation and also sterilized to protect future generations and prevent the continued breeding of harm'.[75]

In addition to the racial hygiene movement taking its cues from developments in Germany, expressly Catholic eugenics of the kind advanced by the Society of Catholic Physicians (St Lukas Gilde) also gained ground in this phase. Taking the 1930 encyclical *Casti connubii* as its compass, the society rejected direct interventions in reproduction such as sterilization, abortion or going so far as to kill unwanted life and thus found itself on a course diametrically opposed to the National Socialist brand of racial hygiene. Education and voluntary restraint from procreation were the methods of choice advanced in these circles to prevent undesired births, but Albert Niedermeyer, the most prominent exponent of Catholic eugenics in Austria, also advocated forced confinement in single-sex labour colonies that would allow those interned to be put to work and force them to contribute towards their upkeep.[76]

With the Anschluss in March 1938, racial hygiene suddenly became a central plank in state policy. Biopolitical practices vastly more radical than all previously contemplated proposals were institutionalized at universities, in public health and social welfare provision and in a host of National Socialist organizations. No direct line can be drawn from the utopian thought experiments of a Julius Tandler or the ideas about eugenics that were compatible with Catholic conceptions of sexuality to the quasi-industrial mass extermination programmes directed against people with intellectual disabilities or mental illness by the National Socialists, although these different biopolitical conceptions had a common denominator in so far as they all rested on a hierarchy of human worth justified with reference to biology. The proponents of socialist eugenics mentioned here, Julius Tandler, Oda Olberg, Karl Kautsky Jun. and Julius Bauer, all died in exile. Ilse Arlt was barred from professional practice as a 'half-Jew' by the National Socialist regime.[77]

The proponents of racial hygiene with pan-German nationalist and increasingly also National Socialist orientations can, however, be seen as having directly paved the way for these subsequent developments. Ignaz Kaup became chair of the Aid League of the German Austrians in Munich in 1934, the organisation that replaced the Combat Ring of the German Austrians (Kampfring der Deutsch-Österreicher im Reich) in that same year and worked in that role to facilitate the National Socialist takeover of power in Austria.[78] The psychiatrist Heinrich Kogerer played a significant role in the *Gleichschaltung* and 'Aryanization' of psychoanalysis in Vienna.[79] After the Anschluss, racial hygiene was rapidly implemented as a new science guiding the field of public health. Some of the protagonists came from Germany, but in other cases it was possible to draw on existing human resources.[80] The Viennese Society for Racial Hygiene played an important role here. Its activities expanded to encompass all of Austria and it became one of the most active groups within the German society.[81]

Notes

1 Translated by Sarah Swift.

2 The concepts of eugenics and racial hygiene were used at least partially as synonyms in the years in question and attempting to separate their meanings precisely is difficult. References to 'eugenics' (*Eugenik*) often invoked scholarly discourses and the international dimension of the phenomenon. 'Racial hygiene' (*Rassenhygiene* or *Rassehygiene*) and 'racial care' (*Rassenpflege*) gradually came to be used ever more narrowly in the meanings they had in German nationalist discourse.

3 Since the mid-1980s, a growing body of literature dealing with the topics treated here has emerged, initially in the form of critical treatments of 'Red Vienna' and its biopolitical strategies (Doris Byer, '"Nation" und "Evolution". Aspekte einer "politischen Anthropologie" im Austromarxismus', in *Zwischen Natur und Kultur. Zur Kritik biologistischer Ansätze*, ed. Hubert Christian Ehalt (Vienna: Böhlau, 1985), 285–314; Doris Byer, 'Sexualität/Macht/Wohlfahrt. Zeitgemäße Erinnerungen an das "Rote Wien"', *Zeitgeschichte* (1987): 442–463; Doris Byer, *Rassenhygiene und Wohlfahrtspflege. Zur Entstehung eines sozialdemokratischen Machtdispositivs in Österreich bis 1934* (Frankfurt am Main: Campus, 1988)), and later in treatments of possible continuities between this period and the National Socialist brand of racial hygiene enforced after 1938 (see Wolfgang Neugebauer, 'Von der Rassenhygiene zum Massenmord. Ideologie, Propaganda und Praxis der NS-Euthanasie in Österreich', *Zeitgeschichte* (2001): 189–199; Wolfgang Neugebauer, 'Von der "Rassenhygiene" zum Massenmord', in *Wien 1938*, ed. Historisches Museum der Stadt Wien (exhibition catalogue, Vienna: Österreichischer Bundesverlag 1988), 262–285; Wolfgang Neugebauer, 'Rassenhygiene in Wien 1938', *Wiener klinische Wochenschrift* 110 (1998): 128–134) and the contributions in Heinz-Eberhard Gabriel and Wolfgang Neugebauer, eds., *Vorreiter der Vernichtung? Eugenik, Rassenhygiene und Euthanasie in der österreichischen Diskussion vor 1938. Zur Geschichte der NS-Euthanasie in Wien, Teil III* (Vienna: Böhlau, 2003). Works on pan-German nationalist 'right-wing' racial hygiene (for instance Thomas Mayer, 'Familie, Rasse und Genetik. Deutschnationale Eugeniken im Österreich der Zwischenkriegszeit', in *Eugenik in Österreich. Biopolitische Methoden und Strukturen von 1900–1945*, eds. Gerhard Baader, Veronika Hofer and Thomas Mayer (Vienna: Czernin, 2007), 162–183) and on Catholic eugenics (Monika Löscher, '*... der gesunden Vernunft nicht zuwider ...*'? *Katholische Eugenik in Österreich vor 1938* (Innsbruck; Vienna; Bozen: StudienVerlag, 2009) both followed. For a broad overview, see also Maria A. Wolf, *Eugenische Vernunft. Eingriffe in die reproduktive Kultur durch die Medizin 1900–2000* (Vienna: Böhlau, 2008); Paul J. Weindling, 'A City Regenerated: Eugenics, Race and Welfare in Interwar Vienna', in *Interwar Vienna: Culture between Tradition and Modernity*, eds. Deborah Holmes and Lisa Silverman

(New York: Camden House, 2009), 81–113, and the contributions in Gerhard Baader, Veronika Hofer and Thomas Mayer, eds., *Eugenik in Österreich. Biopolitische Methoden und Strukturen von 1900–1945* (Vienna: Czernin, 2007). On population policy and anthropology, see also Brigitte Fuchs, *'Rasse', 'Volk', Geschlecht. Anthropologische Diskurse in Österreich 1850–1960* (Frankfurt am Main: Campus, 2003); Gudrun Exner, Josef Kytir and Alexander Pinwinkler, *Bevölkerungswissenschaft in Österreich in der Zwischenkriegszeit. Personen, Institutionen, Diskurse (1918–1938)* (Vienna: Böhlau, 2004).

4 Thomas Mayer, 'Austria', in *The History of East-Central European Eugenics, 1900–1945: Sources and Commentaries*, ed. Marius Turda (London: Bloomsbury Academic, 2015), 4–71, 4. Max Gruber was an important figure in the Viennese public health system until he moved to Munich in 1903.

5 Sophie Ledebur, 'Die österreichische Irren- und Strafrechtsreformbewegung und die Anfänge eines eugenischen Diskurses in der Psychiatrie um 1900', in *Eugenik in Österreich. Biopolitische Methoden und Strukturen von 1900–1945*, eds. Gerhard Baader, Veronika Hofer and Thomas Mayer (Vienna: Czernin, 2007), 231–232. Further examples of thoughts on eugenic sterilization voiced from relatively early on in Austrian psychiatry discourse are given there.

6 Klaus Taschwer, 'Darwin und die frühe Eugenik in Wien: Wie und warum der Soziallamarckismus in Österreich die biopolitischen Diskussionen rund um den ersten Weltkrieg bestimmte', in *Darwin in Zentraleuropa. Die wissenschaftliche, weltanschauliche und populäre Rezeption im 19. und frühen 20. Jahrhundert*, eds. Herbert Matis and Wolfgang L. Reiter (Vienna: LIT Verlag, 2018), 343–360, 354, fn. 21.

7 Mayer, 'Austria', 4–71, 4; Feliks J. Bister, 'Rudolf Goldscheid und die Österreichische Liga für Menschenrechte', in *Wissenschaft, Politik und Öffentlichkeit: von der Wiener Moderne bis zur Gegenwart*, eds. Mitchell G. Ash and Christian H. Stifter (Vienna: WUV Universitätsverlag, 2002), 321–328, 322.

8 Cited from Thomas Mayer, '"... daß die eigentliche österreichische Rassenhygiene in der Hauptsache das Werk Reichels ist". Der (Rassen-)Hygieniker Heinrich Reichel (1876–1943) und seine Bedeutung für die eugenische Bewegung in Österreich', in *Vorreiter der Vernichtung? Eugenik, Rassenhygiene und Euthanasie in der österreichischen Diskussion vor 1938. Zur Geschichte der NS-Euthanasie in Wien, Teil III*, eds. Heinz-Eberhard Gabriel and Wolfgang Neugebauer (Vienna: Böhlau, 2003), 65–98, 69.

9 Ibid., 69–70.

10 Ibid., 71.

11 Mayer, 'Austria', 4–71, 4–5. See also Reichel's obituary for Wlassak: Heinrich Reichel, 'Zum Gedächtnis Dr. Rudolf Wlassaks', *Wiener klinische Wochenschrift* 44 (1931): 544.

12 Goldscheid's main work, *Höherentwicklung und Menschenökonomie* [Higher Development and the Economics of Human Beings] appeared in 1911 and sought (as its subtitle proposed) to establish 'foundations of social biology', a discipline that would, he postulated, deal with the 'prerequisites for national health [*Volksgesundheit*] and fitness [*Volkstüchtigkeit*]' (Rudolf Goldscheid, *Höherentwicklung und Menschenökonomie. Grundlegung der Sozialbiologie* (Leipzig: Klinkhardt, 1911), XIII.) Goldscheid's declared purpose was to derive a foundation for sociology from the natural sciences, and he foregrounded the biological processes of the reproduction of the human species in his analysis of society. On the basis of Darwinian evolutionary theory, he developed the fundaments of a theory of society that had the rational administration of humankind as 'organic capital' as its main postulate. Goldscheid's significance in the context of this contribution is chiefly due to the strong influence he exerted on the political actors behind Red Vienna and

especially on Julius Tandler. The 'rational administration of organic capital' is a core principle found in many of Tandler's public utterances from 1917, at the latest, onwards; see, for example, Julius Tandler, 'Volksgesundheit und Volkswohlfahrt', *Arbeiter-Zeitung* 5.6.1917; Julius Tandler, 'Die Gefahren der Minderwertigkeit. Vortrag am 13.2.1928 für den Bund für Volksaufartung und Erbkunde', *Das Wiener Jugendhilfswerk. Jahrbuch 1928*, 3–22, 6. Goldscheid's attitude towards eugenics was marked by contradictions: he was strongly opposed to a eugenics agenda that chose to see inheritance and selection as the only relevant mechanisms of human evolution and development and that possibly even saw every form of selective pressure as positive. But he also noted approvingly that Galton had placed a high value on combating natural and cultural counterselection and had thus avoided falling into the simplistic thinking of many of his later adherents. For more on Goldscheid, see (among other literature) Gudrun Exner, 'Rudolf Goldscheid (1870–1931) and the Economy of Human Beings: A New Point of View on the Decline of Fertility in the Time of the First Demographic Transition', *Vienna Yearbook of Population Research* 2 (2004): 283–301; Doris Byer, *Rassenhygiene und Wohlfahrtspflege. Zur Entstehung eines sozialdemokratischen Machtdispositivs in Österreich bis 1934* (Frankfurt am Main: Campus, 1988).

13 On this, see Klaus Taschwer, 'Darwin und die frühe Eugenik in Wien: Wie und warum der Soziallamarckismus in Österreich die biopolitischen Diskussionen rund um den ersten Weltkrieg bestimmte', in *Darwin in Zentraleuropa. Die wissenschaftliche, weltanschauliche und populäre Rezeption im 19. und frühen 20. Jahrhundert*, eds. Herbert Matis and Wolfgang L. Reiter (Vienna: LIT Verlag, 2018), 343–360; Johannes Feichtinger, 'Krisis des Darwinismus? Darwin und die Wissenschaften des Wiener Fin de Siècle', in *Ibid.*, 63–86. From a Lamarckian standpoint – if one assumes, in other words, that it is possible for acquired characteristics to be passed on to the next generation – a broad zone of overlap exists between eugenics measures and social medicine or social welfare interventions and these fields cannot be separated with precision. Julius Tandler repeatedly affirmed this view (Julius Tandler, 'Was ist Konstitution?', *Wiener klinische Wochenschrift* 43 (1930): 318–319, 319). It follows that most of the medical and social welfare reforms implemented especially in Red Vienna cannot be assigned to one category or the other without ambiguity; with only a handful of exceptions, these were measures that would have been held to be eugenically ineffective or even counterproductive by the exponents of a 'hard' inheritance theory oriented towards August Weismann (1834–1914). From 1885 on, Weismann rejected the possibility of the inheritance of acquired characteristics entirely in his germ plasm theory: August Weismann, *Die Continuität des Keimplasmas als Grundlage einer Theorie der Vererbung* (Jena: Gustav Fischer, 1885). Exponents of a 'hard' form of race hygiene concluded from this that efforts to improve the living conditions of current generations would be eugenically ineffective if they were not complemented by an element of selection. The Biologische Versuchsanstalt (the Viennese biological research institute in the Prater known as the 'Vivarium') is an example for the influence of Lamarckism on biological research; see Veronika Hofer, 'Rudolf Goldscheid, Paul Kammerer und die Biologen des Prater-Vivariums in der liberalen Volksbildung der Wiener Moderne', in *Wissenschaft, Politik und Öffentlichkeit: von der Wiener Moderne bis zur Gegenwart*, eds. Mitchell G. Ash and Christian H. Stifter (Vienna: WUV Universitätsverlag, 2002), 149–184.

14 Austrian State Archive/Archive of the Republic (hereafter AT-OeStA/AdR), Bundesministerium für soziale Verwaltung (hereafter BMfsV), Volksgesundheitsamt (hereafter VG), 1584, Hebammen, Leopold Moll, 'Die Säuglingsfürsorgerin. Zur Einführung eines neuen weiblichen Berufes', 1913.

15 See, for example, Julius Tandler, 'Die Gefahren der Minderwertigkeit. Vortrag am 13. 2. 1928 für den Bund für Volksaufartung und Erbkunde', *Das Wiener Jugendhilfswerk. Jahrbuch 1928*: 3–22, 6.

16 Julius Wagner-Jauregg, 'Ueber erbliche Belastung. Antrittsvorlesung gehalten bei Uebernahme der II. Psychiatrischen Klinik in Wien', *Wiener klinische Wochenschrift* 15 (1902): 1153–1159.

17 Julius Tandler, 'Krieg und Bevölkerung', *Wiener klinische Wochenschrift* 29 (1916): 445–452, 445.

18 Ibid., 447–448.

19 Erwin Stransky, 'Krieg und Bevölkerung', *Wiener klinische Wochenschrift* 18 (1916): 555–558, 557.

20 Anton Weichselbaum, 'Diskussionsbeitrag zum Vortrag "Krieg und Bevölkerung" von Julius Tandler', *Wiener klinische Wochenschrift* (1916): 500–501.

21 Julius Tandler, 'Krieg und Bevölkerung', *Wiener klinische Wochenschrift* 29 (1916): 445–452, 450.

22 On this, see Helmut Weihsmann, *Das Rote Wien: Sozialdemokratische Architektur und Kommunalpolitik 1919–1934* (Vienna: Promedia, 2002). On Julius Tandler, see Peter Schwarz, *Julius Tandler. Zwischen Humanismus und Eugenik* (Vienna: Edition Steinbauer, 2017).

23 Josef Gold, 'Fürsorgeerziehung und allgemeine Jugendfürsorge', *Blätter für das Wohlfahrts- und Armenwesen der Stadt Wien* 17, no. 193 (1918): 1–14. The expansion of the reference in the journal title from 'poor relief' to 'poor relief and welfare' highlights the transition from traditional charity to the new welfare practices.

24 Ibid., 2.

25 Josef Gold, 'Die Organisation der Säuglings- und Kleinkinderfürsorge', Zeitschrift für Kinderschutz und Jugendfürsorge 4 (1916): 106ff., 106; cited from Alexander Brunner, Über den Wandel im Umgang mit Armut, Krankheit und Abweichung. Beitrag zur Theorie- und Sozialgeschichte des Fürsorge- und Wohlfahrtswesens in Österreich im ersten Drittel des Zwanzigsten Jahrhunderts. Teile 1–2 (doctoral thesis, Vienna: 1996), 437.

26 See, for example, Felix Tietze, 'Säuglingsfürsorge und Rassenhygiene', *Wiener Medizinische Wochenschrift* 34 (1926): 1011–1016, who stressed the eugenically unproblematic nature and even the eugenic utility of infant welfare efforts.

27 Karl Sablik, *Julius Tandler. Mediziner und Sozialreformer. Eine Biographie* (Vienna: A. Schendl, 1983): 140–141. In June 1917, Julius Tandler published an appeal in the *Arbeiter-Zeitung* workers' newspaper that once again highlighted the connection between war and health policy: 'Among all the goods that have suffered severe harm in this war, the loss of organic capital, expressed by counting the people who have perished, is the very greatest. ... The war should, will and must convince humanity that a strong and comprehensively healthy national body is an essential prerequisite for the existence of every state': Julius Tandler, 'Volksgesundheit und Volkswohlfahrt', *Arbeiter-Zeitung*, 5 June 1917.

28 Ella Lingens, 'Gesundheitswesen', in *Die Zweite Republik*. Vol. 2, eds. Erika Weinzierl and Kurt Skalnik (Vienna: 1972), 253–281, 260.

29 Paul Slezak, *Geschichte der österreichischen Sanitätsverwaltung* (Vienna: Urban und Schwarzenberg, 1956), 47.

30 Ignaz Kaup, 'Was kosten die minderwertigen Elemente dem Staat und die Gesellschaft?', *Archiv für Rassen- und Gesellschaftsbiologie* 10 (1913): 723–748. Kaup was not only concerned with identifying opportunities to make savings but also with protecting society from carriers of supposed hereditary defects. Using the metaphor of vermin (*Schädlinge*, literally damagers)

for the individuals in question semantically leaves no possibility but elimination: 'Our healthy offspring are entitled to be protected from ruin by verminous damagers of the germ line [*Keimschädlinge*], and every progressive nation is obliged to reduce the cost burden of inferiors as far as possible'.

31 Ignaz Kaup, 'Säuglingssterblichkeit und Bevölkerungspolitik', *Mitteilungen des Volksgesundheitsamtes* 3 (1919): 76–89. Shortly after the end of the war, Kaup experienced a further career boost. On 1 December 1918, the Ministry of Public Health became a state office of public health headed by Kaup. This state office was then integrated (as the Public Health Office) into the State Office of Social Administration headed by Ferdinand Hanusch in March 1919. In May 1919, Julius Tandler became the new head of the Public Health Office (until October 1920): Paul Slezak, *Geschichte der österreichischen Sanitätsverwaltung* (Vienna: Urban und Schwarzenberg, 1956), 48–49.

32 *Gesetz vom 1. Oktober 1920, womit die Republik Österreich als Bundesstaat eingerichtet wird (Bundes-Verfassungsgesetz)* [Austrian Federal Constitutional Law]. Its author Hans Kelsen (1881–1973) was a member of the Austrian League for National Regeneration and Heredity (Österreichische Bund für Volksaufartung und Erbkunde): Thomas Mayer, 'Austria', in *The History of East-Central European Eugenics, 1900–1945: Sources and Commentaries*, ed. Marius Turda (London: Bloomsbury Academic, 2015), 11.

33 Ibid., 11.

34 Thomas Mayer, '"... daß die eigentliche österreichische Rassenhygiene in der Hauptsache das Werk Reichels ist". Der (Rassen-)Hygieniker Heinrich Reichel (1876–1943) und seine Bedeutung für die eugenische Bewegung in Österreich', in *Vorreiter der Vernichtung? Eugenik, Rassenhygiene und Euthanasie in der österreichischen Diskussion vor 1938. Zur Geschichte der NS-Euthanasie in Wien, Teil III*, eds. Heinz-Eberhard Gabriel and Wolfgang Neugebauer (Vienna: Böhlau, 2003), 65–98, 73–74.

35 Michael Hubenstorf, 'Österreichische Ärzteemigration', in *Vertriebene Vernunft I. Emigration und Exil österreichischer Wissenschaft 1930/1940*, ed. Friedrich Stadler (Vienna: Jugend und Volk, 1987), 359–415, 372.

36 Mayer, '"... daß die eigentliche österreichische Rassenhygiene"', 65–98. On Arlt, see, among other sources, Cornelia Frey, *'Respekt vor der Kreativität der Menschen' – Ilse Arlt: Werk und Wirkung* (Leverkusen: Budrich, 2005).

37 Heinrich Reichel, *Die Hauptaufgaben der Rassenhygiene in der Gegenwart* (Vienna: Volksgesundheitsamt, 1922), 12–13. An additional demand – for a comprehensive register where 'characteristics of relevance for an inherited and hereditary state of health and, if possible, also current and previous states of disease' could be recorded and used to provide marriage advice – anticipated the 'hereditary biological inventory' subsequently maintained under National Socialism: Heinrich Reichel, 'Zur Frage des gesundheitlichen Ehekonsenses', *Wiener klinische Wochenschrift* 35, no. 12 (1922): 274–276.

38 AT-OeStA/AdR BMfsV VG, 1650, Geschlechtskrankheiten, 5458/1920, Volksgesundheitsamt an Wexberg, 18.3.1920.

39 AT-OeStA/AdR BMfsV VG, 1749, 99/1922, Daten der Prostitution.

40 AT-OeStA/AdR BMfsV VG, 1802, 63268/1923, Polizeidirektion an Volksgesundheitsamt, 16.10.1923.

41 Gabriele Czarnowski, 'Eheeignung und Ehetauglichkeit. Körpereinschreibungen im administrativen Geflecht positiver und negativer Rassenhygiene während des Nationalsozialismus', in *Eugenik in Österreich. Biopolitische Methoden und Strukturen von 1900–1945*, eds. Gerhard Baader, Veronika Hofer and Thomas Mayer (Vienna: Czernin, 2007), 312–344, 312.

42 Ibid., 312.

43 Doris Byer, *Rassenhygiene und Wohlfahrtspflege. Zur Entstehung eines sozialdemokratischen Machtdispositivs in Österreich bis 1934* (Frankfurt am Main: Campus 1988), 145–146.
44 Offizieller Führer durch die Hygiene-Ausstellung Wien 1925 in Verbindung mit der Ausstellung 'Der Mensch' vom deutschen Hygiene-Museum, Dresden (Vienna: 1925), 21–22.
45 Heinrich Reichel and Hermann Muckermann, *Grundlagen der Vererbungswissenschaft und Eugenik: Acht Vorträge von Heinrich Reichel und ein Vortrag von Hermann Muckermann, gehalten in der 'Ravag' im Rahmen der 'Stunde für Volksgesundheit'* (Vienna: Wiener Gesellschaft für Rassenpflege (Rassenhygiene), 1930). On the popularization of eugenics and racial hygiene in Vienna, see also Monika Löscher, 'Zur Popularisierung von Eugenik und Rassenhygiene in Wien', in *Wissenschaft, Politik und Öffentlichkeit: von der Wiener Moderne bis zur Gegenwart*, eds. Mitchell G. Ash and Christian H. Stifter (Vienna: WUV Universitätsverlag 2002), 233–320.
46 Byer, Rassenhygiene und Wohlfahrtspflege, 144–148.
47 Karl Kautsky Jun., 'Die Eheberatungsstelle der Gemeinde Wien', *Blätter für das Wohlfahrtswesen* 29 (1930): 309.
48 Karl Kautsky Jun., 'Die Eheberatung im Dienste der Wohlfahrtspflege', *Blätter für das Wohlfahrtswesen* 24 (1925): 26–27, 26.
49 Karl Kautsky Jun., 'Weitere Erfahrungen aus der Eheberatung', *Die Bereitschaft* 5 (1925): 13–15, 14.
50 Karl Kautsky Jun., 'Fünf Jahre öffentliche Eheberatung', *Blätter für das Wohlfahrtswesen der Stadt Wien* (1928): 23–24, 24.
51 Thomas Mayer, Akademische Netzwerke um die 'Wiener Gesellschaft für Rassenpflege (Rassenhygiene)' 1924 bis 1948. (Diplom thesis, Vienna: 2004), 74.
52 Karl Kautsky Jun., 'Ärztliche Ehefragen', *Die Bereitschaft* 8, no. 3 (1927): 11–14, 14.
53 Victor Gegenbauer, 'Über soziale Hygiene', in *Einführung in die soziale Hygiene. Erster Teil*, ed. Gemeinde Wien (Vienna: Gemeinde Wien, 1930), 3–13, 7.
54 Victor Gegenbauer, 'Alkoholismus', in Einführung in die soziale Hygiene. Fünfzehn Aufsätze des städtischen Gesundheitsamtes für Fürsorgerinnen und Sanitätsrevisoren. Zweiter Teil, ed. Gemeinde Wien (Vienna: Gemeinde Wien, 1931), 56–82, 69–70. For an example of the problem of alcoholism being expressly linked with racial hygiene, see Ernst Gabriel, 'Rassenhygiene und Alkoholismus. Vortrag am 1. Oktober 1935 in der "Wiener Gesellschaft für Rassenpflege (Rassenhygiene)"'. *Archiv für Rassen- und Gesellschaftsbiologie* 29 (1935): 420–437.
55 AT-OeStA/AdR BMfsV VG, 2089, Alkohol, 64791-8/1931, 7. Österreichischer Alkoholgegnertag, 21.–23.11.1931.
56 Karl Kautsky Jun., *Der Kampf gegen den Geburtenrückgang. Kapitalistische oder sozialistische Geburtenpolitik?* (Vienna: Verlag der Wiener Volksbuchhandlung, 1924), 19. Attempted abortion was punishable with terms of imprisonment between six months and up to a year, while the completed offence attracted between one and five years of imprisonment.
57 Gertrud Berneck, 'Schwangerschaftsunterbrechung und Bevölkerungspolitik. Protokoll der Tagung der Vereinigung sozialdemokratischer Ärzte vom 24. und 25. Mai 1924', *Wiener Medizinische Wochenschrift* 74 (1924): 1387–1389.
58 Kautsky Jun., *Der Kampf gegen den Geburtenrückgang*, 28.
59 Oda Olberg, *Die Entartung in ihrer Kulturbedingtheit. Bemerkungen und Anregungen* (Munich: E. Reinhardt, 1926), 50. Olberg called for sterilization on eugenic grounds to be made possible, for example, ibid., 140–141.

60 AT-OeStA/AdR BMfsV VG, 1650, Geschlechtskrankheiten, 1920, Österreichs Völkerwacht, 'Unser Programm!'.

61 Mayer, 'Austria', 4–71, 9–10; Mayer, '"... daß die eigentliche österreichische Rassenhygiene"', 65–98, 71.

62 Exner, 'Rudolf Goldscheid', 283–301, 286; Paul J. Weindling, 'A City Regenerated: Eugenics, Race and Welfare in Interwar Vienna', in *Interwar Vienna: Culture between Tradition and Modernity,* eds. Deborah Holmes and Lisa Silverman (New York: Camden House, 2009), 81–113.

63 Alexander Pinwinkler, 'Minderheitendiskurse in der Bevölkerungsstatistik in Österreich 1900 bis 1945', in *Eugenik in Österreich. Biopolitische Methoden und Strukturen von 1900–1945,* eds. Gerhard Baader, Veronika Hofer and Thomas Mayer (Vienna: Czernin, 2007), 257–283.

64 Mayer, '"... daß die eigentliche österreichische Rassenhygiene"', 65–98, 75; Mayer, 'Austria', 4–71, 11.

65 Ibid., 4–71, 7.

66 See, for instance, Julius Tandler, 'Was ist Konstitution?', *Wiener klinische Wochenschrift* 43 (1930): 318–319, 319.

67 Felix Tietze, 'Sterilisierung zu eugenischen Zwecken', *Volksaufartung, Erbkunde, Eheberatung* 4, no. 8–9 (1929): 169–212, 199.

68 Here, too, critical voices emerged, among them Viktor Lebzelter, 'Grundsätzliches zur Rassenhygiene', *Mitteilungen der Anthropologischen Gesellschaft Wien* 55 (1925): 361–362, who rejected the politicization of anthropology by the 'Munich School' of racial hygiene without, however, fundamentally ruling out calls for an active and eugenically founded population policy.

69 Katja Geisenhainer, *'Rasse ist Schicksal'. Otto Reche (1879–1966). Ein Leben als Anthropologe und Völkerkundler* (Leipzig: Evangelische Verlagsanstalt, 2002).

70 Heinrich Reichel, *Die Hauptaufgaben der Rassenhygiene in der Gegenwart* (Vienna: Volksgesundheitsamt, 1922), 13, 16.

71 Julius Bauer, 'Erbpathologie und ihre praktischen Konsequenzen', *Wiener klinische Wochenschrift* 47 (1934): 1460–1462.

72 Heinrich von Kogerer, 'Psychiatrie und eugenische Gesetzgebung', *Wiener klinische Wochenschrift* 48 (1935): 1262–1265.

73 Julius Wagner-Jauregg, 'Ueber Eugenik', *Wiener klinische Wochenschrift* 44 (1931): 1–6, 5–6.

74 Julius Wagner-Jauregg, 'Zeitgemäße Eugenik', *Wiener klinische Wochenschrift* 48 (1935): 1–5, 1.

75 Adolf Lorenz, 'Die Welt ohne Krüppel! Nach einem im ärztlichen Fortbildungskurs am 29. Mai 1937 gehaltenen Vortrage', *Wiener Medizinische Wochenschrift* 88 (1938): 1143–1146, 1144–1146. Lorenz was the father of the later Nobel Prize winner Konrad Lorenz (1903–1989), who publicly advocated for elements of the National Socialist race ideology during the Nazi regime and never subsequently abandoned certain eugenic patterns of thinking; see Benedikt Föger and Klaus Taschwer, *Die andere Seite des Spiegels. Konrad Lorenz und der Nationalsozialismus* (Vienna: Czernin Verlag, 2001).

76 Albert Niedermeyer, 'Ist Sterilisierung das wirksamste Mittel zur Verhütung erbkranken Nachwuchses? (Bemerkungen zu H. Kogerer, S. 1262)', *Wiener klinische Wochenschrift* 48 (1935): 1578–1584, 1583. For more on Niedermeyer and Catholic eugenics, see Löscher, '... *der gesunden Vernunft nicht zuwider...*'.

77 https://www.geschichtewiki.wien.gv.at/Ilse_Arlt (accessed 25 August 2020).

78 Michael Hubenstorf, '"Medizin ohne Menschlichkeit". Die Wiener Medizin und der Nationalsozialismus – 50 Jahre danach. Teil 2', *Wiener Arzt* 6 (1995): 16–30.

79 Birgit Johler, 'Zur Praxis August Aichhorns 1938–1944. Entwurf eines "Soziogramms" auf Grundlage seiner Patientenkalender' (paper presented at Psychoanalyse in totalitären und autoritären Regimen, Wiener Psychoanalytische Akademie, 28 November 2008).

80 See, for example, for Vienna Herwig Czech, Erfassung, *Selektion und 'Ausmerze'. Das Wiener Gesundheitsamt und die Umsetzung der nationalsozialistischen 'Erbgesundheitspolitik' 1938 bis 1945* (Vienna: Deuticke, 2003).

81 Wolfgang Neugebauer, 'Rassenhygiene in Wien 1938', *Wiener klinische Wochenschrift* 110 (1998): 128–134.

3 'Each Jewish Child Is Precious'

Survivor Community in Poland and Its Biopolitical Discourses[1]

Natalia Aleksiun

Watching over the retreat of the Germans in Drohobycz (Drohobych in present-day Ukraine), Adela Hilzenrad commented in July 1944, 'That sight brought me much satisfaction. But where was the joy I hoped to feel? I didn't feel it. There was no joy because I knew what these green uniforms and helmets left behind. They left a cemetery with our dearest in it. When I look at these uniforms I cry with happiness, but my lips curse them. I couldn't do anything else'. Juxtaposing the image of a cemetery – that symbolized not only her personal loss but also an aftermath of a communal genocide – she still tried to make plans for after liberation. Cautiously, she began to envision rebuilding her family's life by raising her son Józio. Rejecting Poland in order to ensure the safety of her only child, she tied her hope for rejuvenation with his future, away from Drohobycz and from Poland more broadly:

> If our child would be saved from this massacre, in which hundreds of thousands of children perished, we have no right to risk his life again. Realistically it was clear to us that no matter in which country we would settle, we would still be Jews. Our thoughts turned to a different homeland, the one true, faraway homeland; about which we heard so much but never thought about settling there. In our real homeland we would never know the senseless and terrible fear of death. There, if we would be attacked, we would defend it because it is our land, our country. There we would never hear the word 'Jew' in a derogatory way. We would never be hurt or denigrated just because we were Jews. If we would have to defend ourselves, we will fight. We will either win or die like human beings, not like animals.[2]

Thus, as was the case of many other survivors, for Hilzenrad, Palestine offered the promise of safety and dignity, in extreme contrast to the humiliation, danger and imminent destruction of Jewish life in the diaspora. Additionally, she anticipated international support for the rehabilitation of the remaining Jews who would seek to rebuild their lives and regain equal rights. Other testimonies of Jews from Poland whose children also survived the Holocaust replicate the same contrast – a cemetery standing in for the Polish Jewish

DOI: 10.4324/9781003161080-5

community on the one hand and on the other hand life, and their children's future away from Poland.[3] Importantly, the either implied or explicit juxtaposition was not limited to these survivors' own biological children.

In an undated testimony, likely recorded in 1947 by the Central Jewish Historical Commission in Poland, a woman recalled her impassioned involvement in locating a Jewish orphan, not related to her, who was being cared for in an orphanage run by nuns in Gliwice, in western Poland. She recalled feeling restless about the fate of the child and her own moral doubts. Should she remove the girl from the Catholic institution and 'give the child to the Jews who constantly wander in the world'? Seeking advice, the witness turned to Edward Rostal, the chairman of a local Jewish committee. His answer was, 'Take the child away. Each Jewish child is precious, there are so few of them. We cannot give up'.[4] He also suggested a strategy: locating a Jew with the same last name as the child in question and introducing him as her relative in order to claim the girl.[5]

This dialogue reveals the discourse of a communal demographic crisis at the heart of public and private conversations among the survivors: both laypeople and elected officials. The sense of loss led to a feeling of urgency and a conviction that no Jewish child could be 'left behind' – and therefore an implicit mission of rebuilding the Jewish national body. Individual survivors, some of them parents before the war, seem to have been eager to ensure the future of the orphaned children who were long left behind in the care of non-Jews.[6] Rather than delving into personal attitudes towards motherhood in the aftermath of the Holocaust, this article pays particular attention to how Jewish communal leaders discussed what lay ahead for Polish Jewry in discourse that focused on new mothers and children seen – to quote Michel Foucault – as a way 'to ensure, sustain, and multiply life, to put this life in order'.[7] Therefore I focus on the discourse promoted by the Centralny Komitet Żydów w Polsce, CKŻP (Central Committee of the Jews in Poland), the most prominent official institution representing Polish Jews in the aftermath of the Holocaust, rather than on informal activities of bodies that sought to locate and 'recover' Jewish children and functioned underground or in semi-legality.[8]

Although they did not represent the state, the CKŻP and its local branches along with other Jewish institutions assisting the survivors, perceived themselves as political bodies representing a minority whose continued existence had been threatened by a genocide. Biopolitical efforts intersected with political culture, discourse on gender and sexuality, and parenthood. Reading these efforts in the Polish Jewish context of the first three years after the Holocaust (1945–1947) suggests a multi-faceted relationship between communal portrayals of parenthood and gender and a hightened pro-natalist turn. In the immediate post-war period, Jewish communal leaders coped with Jewish flight from Poland and promoted motherhood, engaging with the question of national rebuilding. Simultaneously, the goal of Jewish activists was not necessarily to place orphans with Jewish parents and in Jewish families, but rather in a Jewish environment, i.e. the orphanage, at times irrespective of the child's upbringing and wishes. In this enterprise, Jewish communal institutions strove to monopolize and mobilize their biopower over the community of survivors. Guided by the goal of the national revival, it was particularly concerned with the physical well-being of Jewish parents, future Jewish mothers and Jewish children.[9]

Political Leadership

In his Holocaust memoir, a leading activist of the left-wing pioneer Zionist organization Hehalutz Hatzair Dror (The Young Pioneer and member of the Żydowska Organizacja Bojowa (Jewish Fighting Organization) in the Warsaw ghetto, Yitzhak Zuckerman (1915–1981), described his personal breakdown following liberation in January 1945:

> Until January, I lived in constant fever of activity. At that time, until the Liberation, I didn't sense the passage of time, I didn't feel how the days went by. There were fears and terror, but I never reached the breaking point. ... After all, I knew everything, but there's a difference between knowing and seeing with your own eyes. You can read all the books and know everything. I think I knew what was happening to the Jews better than anyone else in Poland. Nevertheless, in light of what I saw 'after the deluge' – that there were no Jews, that Poland was without Jews – I broke down.[10]

However, Zuckerman emerged from this moment of hopelessness to engagement in collective efforts on behalf of the community of survivors in Poland. What propelled him was his political commitment to Zionism which gave meaning to his renewed activism and a sense of urgency.[11] For those who had long been active in the Zionist movement, the moment of liberation indicated a clear call for action on behalf of their organization, their party or more broadly a Zionist cause. The movement was to take charge of the survivors' collective Jewish future and by doing so ensure the national revival. After Warsaw was liberated, Zuckerman continued to reflect on the future of the movement and practical steps that needed to be taken:

> The day the Red Army entered Warsaw, we felt like orphans; we had a sense that there was no Jewish people anymore. We had no estimate, we didn't know how many were left. ... We decided to start assembling remnants. We didn't reach most of the people because the Jews couldn't find us or we couldn't find them. Instead of thousands, we now had hundreds.[12]

However, what seems to have been overlooked is his engagement in a biopolitical project of nation-building for which women and children were essential. Indeed, one of the important turning points for him was a chance encounter in Częstochowa. Visiting the town in search for Jews, he would walk the streets in hope for a clue.[13]

> In the place I entered, I saw two adjoining rooms with a very small transom between them. Suddenly, I heard singing from the other room. I asked who was there and was told it was Jewish children, a group of Jewish sixteen-year-olds. I was curious, I went in, and asked where they were from. They told me they had been in hiding for a long time. The children had been in Camp Hasag and were now going to a Polish school. ... They were all orphans. Their tale made a great impression on me. ... We started talking. I told them about Eretz Israel, about the youths. I said they didn't have a future here as Jews, since they were going to Polish school. I told them we were a Halutz movement, forming kibbutzim; and if they wanted, we would gladly take them. I gave them my address in Warsaw: Poznańska 39.[14]

What Zuckerman's memoir only managed to allude to was the particular status of these teenagers who were miraculously discovered. These were mostly young Jewish women – a fact that becomes clear upon reading their names identified in a footnote.[15] Elsewhere in his memoir he referred to locating the same group as finding 'young Jews' in Częstochowa, who later established a training kibbutz in Warsaw.[16] Zuckerman's recollection refers to the centrality of the process of recovering Jews, who while having survived the Holocaust, may have found themselves in the process of becoming 'lost' to their nation. While Zuckerman does not elaborate on the gender of the orphans, he identified only young women among them. Their future was of essence to the national body: they were both 'children' and future mothers. At the same time they could be directed into Zionism. For Zuckerman, this particular recovery proved a story of unmitigated success. Like Zuckerman, other Jewish political and communal activists realized that in the aftermath of the war, Jewish children who had survived on the 'Aryan side' and in camps continued living with their foster families, wandering under an assumed Christian identity, in orphanages run by religious orders and in groups of adolescents, such as the one in Częstochowa. Some ethnic Poles relinquished Jewish children after the war, in expectation of financial remuneration. Others were driven by an understanding that these children 'belonged with the Jews'.[17] Some children and youth sought contact with Jews and Jewish institutions,[18] but others needed to be located and convinced to come to live among Jews.

Institutional Biopolitics

Zuckerman visited Częstochowa and other sites in Poland under the framework of the umbrella Jewish organization in Poland – the CKŻP. Formed in the fall of 1944 in Lublin, the Central Committee, claimed to represent Polish Jewry vis-à-vis Polish authorities and abroad.[19] From its very inception, it listed the care for Jewish children as one of its key goals. This, of course, was part of a broader mission of initiating organized actions to provide for the survivors while speaking on their behalf. According to the statutes of the Central Committee, it promised to care for children, and in particular orphans, by organizing childcare centres, kindergartens and orphanages.[20] Likewise it sought to organize health care for the Jewish population and tend to the needs of the repatriated Jews.[21] At the first plenary meeting of the Central Committee on 2 February 1945 in Lublin, the participants concluded that the committee needed to delegate representatives to all the towns with Jewish population who would intervene with local authorities on behalf of the Jews, helping organize soup kitchens and employment. As its key goal, the committee was to 'engage with the fate of the children who ought to be sent to Otwock'.[22] The note concerning Otwock – the site of a Jewish sanatorium before the war – signalled the committee's plan to establish Jewish institutions devoted to restoring the health of child survivors. In the early protocols of the Central Committee, where its members regularly requested data about the situation of the Jews in various towns, their discussions noted the number of children among the general population of survivors.[23] A comprehensive physical rehabilitation of children tied with helping their mothers guided the idea behind creating and furter developing Jewish communal institutions as early as spring 1945. When planning its work for May 1945, the committee envisioned opening a clinic for mothers and babies and an ambulatory for children and youth. In Łódź, the committee supervised organizing a kindergarten for 100 children for working mothers to offer them a place for 8 hours a day and full meals.[24]

The Central Committee saw its role as divided into several stages, at first as giving assistance to Jewish men and women emerging from hiding places and expanding it into care for children and founding children's homes.[25] It allocated funds for individual children and took on the role of reimbursing non-Jews who had sheltered Jewish children. For example, when in April 1945, someone with the surname of Bitter who was from Skarżysko-Kamienna asked the committee for assistance in paying the 'Aryan caretakers' of her (or his) child, the committee decided on allocating 5,000 złoty for this purpose.[26] Repeatedly, Jewish activists who were members of the committee expressed concern about the situation of the children that were still under the care of 'Aryans' and who were kept as a security for the future payment. In late April 1945, the committee declared that such children ought to be moved to nascent Jewish institutions without delay.[27]

Similarly, the American Jewish Joint Distribution Committee (Joint), when it was permitted to carry out work in Poland in 1945–1947, placed expenses for Jewish children at the heart of its budgetary provisions.[28] In January 1946, the JDC promised to allocate funds for 2,000 children in

Jewish institutions throughout Poland and for 2,000 children in open care. Additional categories included caring for the youth, the elderly and the disabled, as well as the demobilized Jewish soldiers and the ill.[29]

Following the repatriation from the Soviet Union, a fury of activities began in support of mothers and children, primarily organized by the Towarzystwo Ochrony Zdrowia Ludności Żydowskiej, TOZ (Society for Safeguarding the Health of the Jewish Population). This organization, originally established in Warsaw in 1921 and funded by memberships, donations and foreign Jewish philanthropies, looked after the welfare of Polish Jewish citizens, promoting their health and the health of their children.[30] In 1946, TOZ organized six 'mother and child' stations responsible for providing medical care.[31] Among these institutions was Dom Położniczy (Maternity Home) which opened in Bytom – an important destination for Polish Jews repatriating to Poland.[32] In Soplicowo, near Otwock, and in Dzierżoniów, in Lower Silesia, special homes for young children began operating tending to new-borns and toddlers who could stay there with their mothers, Dom Matki i Dziecka (Mother and Baby Home).[33] Last but not least, a home for new-borns was set up in Cracow, Dom Małego Dziecka (Infant Child Care Home).[34] Building on their pre-war expertise in supporting Jewish mothers to raise healthy children, the new institutions actively sought to protect and improve the health of Jewish children. But they also faced problems specific to the population repatriated from the Soviet Union. For example, in Wałbrzych, Dr M. Schneebaum, who headed the Clinic for Mothers and Children, reported that the personnel of the home struggled with malaria – a condition unknown to them before the war, which was brought by Jews returning to Poland from Central Asia. The report mentioned over 30 cases of malaria among Jewish children.[35] Moreover, TOZ sought to connect 'lonely' (osamotnione) children with Jewish families abroad. Importantly, it sent abroad not only 'nicely done photographs' of the children selected for this form of assistance but also information about their physical health and measurements of their height and chest.[36] In order to facilitate the emotional connection, children were encouraged to create a bond with their 'guardians' abroad by sharing with them details about their experiences and family history. Financial assistance sent from abroad was seen as essential in restoring these children's health.[37]

Recognizing the importance of Jewish children's health needs and the vital role that the children played in the continuity of the Jewish people, the TOZ established institutions devoted to the care for the mothers and their young children. This very much paralleled the pre-war activities of the organization. However, the context of the Holocaust infused these patterns with a sense of particular urgency. Jewish institutions sought to fill the familial and communal void. In Soplicowo, 'From 8 am to 4 pm, mothers help with bathing the children, moving their beds, washing and cleaning the rooms'.[38] It is unclear if other young children were orphans, or if their mothers were caring for other family members, since the number of children was higher than that of the mothers.[39] The reports from Soplicowo decried the conditions in the home and the lack of sufficient equipment without commenting on the quality of the care provided by the mothers, who likely could not rely on other female family members such as their own mothers and older sisters to introduce them into parenting routines. An incentive awaited mothers whose children were leaving the home. They would receive financial and material assistance. For example, a Ms Kotek received some 7,000 złoty in addition to 2 sweaters, 2 tights, 2 pieces of clothing, 3 warm blankets, 1 large blanket, 1 coat and 2 bedsheets, among other such items.[40] These were precious items in a situation of post-war misery and prevalent shortages, especially for the new mothers who likely lacked the support of their extended families or grass-root communal networks.

Jewish Reproduction as a National Threat

The Jewish communal leaders' promotion of motherhood and the value the leaders placed on Jewish children were not shared by the general Polish population. In fact, they elicited quite negative responses. Henryk Kopilewicz survived the Holocaust in the Lwów (today Lviv, Ukraine) and Borysław (today Boryslav, Ukraine) ghettos and in hiding and was later sent to the Plaszow and Mauthausen camps. Longing for Poland, he decided to return to Cracow, where he received some help from the Jewish committee and was eventually sent to a sanatorium in the mountain town of Zakopane. Travelling there on the train, he witnessed alarming conversations among passengers that deeply shocked him. His stereotypically 'non-Jewish appearance' made him a trustworthy partner for conversations. Eavesdropping, Kopilewicz learned about the myths that existed among the Poles, ones in which Jews continued to occupy the exaggerated position as beneficiaries of aid and communist policy and thus as exploiters of Poles. Kopilewicz heard that as a Pole returning from Mauthausen he had no support. On the other hand, he learned from the other travellers that Jews returning to Cracow allegedly received 50,000 złoty and coupons for clothes and coats. Jews, in the minds of these Poles, were perceived as unduly privileged. 'The government assigned a load of money for the Jewish women who give birth so that the accursed tribe multiplied', Kopilewicz retold his conversation in a testimony he submitted to the Jewish Historical Commission.[41] This offers a glimpse into some ordinary Poles' understanding of Jewish biopolitics. Indeed, the attitude towards Jewish children which perceived them as a threat to the national interests of the ethnic Polish community led to armed attacks on Jewish orphanages in Zakopane and Rabka.[42] They resulted in the decision to evacuate many of the children from Poland.

Holding onto the Children as a Way of Holding onto the National Future

The centrality of national recovery – which was to be achieved by regaining control of the Jewish children, caring for their physical well-being and assuring that new Jewish children would be born in the aftermath of the Holocaust – was hardly understood in the same fashion by Jewish communal activists. This tension came to the fore when the members of the Central Committee encountered competition over the children's futures. For once, they disagreed about prioritizing children's physical safety. In January 1946, the members of the presidium argued bitterly about the invitation extended by the Jewish community in Finland who were willing to host and educate a group of 50 children aged 6–12. The umbrella organization of Polish Jewry engaged in bitter argument over the content of the invitation as it was being presented by the Ministry of Foreign Affairs. This was because it pointed to the Polish authorities' support for the project. While some members of the committee, including Zionist representatives, supported the idea as well and considered it beneficial for the children, others expressed doubts.[43] One of the leaders of the Jewish underground in the Warsaw ghetto and a representative of the left-wing Zionist Poale Zion in the Central Committee Adolf Berman (1906–1978) argued that Jewish children in Poland ought to either stay in Poland or be sent to Palestine. Instead, he suggested to ask the Finnish Jews to send the 'complete equipment of a children's home' to Poland. The Bundists and communists were similarly ambivalent. In particular, Leo Finkelstein (1895–1950) spoke against it, arguing that the children were in the care of the Central Committee and should not be torn away from their routines. A communist member of the committee – Marek Bitter (1903–1965) – maintained that new surroundings cannot be good for the children.

At the same meeting, the committee discussed the offer of the World Jewish Congress to send 1,000 children to Sweden, where they would stay until they were able to emigrate to Palestine. The cost of which would be covered by the World Jewish Congress. But Paweł Zelicki (b. 1901) – another communist member of the committee – responded that many Jewish children were still in the hands of Christians and recovering them was costly. He believed that this goal – discussed regularly at committee meetings – was far more important than sending children away. A representative of the World Jewish Congress visiting Poland, Dr Samuel Margoshes (1887–1968), a Yiddish journalist and Zionist activist, was willing to support the offer stating that children in the hands of Christians belonged to the Yishuv (Jewish settlement) in Palestine.[44] The question of the children that were invited to recuperate in Sweden returned at the meeting of the CKŻP in March 1946.[45] A Zionist activist who also arrived in Poland on behalf of the World Jewish Congress, Zerach Wahrhaftig (1906–2002), argued that given the political unrest in Poland and the forced closing of the children's home in Zakopane, sending the children to Sweden was necessary.

In April 1946, the Central Committee faced a similar dilemma. The Jewish organization caring for orphans (Oeuvre de Secours aux Enfants, OSE) declared their desire to invite 100 Jewish children from Poland to Mexico, where they would be placed with Jewish families.[46] Thus, there would be no concerns about the children being raised in a non-Jewish environment. As in the case of Finland, Poland's Ministry of Foreign Affairs supported the initiative. Likewise, the Central Committee supported the idea across political divisions. Only left-wing Zionist representative, Adolf Berman, noted a slight reservation, stating again that the children ought to be sent to Palestine or stay in Poland. However – he continued – given the situation in the country, he was in favour of sending the children not only to Mexico but to other countries willing to take them in.[47] In these discussions, the committee not only asserted its right to decide where and how surviving Polish Jewish children should be raised but also what degree of physical danger to their lives was acceptable and what prompted calls for immediate evacuation.

Limited Biopower

The tensions surrounding the future of Jewish children lay bare the conflicted discourses about biopolitics vis-à-vis the Jewish future. At the same time, the allocation of resources was discussed in the broader context of Polish society after the war. Even in the direst period, on the eve of the mass repatriation from the Soviet Union, Jewish organizations feared that they could be perceived as too sectarian and concerned only with their own body politics. Therefore, as part of the relations with non-Jewish Poles, Jewish activists advocated for Christian children to be included in the material assistance that was earmarked for Jewish children. In early January 1946, members of the Central Committee of the Jews in Poland criticized the Joint for distributing assistance among non-Jewish children during the holidays – something that should have been done via the committee apparatus. However, Salo Fiszgrund (1893–1971), a Bundist representative in the presidium of the Central Committee, argued that these gestures were important as they showed that 'despite experiences and injustices, Polish Jews remember their countrymen in need'.[48]

The community of survivors engaged in biopolitics in the context of extreme insecurity. Not only was the discourse of rebuilding the nation complicated by the Jewish survivor community's minority status but also by the sense of a continued physical threat to the lives of the precious children who represented the hope of a future. In this sense, the story with which I opened this article is particularly telling. When Fischbein – the local Jewish merchant who agreed to carry out a mission acting as a relative – returned home from Gliwice with the Jewish orphan, a girl named Michasia, she became very sick. After a visit from a nun – who complained about what happened when a child missed her familiar surroundings and suggested that she be returned to the Catholic institution – her condition worsened. The child then developed a high fever and was diagnosed with a ruptured appendix. Subsequently, the woman who had first taken an interest in Michasia and orchestrated her removal from the Catholic orphanage called for a Polish non-Jewish doctor to see the child and insisted that she be treated at a non-Jewish hospital and by non-Jewish medical personnel. She commented in her testimony: 'I took into consideration that if the child died, the nuns could have suspected that the Jews had poisoned her in order not to return her to the Polish [i.e., Catholic] orphanage. This was after the Kielce pogroms [sic]'.[49] More importantly, her caution or, rather, a sense of limited biopower was shared by the members of the local Jewish committee who agreed the girl needed to be treated by non-Jews. Referencing the brutal pogrom in Kielce, which was triggered by a blood libel accusation, in reference to the treatment of a Jewish orphan in Silesia, testifies to the limits of Jewish biopower and autonomy.[50]

Conclusions

For the Jewish survivors' community in Poland in the immediate aftermath of the Holocaust, the communal and individual goals of rebuilding seem to have aligned. Survivors and political bodies claiming to represent them looked at parenthood and reproduction as a victory over Hitler, both on a personal and national level. Therefore, Jewish communal institutions after the Holocaust sought social and political power over collective Jewish life by supporting parents in general, but especially young mothers and their children, and by extensive efforts to recover and care for Jewish children, many of them orphans. In this respect, this biopolitical discourse and investment in caring for Jewish children and creating conditions that would encourage survivors to have children resemble the context studied thoroughly in the displaced persons (DP) camps.[51] As in the British and American occupation zones, Jewish umbrella organizations stepped forward to provide for new Jewish parents and parents in spe and to guide them through the process of physical revival. In Poland, this spirited activity took place vis-à-vis the different political and social contexts of a gradual communist takeover and ongoing anti-Jewish violence. Both internally and externally, they walked a thin line between the physical rebuilding of an ethnic minority who had just faced almost complete extinction and a cautious integration in Poland, or, alternatively an exodus from Eastern Europe.

Notes

1 I would like to thank Joanna Sliwa and Katarzyna Person for their comments on an early draft of this article.
2 United States Holocaust Memorial Museum (USHMM), RG 2011.287.1, Hilzenrad family papers, 'Kiedy bestja się budzi … Przeżycia z okresu okupacji niemieckiej, czerwiec 1941-sierpień 1944 r'. (When the Beast Awakens …

Experiences in times of the German occupation, June 1941 to August 1944.) I am grateful to Marcel Drimer for making the English translation available to me.

3 See Esther Stermer, *We Struggle to Survive* (Montreal: Jewish Institute of Higher Research, 1975), 115–117, 120–123. See also Natalia Aleksiun, 'Imagined Motherland: Zionism in Poland after the Holocaust', in *Polin: Studies in Polish Jewry*, vol. 35; *Promised Lands: Jews, Poland, and the Land of Israel*, eds. Antony Polonsky, Francois Guesnet and Scott Ury, 222-232, (forthcoming, 2023).

4 Archiwum Żydowskiego Instytutu Historycznego (Archive of the Jewish Historical Institute, AŻIH), 301/3010, Wyciąg z protokołu [Excerpt from a protocol], 1.

5 AŻIH, 301/3010, 1. She located a Jewish man who agreed to play the role of an uncle. Interestingly, he first inquired about her organizational affiliation but then seemed moved by the role he was asked to play.

6 See Moshe Malz, *Years of Horror. Glimpse of Hope. The Diary of a Family in Hiding* (New York: Shengold, 1993), 134–135.

7 Michel Foucault, *The History of Sexuality, vol. 1: The Will to Knowledge* (New York: Vintage Books, 1978/1990), 138.

8 On this subject, see Emunah Nachmany-Gafny, *Dividing Hearts: The Removal of Jewish Children from Gentile Families in Poland in the Immediate Post Holocaust Years* (Jerusalem: Yad-Vashem, 2009); Nachum Bogner, *At the Mercy of Strangers: The Rescue of Jewish Children with Assumed Identity in Poland* (Jerusalem: Yad-Vashem, 2001); Anna Bikont, *Cena: w poszukiwaniu żydowskich dzieci po wojnie* (Wołowiec: Czarne, 2022).

9 See Michel Foucault: *Security, Territory, Population. Lectures at the Collegé de France, 1977–78* (New York: Palgrave, 2007), 1.

10 Yitzhak Zuckerman, *A Surplus of Memory: Chronicle of the Warsaw Ghetto Uprising* (Berkeley, CA: University of California Press, 1993), 457–458.

11 Zuckerman, *A Surplus of Memory*, 574.

12 Ibid., 565.

13 Ibid., 587.

14 Ibid., 588.

15 Zuckerman, *A Surplus of Memory*, 588, note 30. For a slightly different version of this encounter, see Yitzhak Zuckerman, *The Polish Exodus: On the 'Bricha' and the Reconstruction of the Pioneer Movement* [in Hebrew] (Tel Aviv: Ghetto Fighters' House and Hakibbutz Hameuchad, 1988), 43.

16 Zuckerman, *A Surplus of Memory*, 574.

17 AŻIH, 301/2734, Testimony of Wiktor Rattner, born 5 August 1935 in Lwów, son of Emil and Anna (née) Wertler. When his testimony was recorded, Rattner lived in an orphanage in Bytom.

18 Nachmany-Gafny, *Dividing Hearts,* 83–90; Bogner, *At the Mercy of Strangers,* 183–192.

19 See David Engel, 'The Reconstruction of Jewish Communal Institutions in Post-War Poland: The Origins of the Central Committee of Polish Jews, 1944–1945', *East European Politics and Societies* 10, no. 1(1996): 85–107.

20 Anna M. Rosner, *Obraz społeczności ocalałych w Centralnej Kartotece Wydziału Ewidencji i Statystyki CKŻP*, (Warsaw: Żydowski Instytut Historyczny, 2018), 161.

21 Rosner, *Obraz społeczności ocalałych*, 161.

22 AŻIH, Prezydium i Sekretariat, 303/I/7, Protocol nr 1 of the plenary meeting of the Central Committee of Polish Jewish, 2 February 1945 at the Central Committee in Lublin, 19/29 Lubartowska Street, 5. Present at the meeting: Dr Sommerstein, Dr Herszenhorn, Zelicki, Zonszajn, Kossower, Dr Berman,

Cukierman, Szklar, Cywia [Lubetkin], Juszyńsi, Danielowa, Turkow. Chairing Dr E. Sommerstein, secretary Z. Barall.

23 See, for example, AŻIH, 303.1/8, Protocol of the Presidium 9 February 1945, 9. Present at the meeting: Dr Sommersten, Dr Berman, Bitter, Zonszajn. Zelicki and Turkow. The Protocol noted the number of Jewish children in Częstochowa and Cracow. It also noted the number of Jewish women who returned from the camps and lived in the Perec House in Warsaw.

24 See AŻIH, 303.1/7, Work schedule of the Central Committee of Polish Jews for May 1945, 33–35.

25 AŻIH, 303.1/11, Protocol nr 5 of the Presidium meeting on 29 January 1946, 24. Present at the meeting: Bitter, Berman, Kossower, Leo Finkelstein, Kameraz, Falk, Zonszajn, Wasser, Prof Sack, and guests from abroad Majerzon from Sweden, Blaugrund from Finland, Dr Margoshes and Dr Sigal as representatives of the World Jewish Congress from the United States.

26 AŻIH, 303.1/7, Protocol nr 9 of the Central Committee of Polish Jews meeting on 13 April 1945, 25–26. Present at the meeting: Dr Sommerstein, Bitter, Zelicki, Zonszajn, Szklar, Berman and Turkow.

27 See AŻIH, 303.1/7, Protocol nr 10 of the plenary session of the members of the Central Committee of Polish Jews meeting on 28 April 1945, 44. Present at the meeting: Dr Sommerstein, Dr Herszenhorn, Bitter, Zelicki, Dr Berman, Turkow, Danielowa, Adw. Gutmacher, Szklar, Zonszajn, Kossower, Szuldenfrei, Fiszgrunt, Sack and Friedman.

28 See Helena Datner, *Po Zagładzie. Społeczna histora żydowskich domów dziecka, szkół, kół studentów w dokumentach Centralnego Komitetu Żydów w Polsce* (Warsaw: Żydowski Instytut Historyczny, 2016).

29 JDC provided funding for opening and sustaining public kitchens, culture and propaganda, funerals and exhumations, historical commissions and productivization. See AŻIH, 303.1/11, Protocol nr 2 of the conference concerning the budget for the Central Committee of Polish Jews, 8 January 1946, 9. See also Anna Sommer-Schneider, *Sze'erit hapleta Ocaleni z Zagłady. Działalność American Jewish Joint Distribution Committee w Polsce w latach 1945-1989* (Cracow: Księgarnia Akademicka, 2014), 37-167.

30 See Ignacy Einhorn, *Towarzystwo Ochrony Zdrowia Ludności Żydowskiej w Polsce w latach 1921–1950* (Toruń: Wydawnictwo Marszałek, 2008).

31 Archiwum Akt Nowych (Archive of New Records, ANN), Ministerstwo Administracji Publicznej (MAP), Dep. Polit., CKŻP, 788.

32 AŻIH, TOZ, 324/536.

33 AŻIH, TOZ, 324/122, 374, 1639–1641.

34 AŻIH, TOZ, 324/1391.

35 TOZ 324/ 579. Dzierżoniów. Oddział Wojewódzki TOZ. *Rok naszej pracy* [Wrocław 1947]. Sprawozdanie z działalności za okres marzec 1946-marzec 1947 r., 39.

36 AŻIH, TOZ, 324/851, Letter of the TOZ Branch in Dzierżoniów to TOZ in Bolków, Jawor county, 18 August 1947, signed by dr. Bayer, Hekselman, 3.

37 See a copy of a letter sent to the TOZ chapter in Bolków on 24 July 1948, signed by dr. Deutschmeister and Hekselman, AŻIH, TOZ, 324/851, 21.

38 AŻIH, TOZ, 324/1834. According to the reports, the centre cared for 19 children with the help of 21 personnel. The report was likely from the fall of 1946.

39 AŻIH, TOZ, 324/1639, 31 August 1946, 7.

40 Do Kierowniczki Domu Dziecka Soplicowo, signed by Director General Dr I. Chain, Referat Opieki nad Matką i Dzieckiem Dr. Z. Golde, Copy of, 11 March 1947, 1861/47, AŻIH, TOZ, 324/122.

41 AŻIH, 302/51, Pamiętnik Henryka Kopilewicza, 54.

42 See Karolina Panz, '"Poles Take Over all of Rabka" – the Microhistory of Ethnic Cleansing', in *No Neighbours' Land: Post-War Europe in a New Comparative Perspective*, eds. Anna Wylegała, Sabine Rutar and Małgorzata Łukianow (New York: Palgrave, 2022), forthcoming. See also idem, '"The Children are in a State of True Panic" Post-War Anti-Jewish Violence in Podhale and Its Youngest Victims', *Yad Vashem Studies* 46, no. 1 (2018): 103–140.

43 AŻIH, 303.1/11, Protocol nr 5 of the Presidium of the Central Committee of Polish Jews, 29 January 1946, 24. Present at the meeting: Bitter, Berman, Kossower, Leo Finkelsten, Kameraz, Falk, Zonszajn, Wasser, Prof. Sack, guests from abroad Majerzon from Sweden, Blaugrund from Finland, Dr Margoshes and Sigal from America as representatives of the World Jewish Congress. Chairing. Marek Bitter, protocol Zanwel Barall.

44 AŻIH, 303.1/11, Protocol nr 5 of the Presidium of the Central Committee of Polish Jews, 29 January 1946, 25.

45 AŻIH, CKZP, 303.1/11. Protocol nr, of the Presidium of the Central Committee of Polish Jews with participation of the representatives of the World Jewish Congress, 11 March 1946, 62–63. Present at the meeting: Bitter, Fal, Kossower, Wasser, Zelick, Zonszajn, Wahrhaftg, chairing Bitter, protocol Gertnerowa.

46 AŻIH, 303.1/11, Protocol nr 24 of the Presidium of the Central Committee of Polish Jews, 8 April 1946, 80. Present at the meeting: Bitter, Zelicki, Sack, Herszenhorn, Zonnszajn, Dr Berman, Kossower, Zachariasz, Kameraz, Grosman, chairing Bitter, protocol Barall.

47 Ibid.

48 AŻIH, 303.1/11, Protocol nr 1 of the plenary session of the Central Committee, 3 January 1946, 7. Present at the meeting: Bitter, Zelicki, Zonszajn, Kameras, Mirski, Grajek, Wertheim, Berman, Fiszgrunt, Zachariasz, Wasser, as a guest [Jacob] Pat – a delegate of the Jewish Workers' Committee in America, chairing Bitter, protocol Barall.

49 AŻIH, 301/3010, 2.

50 On the pogrom in Kielce see Joanna Tokarska-Bakir, *Pod klątwą. Społeczny portret pogromu kieleckiego*, t. 1–2, (Warszawa: Czarna Owca, 2018).

51 See Atina Grossmann, *Jews, Germans, and Allies: Close Encounters in Occupied Germany* (Princeton, NJ: Princeton University Press, 2007); Margarete Myers Feinstein, "Jewish Observance in Amalek's Shadow: Mourning, Marriage, and Birth Rituals among Displaced Persons in Germany", in: *We Are Here. new approaches to Jewish displaced persons in postwar Germany*, ed. Avinoam Patt and Michael Berkowitz (Detroit: Wayne State University Press, 2010), 257-288.

4 'Marital Intercourse Means Togetherness and Parenthood'

The Biopolitics of Catholic Marriage Preparation in Poland during the 1970s

Agata Ignaciuk

Introduction

In February 1969, mere months after publication of the Encyclical *Humanae Vitae*, in which Pope Paul VI reiterated the central role of fertility in Catholic marriage and banned all 'artificial contraception', the Polish Episcopate released an *Instruction to Priests on the Preparation of the Laity for the Sacrament of Marriage and on Chaplaincy of Families.*[1] This document, in direct dialogue with the Encyclical, initiated the expansion and institutionalization of Catholic marriage preparation in Poland in development since at least the beginning of the century.[2] In the late 1950s, the Polish Catholic hierarchy had promoted pronatalism and large families in stark contrast to the moderately anti-natalist stance of the communist authorities.[3] Attempts were made to thwart state population policies that legalized abortion in 1956, and those that, from 1957 onward, promoted the use of contraception, particularly through *Duszpasterstwo Służby Zdrowia,* a healthcare ministry providing spiritual advice for medical professionals. In addition to the Catholic press, sermons during Sunday Mass and religious lessons across the country were important vehicles for the transmission of Catholic biopolitics to the broader community of followers.[4] The formalization and intensification of Catholic marriage preparation was a key element of the increasing Catholicization of Polish society during the late 1960s and 1970s.[5] Through analysis of marriage preparation course guides released during the 1970s, this chapter explores the development of Catholic marriage expertise and how this dialogued with the concurrent processes of expertization in relation to sexuality and the broadly defined family sciences[6] both in Poland and transnationally.

In Poland these expertization processes intensified from the late 1950s onward, fuelled by the unprecedented rise and mainstreaming of state-sponsored family planning and sex education activities.[7] Many experts in these areas were linked to the Society for Conscious Motherhood, a semi-autonomous organization revived from interwar urban birth control activism and reinforced through membership in the International Planned Parenthood Association.[8] Activities centred around the notion of a 'culture

DOI: 10.4324/9781003161080-6

of sexuality': understood as defining and promoting a 'healthy' sexual relationship within marriage and framed as beneficial for the (socialist) society and the nation.[9] Historian Natalia Jarska has argued that the state-sponsored sex education project of the late 1950s and 1960s was an ambiguous modernization process: intended to counter the 'backwardness' of Catholic sexual norms, it simultaneously and stringently inscribed sexuality within the institution of the family.

The 1970s in Poland witnessed an increase in the public profiles of sexology, demography and the sociology of the family, as well as mounting cooperation between scientific communities and the state-socialist leadership.[10] This cooperation blossomed in the context of the rising governmental preoccupation with the falling population growth rate, prompting increased investment in welfare policies that supported families, such as maternity benefits.[11] This pronatalist shift in population policy brought the state into alignment with the reproductive values of the Polish Catholic Church, an alliance personally endorsed by the leader of the Polish United Workers' Party throughout the 1970s, Edward Gierek.[12] Following Erik G. Huneke, historian Barbara Klich-Kluczewska has argued that at the time this alignment was taking shape, state-socialist biopolitics in Poland were shifting from repressive to relatively 'soft'.[13] This chapter will provide further nuances to this argument, by focusing on the Polish Catholic Church's population management efforts within the new configuration of alignment rather than antagonism.

As anthropologist Agnieszka Kościańska has demonstrated, in a similar way to state-socialist biopolitics, 1970s Catholic sexology – the science of marriage – was increasingly drawing on rationality and scientific knowledge. The marriage preparation guides explored in this chapter exemplify the construction and mainstreaming of Catholic sexual expertise that blended 'science' and 'faith'. This blending, as Kościańska has highlighted, had been dynamized by the Encyclical *Humanae Vitae*, which explicitly incorporated medicine and psychology into Catholic ethical rationales.[14] This examination of Catholic marriage preparation materials – a particular case of Catholic reproductive management –contributes to recent historical research calling for an analysis of the interaction and interlocution between the Polish church and the Polish state. The rigorous inspection of Catholic biopolitics in relation to state biopolitics during the 1970s enriches our understanding of the operational modes of Polish population administration in the state-socialist era as well as the present day.[15] In what follows, I will first outline the second half of the twentieth-century history of Catholic marriage preparation in Poland within a context of competition with secular sex and family planning education. Second, I will discuss my sources: the marriage preparation guides produced during the 1970s that were aimed at the priests and laity engaged in delivering Catholic marriage preparation courses. Finally, I analyze the representations of birth control practices and marital sexuality in these guides, highlighting singularities and similarities in their framing of Catholic discourse and mainstream sociological and medical expertise.

Catholic Marriage Preparation in State-Socialist Poland

Catholic marriage preparation courses, the systematic analysis of which has thus far sparked limited interest within the history of Polish sexuality, were a form of sex education that the vast proportion of Polish society under state-socialism were exposed to and which, as this chapter will show, competed with and at the same time complemented state-sponsored family planning and sex education campaigns.[16] Following the legalization of abortion in 1956, the Society for Conscious Motherhood was assigned the task of launching a mass campaign to popularize contraception, through lectures, radio programmes and high-print-run brochures. This campaign was most intense during the late 1950s and the first half of the 1960s.[17] Although public and state-sponsored sex education was introduced to primary school curricula in 1969 and formalized as a specific subject entitled 'preparation for socialist family life' during the mid-1970s, by the end of that decade, only one-third of schools were delivering sex education classes; these were only made mandatory in 1986.[18] Marriage preparation courses, on the other hand, had a potentially far wider coverage. In 1976, 82 per cent of all Polish marriages were conducted in a Catholic church; in 1980, this figure peaked at 97.3 per cent. While this percentage decreased slightly over the following years (94.4 per cent in 1985, 92.8 per cent in 1988), it is fair to speculate that the vast majority of Poles coming of age in the 1970s would have been exposed to some kind of Catholic marriage preparation content.[19] One small late-1980s study of urban and rural women's contraceptive practices concluded that premarital courses were the second most important source of knowledge about family planning in the city and the countryside alike, surpassed only by 'mass media'.[20]

Catholic marriage preparation was broad in scope and conceived of as a long-term process. From the late 1950s onwards, the Polish Episcopate recommended that specific marriage preparation content be provided for children, young people and adults at every stage of their religious education. This 'long-term preparation' was to be delivered to schoolchildren during retreats (*rekolekcje*) and during religious lessons held in every parish (since religion had been removed from public education in 1961), as well as to young adults during marriage preparation courses and catechesis, and to the affianced through 'immediate preparation', which concluded with a prenuptial exam. The 1969 'Instruction to Priests on the Preparation of the Laity for the Sacrament of Marriage and on Chaplaincy of Families' made 'immediate preparation' mandatory for couples wanting a Catholic marriage, unless they had previously completed a marriage preparation course for young adults. The Episcopate deemed that such courses, consisting of a series of lectures combined with worship and prayer, should be made available in every diocese. The distinctive element of the mandatory immediate marriage preparation was more in-depth and even personalized training in the 'natural regulation of conceptions', the term used to denominate the recommended system of fertility awareness that blended science with faith. This training was ideally to be offered by female fertility awareness instructors. The network of these instructors, initially unevenly distributed and concentrated in specific jurisdictions such as Cracow, under the future Pope John Paul II and Archbishop Karol Wojtyła, started to develop in the early 1960s and expanded rapidly in number and geographical coverage during the 1970s.[21]

During the 1960s and 1970s, local dioceses and lay Catholic intellectuals elaborated several guides to support priests and secular believers responsible for the organization of marriage preparation courses for young adults and the affianced. In this chapter, I examine ten such guides, produced in seven Polish cities (Gorzów Wielkopolski, Cracow, Łódź, Poznań, Pelplin, Warsaw and Lublin) between 1970 and 1979. I acceded most of the guides through the archives of the Cracow Metropolitan Curia and the Warsaw Catholic Intelligentsia Club (CIC) archives located in Warsaw's Central Archives of Historical Records. The Cracow Archdiocese was amongst the first to establish a specific Department of Chaplaincy of Families. Under the spiritual leadership of Archbishop Wojtyła, elected in 1963, the department became a leading 'think-tank' in marriage preparation, following the spirit of the Encyclical *Humanae Vitae*.[22] The CIC, an independent organization with branches in many Polish cities, had played an important role in popularizing the ideas of the Second Vatican Council in Poland, expanding notions about the purpose of marital sexuality from primarily reproductive, to reproductive and bond-building. The council also elaborated on the notion of 'responsible parenthood': rational, conscience-informed decision-making by a married couple in planning the number and spacing of offspring.[23]

Catholic Marriage Preparation Training Guides: Methodological Challenges

Three of the guides I analyzed were produced by the hierarchy, four by secular Catholics and the remaining three scripts by a combination of priests and lay Catholic intellectuals, most of the latter with links to the CIC. The majority were aimed at the affianced in immediate marriage preparation, but the authors of others suggested they could also be used in the long-term marriage preparation of all young adults. A guide by the Collaborators of the Poznań Chaplaincy of Families focused specifically on long-term preparation for children aged 7–12 and their parents, while another, by the Department of the Chaplaincy of Families of the Warsaw Metropolitan Curia (1978), targeted instructors of the aforementioned fertility awareness training in the spirit of responsible parenthood as informed by the *Humanae Vitae*.

By the late 1950s, the marketplace for marriage advice publications was becoming rather crowded, with the Society for Conscious Motherhood and its affiliated doctors publishing high-print-run manuals focusing on family planning and sexuality for married women and couples. The prescriptive literature specifically aimed at Catholics gained prominence in the 1970s, when influential books such as *Marriage Upon Us* by the Catholic intellectual and CIC activist Andrzej Wielowiejski appeared, and others, including *Catholics and Family Planning*, first published in the 1960s, were re-edited and expanded in length and print run.[24] Unlike these published manuals aimed directly at affianced and young married couples, the guides I analyze here had a different target audience: those responsible for organizing and delivering Catholic marriage preparation courses. While some were published by local dioceses in extremely short runs, others circulated as scripts. Many went unsigned, making it difficult to attribute authorship, a familiar situation with Catholic teaching materials. However, careful analysis reveals appropriated and often unacknowledged references that would amount to plagiarism in published material, but here perhaps represent the ideas of collective authorship and collage-style writing, in which various sources and arguments are combined in a discourse to serve a specific purpose. I will provide examples of this later in the chapter. In the Polish material, the authorship difficulty is further aggravated by the inherent instability of the mutual tolerance between the Church and communist authorities. The latter, as historian Natalia Jarska has shown, framed sexual governance, and specifically the form of abortion law and access, as an arena in which Church influence could either be accepted or challenged.[25] Therefore, we can speculate that communist authorities tightened or relaxed direct and indirect control mechanisms – such as, respectively, censorship and availability of paper – on what printed Catholic materials could circulate. In this context, the blurred authorship of internal marriage preparation manuals could also be a resistance strategy.

Despite these challenges, the preliminary selection of marriage preparation training material I present here is illustrative of local diversity and the variety of actors – clerical and secular – involved in the design and delivery of preparation for Catholic marriage in Poland during the 1970s and the following decades. In addition to sample lectures and syllabi, this material provides a valuable insight into how the hierarchy and local departments of the Chaplaincy of Families – created in local curiae and archdioceses in a number of Polish cities from the late 1950s onwards[26] and which played an important role in supporting the delivery of marriage preparation – imagined the very concrete protocols of this delivery.

In addition to draft syllabi and lecture content, these protocols included accompanying prayers and songs. Emphasis was often placed on the key role of interaction between speaker and participants, including recommendations to 'discreetly' set out 'question boxes' whereby participants could deposit their questions anonymously[27] and, towards the end of the 1970s, work in small groups to collectively address 'difficult questions'.[28] These explicitly inclusive methodologies echoed concurrent trends in Polish sexology, which, as Agnieszka Kościańska has shown, was shaped by intense exchanges between experts and their readers and patients.[29] Another characteristic of these guides, illustrated in the aforementioned mixed authorship, was an emphasis on cooperation between hierarchy and laity in course delivery, as embedded in the 1969 Episcopal Instruction. While parsons were expected to supervise the course, the Episcopal Instruction and guides explicitly stated that some lectures – especially those relating to reproductive anatomy and physiology, sexuality and contraception – were to be delivered by secular Catholics.

While a number of guides mention the possibility of inviting Catholic doctors or psychologists to present some lectures, most also promoted another category of expert: 'serious and intelligent women'.[30] The earliest of the guides analyzed here, produced by the diocese with the see in Gorzów Wielkopolski, which covered 1/7th of Polish territory after the Second World War,[31] argued that women were particularly appropriate for delivering talks on those topics less suitable for priests. Also illuminating the challenges of introducing sex into the presbyterium, this guide insisted that when 'strictly medical topics' were to be discussed, the monstrance should be removed from the room, an indirect indication of a sense of shameful unholiness persistently linked to the reproductive body.[32] What validated the expertise of secular Catholics, and of Catholic women in particular, was the 'competence, special preparation [with regards to cycle-observation-based "regulation of conceptions"] and long family and marital experience'.[33] An additional validation, necessary for any female instructor, physician and psychologist invited to deliver specific course content, was bestowal by the local hierarchy of 'a mission', an indispensable credential.[34]

These guides tell us little about how attendees reacted to the courses, whether they questioned or rejected the values and ideas to which they were introduced, and cannot reveal the actual delivery of courses in local settings, even if they were locally produced. However, authors of some sample lectures underlined that they had 'actually delivered them in a number of parishes'.[35] Others include handwritten corrections, crossings-out and comments, perhaps showing adaptation of the proposed content to the predilections of the priest or laywoman delivering the catechesis.[36] What this material does showcase is the construction of particular expert discourses on sexuality: Catholic expert discourses, which have largely been ignored by historians. Notable exceptions include, in the European context, contributions to the recently edited collection by Alana Harris, as well as work by Wannes Dupont and Lucia Pozzi.[37] In the Polish context, critical engagement with the history of Catholic family planning is still embryonic. With the aforementioned recent exceptions, including the scholarship of Agnieszka Kościańska, Barbara Klich-Kluczewska, Sylwia Kuźma-Markowska and Natalia Jarska,[38] most of the histories of Catholicism and sexuality/contraception have been memoirs of professional and spiritual experiences by priests and laity personally involved in the Chaplaincy of Families. The relatively limited body of conservative-Catholic historiography has focused heavily on the Church's anti-abortion campaigns between 1956 and 1966.[39] The preliminary analysis in this chapter will include and historicize Catholic premarital expertise, showcasing exchanges and dialogue between the hierarchy and laity during the expansion and intensification of the infrastructure for 'Catholic family planning' delivery in Poland, an infrastructure that has grown immensely ever since. In 2017, there were over 2,500 family counselling centres in Poland, most of which are on a parish level.[40]

The guides I analyze here cover similar topics, including the Catholic conception(s) of love, the sacrament of marriage (including its liturgic, legal and social aspects), sexual ethics and responsible parenthood. This framework has changed little up to the present day. In February 2019, I interviewed a female psychologist who has been an instructor in marriage preparation courses in Sieradz, a small town in central Poland, since the 1980s. A photocopy of the contemporary local marriage preparation programme she provided listed much the same issues as those raised during the 1970s.[41] Given this continuity, my analysis of the key themes raised in marriage preparation guides takes consensus and diversity as the main axes. The two issues that have been most represented, winding through all the guides analysed here, are abortion and contraception. Their centrality is hardly a surprise, given that the intense medicalization and institutionalisation of both practices from the late 1950s has been decried by the Polish Catholic Church and was the rationale for mobilizing the promotion of alternatives. Contraception and abortion, as Kateřina Lišková, Natalia Jarska, and Gabór Szegedi have noted, have been the key elements of state-sponsored sex education in East-Central Europe.[42]

Contraception and Abortion

In Poland, contraceptives, especially female contraceptives such as barrier methods, and from the late 1960s onwards, intrauterine devices, were strongly promoted as healthier alternatives to abortion, which was unequivocally framed as being harmful.[43] However, in Catholic marriage preparation guides of the 1970s, contraception and abortion were represented as being both physically and morally harmful options that would lead to the destruction of love, mutual mistrust and eventually, divorce.[44] Contraception was habitually depicted as 'primitive and vulgar, depriving the sexual act from what is most valuable – the complete surrender'.[45] All the guides analyzed here emphasised that physical harm could result from contraceptive practices, but any references to medical authority as confirmation were rather vague: '*it is said* that some chemical contraceptives cause cancer; *some assert* that their consequences will be seen only in next generations'[46] (my emphasis).[47] In addition to transmitting the idea that contraceptive methods, including unmedicalized techniques such as coitus interruptus, were holistically harmful, they also suggested they were inefficient, selectively using the authority of organizations such as the World Health Organization (WHO) to support their claims. A guide by the Chaplaincy of Families in Łódź quoted the 'WHO technical report no. 360' – probably the 1967 report on *Biology of Fertility Control by Periodic Abstinence* – to claim that condoms had a failure rate of 16 per cent: the original WHO report did not mention condom use at all.[48] The same guide quoted an untraceable 1961 study on 'chemical contraception' proving a failure rate of between 26 and 42 per cent. In contrast, but with no studies to support it, the authors of the guide claimed, 'the periodic abstinence method is practically infallible'.[49]

The equation of abortion with murder was present in all the guides. Many used war and/or genocide metaphors – 'In Poland, we are now responsible for genocide because during the past decade we murdered more human beings than [were murdered] in Auschwitz'[50] – and emphasised the responsibilities of Polish couples towards a 'nation' that needed them to produce more than two children.[51] The 1972 Łódź dioceses guide stated, 'I dare to say that while once the fate of Poland was decided in the battlefield, now these battles are taking place in our families, especially the young ones'.[52] Many scripts recommended the use of visual and textual materials to construct or strengthen ideas about foetal personhood, such as slides with pictures of foetuses. At times, these foetuses were given names, such as 'Jaś' in the 1978 Warsaw Metropolitan Curia script for the affianced.[53] Other guides referred to a magazine article, 'The secret of nine months', originally published in the French *Elle* magazine and reprinted in 1963 in *Kobieta i Życie*, a popular Polish magazine sponsored by the party-affiliated Women's League.[54] The article, rather than reproducing foetal images, discussed the development of an embryo and foetus month by month. When used for Catholic marriage preparation the article was enveloped in pointers to strengthen the emotional and ideological construction of foetal personhood. A 1967 bibliography compiled by the Cracow Department of the Chaplaincy of Families referred to the article as describing 'the prenatal development of a baby' and suggested it be accompanied with the statement that 'from the first moment of conception it is a human being'.[55] The article continued to be a recommended resource in guides throughout the 1970s.[56] Towards the end of the decade, the 1978 Warsaw Metropolitan Curia's script encouraged use of the article with images representing embryonic and foetal development, suggesting that the circulation and political use of foetal visuals had become more extensive in Poland. This collage-like technique of blending – and bending – various resources and sources of authority, voiding or packing them with meaning, was, as I suggested earlier, a common feature of Catholic marriage preparation materials. Similar usage of scientific authority has also been documented by Agnieszka Kościańska in her analysis of sex education debates in the pages of the Catholic magazine, *Miłujcie się*, during the early 1990s.[57]

Acclaim for periodic abstinence, or the natural regulation of conceptions, was unanimous in the guides I analyzed. Marital love was represented as universally, essentially and inevitably fertile: 'marital intercourse means togetherness and parenthood', as a Cracow guide from 1971 preached,[58] a representation clearly linked to the idea of contraception as a threat to the true course of love. These conceptions of marital love were directly inspired by the Encyclical *Humanae Vitae,* which in the majority of guides I analyzed was presented as a thread bringing together the various proposed lectures. The guides were also clear about their aspiration to popularize the Encyclical.[59] The aforementioned fertility awareness training guide produced by the Warsaw Metropolitan Curia in 1978 explicitly detailed what the Encyclical was and recommended that the instructors bid farewell to the affianced with a lengthy quote from the *Humanae Vitae.*[60] This perhaps suggests that by the late 1970s, the papal document had not been as widely disseminated as the Episcopate had initially hoped. Some contemporary scripts omitted mention of the Encyclical and constructed their arguments around Vatican II.[61] Despite pressure from the hierarchy, as Agnieszka Kościańska has also argued, it seems that the persistent presence – perhaps even prioritization – of Vatican II in some marriage preparation material demonstrates its status as an ongoing point of reference for more progressive Catholic intellectuals, such as those linked to the CIC.[62]

Marital Sexuality, Gender and the Natural Regulation of Conceptions

Some other key issues that the guides took slightly different positions on – either linking their orientation to *Humanae Vitae* or Vatican II – were the interconnected ideas relating to gender roles and sexual pleasure. Many of the guides presented a rigid concept of gender roles, detailing how men and women 'naturally' behaved, both professionally and in a couple. Such ideas were extensively developed in one of the guides in my sample targeted at instructors of schoolchildren and their parents.[63] This is not surprising: as Kateřina Lišková, Natalia Jarska and Gabór Szegedi have shown, gender differences, or what the Catholic hierarchy understood as the 'psychological differences between men and women', had been one of the main axes of Catholic long-term marriage preparation for schoolchildren since the end of the 1950s. Gender differences were also the central element of secular sex education in Poland, which promoted an ambiguous blend of formal equality between the sexes while emphasizing their 'cultural and biological differences'.[64] Agnieszka Kościańska has shown how the institutionalization of sexology in the 1970s and 1980s was accompanied by sex experts proactively shaping and popularizing gender stereotypes, especially relating to the binary of passivity/activity in initiating and performing heterosexual sex acts.[65] All the guides analyzed here were resolute that gender and sexual differences existed and could be summarized by the frequently repeated sentence, 'a man wants to be somebody in life, a woman wants to be somebody for someone'. This sentence can also be found in Catholic-inspired sex education materials used in Polish schools today.

A few of the 1970s marriage preparation training guides did offer more flexible advice on the practical aspects of partnership, emphasizing that partners, while 'naturally' suited to their predetermined family roles – women to nurture, men to financially support and 'represent' the family to the outside world – could and should exchange these if necessary.[66] Other authors – both from the hierarchy and the laity[67] – recognised the 'dilemmas of modern mothers' in relation to professional careers 'to which they prepared themselves during 5 years of studies [a university degree]'.[68] They encouraged women to take advantage of the 3-year unpaid maternity leaves, one of the key measures of the 1970s state family policy the Catholic Church commended. One guide emphasized that 'if a child can be well-looked after by an aunt or a grandma, and mother is a recognized and needed employee, perhaps she will have to go back to work after leave'.[69] However, the example provided of a 'recognized and needed employee' was a 'constructor of spaceships', perhaps symptomatic of the exceptionality of such a situation, as well as the highly masculinized ethos of engineering in state-socialist Poland. No involvement in raising the child by a father was mentioned.

As for the sex act itself, there was – and, as anthropologist Esther Peperkamp has shown, continues to be – a consensus that sex was to be triggered by love, not desire, and was a thoroughly spiritual act, as was marital love itself. To use Peperkamp's description, the marital act had in fact three participants: the (heterosexual) spouses and God.[70] Masturbation, or, as the Polish word used in the 1970 Gorzów guide framed the act, 'self-rape', was the ultimate 'egoism, unbridled search for pleasure and inability to love with the sense of sacrifice': the antithesis of God-blessed sexuality.[71] Marital sexuality was sanctioned pleasure. 'Reaching and experiencing mutual love'[72] – a euphemism for orgasm – was in this sense a by-product of mutual subordination, sacrifice and purity within the sex act. At the same time, some guides were explicit about the legitimacy of 'mutual tenderness', meaning foreplay, needed to accomplish this, such as the 1978 Warsaw manual for Family Counselling Centre instructors that offered intensive premarital training over three meetings, a brevity that perhaps explains the relative explicitness of the sexual advice.[73] However, this 'tenderness', as Peperkamp also noted, was only legitimate as a preliminary to the 'natural' intercourse that terminated with ejaculation within the vagina: in any other context, it was sinful. The degree of this sinfulness did vary. The 1970 Gorzów guide, for instance, insisted that wives whose husbands practiced withdrawal, despite their attempts to convince them otherwise, were not engaged in their husbands' sin. However, if a husband used contraceptive devices, the wife would need exceptional reasons to agree to intercourse, and any enjoyment she felt would be a sin.[74] Guides produced by the hierarchy emphasized that, although, and perhaps also because, sexual intercourse could be a merit in the eyes of God, 'one spouse cannot deny it to the other without a serious reason'. Among these reasons, in addition to a husband practicing contraception, the Gorzów guide cited illness and drunkenness, but stressed that 'to deny the marital right lightly is sin'.[75] A guide produced by the Chaplaincy of Families in Łódź extended and gendered these indications, suggesting that 'when the wife is feeling unwell, she is tired, sleepy and only wishes to rest, encouraging her to have intercourse is denial of love. So would be showing a wife disapproval because her mood (*samopoczucie*) forces the husband to give up on the intercourse he eagerly anticipated'.[76]

In this context of pleasurable and somewhat compulsory marital sexuality, the natural regulation of conceptions – the Catholic implementation of the rhythm method – was a moral system intended to train spouses, particularly the husband, in the spirit of love-embedded sacrifice.[77] This sacrifice was also a crucial element in responsible parenthood. While all the manuals insisted the purpose of marital love was to produce abundant offspring, they also underlined the responsibility that reproduction entailed and provided differing advice to guide couples towards 'responsible' decisions. The Kuria Chełmińska's 1974 guide, for instance, included a comprehensive list of reasons for practicing the natural regulation of conceptions through 'periodic abstinence'. These included a wife's ill health, a lack of resources to provide for further children, and ethical reasons, such as when the couple wished to cure themselves of certain unethical practices, probably a reference to *coitus interruptus*.[78] The guide also mentioned *eugenic* reasons taken after seeking advice from a *serious* doctor (my emphasis). The use of 'eugenic' as a legitimate denominator of potential foetal malformations in a guide produced by the Catholic hierarchy, which emphasised that pregnancy should be avoided in such a case as termination was not an option, is particularly interesting given the current use of 'eugenic abortion' in anti-abortion discourses in Poland today: the negative connotations of 'eugenics' are far greater now than half a century earlier. Finally, this and a number of other guides explicitly refer to a lack of independent, adequate housing: 'a child over 3 years of age should not share their parents' bedroom'.[79] In light of the endemic housing crisis in the People's Republic, this consideration had the potential to significantly stifle reproduction within Polish Catholic families, despite waiting periods for cooperative flats being shorter for couples with young children.[80] These ways of delimiting responsible parenthood, which in practice could be applied to the majority of young married couples in Poland, are inherently contradictory as a system for putting fertile love into practice. Another contradiction, as noted in Esther Peperkamp's ethnographic study of young people practicing the natural regulation of conceptions in Poland during the 2000s and also present in my material, is the insistence on the high effectiveness of cycle observation in preventing births, thus potentially restricting the fertile aspects of sexuality to a minimum.[81] While a number of guides provided detailed scripts of natural regulation training sessions,[82] others limited such practical advice to outlining the advantages of the method – 'periodic abstinence is one of the conditions of love, of preserving physical attractiveness, of preventing depression. It is a true love test …'[83] – and listing useful references, before directing couples to Catholic marital counselling centres for fertility awareness training. Amongst the references cited, publications by the Catholic gynaecologists, Włodzimierz Fijałkowski and Teresa Kramarek, were especially prominent. During the 1970s, Włodzimierz Fijałkowski published a number of books on fertility awareness, targeted at both doctors and the general public, through the state medical publisher, Państwowy Zakład Wydawnictw Lekarskich.[84] Teresa Kramarek's booklets on the regulation of conceptions based on temperature observation, and later, on ovulation symptoms and temperature observation, circulated from the mid-1960s onwards outside state-sponsored publication channels,[85] an asymmetry worthy of further exploration.

Conclusion

In this chapter, I have argued that Catholic sexual expertise should be systematically included in historical explorations of sexual expertise and biopolitics in state-socialist Poland. As an omnipresent form of sex education, the Catholic marriage preparation guides I have analyzed, while diverse, promoted a number of the ideas popularized by sex experts and state-sponsored sex education programmes, and can be understood as yet another example of alignment between state and church biopolitics in Poland during the 1970s. Amongst these common threads, the two most significant are the indivisible triad of love-sex-marriage and the more or less ambiguous articulation of gender roles, with uneasy conciliations between 'equality' and 'difference'. The key, irreconcilable differences are the representations of 'artificial' contraception and abortion. In state-sponsored discourses, contraception was the vital prophylaxis to dangerous abortion. In Catholic marriage preparation guides, contraception itself was dangerous and abortion equalled murder. Poland is a particularly illustrative example of the expansion of channels through which Catholic sexual expertise has been promoted since the 1970s. These channels, in addition to premarital courses, include the increasingly institutionalized and expanding network of Catholic family counselling centres and the recent (launched in 2016) substitution of in-vitro fertilization by Na-Pro-Technology techniques, intimately linked to the natural regulation of conceptions in state-sponsored infertility treatment. In this context, historicizing and de-homogenizing Catholic sexual expertise has the potential to shed new light on both past and present Catholic engagement with reproduction in Poland.

Notes

1 Alana Harris, ed., *The Schism of '68: Catholicism, Contraception and Humanae Vitae in Europe, 1945–1975* (Cham: Palgrave McMillan, 2018). This chapter is a result of the research project 'Catholicizing Reproduction, Reproducing Catholicism: Activist Practices and Intimate Negotiations in Poland, 1930 – Present' (National Science Centre, Poland grant no. 2019/33/B/HS3/01068).

2 Sylwia Kuźma-Markowska 'Marx or Malthus? Population Debates and the Reproductive Politics of State-Socialist Poland in the 1950s and 1960s', *The History of the Family* 25, no. 4 (2020): 576–598 (585); Magdalena Gawin, 'The Social Politics and Experience of Sex Education in Early Twentieth-Century Poland', in *Shaping Sexual Knowledge: A Cultural History of Sex Education in Twentieth Century Europe,* eds. Lutz Sauerteig and Roger Davidson (New York: Routledge, 2009), 217–235; Jerzy Buxakowski, *Wprowadzenie do teologii duszpasterstwa rodzin* (Pelpin: Bernardium, 1999), 358; Episkopat Polski, 'Instrukcja Episkopatu Polski dla duchowieństwa o przygotowaniu wiernych do sakramentu małżeństwa i o duszpasterstwie rodzin', in Wydział Duszpasterstwa Rodzin (1972), *Konferencje dla nupturientów* (Łódź), 2. Catholic Intelligentsia Club (henceforth CIC). Central Archives of Historical Records, 2/2212/547.

3 Kuźma-Markowska, 'Marx or Malthus', 582.

4 Agata Ignaciuk, 'No Man's Land? Gendering Contraception in Family Planning Advice Literature in State-Socialist Poland (1950s–1980s)', *Social History of Medicine* 33, no. 4 (2019): 1327–1349; Sylwia Kuźma-Markowska, and Agata Ignaciuk, 'Family Planning Counselling in State-Socialist Poland, 1950s–1980s', *Medical History* 64/2 (2020): 240–266; Barbara Klich-Kluczewska, 'Biopolitics and (Non-)Modernity: Population Micro-Policy, Expert Knowledge and Family in Late-communist Poland', *Acta Poloniae Historica* 115 (2017): 151–174.

5 Agnieszka Kościańska, *To See a Moose: The History of Polish Sex Education* (New York: Berghahn Books, 2021).

6 Klich-Kluczewska, 'Biopolitics and (Non-)modernity'.

7 Ignaciuk, 'No Man's Land?'; Kuźma-Markowska and Ignaciuk, 'Family Planning Counselling'.

8 Sylwia Kuźma-Markowska, 'Międzynarodowe aspekty działalności Towarzystwa Świadomego Macierzyństwa w latach 50. i 60. XX w.', in *Problem kontroli urodzeń i antykoncepcji. Krytyczno-porównawcza analiza dyskursów,* eds. Bożena Płonka-Syroka and Aleksandra Szlagowska (Wrocław: Uniwersytet Medyczny im. Piastów Śląskich, 2013), 265–282.

9 Natalia Jarska, 'Modern Marriage and the Culture of Sexuality: Experts between the State and the Church in Poland, 1956–1970', *European History Quarterly* 49, no. 3 (2019): 467–490 (467–469).

10 Klich-Kluczewska, 'Biopolitics and (Non-)Modernity', 156; Kościańska, *To See A Moose* Agnieszka Kościańska, *Gender, Pleasure, and Violence: The Construction of Expert Knowledge of Sexuality in Poland* (Bloomington, IN: Indiana University Press, 2020); Barbara Klich-Kluczewska, *Family, Taboo and Communism in Poland, 1956–1989* (Berlin: Peter Lang, 2021); Kateřina Lišková, Natalia Jarska and Gábor Szegedi, 'Sexuality and Gender in School-Based Sex Education in Czechoslovakia, Hungary and Poland in the 1970s and 1980s', *The History of the Family* 25, no. 4 (2019): 550–570.

11 Jarska, 'Modern Marriage', 469; Eva Fodor et al., 'Family Policies and Gender in Hungary, Poland and Romania', *Communist and Post-Communist Studies* 35, no. 4 (2002): 475–490; Piotr Perkowski, 'Wedded to Welfare?

Working Mothers and the Welfare State in Communist Poland', *Slavic Review* 76, no. 2 (2017): 455–480.

12 Kuźma-Markowska, 'Marx or Malthus', 17; Mikołaj Kozakiewicz, ed., *Wychowanie seksualne i planowanie rodziny w Polsce. Przeszłość, teraźniejszość, przyszłość. 40-lecie Towarzystwa Rozwoju Rodziny 1957–1997* (Warszawa: Movex, 1997), 208; Mikolaj Kozakiewicz, 'The History and Politics of Planned Parenthood in Poland', in *Planned Parenthood in Europe the 1980s: A Human Rights Perspective*, eds. Philip Meredith and Lyn Thomas (London: IPPF Europe, 1985), 183–192 (185).

13 Klich-Kluczewska, 'Biopolitics and (Non-)Modernity', 158, 173.

14 Kościańska, *To See a Moose.*

15 Kuźma-Markowska, 'Marx or Malthus', 19; Michael Zok, 'Wider die "angeborene und nationale Mission der Frau"? Gesellschaftliche Auseinandersetzungen um Abtreibungen in Polen seit der Entstalinisierung', *Zeitschrift für Ostmitteleuropa-Forschung/Journal of East Central European Studies* 68, no. 2 (2019): 249–278 (253–254).

16 One exception is Agnieszka Kościańska's examination of *Marriage Upon Us* (first edited in 1972 and re-edited in 1974 and 1988). This popular marriage textbook authored by Andrzej Wielowieyski, long-time president of the Catholic Intelligentsia Club in Warsaw, represented a vision of Catholic marriage and sexuality parallel to the ideas of Vatican II. See Kościanśka, *To See a Moose*; Agnieszka Kościańska, 'Humanae Vitae, Birth Control and the Forgotten History of the Catholic Church in Poland', in *The Schism of '68: Catholicism, Contraception and Humanae Vitae in Europe, 1945–1975*, ed. Alana Harris (Cham: Springer International Publishing, 2018), 187–208.

17 Ignaciuk, 'No Man's Land?'.

18 Lišková, Jarska and Szegedi, 'Sexuality and Gender', 11; Kościańska, *To See a Moose.*

19 Główny Urząd Statystyczny, *Rocznik statystyczny 1976* (Warszawa: GUS, 1977), 36; Lucjan Adamczuk and Witold A. Zdaniewicz, *Kościół Katolicki w Polsce, 1918–1990: rocznik statystyczny* (Warszawa: GUS, 1991), 171.

20 Ada Dubowska, Halina Skurzok and Tamara Krystian, 'Socjologiczne problemy antykoncepcji w opinii kobiet miasta i wsi', *Ginekologia Polska* 60/2 (1989): 78–85 (82).

21 Buxakowski, *Wprowadzenie do teologii*, 359.

22 Władysław Gasidło, *Duszpasterska troska Kardynała Wojtyły o rodzinę* (Kraków: Czuwajmy, 1996), 7.

23 Kościańska, *To See a Moose.*

24 Kościańska, 'Humanae Vitae'; Kuźma-Markowska and Ignaciuk, 'Family Planning Counselling'.

25 Jarska, 'Modern Marriage'.

26 E.g. in Cracow in 1957. Gasidło, *Duszpasterska troska*, 17.

27 Diecezja Gorzowska, *Materiały na kurs przedmałżeński* (Gorzów Wielkopolski, 1970). CIC, Central Archives of Historical Records, 2/2212/383.

28 Maria Braun-Gałkowska, *Przygotowanie do małżeństwa. Opracowanie* (Lublin, 1979). CIC, Central Archives of Historical Records, 2/2212/396.

29 Kościańska, *Gender, Pleasure and Violence.*

30 Diecezja Gorzowska, *Materiały na kurs przedmałżeński,* 13.

31 https://diecezjazg.pl/o-diecezji/ (accessed 14 January 2020).

32 Diecezja Gorzowska, *Materiały na kurs przedmałżeński*, 30. See also Kuźma-Markowska and Ignaciuk, 'Family Planning Advice'.

33 Duszpasterstwo Rodzin Archidiecezji Krakowskiej, *Materiały do dalszego i bliższego przygotowania do małżeństwa* (Kraków, 1971), 121. Department of the Chaplaincy of Families, Archives of the Cracow Metropolitan Curia, box 7.

34 Kuria Biskupia Chełmińska, *Cykl dziesięciu katechez przedmałżeńskich* (Pelplin: Kuria Biskupia Chełmińska, 1974 [published guide]).
35 Diecezja Gorzowska, *Materiały na kurs przedmałżeński*, 34.
36 Kuria Biskupia Chełmińska, *Cykl dziesięciu katechez*, for example on p. 3.
37 Contributions to Harris, *The Schism of '68*; Lucia Pozzi, 'Chiesa cattolica e sessualità coniugale: l'enciclica Casti connubii', *Contemporanea, Rivista di storia dell'800 e del '900* 3 (2014): 387–412; Lucia Pozzi, *The Catholic Church and Modern Sexual Knowledge, 1850–1950* (Cham: Palgrave MacMillan, 2021); Wannes Dupont, 'Catholics and Sexual Change in Flanders', in *Sexual Revolutions*, eds. Gert Hakma and Alain Giami (Basingstoke: Palgrave Macmillan, 2014), 81–98.
38 Also, Esther Peperkamp, 'The Fertile Body and Cross-Fertilization of Disciplinary Regimes: Technologies of Self in a Polish Catholic Youth Movement', in *Exploring Regimes of Discipline: The Dynamics of Restraint*, ed. Noel Dyck (New York: Berghahn Books, 2008), 113–134. Polish translation: 'Płodne ciało i wzajemne zapładnianie reżimów dyscyplinarnych. "Techniki siebie" w pewnym katolickim ruchu młodzieżowym', in *Antropologia seksualności. Teoria, etnografia, zastosowanie*, ed. Agnieszka Kościańska (Warszawa: Wydawnictwa Uniwersytetu Warszawskiego, 2012): 218–239.
39 These memoirs and similar accounts include: Gasidło, *Duszpasterska troska*; Buxakowski, *Wprowadzenie do teologii*; Elżbieta Sujak, *Charyzmat zaangażowania. Życie Teresy Strzembosz* (Warszawa: Instytut Wydawniczy PAX, 1983); Włodzimierz Fijałkowski, *Moja droga do Prawdy* (Katowice: Księgarnia Św. Jacka, 1991); Kazimierz Majdański, *Ocalić prawdę o rodzinie* (Łomianki: Pomoc Rodzinie, 2000); Benedykta Perzanowska, *Teresa Strzembosz i jej dzieło* (Łomianki: Fundacja 'Pomoc Rodzinie', 2010); Piotr Sukiennik, 'Rys historyczny działalności duszpasterstwa rodzin w Polsce ze szczególnym uwzględnieniem Archidiecezji Krakowskiej', *Studia nad Rodziną* 10, no. 1 (2006): 315–322.
40 Wojciech Sadłoń, *Annuarium statisticum ecclasiae in Polonia* (Warszawa: Instytut Statystyki Kościoła Katolickiego, 2019), 40–42.
41 Anna Putyńska, psychologist and marriage preparation instructor. Interview by Agata Ignaciuk in Sieradz, 14 February 2019.
42 Lišková, Jarska and Szegedi, 'Sexuality and Gender', 16.
43 Ignaciuk, 'No Man's Land'; Agata Ignaciuk, 'Innovation and Maladjustment. Contraceptive Technologies in State-socialist Poland, 1950s-1970s,' *Technology and Culture* 63, no. 1 (2022): 182-208.
44 Kuria Biskupia Chełmińska, *Cykl dziesięciu katechez*, 69.
45 Wydział Duszpasterstwa Rodzin, *Konferencje dla nupturientów*, 42.
46 Duszpasterstwo Rodzin Archidiecezji Krakowskiej, *Materiały do bliższego i dalszego przygotowania*, 123. Other examples of representing contraception as unhealthy: Duszpasterstwo Rodzin Archidiecezji Krakowskiej, *Konferencje dla narzeczonych*, 44–45. Department of the Chaplaincy of Families, Archives of the Cracow Metropolitan Curia, box 1. Wydział Duszpastestwa Rodzin, *Konferencje dla nupturientów* (1975), 43.
47 Also, in Kuźma-Markowska and Ignaciuk, 'Family Planning Advice'.
48 World Health Organization, *Biology of Fertility Control by Periodic Abstinence. Report of a WHO Scientific Group* (Geneva: WHO, 1967).
49 Wydział Duszpasterstwa Rodzin, *Konferencje dla nupturientów*, 43.
50 Diecezja Gorzowska, *Materiały na kurs przedmałżeński*, 199.
51 Duszpasterstwo Rodzin Archidiecezji Krakowskiej, *Materiały do bliższego i dalszego przygotowania*, 10.

52 Wydział Duszpasterstwa Rodzin, *Konferencje dla nupturientów*, 44.
53 Wydział Duszpasterstwa Kurii Metropolitalnej Warszawskiej, *Spotkania z narzeczonymi w punkcie poradnictwa rodzinnego* (Warszawa: Kuria Metropolitalna, 1978) (published guide).
54 'Tajemnica dziewięciu miesięcy', *Kobieta i Życie* 32/653 (1963): 13.
55 Duszpasterstwo Rodzin Archidiecezji Krakowskiej, 'Duszpasterstwo Rodziny. Zeszyt Pierwszy'. Department of the Chaplaincy of Families, Archives of the Cracow Metropolitan Curia, 1967, box 1.
56 Duszpasterstwo Rodzin Archidiecezji Krakowskiej, *Materiały do bliższego i dalszego przygotowania*; Wydział Duszpasterstwa Kurii Metropolitalnej Warszawskiej, *Spotkania z narzeczonymi.*
57 Kościańska, *To See a Moose.*
58 Duszpasterstwo Rodzin Archidiecezji Krakowskiej, *Materiały do bliższego i dalszego przygotowania*, 23–24.
59 For example, Diecezja Gorzowska, *Materiały na kurs przedmałżeński*, 194; Duszpasterstwo Rodzin Archidiecezji Krakowskiej, *Materiały do dalszego i bliższego przygotowania*, 23–24, 194; Kuria Biskupia Chełmińska, *Cykl dziesięciu katechez*, 62–63; Duszpasterstwo Rodzin Archidiecezji Krakowskiej, *Konferencje dla narzeczonych*, 1975, 28.
60 Wydział Duszpasterstwa Rodzin Kurii Metropolitalnej Warszawskiej, *Spotkania z narzeczonymi.*
61 Szałkowska, Janina, Konferencje dla narzeczonych, 4. CIC, Central Archives of Historical Records, 1977, 2/2212/389.
62 Kościańska, *To See a Moose.*
63 Współpracownicy Duszpasterstwa Rodzin, Problem rodziny i małżeństwa w wychowaniu i katechizacji. Konferencje dla rodziców, pogadanki dla dzieci (Poznań), 66. CIC, Central Archives of HRecords, 1974, 2/2212/396.
64 Lišková, Jarska and Szegedi, 'Sexuality and Gender', 5–6.
65 Kościańska, *Gender, Pleasure and Violence.*
66 Duszpasterstwo Rodzin Archidiecezji Krakowskiej, *Materiały do dalszego i bliższego przygotowania*, 58–59.
67 Kuria Biskupia Chełmińska, *Cykl dziesięciu katechez*; Szałkowska, *Konferencje dla narzeczonych*, 4–5.
68 Ks. Kazimierz Benkowski in Kuria Biskupia Chełmińska, *Cykl dziesięciu katechez.*
69 Szałkowska, *Konferencje dla narzeczonych*, 4–5.
70 Peperkamp, 'Płodne ciało', 227.
71 Diecezja Gorzowska, *Materiały na kurs przedmałżeński*, 93.
72 Wydział Duszpasterstwa Rodzin Kurii Metropolitalnej Warszawskiej, *Spotkania z narzeczonymi*, 17.
73 Ibid., 17.
74 Diecezja Gorzowska, *Materiały na kurs przedmałżeński*, 234–235.
75 Ibid., 229–230.
76 Wydział Duszpasterstwa Rodzin, *Konferencje dla nupturientów*, 36.
77 Peperkamp, 'The Fertile Body'.
78 Kuria Biskupia Chełmińska, *Cykl dziesięciu katechez*, 68.
79 Duszpasterstwo Rodzin Archidiecezji Krakowskiej, *Materiały do dalszego i bliższego przygotowania*, 118. Housing argument also in Wydział Duszpasterstwa Rodzin Kurii Metropolitalnej Warszawskiej, *Spotkania z narzeczonymi*, 35; Kuria Biskupia Chełmińska, *Cykl dziesięciu katechez*, 69.
80 Jarosz, Dariusz, *Mieszkanie się należy ...: studium z peerelowskich praktyk społecznych* [Entitled to a Flat ...: A study of Polish state-socialist social practices] (Warszawa: ASPRA, 2010).

81 Wydział Duszpasterstwa Rodzin, *Konferencje dla nupturientów*, 55.
82 Wydział Duszpasterstwa Rodzin Kurii Metropolitalnej Warszawskiej, *Spotkania z narzeczonymi*.
83 Duszpasterstwo Rodzin Archidiecezji Krakowskiej, *Materiały do dalszego i bliższego przygotowania*, 65.
84 Włodzimierz Fijałkowski, *Biologiczny rytm płodności a regulacja urodzeń* (Warszawa: Państwowy Zakład Wydawnictw Lekarskich, 1971); Włodzimierz Fijałkowski, *Naturalny rytm płodności* (Warszawa: Państwowy Zakład Wydawnictw Lekarskich, 1976).
85 Teresa Kramarek, *Metoda termiczna regulacji poczęć*, 1966 [located in the Department of the Chaplaincy of Families, Archives of the Cracow Metropolitan Curia, box 7]; Teresa Kramarek, *Metoda objawowo-termiczna regulacji cząć*, 1969 [printed brochure without publication details]. The catalogue of the Polish National Library lists further copies of the brochure published in 1972, 1973 and 1976, but again, without publication details.

5 Whose Children?

Pronatalist Incentives and Social Categorization in Socialist Romania

Corina Doboș

The second article of the 1965 Constitution of the Socialist Republic of Romania reads that 'People's power is based on the workers – peasants' alliance[1]. In close union, the working class – the leading class of society – the peasantry, the intelligentsia and the other categories of working people, regardless of their nationality, are building the Socialist system, and creating the conditions for the transition to communism'.[2] The 1975 *Dicționar politic* (Political Dictionary) reiterated that 'nowadays Romanian society is made out of social classes and categories that actively contribute to productive work, producing both material and spiritual goods, collaborating and working together for the building of socialism in Romania'.[3] The dictionary affirmed that the working class was the leading force of socialist society,[4] and mentioned that the working peasants were the ally of workers in the building of socialism.[5]

However, in spite of the claimed alliance between the peasantry and workers, who made up the most numerous social category in the country, the peasantry was left behind in the social hierarchy forged in socialist Romania. Building on my previous research into Nicolae Ceaușecu's pronatalist program, the present chapter addresses the ideological dimensions of Ceaușescu's pronatalist welfare by examining the way in which the reproduction of different social categories was encouraged or discouraged through family and maternity provisions. Specifically, I analyze the way the Romanian state addressed the differentiated fertility of peasants and workers, through various financial and social measures, to reveal how pronatalist incentives were used as mechanisms of social categorization.

Taking into consideration the capacity of social classifications 'to generate social realities rather than simply reflect them',[6] the analysis of the way pronatalist incentives and provisions were used by the Ceaușescu regime as mechanisms of social categorization represents a way to investigate the giant effort undertaken by state socialist regimes to 'transform society in the image of certain ascribed qualities'.[7] When comparing the reproduction policies used in Nazi Germany and in the Stalinist Soviet Union, David Hoffmann and Annette Timm explained that even if these policies were pursued in illiberal regimes where 'individual liberties were rejected

DOI: 10.4324/9781003161080-7

in favour of two quite different collectivist projects',[8] the dissimilarities in the reproductive goals and means to attain them produced 'quite different policies toward reproduction'.[9]

If one goes beyond the totalitarian paradigm that opposes individual liberties and options to state intrusion in the private sphere and looks at the social content of Romanian pronatalism and to the social hierarchies these mechanisms were creating, new aspects of Ceauşescu's pronatalism can be identified. The examination of the social hierarchy that pronatalist welfare contributed to can reveal the intricate web of (often conflicting) welfare provisions, social hierarchies, scientific facts, professional interests, political goals and ideological tenets behind public policymaking and implementation in a state socialist regime.

My analysis will be pursued against the context of social research and knowledge production on fertility and social differentiation undertaken in pre-war and post-war Romania. My main research hypothesis is that the pronatalist welfare measures were used as mechanisms of class discrimination of the peasantry, as a means of social engineering to achieve qualitative goals defined in ideological terms, rather than quantitative objectives defined in demographic terms.

Introduction: Current State of Research

In October 1966, the Ceauşescu regime drastically limited the access to abortion on demand in Romania through Decree 770/1966. This ban would last until the regime's last days and was outlawed in the furore of the Romanian revolution in December 1989. While in the long run, the ban had doubtful demographic consequences, it had tragic consequences especially for women and children. Self-inflicted abortions, together with abortive manoeuvres performed by different abortion providers had often had dramatic consequences for women's health and lives. More than 12,000 women – most of them mothers already – died as they tried to get rid of the unwanted pregnancies, leaving behind broken families and thousands of orphans. Many children were abandoned and most of them were put in dreadful 'care' facilities, only to die from cold, hunger and unspeakable abuse.[10]

Given the traumatic experiences and tragic outcomes of Ceauşescu's pronatalism, it is not surprising that prior research insisted upon the negative, repressive facets of the Romanian pronatalist policies, focusing on the terrible consequences the severe ban on elective abortion (implicated from 1966 to 1989) had for the lives of the many and for society as a whole.[11] The socio-economic measures destined to support families, mothers and children in communist Romania remain understudied, with few attempts made to systematically research these policies.[12]

Some studies focused on different components of Ceauşescu's pronatalism, such as expert knowledge formation, policy-making processes, institutional networks, welfare provisions, and demographic outcomes.[13] They have pointed out diverse socio-economic measures destined to support families, mothers and children: maternity leaves, family allowances and other types of financial support for families with children and single mothers, childcare facilities, free health services, free education, etc. Most of these provisions existed well before 1966 and were part of the general welfare program assumed by the communist regime in the first post-war decades; some of them were adopted under direct Soviet influence. The measures aimed to support maternity and birth rates were common in the actually existing socialist regimes of Eastern Europe, however, their content and conditions of applicability differed greatly from Eastern European country to country, shaped by local traditions, knowledge and dynamics of governance. Compared to similar measures taken elsewhere in the region (especially in GDR, Czechoslovakia and Hungary), the socio-economic measures to support motherhood, children and family implemented in post-war Romania were financially modest, quite inflexible and much less creative, especially in regard to the support given to working and single mothers and childcare facilities.[14] The situation remained unchanged even after 1966, when these measures assumed an explicitly pronatalist character.

Previous research also highlighted some of the important ideological dimensions of Ceauşescu's pronatalism, as well as its contribution to the formation of new socialist subjectivities and gender construction in socialist Romania. Special attention was given to the fundamental role that the pronatalist policies played in the institutionalization of the communist dictatorship, as exemplified in the discursive construction of both socialism and nationalism in Ceauşescu's Romania. The ideological tropes of pronatalism legitimized the state control of individual lives and bodies.[15] As I will demonstrate, the examination of the social categorization implications of the Ceauşescu regime's welfare system can reveal some unknown ideological implications of Ceauşescu's pronatalism.

Social Classes, Social Estates, Social Categories and a Classless Society

My interest in the social hierarchies created with the help of pronatalist welfare provisions was raised by the brilliant analysis of 'class discrimination' in Soviet Russia undertaken by Sheila Fitzpatrick. She was able to identify three layers of meaning circumscribing the construction of social class in Soviet Russia. She defined the difference between a Marxist socio-economic conception of class as 'something to which a person belongs by virtue of his socio-economic position and relationship to the means of production' and a social estate 'which is first and foremost a legal category that defines an individual's rights and obligations to the state'. This allowed her to conclude upon the paradoxical character of class structure in Soviet Russia, upon 'the peculiar conjunction of two incompatible concepts, ascription and Marxist class', the outcome being that 'class became an ascribed category in Russia after the revolution'.[16] She also identified a *virtual social class* – the outcome of Marxist categories of social analysis applied in the realm of social statistics, as Soviet statisticians 'painstakingly built such categories into their data, including the volumes of the 1927 population census dealing with occupation'.[17] This *virtual class society* was 'a representation, whose purpose was to sustain the illusion of classes'.[18]

Fitzpatrick pursued an examination of the 'structure of class discrimination' in Soviet Russia, identifying several instances, domains and situations where the ascription to a certain class worked as a 'stigma', limiting different categories of citizens to move, study, vote, eat, get a job or a qualification, housing, etc.[19] In command economies, where the state acted as the main (re)distributor and allocator of resources, 'the main way class was significant in Soviet society was as a state classificatory system determining the rights and obligations of different groups of citizens. ... In the Soviet context, "class" (social position) was an attribute that defined one's relationship to the state'.[20]

In the case of the Socialist Republic of Romania, the question of social categorization also has different layers of meaning, depending upon the level of analysis employed. In her study dedicated to Ceauşescu's pronatalism, Gail Kligman quoted Nicolae Ceauşescu, Secretary General of the Romanian Communist Party, who at the national conference of the party (1972) had stated that:

> In the socialist society, a process has begun to make the village more like the city, to encourage the gradual disappearance of classes, and [to give rise to] the homogenization of society, gradually erasing the fundamental differences between physical and mental labour.[21]

According to Kligman, Ceauşescu's pronatalism also played a fundamental role in the realization of social homogenization which, 'fully elaborated by the mid-1980s, was meant to produce social equality by rendering social differences insignificant. Race, gender, and ethnicity were all to be homogenized, as were spatial and other distinctions'.[22] She considered that under the trope of social homogenization, the political ideal of a classless society specific to communist regimes, had become reality in the case of the Socialist Republic of Romania, and that Ceauşescu's pronatalism had played a fundamental role in the realization of social homogenization.

However, different political documents, sociological and statistical studies, laws and policies issued and implemented in the Socialist Republic of Romania seem to indicate that the building of socialism in Romania did produce a specific social hierarchy, and that the classless society represented only a (political) ideal of the (utopian) communist society to come. As I will show, the building of socialism in post-war Romania did not erase social differentiation among different socio-economic and professional groups created through the socialist transformation of the country. This differentiation was not only debated and studied by social researchers,[23] but actively promoted by the communist state through the welfare measures integral to Ceaușeasu's pronatalist program (1966–1989).

The theme of social homogenization surfaced in the political agenda in 1968, when it was formulated as one of central committee's theses for the Xth Congress of the Romanian Communist Party (1969):

> Our society experiences, as it advances on the path of socialism, a growing homogenization based on the gradual elimination of the essential differences between social categories, between village and city, between physical and intellectual work, [based] on the commonality of economic, political, and ideological interests of all working-class people.[24]

Adela Hîncu convincingly argued that the theme of social homogenization, in spite of the massive ideological connotations, was 'not accepted without qualification', being vividly debated and extensively studied by social researchers especially during the 1970s.[25]

In the social and statistical studies pursued in the wider context of de-Stalinization 'social category' became one of the main analytical categories of social research. Starting with the second half of the 1950s, throughout the 1950s and especially the 1970s, social category emerged as a central trope of post-war social research, and was used extensively to study the changes in social structure generated by the socialist transformation of the country.[26] The 1956 Census was the first one that openly investigated the social group to whom a respondent belonged, defined as such not only by the profession but also by the position the respondent had in the relations of production.[27] The 1956 census made use of 11 categories to investigate the social structure produced by the socialist transformation of the country including: workers, clerks, cooperative peasants, cooperative craftsmen, individual peasants, individual craftsmen, tradesmen, self-employed [*liber-profesioniști*], etc.,[28] while the 1966 census used seven social categories in order to research and present the social structure of the country including: workers, intellectuals-clerks, cooperative peasants, independent peasants, craftsmen, etc.).[29]

During the 1960s, when the conditions of social knowledge production were further improved, sociology was disciplinary and institutionally reinstated.[30] The new infrastructure for social research was paralleled by a selective recuperation of the social research undertaken during the 1950s and early 1960s.[31] At the end of the 1960s, social categories thus became a matter of theorization and debate, and in the 1970s became one of the main interests for social research.[32]

In the late 1960s, an increasing number of social researchers in Romania and Eastern Europe insisted upon the necessity of passing the strict economic definition proposed by Lenin in 1919 – to recognize and debate the specific social positions and roles undertaken by different professional groups created by the socialist transformation of the country.[33] The sociologist Mihai Cernea convincingly showed that the 'disappearance' of social classes in socialist society must to be understood as the eradication of antagonist classes, but not of social groups, as the building of socialism contributed to a diversification of socio-professional groups.[34] He specialized in the study of the rural world and acknowledged the economic hardships and social inequalities cooperative peasants were struggling with.[35] According to Adela Hîncu, Cernea showed that 'social inequalities were preserved under socialism, that they should be treated as a fact and studied accordingly (for instance, the role of the family in reproducing socio-economic and cultural inequalities), and that what would have been of interest was an analysis of the actual political measures taken to reduce them'.[36]

Other forms of class discrimination could also be detected in the realm of education, as the access to different forms of education and formation was restricted for those children whose parents belonged to different stigmatized social and political categories: rich peasants (*chiaburi*, the Romanian equivalent of *kulacs*), former employers, former owners of plants and of estates, those who were condemned for different sorts of political crimes, etc.[37]

The *Dicționar politic* confirmed that the classless society would be characteristic of a communist society only when Romania had advanced to that stage of social and political organization.[38]

All these elements – whether of an ideological and/or political nature or coming from social research and statistics or from the sphere of public policies – indicate the existence of a social hierarchy led by the workers in socialist Romania, with social homogenization and a classless society being rather an ideological ideal to be achieved only in a future communist society. Whether or not this structure was one of the social classes (either resulting from socio-economic conditions and production relations or just scientific representations) or one of the social estates (resulting from different ascription practices run by the Romanian state), or a mix of both – is not the subject of the present research and needs to be further investigated. I will further proceed to an examination of the content of welfare measures destined to support mothers and children and families, and to raise birth rates, that were discussed and implemented in socialist Romania, as well as to the research of rural fertility undertaken by various population researchers in twentieth-century Romania.

The Socialist Transformation of Agriculture, Population Research and Welfare Schemes in the First Two Post-War Decades

The demographic evolution of Romania between 1947 and 1955 was characterized by a (slow) recuperation of birth rates and fertility rates, accompanied by sharp decreases in mortality levels, especially in infant mortality and a significant prolongation of life expectancy,[39] as well as a combined effect of the massive improvements and investments made in healthcare services, especially vaccination and enhanced accessibility to healthcare.[40]

The socialist transformation of the economy and society was well on its way after 1947, marked by the transformation of property relations, the implementation of command-economy structures and the beginning of collectivized agriculture.[41] These changes were paralleled in the 1950s by increased rates of population growth, which were comparable with interwar levels. After 1958, the socialist transformation of the economy greatly accelerated, a consequence of the massive industrialization, urbanization, and the collectivization and mechanization of agriculture.[42] Even though the birth rates began to diminish in the second half of the 1950s, a combined effect of the massive transformation society and economy experienced in an accelerated manner after 1958, and of the liberalization of access to abortion on demand (1957), population growth rates sustained high levels throughout the 1950s, given the steady decrease in mortality rates.[43]

During the 1950s, the communist government did not seem preoccupied with the decrease in birth rates and fertility rates, which became more prominent in the second half of the 1950s.[44] Public policies addressing population dynamics continued to focus on providing better medical care to mothers and children.[45] The efforts paid off, as the continuously declining infant mortality rates reflected the improvement in healthcare standards for pregnant women and newborns.[46]

The little interest manifested by the new regime for direct intervention upon birth rates in the 1950s was mirrored by the marginal status demographic research had during the 1950s and in the first half of the 1960s, particularly when compared with the prominent status of the discipline and its research infrastructure enjoyed before 1948 (especially during the Ion Antonescu regime).[47] The autumn of 1957 decision to legalize abortion upon request during the first three months of pregnancy established some of the most permissive conditions under which the interruption of pregnancy could be performed at that time in the world.[48] This decision was apparently motivated by the need to attract more women into the workforce[49] and was taken without prior consultation with health professionals.[50] This confirms the minor status of demographic research in Romania during the 1950s.

The definitive results of the 1956 population census, which were issued in 1959, prompted the publication of some articles on demographic themes published in *Revista de statistică* [*Journal of Statistics*]. These articles were rather optimistic regarding demographic dynamics registered in the 1950s (especially by the massive decreases in infant mortality), determined by the investments the communist regime made in healthcare, education and housing.[51]

Maternity Support and the Childcare System during the 1950s

Under these circumstances, the welfare support offered to families, mothers and children designed in the 1950s seemed to have more to do with the general welfare commitments undertaken by the communist regime under Soviet influence in Romania and elsewhere in Eastern Europe than with a specific pro-natalist agenda.

During the 1950s, the state support system for families remained relatively underdeveloped (especially in comparison with other countries from the region), in spite of the fact that the 'constitutions of 1948 and 1952 asserted special state protection for the family'.[52] The support for families with children was heavily shaped by the Soviet influence[53] and included prizes for 'hero-mothers',[54] those women who had given birth and raised 10 children or more and which resembled the 'privileges granted to the predominantly male, Heroes of Socialist Work'.[55]

Starting in 1950, cash prizes were granted to families with four or more children.[56] These prizes were paid out if at least one of the parents, or the single mother, was employed or a member of the agricultural cooperatives or state farms, until the child turned four. Single mothers could benefit from this grant until the child turned 12, starting with the first child. The same decree instituted the birth grants, which were allotted starting with the birth of the tenth child.[57] These first child benefits were given to working people (employees), which at that time included the collectivized peasants, who were very few at the incipient stage of the collectivization process.[58] At the same time, employed women were granted a maternity leave of 80/90 days (35 before giving birth and 45–55 days afterwards upon a physician's recommendation); there were breastfeeding breaks, or leaves to take care of their sick children if they were younger than two.[59] The benefits that addressed the employed female population were probably also used to attract women to the labour market.[60] The childcare services given to working people, and to working mothers in particular, also comprised the (slow) development of a public network of nurseries and kindergartens.[61] These facilities were also supposed to be implemented in the rural areas, but very few agricultural cooperatives assumed the responsibility of organizing them.[62]

In 1956, the first form of child allowance was introduced and was intended for the children of 'workers and retired employees'.[63] This monthly allowance was granted until children turned 14, and was contingent upon whether the parents were active or retired state employees, or if they were students, workers, or PhD students, writers, painters, sculptors – or members of the creative unions. The amount of this allowance was a standard 100 lei, but the allowance was granted in inverse proportion with the family revenue, and with the rank of the children. If the employee lost their job, the allocation was still granted until they were hired again, but not for more than three months. In exceptional cases, the allocation could also be granted to people who were not active or retired employees, students, or members of the creative unions (single mothers, or married women with husbands who were not able to work).

Things started to change at the beginning of the 1960s, as the decrease in birth rates that were accelerating in the rural world after 1958 began to be perceived by population researchers as dangerous for the country's future.[64] The growing public attention given to population dynamics during the 1960s can be understood in connection with the crucial role population came to play in the plans of rapid economic development envisaged by the state socialist regimes in Romania, and in Eastern Europe more generally.[65] The size, age, structure and specialization of the working force represented a key variable for the success of the developmental plans built around industrialization projects envisaged by the party-state in Romania.[66]

Rural Fertility Research

The main concerns were related to the fertility decline of the rural world, which accelerated after 1958, when the last and most accelerated phase of agriculture collectivization began. The fundamental role rural fertility played for the country's population dynamics, and the anxieties provoked in the 1960s by the massive drop in rural birth rates have their roots in the interwar studies regarding the regional dynamics of fertility in greater Romania.[67] The pro-populationist narrative created before 1945 fit the paramount nationalist discourse of the interwar era, and starting with the 1960s, its heritage was reconfigured and rewritten into post-war Romania to support the developmental goals of the communist regime. In the 1960s, the older ideas about the benefits of a growing ethnic Romanian population were rewritten in a different economic, political and social context with the help of new statistical tools and economic theories.

The interwar studies of declining rural birth rates were performed in the 1930s in a different context of demographic knowledge production. The main research interest of interwar demography was the study of the ethnic composition and dynamics of greater Romania and what the possibilities were of altering them in order to increase the percentage of ethnic Romanians in the country in general, and in towns in particular.[68] Taking into consideration the differentiated fertility rates of various ethnic groups and their regional distribution (higher for the Romanians concentrated in the rural areas, and lower for Germans, Jews and Hungarians concentrated in urban spaces), the maintenance of higher birth rates in the rural areas represented a prerequisite condition for the achievement of the *Romanianization* of towns.

In a work published in 1940, the physician Sabin Manuilă (1894–1964), a key figure of interwar demographic research, elaborated on the complicated statistical equation of Romania's ethnic structure dynamics, the regional composition of Romania's population, its rural and urban distribution and differences in birth dynamics of the urban and the rural population:

> The process of migration from the villages to towns is of special importance for the evolution for it has been established that every 3 or 4 generations the town population is renewed which will change also the ethnic composition of the minority towns in the regions with a Romanian population. It is necessary to consider directing the population movement towards the town and the semi-urban centres of the frontier zones ... In conclusion, the demographic ideal followed in the process of urbanization is the integration as regards the number and the economic power of the Romanian element in the town-life of the country, at least in the same proportion in which it is represented in the rural life and the country's army, which will ensure for its citizens peace, and educational and economic progress.[69]

The assessment of the evolution of birth rates between 1920 and 1929 showed that births rates decreased from 39 per cent (1920) to 34 per cent (1929), presenting a 'tendency of decrease', 'due in major part to the very low birth rate of the new annexed provinces'.[70] The situation was considered to be dramatic even in the region of Banat, where 'immediate biological health measures' were needed, in order to correct a 'biological atrophy of the population, which cannot be the result of a high degree of economic evolution, as this would tend to diminish the deathrate at the same time. It is therefore against mortality that urgent measures have to be taken, and against infant mortality, as this is for Banat one of the highest in the whole country'.[71]

Both Sabin Manuilă and Petre Râmneanţu (1902–1991), another key figure of interwar Romanian demography,[72] came from Banat, and fear of depopulation seems to have influenced their career choices. Manuilă confessed that his interest in demography was mainly determined by a deep concern for the decreasing birth rates in Banat. The anxieties related to Banat 'depopulation' were shared by other influent physicians involved in public health,[73] and this led to the organization of a modernized system of vital statistics in Romania. Because of 'the low birth rate in Transylvania and to the decrease in the population of Banat, the Transylvanian scientists were the first to agitate in favour of organizing the vital statistics in Roumania. Previous to the year 1930, the problem of the population had been tackled for social reasons (impropriation and colonization) or economic ones (conversion of agricultural debts)'.[74]

Previous research on (rural) depopulation concentrated thus on the region of Banat and represented an important precedent for how reproductive rural practices were researched, for the formation of demographic reasoning regarding the influence that 'social factors, hygiene, economic factors and culture'[75] have on birth rates. In the mid-1930s, Râmneanţu conducted systematic research on the 'depopulation of Banat', focusing on three villages (Văradia, Banloc and Jablanița), which was considered representative for the entire region's depopulation patterns, all of them with a majoritarian ethnic Romanian population. These villages were closely observed and investigated in the summer of 1934 by a research team composed of social care nurses and physicians and was coordinated by Râmaneamțu.[76]

After ruling out the biological and demographical factors that contributed to the situation, Râmneanțu concluded that the most important element that determined the declining birth rate was a drop in women's fertility (number of births/women of a fertile age) in the countryside.[77] In order to obtain more detailed information on the causes that contribute to depopulation Râmneanțu and his team undertook a complex investigation of the families living in the three villages, in order to clarify 'the positive and negative correlations between demographic phenomena and the economic, social, cultural and hygienic standards of population'.[78] He concluded that the birth rates were in an inverse proportion with wealth, as well as with the cultural and social status.[79] He considered that it was a mechanism of behavioural imitation that explained the spread of smaller families from wealthier categories – who also enjoyed a superior social status – towards poorer categories that had a lower social status. The village intellectuals were considered the engines of change, because it was from them that the richer peasant families learned that it is preferable to have fewer children, and this mechanism of imitation propagated top-down along the social hierarchy.

Social-care nurses also gave questionnaires to hundreds of women from rural areas to find out details regarding their reproductive behaviours and choices (number of pregnancies, number of born children, stillbirths, the use and type of contraceptive methods, the existence, methods and number of pregnancy interruptions). After reviewing the answers regarding contraceptive practices, it was concluded that the main cause of these differences between fertility and fecundity (number of pregnancies/number of live births), was represented by the women's frequent appeal to induced abortion.[80] Most of the women in Văradia (51 per cent) appealed to abortion only after using a contraceptive method (such as vaginal douches with different substances and/or *coitus saxonicus*) that failed.[81] The investigators also found out about other contraceptive methods used by women – the most common being *coitus interruptus* and the application of different types of vaginal pessaries: contraceptive methods that were the most efficient in preventing a pregnancy.[82] Ramneantu advanced a socio-psychological explanation for the reasons behind the decision to limit the number of births, namely 'women's vanity' and the materialist orientation of the couple. This vanity was expressed by both women's and young girl's lust for clothing and luxury, their interest in gossiping and conspiring, coupled with their very inefficient household management and lack of skills in rearing children, an effect of the general lack of education of the young girls, who usually abandoned primary school before graduation to start a conjugal life.[83] The limitation of the number of children constituted a way of maintaining a higher living standard for the rest of the family and easier living, in general.[84]

Even though the number of marriages (nuptiality) did not seem to have decreased significantly in the families with higher social status, education and wealth, which also had the lowest fertility levels, a thorough analysis showed the dissolution of the family institution among all social groups. The mounting number of separations, divorces and different types of *concubinajes*, as well as children born out of wedlock, seemed to have a negative effect upon birth rates in Văradia.[85]

Professing an explicit pro-natalist attitude, a rather patriarchal perspective on gender roles and a paternalistic view over the relationship between state and citizens, something which was quite common with medical professionals of the epoch, Râmneanţu also underlined the negative effects that the young girls lack of education and early-aged coupledom had on fertility rates. Moreover, he addressed the question of reproductive behaviour as determined by multiple causes: economic, cultural, educational, social, psychological, civilizational and biological, to try and offer a complex explanation of villagers' reproductive choices, underling the importance that psychological factors and social roles had over economic factors.

During the (first) post-war decades, the rural world continued to be considered the main source of population growth in the country. Under the new social, economic and political conditions, what was at stake was not the success and pursuit of the (explicitly ethnic) *Romanianiziation* of the urban centres, but rather the success of the massive plans of industrialization undertaken by the communist regime, and which was heavily dependent on the rural workforce provided after the 'socialist transformation of agriculture.'[86]

This transformation was officially completed in April 1962. At this time, more than 90 per cent of Romania's agricultural land was organized under different forms of socialist property (30 per cent in the form of State Agricultural Enterprises (SAE) [*Întreprinderi Agricole de Stat*], 60 per cent in the form of Agricultural Cooperatives of Production (ACP) [*Cooperative Agricole de Producţie*]) and 10 per cent remained in the property of private owners ('individual peasants').[87]

These transformations resulted in major changes to the social structure of the rural world. While in the 1956 census, the number of collectivized peasants represented only 3.4 per cent of the total population of the country and the individual peasants represented 51.2 per cent,[88] the situation dramatically changed after the socialist transformation of agriculture.

Gheorghe Retegan (1916–1998), a former sociologist specializing in demography at the beginning of the 1960s, published several demographic studies; for unclear reasons, some of them were signed as 'Şerbu'.[89] In these studies, he showed that the number of inhabitants of new and old towns that assumed extended industrial capacities during the socialist transformation of the country increased dramatically in the 1950s. He also demonstrated that the main two causes that contributed to the increased urban population were the significant drop in mortality rates registered in these new and old industrial centres and the massive migration from the countryside of the working force available after the socialist transformation of agriculture.[90]

In 1962, Retegan published a crucial study dealing with the evolution of fertility in Romania between 1900 and 1960.[91] Retegan was the first to reconstitute both the general and specific fertility rates of fertile women in Romania for the first 60 years of the twentieth century, and the data provided in this study continues to be referential for the study of fertility in Romania.[92] While the analysis of the declining birth rates was attempted before his time, Retegan was the first to address the evolution of this index (fertility measurements were considered more accurate than birth rates for population forecasts) and to trace the continuous decrease of the general fertility rates after 1920, and the intensity of this decrease after 1955.[93]

In the study, special attention was given to differentiated fertility: the fertility rates of various groups defined according to age, urban/rural distribution and social category. While the latter could not be studied because of lack of proper data, Retegan was able to calculate fertility evolution in relationship with different age groups and rural/urban distribution. Retegan's computations and estimations of fertility dynamics were the first of this kind undertaken in Romania and brought an essential contribution in showing the general trend of fertility decline experienced by Romania during the first half of the twentieth century.[94]

Retegan also analyzed differentiated fertility rates in relationship to the 'social environment' of women, which was equated with their place of residence. He was able to compute general fertility rates on rural/urban distribution for the years 1920–1939 and 1946–1960, presenting five year averages.[95] These estimates allowed Retegan to conclude that even if the General Fertility Rate (GFR) in urban areas was much lower than in rural areas, the post-war evolution numbers were much better than in rural areas: while the GFR for urban areas constantly increased after the Second World War, reaching a maximum of 68.7 live births (1951–1955), the GFR continuously diminished in the rural areas, reaching a low of 90.9 in 1956–1960.[96] In the long run, Retegan concluded that while the GFR increased in urban areas with 2.1 per cent between 1920 and 1960, they decreased by more than 40 per cent in the rural areas for the same period of time.[97] These evolutions were explained by Retegan as caused by the 'elimination of contradictions between village and town', as the accentuated decrease of rural fertility and much smaller decrease in the urban areas suggested the 'accentuated similarities of reproductive behaviour of the population living the two different social environments'.[98]

Between 1962 and 1964, the physician Alexandru Pescaru, a specialist in hygiene and public health, designed and carried out several fertility surveys in both rural and urban areas. Given 'the importance rural birth rates have for the general level of birth rates in [the] country', and by taking into consideration the important decrease in birth rates Romania experienced in parallel with 'socialist industrialization, collectivization of agriculture and cultural revolution', in 1964 Pescaru carried out a fertility survey in five villages from four different regions of Romania (Movila-Mireşti, Orţişoara, Coţofenii din Faţă, Ciorocul Mare, Mădăraş).[99] The data was obtained from the answers to a questionnaire, which was given to women from 432 households from the 5 villages with the help of local medical nurses, and supplemented with data provided by the local dispensaries and the local cooperatives of agricultural production.[100] The questionnaire had 32 questions, related to household membership (number of people living under the same roof, the social category of the head of the household prior to collectivization, number of couples living under the same roof, number of the household members able to work), household incomes, a woman's schooling level, her civil status, the number of births she had, the number of her living children, the number of children her mother and grandmother had given birth to and the years when her children were born.

From the answers received, Pescaru reached important conclusions regarding the changes rural 'demographic behaviour' had suffered between 1955 and 1964, the decade when the socialist transformation of agriculture was accomplished. He observed that while the size of household membership did not decrease in the 10 years under investigation, its 'fertility potential' decreased because of the age structure of its members and the decline in the proportion of fertile women.[101] This evolution was determined by diminished birth rates registered during the Second World War and by the important migration of rural youth to urban centres.[102] He observed the general trend of diminishing fertility rates, confirmed by the growing proportion of women who had given birth to one to two children maximum (74 per cent of the respondents of fertile age), especially when compared with their grandmothers (where the proportion of women with maximum two children was only 29.5 per cent). At the same time, the proportion of women with three or especially four children had decreased from 56.8 per cent (in the grandmothers' generation) to 7.9 per cent in the respondents' generation.[103]

Pescaru also investigated the number of children considered ideal by the respondents and concluded that most of them (72 per cent) wished to have two children at most, and that only 70 per cent of those who wished to have three or more children actually had them. Most of the married women (133 out of 207) had the number of children they considered ideal, or more, and only 54 of them had less children than they wanted. In order to limit the number of children, more than 40 per cent of the respondents had suffered interruptions of pregnancy, most of them women who already had two children.[104] Given these and other findings, Pescaru concluded pessimistically that 'for the rural areas under investigation it can be presumed that fertility rates would stabilize at minimum levels, as confirmed by birth and fertility rates in the country'.[105]

Despite these worrying findings about the declining rural fertility and birth rates, the welfare schemes addressing mothers and children were not expanded in the 1960s to address the demographic dynamics generated by the socialist transformation of the rural world.

Maternity Support and the Child Care System, 1960–1965

During the first part of the 1960s, the welfare scheme addressing mothers and children became more comprehensive and articulate, probably in the attempt to curtail the decrease of birth rates that were becoming ever more worrying.[106] However, the children of peasant were (again) left aside.

In 1960, a new form of child allowance was designed.[107] This financial support again addressed those who were employed with permanent work contracts, employees in training or higher education, and its value was in an inverse proportion with family revenue and the child's rank, and also depended upon the place of residence (the sum was significantly higher for those residing in urban areas). Despite the differentiated sums allotted to the residents of the rural and urban areas, neither the children of the Agricultural Cooperatives of Production (ACP) peasants, nor those of the independent peasants were covered by this financial support.[108]

In 1965, maternity leaves were extended to 112 days, paid with 90 per cent of the last salary for the employees with at least 12 months seniority in work, and with 70 per cent of the last salary for the female employees who had less than 12 months seniority. In case of the employees who did not have an undetermined work contract, they could benefit from the maternity leave only if they had at least 4 months of seniority in the last 12 months before the maternity leave or at least 10 months of seniority in the last 2 years before the maternity leave.[109]

The main elements of the mother and child support systems (maternity leaves and child allowance) were conditioned by employment and were mainly intended to contribute to employee welfare. However, a significant part of the country's population was left aside: the peasants, be they independent or members of the recently created ACP whose numbers were significantly augmented after 1962. Nevertheless, the nationwide access to free medical services represented a priority of governance, and while the social support for motherhood remained fragmented, and conditioned by employment status, the access to medical services and medical support for pregnant women was not.

Ceauşescu's Pronatalism, 1966–1989: Socio-Economic Incentives and Social Hierarchies

After the death of Gheorghe Gheorghiu Dej in 1965, Nicolae Ceauşescu[110] became the new Secretary General of the Romanian Communist Party (RCP). Within the political context created by the regime change of

1965–1966, different bodies of statisticians and health professionals synthesized the findings of several studies published in the first half of the 1960s on the decline of birth and fertility rates in order to put forward different policy proposals designed to raise the birth rates of the country. These syntheses and proposals were not published, as they were working documents of the ministry of health and of the RCP.[111]

The studies from 1965 to 1966 adapted their rhetoric to the political realities of 1966 Romania, presenting the accentuated decrease of birth and fertility rates as integral part of the successful socialist transformation of the country, an adaptation to the significant decrease of mortality rates and to the general increase of educational and living standards. The fall of the birth and fertility rates of the rural world was introduced between the lines of this general narrative of success by the studies issued in the first half of 1966, especially by a study from February 1966. By presenting the evolution of birth rates between 1938 and 1965 (Table 5.1), these studies insisted that the decline of birth rates in the rural areas, which accentuated during the 1950s and was sharper than in the urban areas, was crucial in explaining the general drop of fertility rates in Romania.[112]

Among the factors identified to have contributed to the sharper decrease of rural birth rates was the massive migration from villages to urban areas,[114] the modest support for families with children in general,[115] and for rural families in particular, because most of the rural children, and mainly the children of the cooperative peasants were not covered by the child allowance.[116]

After the socialist transformation of agriculture was accomplished in 1962, cooperative peasants came to represent the second largest social category of the country, as most of the peasants had become members of the CAP (representing 58.2 per cent of the rural population).[117] Cooperative peasants (7,365,179 persons) represented in 1966 38.6 per cent of the total population. They were outnumbered only by 'workers' (7,624,981 persons, representing 39.9 per cent of the total population, but the peasantry (reuniting cooperative peasants and individual peasants) continued to represent the most numerous social group in the country (around 43 per cent of the total population).[118]

Table 5.1 Birth rates in Romania, 1938–1965, for the entire country, urban and rural areas[113]

	1938	*1948*	*1955*	*1965*
Overall	29.5	23.9	25.6	14.6
Urban	18.7	16.4	20.6	12.1
Rural	23.6	26.2	27.4	15.9

Source: Romanian Ministry of Health, Studiu, *Studiu privind situaţia natalităţii din RSR* (1966), f. 107.

Taking into consideration the demographic potential the rural world had for the entire country, on the one hand, and the alarming decrease in birth rates in the rural world, on the other hand, policy proposals put a particular emphasis on the reorganization of the child allowance system, as the existing system of child allowance 'covered only 2,500,000 children, while 2,200,000 children, predominantly those of the cooperative peasants, were left aside'.[119] A new allowance system was proposed, which was supposed to support the increase of birth rates in the rural environment, especially for the peasants working in the collective farms system.[120]

The studies from 1966[121] problematized the worrying change in the peasants' reproductive behaviour brought about by the socialist transformation of agriculture and the substantial changes to the traditional rural world severely affected by massive urban migration and by the creation of cooperative farms. In addition to stricter rules and mild restrictions on the conditions under which abortions on demand could be allowed, proposals insisted upon different types of social and economic incentives meant to stimulate birth rates: better housing facilities for families with children, longer maternity leave, cash payments starting with the third birth child, improved and sufficient child care facilities and the promotion of modern contraception.[122]

The last version of these working documents[123] was sent to the highest political decision-makers and discussed in detail in a meeting in August 1966.[124] Both the analysis and proposals advanced by the ministry of health were received with deep mistrust by the political decision-makers; politicians considered extended access to abortion as a key reason for the decrease in birth and fertility rates. The ministry of health was sacked and a new set of measures built around severe restrictions on abortion on demand were soon adopted. Decree 770/1966,[125] regulating the conditions of legality under which a uterine curettage could be performed, represented the cornerstone of Ceauşescu's pronatalism.[126] The policy aimed to raise the birth rate in socialist Romania was marked by a growing emphasis placed on repressive means to attain demographic goals, expressed in practices of (secret) police control and 'preventive' surveillance, criminal law regulations and show-trials.[127]

While health professionals and statisticians succeeded in presenting the decrease of the birth rate as a serious enough issue to raise political concern and state intervention, they failed to convince party officials of the accuracy of their analysis. Population researchers promoted an intricate image of population dynamics, but the way that the political circles received their analysis simplified the nuanced semantic universe of 'population' depicted in these studies. The socio-economic incentives proposed in the 1965–1966 studies, designed to stimulate birth rates by offering improved conditions and childcare facilities for working mothers and to financially support the families with many children, were received with equal mistrust by the political decision-makers.[128] Even if the child allowance system gained more and more financial significance over the years, it continued to be connected with the existence of a wage, thus addressing mainly employees in general, and workers in particular. It was only in 1977 that a regular support for mothers, members of the cooperative farms and for the children of the cooperative peasants was introduced: mothers were entitled to 60 days of paid maternity leave (pre-natal and paternal leave), less than half than the maternity leave destined to employees.[129] Cooperative peasants were entitled to a monthly child allowance (starting with the first child), whose amount increased with the rank of the child (starting with the sixth until the ninth child).[130] The award was granted only in the month when at least one parent had worked a minimum of 15 days for the cooperative farm, and realized all the assigned productivity targets.[131] The value of this award of was much smaller than the child allowance granted to the rural residents who were employees: while the cooperative peasants were entitled to 50 lei for each child from the first to the fifth, the employees residing in the rural area were entitled to 80–140 lei for the first child (in inverse proportion with the revenue), and more starting with the second child.[132]

In 1985, the conditions under which the grant was allotted were slightly revised (the beneficiaries received this grant on the condition that they worked at least 20 days in the respective month at the cooperative farm).[133] The grant value doubled (100 lei for the first and second child, 200 lei for the third and the fourth and 300 lei for the fifth and following children), but continued to be smaller than the monthly allowances allotted to the rural employees.[134]

Conclusion

The analysis on the maternal and child welfare support system both before and after 1966 revealed the small effort made by the state to promote the reproduction of the peasantry, especially in comparison with other social and professional categories. The absolute and relative size of the peasantry continued to diminish after 1966, as confirmed by the 1977 census: the number of collectivized peasants sunk to 4,950,014 persons, representing less than 23 per cent of the total population, while the individual peasants' number also decreased to 818,150 or 3.7 per cent of the total population.[135]

The reluctance to support the reproduction of peasantry, a social category whose demographic potential seemed diminished by the socialist transformation of agriculture, and whose importance for the demographic future of the country was underlined by population researchers several times, suggests the pervasiveness of a certain negative attitude towards the peasantry, whose socialist conversion was often conducted in the brutal terms of a class war.[136] The party's unchallenged commitment to rapid industrialization and to the expansion of the working class,[137] together with the perceived social, cultural, political, and economic threat understood to be residing in the countryside, 'resulted in the mobilization, control and integration of the peasantry into the socialist system'.[138] While the repressive sides of pronatalism addressed the entire population, where pronatalist incentives were concerned, preference was given – from beginning to end – to the workers as they represented the social category whose existence guaranteed and legitimized the existence of the political regime itself.[139]

During the first decades of building socialism under the Gheorghiu-Dej regime (1948–1965), the measures to support working (employed) mothers and the birth of wage-earner's children can be understood as part of the general effort of proletarianization of the peasantry in order to create social structures that were crucial for the success of the socialist construction under the guidance of the Leninist principle of the 'dictatorship of the proletariat'.[140]

The maintenance, despite the suggestions given by population researchers, of the stimulative measures preferentially addressing the wage-earners during the assumed pronatalist policy promoted by the Ceaușescu regime, shows that this principle was still at work in late socialism. Thus, the pronatalist measures taken after 1966 had not only a strict quantitative goal – such as the general growth of population but also a qualitative one – the reproduction of those social categories deemed most appropriate for the accomplishment of Romania's version of the socialist project. Whereas in interwar Romania, these qualities were mostly ethnically defined, in postwar Romania, these qualities were socially assigned, as the socio-economic pronatalist incentives also represented important tools to operate a social categorization defined by powerful ideological presuppositions.

Despite the reformation of the child allowance and maternity support system that started in 1967 in the context of the pronatalist program implemented by Ceaușescu regime, and of the demographic potential of the rural potential acknowledged by population researchers, different measures destined to support rural fertility in general, and that of cooperative peasants, in particular, never materialized.

The analysis of the complicated system created to support higher birth rates in Romania allows us to reconsider the way pronatalist incentives were used for the building of a socialist nation in Ceaușescu's Romania, thus being instrumental in forging a new social hierarchy, structured by the (ideologically presumed) loyalty to the socialist project. While population researchers recommended the encouragement of the reproduction of the peasantry, as the social category with the highest demographic potential in the country, the pronatalist measures put in practice by the Ceaușescu regime addressed the peasants only marginally. These measures rather served as mechanisms of social engineering, to support the proletarianization of peasants and contributed to the achievement of ideological goals and not of demographical objectives. They did not address the citizens of socialist Romania equally, and instead produced (new) hierarchies based on class discrimination.

Notes

1 This research was supported by the Unitatea Executiva pentru Finantarea Invatamantului Superior, a Cercetarii, Dezvoltarii si Inovarii [PN-III-P1-1.1-PD-2016-1720], project: *Crafting demographic knowledge in the 20th century: Population and development in an Eastern European periphery* (DEMOECRO), https://demohistory.wordpress.com/.

2 *Constitution of the Socialist Republic of Romania* (Bucureşti: Meridiane Publishing House, 1975), art. 2. Acknowledgement: This work was supported by the Unitatea Executiva pentru Finantarea Invatamantului Superior, a Cercetarii, Dezvoltarii si Inovarii [PN-III-P1-1.1-PD-2016-1720], project: *Crafting demographic knowledge in the 20th century: Population and development in an Eastern European periphery* (DEMOECRO), https://demohistory.wordpress.com/

3 Ionel Achim, ed., *Dicţionar Politic* (Bucureşti: Editura politică, 1975), 111.

4 Ibid.

5 Ibid., 600.

6 Michael Geyer and Sheila Fitzpatrick, 'Introduction: After Totalitarianism, Nazism and Stalinism Compared', in *Beyond Totalitarianism: Stalinism and Nazism Compared*, eds. Michael Geyer and Sheila Fitzpatrick (Cambridge: Cambridge University Press), 36.

7 Christopher R. Browning and Lewis H. Siegelbaum, 'Frameworks for Social Engineering and the Nazi *Volksgemeinschaft*', in Ibid., 231.

8 David L. Hoffmann and Annette F. Timm, 'Utopian Biopolitics: Reproductive Policies, Gender Roles and Sexuality in Nazi Germany and the Soviet Union', in Ibid., 87.

9 Ibid.

10 L.M. Jinga, 'Mortalitatea infantilă în România.1965–1989', in *Politica pronatalistă a regimului Ceauşescu*, eds. L.M. Jinga and F.S. Soare, vol. 2 (Iaşi: Polirom, 2011), 187–196; and L.M. Jinga, 'Copilărie şi abandon familial în România anilor '80', in *Copilăria românească între familie şi societate (secolele XVII–XX)*, ed. Nicoleta Roman (Bucureşti: Nemira, 2015), 314–342.

11 Gail Kligman, *The Politics of Duplicity: Controlling Reproduction in Ceauşescu's Romania* (Berkeley, CA: University of California Press, 1998).

12 Corina Doboş, 'Măsurile socioeconomice de stimulare a natalităţii şi susţinere a familiei din România ceauşistă (1966–1989)', in *Politica pronatalistă a regimului Ceauşescu. Vol. 1: O Perspectivă comparative*, ed. Corina Doboş (Iaşi: Polirom, 2010) and T. Inglot et al., *Continuity and Change in Family Policies of the New European Democracies: A Comparison of Poland, Hungary and Romania* (2011, NCEER Working Paper, available at https://www.ucis.pitt.edu/nceeer/2011_825-10_Inglot1.pdf).

13 Corina Doboş, ed., *Politica pronatalistă a regimului Ceauşescu. Vol. 1: O Perspectivă comparative* (Iaşi: Polirom, 2010); L.M. Jinga and F.S. Soare, eds., *Politica pronatalistă a regimului Ceauşescu*, vol. 2 (Iaşi: Polirom 2011); T. Rotariu et al., *Demografia României în perioada postbelică 1948–2015* (Iaşi: Polirom, 2017); Inglot et al., *Continuity of Change*.

14 Doboş, 'Măsurile socioeconomice', 276–280.

15 Kligman, *The Politics of Duplicity*, 7, 11, 245.

16 Sheila Fitzpatrick, 'Ascribing Class: The Construction of Social Identity in Soviet Russia', *The Journal of Modern History* 65, no. 4 (1993), 745, 768.

17 Ibid., 769.

18 Ibid.

19 Sheila Fitzpatrick, *Everyday Stalinism: Ordinary Life in Extraordinary Times: Soviet Russia in the 1930s* (New York and Oxford: Oxford university Press, 1999), 11–13.
20 Ibid., 12.
21 Kligman, *The Politics of Duplicity*, 33.
22 Ibid.
23 Adela Hîncu, *Accounting for the 'Social' in State Socialist Romania, 1960s–1980s: Contexts and Genealogies* (Budapest: Central European University, 2019).
24 *Tezele C.C. al P.C.R. pentru Congresul al X-lea al Partidului Comunist Român,* apud Hîncu 2019, 140.
25 Hîncu, *Accounting,* 140–143, 150.
26 Ibid., 140–152.
27 Recensămînt, *Recensământul populației din 21 februarie 1956.* Vol.: *Structura social-economică a populației:populația activă, populația pasivă, grupe sociale, ramuri, subramuri de activitate* (București: Direcția Centrală de Statistică, 1960), 5–6.
28 Ibid., XII–XIII.
29 Recensămînt, *Recensământul populației și locuințelor din 15 martie 1966.* Vol. 1: *Rezultate generale. Partea I-populație* (București: Direcția Centrală de Statistică, 1969), 364, table 23.
30 Ștefan Bosomitu, 'In the Age of "Misery": The Romanian Sociology During the Communist Regime (1948–1977)', in *N.E.C. Ștefan Odobleja Program Yearbook 2011–2012* (București: New Europe College, Institute for Advanced Studies, 2012); and Z. Rostás, 'The Rehabilitation of Romanian Sociology after Stalinism', in *The Social Sciences in the 'Other Europe' Since 1945*, eds. Adela Hîncu and Victor Karady (Budapest and New York: CEU University Press, 2018), 117–138.
31 M. Mănescu, 'Cercetarea sociologică a nivelului de trai a populației. Schema generală a sistemului sociologic de indicatori ai nivelului de trai al populației', in *Teorie și metodă în științele sociale. Vol. III: Economie. Drept. Statistică. Sociologie*, ed. Institutul de Filozofie al Academiei RSR (București: Ed. Politică, 1966), 7–24; C. Morgescu et al., 'Influențe ale procesului de industrializare asupra mobilității sociale – Pe exemplul României. In Institutul de Filozofie al Academiei RSR', in *Teorie și metodă în științele sociale. Vol. III: Economie. Drept. Statistică. Sociologie*, ed. Institutul de Filozofie al Academiei RSR (București: Ed. Politică, 1966), 33–47; H. Stahl and I. Matei, 'O experiență de documentare sociologică în materia de sistematizări teritoriale', in *Cercetări sociologice contemporane*, ed. Miron Constantinescu (coord.) (București: Ed. Științifică), 283–296; and P. Grigorescu, 'Concrete sociological investigations performed at the Institute of Economic Research', *Romanian Journal of Sociology* IV–V (1966): 319–321.
32 Hîncu, *Accounting*, 150.
33 Ibid., 145–146.
34 M. Cernea, 'Structura socială a României. Schimb de păreri', *Partidul Muncitoresc Romîn, Lupta de clasă* 49, no. 7 (1969), 58–59; and Hîncu, *Accounting*, 142.
35 M. Cernea, 'Schimbări ale structurii familiei țărănești în cooperativele agricole', in *Revista de filozofie* 16, no. 8 (1969): 1009–1022; M. Cernea, 'Omogenizarea socială în România', *Viitorul social* 3, no. 2 (1974): 440–441; and M. Cernea, *Sociologia cooperativei agricole* (București: Editura Academiei RSR, 1974).
36 Hîncu, *Accounting*, 152.

37 Comisia Prezidenţială pentru Analiza Dictaturii Comuniste din Romania, *Raport Final* (2006), 483–485.
38 Achim, ed., *Dictionar Politic*, 110–111.
39 Rotariu et al., *Demografia României*, 19, Table 2.1; V. Gheţău, 'Evoluţia fertilităţii în România de la transversal la longitudinal', in *Revista de Cercetări sociale* 1 (1997), 3–85; and V. Gheţău, 'L'évolution de la fécondité en Roumanie', *Population* 33, no. 2 (1978), 425–439.
40 Rotariu et al., *Demografia României*, 20–24.
41 B. Murgescu, *România şi Europa. Acumularea decalajelor economice (1500–2010)* (Iaşi: Polirom, 2010), 336.
42 J. Montias, *Economic Development of Communist Romania* (Cambridge, MA: MIT Press, 1967); K. Jowitt, *Revolutionary Breakthrough and National Development: The Case of Romania, 1944–1965* (Berkeley, CA: University of California Press, 1971); Murgescu, *România şi Europa* and M. Mărginean, *Ferestre spre Furnalul Roşu. Urbanism şi cotidian în Hunedoara şi Călan (1945–1968)* (Iaşi: Polirom, 2015).
43 Population growth rates: 15.4 (1928), 10.1 (1939), 6.0 (1946), 1.4 (1947), 8.3 (1948), 13.9 (1949), 13.8 (1950), 12.2 (1953), 13.3 (1954), 15.9 (1955), 14.3 (1956), 12.7 (1957), 12.9 (1958), 10 (1959), 10.4 (1960), 8.8 (1961), 7.0 (1962), 7.4 (1963), 7.1 (1964), 6.0 (1965), 6.1 (1966), 18.1 (1967), see V. Gheţău, 'Evoluţia fertilităţii în România', in *Revista de Cercetări sociale,* 29–32, Table A1. Gheţău 1997, 29–32, table A1.
44 Rotariu et al., *Demografia României*, 45–46, esp. fn 20; and V. Gheţău 'Evoluţia fertilităţii în România de la transversal la longitudinal', in *Revista de Cercetări sociale* 1 (1997), 7–8.
45 Inglot et al., *Continuity and Change*, 40.
46 T. Rotariu et al., *Demografia României*, 23–24; and Studiu, *Unele probleme privind dinamica sporului natural al populaţiei din Republica Socialistă Romania* (Bucureşti: Ministry of Health Archives, Bucharest, Fund Cabinetul 1, file nr. 69/1966, unnumbered, 1965), 6.
47 Corina Doboş, 'Swinging Statistics: Population Research and Political Construction in 20th Century Romania', *History of Communism in Europe* 9 (2018): 112–115; and V. Solonari, *Purifying the Nation: Population Exchange and Ethnic Cleansing in Nazi-Allied Romania* (Baltimore, MD: Johns Hopkins University Press, 2009), 75–94.
48 Decret 463, 'Decret privind încuvinţarea întreruperilor de sarcină', in *Buletinul Oficial al MAN al R.P.R.*, 26, 30.09.1957.
49 V. Trebici, Interview with Vladimir Trebici, 'Mărturii din Arhiva Radio: 98 de ani de la naşterea acad. V. Trebici', http://arhiva.rador.ro/info4.shtml?cat=1281&news=388215; Kligman, *Politics of Duplicity*, 23; and Jill Massino, 'Worker under Construction: Gender, Identity and Women's Experiences of Working in State Socialist Romania', in *Gender Politics and Everyday Life in State Socialist Eastern and Central Europe*, eds. Shana Penn and Jill Massino (New York: Palgrave Macmillan, 2009) 14–15.
50 A. Matioc and R. Costa, 'Problema întreruperii saricinii la cerere', *Obstetrica şi Ginecologia* 10, no. 3 (1963): 193–202; V.D. Zlătescu, 'La politique de population en Roumanie: l'impératif de croissance démographique et ses moyens de réalisation', in *Natalité et politiques de population en France et en Europe de l'Est*, ed. Institut national d'études démographiques (Paris: PUF, 1982), 235-248; and V. Trebeci, *Interview*, 1997.
51 I. Ferenbac, I. Mada and Gh. Lungu, 'Natalitatea, mortalitatea şi sporul natural al populaţiei din R.P.R', *Revista de statistică,* 8, no. 3 (1959): 51–58; I. Iscovici, 'Dezvoltarea populaţiei R.P.R. pe drumul socialismului', *Revista de*

statistică, 8, no. 8 (1959): 50–58; and I. Mada, 'Creşterea în perspectivă a numărului populaţiei RPR', *Revista de statistică*, 9, no. 5–6 (1960): 64–70.
52 Inglot et al., *Continuity and Change*, 40.
53 Ibid., 39.
54 Decret 195, 'Decretul nr. 195/1951 privind instituirea titlului de onoare de Mamă Eroină, a ordinului Mamă Eroină, a ordinului Gloria Maternă şi a Medaliei Maternităţii', in *Buletinul Oficial al MAN al RPR*, 109, 08/11/1951.
55 Inglot et al., *Continuity and Change*, 41.
56 Decret 106, 'Decret privind înfiinţarea ajutorului familial de stat', *Buletinul Oficial al MAN al RPR*, 39, 29/04/1950.
57 Ibid., art. 5.
58 E. Mesaroş, 'Indicatorii demografici ai populaţiei rurale înainte şi după colectivizarea agriculturii', *Revista de statistică* 21, no. 6 (1972): 58.
59 Codul Muncii, 'Legea nr.3 din 30 Mai 1950', *Buletinul Oficial al MAN al RPR*, 50, 8/06/1950 art. 89–93.
60 Massino, 'Worker under Construction', in *Gender Politics and Everyday Life in State Socialist Eastern and Central Europe*, 14–15.
61 Inglot et al., *Continuity and Change*, 42.
62 Ibid.
63 Decret 571, 'Decret privind acordarea unei alocaţii de stat copiilor muncitorilor şi pensionarilor', in *Buletinul Oficial al MAN al RPR*, 28, 5/11/1956.
64 Corina Doboş, 'Disciplining Births: Population Research and Politics in Communist Romania', *The History of the Family* 25, no. 4 (2020): 559–626.
65 P.R. Gregory, 'Fertility and Labor Force Participation in the Soviet Union and Eastern Europe', *Review of Economics and Statistics* 64, no. 1 (1982); and Kligman, *The Politics of Duplicity*, 19–20.
66 Murgescu, *România şi Europa*, 336–341.
67 Corina Doboş, 'Global Challenges, Local Knowledges: Politics and Expertise at the World Population Conference Bucharest, 1974', *East Central Europe* 45, no. 2 (2018): 231–232; and M. Bucur, *Eugenics and Modernization in Interwar Romania* (Pittsburgh, PA: University of Pittsburgh Press, 2002), 188, 227.
68 Doboş, 'Swinging Statistics', *History of Communism in Europe* 9 (2018): 112–114.
69 S. Manuilă, *Structure et évolution de la population rurale* (Bucureşti: ICS, 1940), English in original.
70 MPR, 'Mişcarea Populaţiei României pe anul 1929', *Buletinul Demografic al României* 1, no. 1 (1932): 48–49.
71 Ibid., 48, English in original.
72 Doboş, 'Global Challenges, Local Knowledges', *East Central Europe* 45, no. 2 (2018): 215–244.
73 Most probably his fellow-physicians from the Faculty of Medicine from Cluj, many of them eugenicists grouped around Dr Ioliou Moldovan, a close friend and mentor of Manuilă. See V. Solonari, *Purifying the Nation*, 75.
74 S. Manuilă, *Structure et évolution de la population rurale*, 67, English in original.
75 P. Râmneanţu, 'Studiu asupra depopulării Banatului. Cauzele depopulării Banatului. Rezultatele anchetei demografice din comuna Vărădia, judetului Caraş', *Buletin Eugenic şi Biopolitic* 6, no. 6–9 (1935): 195.
76 Ibid.
77 Ibid., 203.
78 Ibid., 215.
79 Ibid., 221–223.
80 Ibid., 238.
81 Ibid., 239–240.

82 Ibid., 239–240, 267.
83 Ibid., 251–252.
84 Ibid., 252–253.
85 Ibid., 246–253.
86 Murgescu, *România şi Europa*, 339–341.
87 D.A. Kideckel, *Colectivism şi singurătate în satele româneşti. Ţara Oltului în perioada comunistă şi în primii ani după revoluţie* (Iaşi: Polirom, 2006); and Raport, 'Comisia Prezidenţială pentru Analiza Dictaturii Comuniste din Romania', in *Raport Final* (2006), 432.
88 Recensămînt, *Recensământul populaţiei din 21 februarie 1956*, XIII.
89 G. R. Serbu, 'Evoluţia numerică a populaţiei oraşelor mari ale RPR, 1859–1959', *Revista de statistică* 10, no. 3 (1961): 37–50; G.R. Serbu, 'Căile de creştere numerică a populaţiei oraşelor mari ale RPR', *Revista de statistică* 10, no. 5 (1961): 26–34; G.R. Serbu, 'Evoluţia fertilităţii populaţiei feminine din R.P.R. în perioada 1900–1960', *Revista de statistică* 11, no. 4 (1962): 43–58 and G. Retegan, 'Necesitatea cercetării complexe a fertilităţii populaţiei în vârstă de reproducere', *Revista de statistică* 13, no. 10 (1964): 68–74.
90 Serbu, 'Evoluţia numerică a populaţiei oraşelor mari ale RPR, 1859–1959', *Revista de statistică* 10, no. 3 (1961): 37–50; and Serbu, 'Căile de creştere numerică a populaţiei oraşelor mari ale RPR', *Revista de statistică* 10, no. 5 (1961): 26–34.
91 Serbu, 'Evoluţia fertilităţii populaţiei feminine din R.P.R. în perioada 1900–1960', *Revista de statistică* 11, no. 4 (1962): 43–58; Doboş, 'Disciplining Births', 559–626.
92 V. Gheţău, 'Evoluţia fertilităţii în România de la transversal la longitudinal', in *Revista de Cercetări sociale* 1 (1997): 3–85.
93 GFR calculated by Retegan – 1946–1950: 92.2; 1951–1955: 90.9; 1956–1960: 79.5 Serbu, 'Evoluţia fertilităţii populaţiei feminine din R.P.R. în perioada 1900–1960', *Revista de statistică* 11, no. 4 (1962): 45, table 1.
94 Doboş, 'Disciplining Births', 605.
95 Retegan advanced the following values for the GFR – for urban areas: 1920–1924: 69.8, 1925–1929: 69.5, 1930–1934: 66.2, 1935–39: 59.1, 1946–1950: 62, 1951–1955: 68.7; 1956–1960: 57.7, and for rural areas: 1920–1924: 168.8, 1925–1929: 159.6, 1930–1934: 137.9, 1935–1939: 127.3, 1946–1950: 120.4, 1951–1955: 99.6; 1956–1960: 90.9. Serbu, 'Evoluţia fertilităţii populaţiei feminine din R.P.R. în perioada 1900–1960', *Revista de statistică* 11, no. 4 (1962): 52, table 4.
96 Ibid., 62.
97 Ibid., 53.
98 Ibid.
99 A. Pescaru, 'Experimentarea unei fişe de anchetă asupra fertilităţii în mediul rural', in Direcţia de Statistică, *Volumul celei de-a 5-a consfătuiri ştiinţifice de statistică: 8–11 decembrie 1965* (Bucureşti: Direcţia Centrală de Statistică 1967), 1302.
100 Ibid., 1303.
101 Ibid., 1304.
102 Ibid.
103 Ibid., 1304–1305.
104 Ibid., 1305.
105 Ibid., 1306.
106 Ibglot et al., *Continuity and Change*, 42.
107 Decret 285, 'Decretul nr. 285/1960 privind acordarea alocaţiei de stat pentru copii', *Buletinul Oficial al MAN al R.P.R*, 14, 10/08/1960.

108 Inglot et al., *Continuity and Change*, 43.
109 HCM 880, 'Hotărârea nr. 880/1965 privind acordarea de ajutoare materiale în cadrul asigurărilor sociale de stat', *Buletinul Oficial al RSR*, 33, 21/08/1965, art. 14–17.
110 Nicolae Ceauşescu (1918–1989), member of the Central Committee of the RCP/RWP (1945–1948, 1952–1989), member of the Politburo (1954–1965), General Secretary of the RCP (1965–1989), member of the Executive Committee of the CC of RCP (1965–1989), President of the State Council (1967–1989), president of the Socialist Republic of Romania (1974–1989).
111 Romanian Ministry of Health, *Unele probleme privind dinamica sporului natural al populaţiei din Republica Socialistă Romania* (Bucureşti, 1965), Ministry of Health Archives, Bucharest, Fund Cabinetul 1, file nr. 69/1966, unnumbered; Romanian Ministry of Health, *Studiu privind situaţia natalităţii în RSR* (1966), Ministry of Health Archives, Bucharest, Fund Cabinetul 1, file nr. 69/1966, unnumbered; Romanian Ministry of Health, *Propuneri de măsuri privind redresarea natalităţii* (1966), Ministry of Health Archives, Fund Cabinetul 1, file nr. 69/1966, unnumbered; Romanian Ministry of Health, *Studiu privind situaţia natalităţii din RSR* (1966), National Archives of Romania, Headquarters, Bucharest, Fund CC al PCR-Cancelarie, file nr. 101/1966, ff. 102–127) and Romanian Ministry of Health, *Propuneri de măsuri pentru redresarea natalităţii în ţara noastră* (1966), National Archives of Romania – Headquarters, Fund CC al PCR-Cancelarie, file nr. 101/1966, ff. 114–125fv.
112 Romanian Ministry of Health, Studiu, *Studiu privind situaţia natalităţii în RSR* (1966), 6; and Romanian Ministry of Health, Studiu, *Studiu privind situaţia natalităţii din RSR* (1966), f. 107.
113 Taken from Studiu 1966b, f. 107.
114 Romanian Ministry of Health, Studiu, *Studiu privind situaţia natalităţii în RSR* (1966), 6; and Romanian Ministry of Health, Studiu, *Studiu privind situaţia natalităţii din RSR* (1966), f. 107.
115 Romanian Ministry of Health, Studiu, *Studiu privind situaţia natalităţii în RSR* (1966), 10.
116 Ibid., 15–16.
117 E. Mesaroş, 'Indicatorii demografici ai populaţiei rurale', *Revista de statistică* 21, no. 6 (1972): 56.
118 Recensămînt, *Recensământul populaţiei şi locuinţelor din 15 martie 1966* (Bucureşti: Direcţia Centrală de Statistică, 1969), 364, table 23.
119 Romanian Ministry of Health, Studiu, *Studiu privind situaţia natalităţii în RSR* (1966), 16.
120 Propuneri, *Propuneri de măsuri privind redresarea natalităţii*, Ministry of Health Archives, Fund Cabinetul 1, file nr. 69/1966, unnumbered, 2.
121 Romanian Ministry of Health, Studiu, *Studiu privind situaţia natalităţii în RSR* (1966); and Romanian Ministry of Health, Studiu, *Studiu privind situaţia natalităţii din RSR* (1966).
122 Doboş, 'Măsurile socioeconomice', 223–263.
123 Romanian Ministry of Health, Studiu, *Studiu privind situaţia natalităţii din RSR* (1966); and Propuneri, *Propuneri de măsuri pentru redresarea natalităţii în ţara noastră* (1966).
124 F.S. Soare, 'Reglementarea accesului la avort şi contracepţia modernă în România comunistă, 1945–1989', in *Politica pronatalistă a regimului Ceauşescu. Vol.1*, ed. Corina Doboş; and Doboş, 'Disciplining Births', 559–626.
125 Decret 770, 'Decret pentru reglementarea întreruperii cursului sarcinii', *Buletinul Oficial al RSR*, 60, 01/10/1966.

126 Under the provisions of the new decree, abortion on demand could be performed at the recommendation of a socio-medical commission that decided upon the request. The interruption of pregnancy was allowed for certain medical conditions or social circumstances: the woman was older than 45 or if she already had 4 children. The surgical intervention had to be performed in a state medical facility in the first 12 weeks of pregnancy. At the same time, the interruption of pregnancies outside the conditions stipulated by the Decree 770/1966 was criminalized: both women who accepted the illegal interruption of pregnancy or who performed abortive methods, as well as abortion providers, were to be punished by two years or more in jail if the abortive manoeuvres resulted in woman's death or of a long-term deterioration of her health. In addition, the medical practitioners who provided interruption of pregnancies outside the conditions of the law were also sanctioned with different restrictions upon their right of medical practice.

127 Kligman, *The Politics of Duplicity*; and Soare, 'Legislaţia penală privind avortul. Cazuri în instanţă', in *Politica pronatalistă a regimului Ceauşescu*, vol. 2, eds. L. Jinga and F.S. Soare (Iaşi: Polirom, 2011).

128 Corina Doboş, ed., *Politica pronatalistă a regimului Ceauşescu. Vol. 1: O Perspectivă comparative* (Iaşi: Polirom, 2010).

129 Lege 4, 'Legea nr. 4 din 30 iunie 1977privind pensiile şi alte drepturi de asigurări sociale ale membrilor cooperativelor agricole de producţie', *Buletinul Oficial al RSR*, 61, 08/07.1977, art. 32 (Lege 4, 1977, art. 32).

130 Ibid., art. 33.

131 Ibid.

132 Decret 246, 'Decret nr. 246 din 28 iulie 1977privind alocaţia de stat pentru copii', *Buletinul Oficial al RSR*, 79, 01/08/1977, art. 3.

133 Decret 410, 'Decret nr. 410 din 26 decembrie 1985privind alocaţia de stat şi indemnizaţia pentru copii, ajutoarele ce se acordă mamelor cu mai mulţi copii şi sotiilor de militari în termen, precum şi indemnizaţia de naştere', *Buletinul Oficial al RSR*, 76, 26/12/1985 art. 16.

134 Ibid., art. 3.

135 Recensămînt, *Recensământul populaţiei şi al locuinţelor din 5 ianuarie 1977*, vol. II. *Populaţie – Structura social-economică* (Bucureşti, Direcţia Centrală de Statistică, 1980), 46, Table III.

136 Raport, 'Comisia Prezidenţială pentru Analiza Dictaturii Comuniste din Romania', *Raport Final* (2006): 432–437.

137 Jowitt, *Revolutionary Breakthrough and National Development*, 112–113.

138 Ibid., 121.

139 Doboş, 'Măsurile socioeconomic', 238, 263.

140 Jowitt, *Revolutionary Breakthrough and National Development*, 108–109, 121.

6 State and Parenthood

Family Planning Policy in Socialist Yugoslavia (1945–1991)

Ivana Dobrivojević Tomić

Introduction

The topic of birth control, reproductive health and state policy in the sphere of family planning in Yugoslav and post-Yugoslav historiography has been either completely neglected or inconsistently researched. This is despite the available sources: especially primary sources from the Family Planning Council found in the Archive of Yugoslavia, as well as periodicals and related demographic, sociological and medical literature. This paper, therefore, will try to shed light on the regulations and practice of family planning in Yugoslavia, not as a means to deny the partial success of socialist Yugoslavian policies in the field, but to reveal the same problems and challenges that both the interwar and post-war state faced. Notwithstanding the changing socio-economic situation in the country, a rise in the standard of living and increased access to contraceptives, abortion – at first illegal and then legal – remained one of the basic 'methods' of family planning for most couples throughout the twentieth century. The socialist authorities, lacking sufficient commitment to the systematic education of young people and the promotion of contraception, but also facing accumulated social problems, chose the easiest path and turned to the gradual liberalization of abortion. Therefore, the initial intention of the legislator was neither emancipatory nor was it intended to give women the right to freely decide about their own bodies; until 1969, it appeared as a strategy serving to repair the health and economic consequences of a large number of illegal abortions.

Abortion and contraception will be given a special attention in this chapter, while certain social measures meant to facilitate the existence of the family, without increasing or decreasing the birth rate, will not be analyzed. However, despite recognizing a need to create 'preconditions for family stability' or providing economic relief or the conditions in 'which a mother-worker will perform maternal functions without exceptional sacrifices and self-denial',[1] the problems were numerous in terms of a child protection policy. For example, the number of available places in nursery schools decreased, the financing of their construction

DOI: 10.4324/9781003161080-8

was unresolved, company management turned a deaf ear to the obligations and problems of single mothers, and there were indicators in court practice that fathers were seldom compelled to pay mandatory alimony after divorce.[2] Although the child allowance doubled the number of its beneficiaries from the moment it was introduced in 1948 until the beginning of the 1980s, the amounts paid out covered only a part of the costs. Therefore 'a family with children was put into a relatively disadvantaged position' by economic and social factors, as estimated in one of the analyses by the Institute of Economics (1981).[3]

The Legacy of the Kingdom of Yugoslavia

At the end of the Great War and before the unification into one state, the various regions of Yugoslavia were at different stages of economic development. The cultural, social and religious dissimilarity based on economic differences deeply affected family, family relations and demographic trends. According to statistics, in 1935, there was an average of 29 births per 1,000 persons in Yugoslavia. The average birth rate concealed a particular demographic phenomenon, as the Sava and the Danube divided the country into two totally different regions: one in the north, where the birth rate was lower and approximated the birth rate of Central and Western Europe, and the other in the south where the birth rate was very high. The more modest the living conditions were, the more localized the economy, the more illiterate the people, and the greater the distance from cultural and economic centres, the higher the birth rate was.[4] The record was held by Vrbas Banovina and Vardar Banovina (40 per mille), and especially the Bosnian counties such as Cazin, Travnik and Jajce, where the number of live births was close to 60 per mille.[5] There was not much speculation regarding reasons for the lack of birth control in the poorest and most underdeveloped parts of the country – Bosnia and Herzegovina, Macedonia, Sandzak, Montenegro and Kosovo. Having children was regarded as the 'will of God' against which one 'should not act', and spouses, especially men, desired numerous offspring. As demonstrated in Vera Stein Erlich's field study conducted in the 1930s, there were sporadic cases where fathers wanted to control the number of children 'but did not know how', since the population in these parts of the country was unaware of contraception methods or of the possibility of intentional miscarriages.[6]

In addition to the fact that the annual natural population increase began to decline under the influence of modernization and the growing economic crisis in 1931, 200,000 new residents a year was a heavy burden on the weak Yugoslav economy.[7] In the more developed parts of the country, which had already undergone a demographic transition in the 1920s, the patriarchal view of children as a primary cause of happiness and (an intangible yet familial) wealth shrank in the face of a rational fear for the existence of the family. Peasants could hardly enlarge their property, and the following generations, due to the constant division of estates, ended up with fewer possessions. Relative agrarian overpopulation, declining agricultural prices and narrowed employment opportunities were some of the main economic and social reasons behind the increased desire for birth control, especially in towns, but also in rural areas such as Slavonia (Croatia), Vojvodina and northern Serbia. The somewhat looser relationships between the sexes, along with the stigmatization of mothers and their illegitimate children added to this trend, although not crucially. Family life in the aforementioned regions was radically transforming during the 1920s and 1930s, and families with one or two children, a rarity in the years leading up to the Great War, became commonplace.

As was the case with many other European countries, sexuality and sexual intercourse in the interwar period was the most rigorously guarded taboo of which little was said, and even less was known. Although one could buy condoms illegally, contraception was forbidden,[8] and the birth of an extramarital child was considered the biggest family embarrassment. The superstitions about conceiving were numerous: it was believed that breastfeeding a child would prevent a new pregnancy and Montenegrins thought that pregnancy was unlikely to occur if a woman was angry or if sexual intercourse was violent.[9] A small group of the educated population in towns were able to inform themselves about sexuality and conception from the articles published in newspapers and women's magazines periodically, as well as from the books published in the *Eros* edition, launched in Zagreb, and the *Library for Sexual Issues* published in Belgrade.[10] Although the 'pandemic outbreak' of abortions endangering the health and lives of women[11] and consequently of families as a whole was openly discussed, especially amongst the professional public such as doctors and lawyers, there were no attempts made to advance the sexual education of the population. The Yugoslav population hardly considered preventative measures as a whole. Although coitus interruptus was familiar to many in different parts of the country, the peasants from the Ogulin area of Croatia felt that because they were deprived of many pleasures due to poverty, they should 'enjoy sex in the true and natural way'. However, there were slight regional dissimilarities: for example, in Slavonia (the region with the highest number of deliberate miscarriages in Yugoslavia), a number of married couples practiced coitus interruptus,[12] and there were cases recorded where women tried to sew primitive condoms from cloth for their husbands.[13] However, such isolated cases of primitive contraception could not significantly influence the widespread practice of intentional miscarriages as the basic method of family planning.

The reasons for abortions were largely the same all over Yugoslavia. The social circumstances, the fragmentation of estates during the inheritance process, as well as the desired number of children were the main reasons that encouraged women to procure miscarriage. Often, women would give birth to the first three children, but in the case of subsequent pregnancies, they would question whether it was a good idea.[14] The decision for the first abortion caused a kind of moral discomfort, while subsequent decisions were reached without thinking, almost automatically. When asked by Dr Aleksandar Petrović, a doctor who conducted research on the everyday life of the peasants in the surroundings of Belgrade: 'Is it a sin to kill children in the womb?' women would counter by asking another question: 'Isn't it a sin to watch children suffer?'.[15] The reduced influence by the church overall and the notion that life begins on the day of one's birth, made it easier for Serbian residents to accept deliberately induced miscarriages as an integral part of daily life.[16] That practice was drily justified by the social circumstances and relative agrarian overpopulation. 'Earlier, in old times, when property was large, we loved children', said one of the older peasants to Dr Aleksandar Petrović, '[e]very new child then meant a new worker in the house. Now [that] property is small ... every new child is a new trouble for a peasant'.

Peasant abortions were performed with quinine, the subject would sit over steaming water, the uterus would be opened with a piece of wood, a spindle or some kind of wire, and various herbs would be placed in the uterus. The peasant women passed on the 'techniques' for deliberate miscarriages, i.e. abortions, to one another,[17] and there was a woman with particular skills in each village who helped others to end unintended pregnancies with as few consequences as possible.[18] While well-to-do city ladies could pay for (illegal) abortions in one of the 'discreet' sanatoriums, which charged as much as 2,000 dinars for the service, an amount equivalent to the quarterly salary of an unskilled worker,[19] a woman of a modest economic standing could not even think of such a 'luxury'. Uterine ruptures, sepsis, severe bleeding and poisoning were just some of the consequences of improperly performed abortions. Year in, year out, the health of women was becoming increasingly threatened and the number of deaths was growing, as evidenced by the autopsy data gathered from the Belgrade Forensic Institute. In spite of the number of doctors and midwives who were ready to help women end their unintended pregnancy for social reasons, a hurried approach, lack of experience, insufficiently sterile conditions and the lack of proper instruments took their toll, thus mortality was still high in the abortions performed by these semi-professionals.[20]

Regional differences regarding abortion techniques were also becoming apparent. In the more economically developed parts of the country, and especially in the more prosperous counties of Slavonia where abortion was an integral part of everyday life before the First World War, women gained a 'greater experience' and more concrete ideas about the anatomy of female genitalia over time. As a result, there were fewer unprofessional abortions performed with spindles and wires than before. An unusual, but certainly representative case, involved a practice in a village in the vicinity of Osijek (Croatia), where women learned the technique of performing abortions with a metal female catheter that was purchased from a local pharmacy. When needed, the communal catheter was shared between the peasant women, who made sure to boil it or disinfect it with brandy before use. Moreover, these women knew how to control the abortion procedure, and as soon as they noticed that things were not going well, they immediately went to a nearby hospital.[21] However, the isolated examples of a kind of 'modernization' in this field were unable to change the sad statistics that testified to the heavy consequences that unskilfully performed abortions left on women's health. Vladimir Bazala, one of the most prominent Yugoslav gynaecologists of the time, wrote:

> We need to ask our hospitals and doctors in practice what today's female clientele looks like … Abortion after abortion, one worse than the other, one harder than the other. Terrible consequences, excess mortality. Is anyone concerned about compiling statistics on our abortions? Has anyone of those who are constantly watching those mutilated, half-dead women after the criminal act of abortion, found themselves raising their voice, both as a doctor and a man, to demand that anything be done to prevent and eliminate or minimize this distress? One could not hear it from anywhere, only the constant request of those who apodictically seek the law against abortion.[22]

The state authorities attempted to combat the growing number of abortions with repressive measures. The penal code, the first common law adopted for the whole country (1929), established abortion as a criminal act punishable with 3–5 years in prison. However, the code also provided for an important novelty that, at least in part, improved the position of women who wanted to terminate pregnancy. A medical indication was introduced, which allowed doctors to terminate a pregnancy to save a woman's health or life. Moreover, the principle of general punishment was also waived in the case of extramarital pregnancies; single girls who had committed abortions themselves could be released from punishment by a court decision.[23] Nevertheless, the penalties were allotted for what amounted to be a dead letter. There were few cases that reached the court, so the number of women, midwives, doctors and surgeons punished for abortions was minimal.[24] Paradoxically, the willingness of state authorities to turn a blind eye to the widespread practice of family planning via abortion could also mean that in some cases the social indicator was not considered a sufficient reason to terminate the pregnancy. Although doctors, lawyers and women's associations were increasingly calling for a partial liberalization of legislation in order to reduce female mortality and morbidity as a result of unskilfully performed abortions, the authorities were not responding.[25] The resolution of the Yugoslav doctors reached at the congress in 1935, which called for support in raising children, opening family counselling centres, and changing the articles of the penal code relating to abortion by respecting the 'socio-economic, mentally hygienic and racially biological moments' was also ignored.[26]

From Illegal to Legal: Abortions and Abortion Legislation in Socialist Yugoslavia

The communist party's rise to power resulted in substantial socio-economic changes in Yugoslav society. The 1946 constitution guaranteed women equal civil and political rights.[27] In terms of legal rights, wives ceased to be subordinate to their husbands in marital relationship status, and spouses were guaranteed the same rights and obligations regarding children. Traditional gender roles changed, women began to choose life partners independently and spouses became more like equal partners. Divorces became more frequent and socially acceptable, and the number of incomplete families and illegitimate births grew.[28] Although socialist modernization led to a significant and unprecedented improvement in the position of women throughout history, it turned out that the state was not fully capable of supporting the laws that were passed, thus the socialist reality largely deviated from an imaginary concept, especially before the end of the 1960s.[29] Motherhood was still emphasized as one of the basic duties of women, and in the case of a divorce, it was almost exclusively the duty of a woman to care for the children in many cases, since avoiding legal obligations primarily in terms of paying very low alimony became a regular pattern of behaviour.[30]

Causes such as rural to urban migrations, the economic independence of young migrants and a life without constant family supervision and control, characteristic for rural areas, favoured a more open expression of emotions, release of sexuality and change of perception about extramarital sex. Love, instead of marriage, became the ideal one dreamed of and aspired to, advanced somewhat by the art of cinematography during the 1950s. Despite sexual liberation, the emotional relationships between men and women continued to be burdened, especially in smaller communities, with old prejudices and conceptions that were not in consistent with freed sexual behaviour. The insufficient knowledge of contraception, together with the belief that engaging in sexual intercourse in some way constituted a formalization of the relationship, generated numerous problems as well. In cases of unintended and unwanted pregnancies, a woman was the one who had to deal with the consequences. The intimate life of women, unlike the intimate life of men, came under the influence of puritanical ideas, and women who tried to live up to their moral beliefs often ended up on the pillar of shame. The number of extramarital pregnancies was steadily increasing and as set out in one report, illegitimate children were born by girls who wanted to get married as a result of believing the promises of young men. The deep-rooted patriarchal views also led to a unanimous condemnation of the social environment, so the prevailing moral standard was one of the main motives for forcing unmarried girls and women to have abortion. Although extramarital pregnancies caused much more public attention and suspicion, abortions were still the most widespread form of family planning, especially among married women.[31] The rationale that led couples to plan small families resembled, in part, those seen before the Second World War. Some of the basic factors that generated an increase in the desire for birth control were economic opportunities, rural impoverishment as a result of the agricultural policy of the new authorities, but also the rapid pace of urbanization, women's employment and the increasing availability of education. A major demographic transformation took place over the course of a generation, and couples, even in new social and political circumstances, continued to plan families in an established way – intentional terminations of pregnancies and primitive methods of contraception, which often bore hallmark of witchcraft and magic until the late 1950s.[32]

There was a certain legal vacuum regarding abortion until 1951. The Penal Code of the Kingdom of Yugoslavia ceased to be valid by the decision of the Anti-Fascist Council for National Liberation of Yugoslavia in February 1945, and the new penal code of 1947 did not even reference abortion.[33] In the absence of other sources, and according to the existing data in the medical literature, we know that abortion commissions were set up by new authorities.[34] Moreover, on the basis of a provisional order, the Croatian Ministry of Health decided on using social indicators for a pregnancy termination from 1945 to 1946, both on its own discretion and on a case-to-case basis. It is impossible to say what the situation was in other republics, due to a lack of sources. Given the rigid centralism at the time, one can only assume that a similar practice existed in other parts of the country. How exactly established commissions worked is difficult to ascertain. The social indicators seem to have been approved only exceptionally in the early post-war years; a total of forty-six pregnancy terminations were performed at the gynaecological clinic in Zagreb in one year. Although the number was rather small, the influential doctors from Zagreb were dissatisfied. They called this practice a 'homicide', complaining that the following problems such as: 'My husband is going abroad'; 'We're moving to Belgrade'; 'I got a job at school', were accepted as social indicators for abortion.[35]

Although the Fifth National Conference of the Communist Party held in 1940 asked for the legalization of abortion 'until the conditions for careless parenting were met', in many aspects, the policy of socialist Yugoslavia against abortion as a form of family planning, up until the early 1950s, paradoxically resembled the practice seen in the Kingdom of Yugoslavia. The health service was limited to assisting women with legal and incomplete abortions – i.e. illegal abortions with complications. The party leaders, engaged in building a new society and dealing with political opponents, ignored the issue of intentional miscarriages, neglecting the consequences of such a method of birth control. The reasons for such a practice were numerous: high infant mortality as a result of illness, hunger, poor hygiene and general poverty, insufficient hospital beds and worn-out hospital infrastructure as well as a lack of doctors – especially gynaecologists. The delicacy and intimacy of the topic were also certain to cause some discomfort at the time. While in the interwar period, the communist party condemned 'dual morality' and advocated for gender equality and the equality of marital and extramarital children, the situation changed once they came to power. Up until the late 1950s, sexual freedom and the light-hearted engagement of young people caused dissatisfaction and discomfort among the party leaders and as a result, the police were authorized to arrest couples for kissing in public.[36]

Abortion was not long regarded as a woman's right to decide regarding her own body. Modelled by the Soviet interwar attitude and practice, abortion was, in the first post-war years, regarded as a 'tool' that was permitted until the construction of a socialist society was complete, at which time the care of mothers and children would be taken over by the state.[37] However, the number of intentionally terminated pregnancies was increasing year in year out[38] and assumed the proportions of true 'epidemic'.[39] The mortality and morbidity of women also increased, as evidenced by incomplete hospital statistics. Increasing numbers of Yugoslav women living in urban areas sought medical help in cases of unprofessionally induced miscarriages that were accompanied by complications. Already in 1948, it was estimated there were more incomplete abortions performed at gynaecological wards in some parts of the country, especially in Slavonia and Vojvodina, than births.[40] Of course, these were more relative than absolute numbers, since until the mid-1950s, due to the lack of hospital capacity, but also due to traditional practices that were dying out, most births were performed at home. Although abortions were a taboo that was only discussed in cases of tragic outcomes,[41] the worrying medical reports about the pernicious consequences of unprofessionally terminated pregnancies all over the country forced the authorities to respond. Therefore, the People's Health Committee of the Federal People's Republic of Yugoslavia required all medical associations and gynaecological wards to formulate their views on the termination of unintended pregnancies. Dr Franc Novak,[42] a renowned Slovenian gynaecologist, was appointed as an abortion specialist. He summarized the views heard at the sessions at gynaecological clinic meetings in Belgrade, Zagreb and Ljubljana, as well as the opinions expressed in the papers of the eminent gynaecologists of the time. In summary, medical professionals observed that abortion should be performed no later than three months into pregnancy, that abortion should not be performed on an outpatient basis but only in certain institutions, that a social indicator should not be a reason for the termination of pregnancy and that contraception should not be included in the concept of prohibited abortion. Although the proponents of the new penal code (1951) initially argued that both abortionists and women who aborted should be punished, the gynaecologists advocated for the impunity of women. Namely, it was believed that in a case of complications due to improperly performed abortions, women would seek medical help faster, which would result in reduction of the number of deaths.[43]

The first step towards the liberalization of abortion was made in 1952 with the adoption of the Regulation on the Execution of a Permitted and Completion of an Initiated Abortion. The regulation set out the indicators for the legal termination of pregnancy – medical, moral, ethical (in the case of incest and rape) and socio-medical, and specified the persons who were authorized to approve the termination of pregnancy as well as the institutions where abortions should take place.[44] Despite the fact that physicians were guided by the very strict criteria for permitting abortions in the first years following the adoption of the regulation, difficult living conditions, extremely low living standards and high housing shortages forced commissions to show greater flexibility in decision-making for health, social and political reasons. Thus, in practice, a poor financial situation became a sufficient reason for approving abortion even though it was contrary to the established regulation. Therefore, already in the mid-1950s, a vicious circle was created from which there was no way out; it persisted as such until the breakup of Yugoslavia. Spouses planned small families with one or two children, and out of ignorance, carelessness or laziness, chose abortion as the basic method of birth control.[45] Despite the efforts made by the state authorities, there was not the sufficient capacity to educate the population and offer a wide range of reliable and cheap contraceptives, nor significantly improve the standard of living, address housing shortages, provide a sufficient number of places in kindergartens, or provide equal working conditions for busy mothers and relief women from the workload that existed both at work and at home. Although the authorities were aware of the fact that the cuts in social welfare benefits (beginning in 1951) and accumulating social problems were some of the causes of the growing number of abortions, it is evident when reading the discussions from various counselling sessions organized around this topic that the party leaders were more concerned about the costs incurred by the type of the family planning used than the health and social implications of (illegal) abortions. Namely, women were mothers and housewives in the new socialist society, but they were also self-managing workers who, like men, had to participate in the construction of socialism and the industrial transformation of the state and society. Therefore, it was not rare that reports on abortions and women's reproductive health in general spoke mostly through the prism of the number of days spent on sick leave and the costs that those absences caused.[46]

In an attempt to restrain the practice of illegal abortions, yet without the willingness to change the legislative framework, the authorities took the path of least resistance, putting pressure on doctors to interpret abortion regulations more flexibly in order that the social circumstances of Yugoslavs would be at least partially facilitated. Such practice provoked dissatisfaction and resentment with gynaecologists who also considered the 'professionally and exactly executed abortion' equally 'harmful and risky'.[47] Looking at the problem of abortion purely from the health aspect, the Second Gynaecological Congress (1953) demanded that the Regulation on Permitted Abortion should be made stricter, that the social indicator should be accepted in combination with the medical, and that pregnant women who had decided to have an abortion should be punished. One demand was to expand the network of counselling centres and infirmaries for women and to specify that abortion, even when performed in hospital, constituted 'a grave injury to a woman, her health and her state of mind'. The authorities were unwilling to hear such doctors' opinions. The resolution passed at the congress elicited a strong response from mass organizations.[48] Vida Tomšič, a Slovenian politician, prominent member of Women's Antifascist Front organization and government spokeswoman for the matter, responded in the daily newspaper *Borba* (Struggle), saying that tightening up the prosecution meant 'following an old, for a socialist country ... wrong and impossible way'. Blaming the gynaecologists for having 'double standards' because they suggested punishing women who opted for abortion but not their partners, she stated that it would be better if 'comrade doctors stayed in the field of medical science' because women should not be discussed as if they were 'a major threat to the lives of children'.[49]

The views expressed in the aforementioned article more or less marked the policy of the Yugoslav authorities on abortion until the adoption of the new regulation in 1960. Although public opinion consisted of the voices of women and some gynaecologists who were advocating for the introduction of a social indicator and even the legalization of abortion, Vida Tomšič opposed it. She supported her arguments by saying that women who wanted to terminate pregnancy were not in an existential threat in the majority of cases since low income, unfinished studies, living in a cramped space or being single could not be considered as sufficient reasons to allow abortion. As the 1952 regulation provided for a social indicator only in cases where the birth of a child – due to particularly difficult financial, personal or family circumstances – would endanger the health of a mother, Vida Tomšič favoured 'a more flexible practice of the commissions themselves' in order to prevent the legalization of abortion.[50] However, from the mid-1950s onward, the 'more flexible' interpretation of the regulations led to over 80 per cent of all legal abortions being approved for socio-medical reasons. 'Everyone who monitored the work of the abortion commission in those years, especially the doctors who worked for them', as stated in one report, 'knew very well that difficult social reasons were hidden under those indicators that medical reasons were added automatically and that they 'would not be able to withstand medical expertise as a deciding factor'.[51] The various interpretation of socio-medical indicators by some institutions and/or commissions opened the way to arbitrary decision-making, thus the number of abortions allowed did not increase equally across the country.[52] Deprived of medical help, a large number of women continued to seek salvation from pregnancy through illegal abortions, risking their health and their lives. Therefore, even a relatively flexible interpretation of the regulation could not substantially change the worrying statistics, which testified that as many as 70 per cent of abortions, even in the late 1950s, were performed illegally and were applied using primitive techniques by non-professionals and under non-sterile conditions.[53]

As a means to keep up with the situation in the country and reduce or prevent illegal abortions, the authorities issued a new Regulation on the Conditions and Procedure for Allowing Abortion in February 1960, in which social indicators became a sufficient reason to perform an abortion.[54] Yugoslavia thus followed the Eastern European trend with the liberalization of abortion in clinics occurring in the Soviet Union (1955), Poland, Bulgaria and Hungary (1956) and Czechoslovakia (1957).[55] The new regulations provided that, except for medical reasons, abortion may also be granted in all cases 'when a pregnant woman can actually be expected to have difficult personal, family or financial circumstances due to the birth of a child'. The requests for permitting abortions were decided by the first instance and second instance commissions, organized in general hospitals, maternity hospitals and gynaecological and obstetric clinics. All women who sought the termination of pregnancy were required to submit an application with accompanying documents that would prove difficult housing conditions, poverty, marital status, the number of children in the family and other issues that posed threats and challenges to existence. Acting on the request, the commissions took into consideration the marital status of the petitioner, the number of children in the family, the possible existence of social illnesses, unresolved housing issues and the like.[56] The regulation stipulated that the commissions should pay special attention to the health and educational work regarding the interpretation of the risks associated with abortion, the benefits of preventive measures and the recommendations to visit contraceptive counselling centres that had been opening throughout the country since 1958. However, the true work with prevention was lacking, partly due to the commissions being overloaded, and partly due to the fact that both federal and republic authorities were late in issuing instructions and guidelines that were supposed to facilitate the work of the commission members.[57] Unwanted pregnancy had the added consequence of putting a woman in difficult social circumstances and whereas legislators considered the permission to abort to be just a 'form of assistance provided by society to a woman', Yugoslavs themselves saw the new regulations as a universal right to abortion. In spite of the fact that the flexibility in decision-making varied from town to town, social indicators became more individualized in practice.[58] Increasingly, women suggested a reluctance to have more children as a primary motive for abortion.[59] The poor educational structure and the lack of health education led women and their partners to regard abortion as the 'simplest' form of contraception, not realizing that it meant a serious medical procedure. Once approved, having an abortion was not a guarantee that the same woman would not refer to the commission again, in two to three months, with the same problem.[60] The results of a survey conducted in 1963 on a sample of 1,000 women showed that 27 per cent of women still considered abortion the most appropriate birth control method even after the first abortion, that 30 per cent of women continued to use the same methods to avoid conception, though already proven unreliable (mainly coitus interruptus and the Ogino-Knaus method), while only 43 per cent of women were ready to accept modern contraceptives.[61]

According to the statistics available, a total of 1,229,692 abortions were performed in Yugoslavia between 1963 and 1967, of which 335,580 were illegal.[62] The adoption of the Regulation on the Conditions and Procedure for Allowing Abortion played a significant role in reducing the number of illegal abortions, which was its primary objective. However, the lack of systematic work to educate the population, coupled with the increasingly flexible interpretation of the regulations, led to a real 'epidemic' of abortions. As early as 1961, the national average for abortions was 1.33 abortions per single birth. The infamous record in reckless family planning was held by the residents of Serbia and Croatia, where there were as many as 2.5–3 abortions per birth. Essentially, doctors had 'turned into abortionists',[63] performing 10 or more abortions a day.[64] It became clear that the legislation needed to be modified a little considering the circumstances. During the discussions, opinions were divided into two groups: the first group favoured a complete ban on abortion in regions where the birth rate was very low and the second group supported the complete liberalization of abortion. Considering the fact that the state did not consider birth control an instrument of population policy, but also the fact that the women, rejected by the second-instance commissions, spoke out that 'they would certainly seek a private person to intervene', a decision was reached in favour of liberalization.[65] The Family Planning Resolution, which was passed at the federal assembly in April 1969, was an introduction to the complete liberalization of abortion and a kind of a national program that attempted to ensure that every child born was wanted by its parents.[66] The right of parents to decide on the number of children in the family and the period of time between childbirths was defined as one of the 'basic human rights' made achievable by the use of contraceptives. According to that, a termination of pregnancy was said to be the least desirable form of birth control, which should be resorted to only as a 'last resort' when an unintended conception had already occurred.[67] Although Yugoslav society reached a partial general agreement towards family planning by the end of the 1960s, the resolution did not pass without resistance and negative reactions. Many physicians still believed that an abortion should be performed for medical reasons only.[68] Scepticism was expressed towards contraception and there were requests heard that contraceptives should only be spared for the married women or women over 40.[69] Representatives of the Roman Catholic Church demanded a complete ban on abortion, even when medical reasons were present. They insisted that a 'conscience clause' be introduced into the law, which would allow doctors and nurses of the Catholic denomination to refuse to participate in performing abortions without consequence.[70] The aforementioned objections and resistance did not delay or change the legislature's intention to liberalize abortion without any restrictions. Already in 1969, a General Law on Termination of Pregnancy was adopted, which contained all kinds of indications for the termination of pregnancy, including personal reasons.[71] Five years later, the right of a person to freely decide on the number of offspring was incorporated into the Yugoslav constitution (1974)[72] and later into the republic and provincial constitutions.[73]

Contraception

Gynaecologists and government officials began to speak about contraception as a basic means of preventing unintended pregnancies, primarily at the beginning of the 1950s. It was only then that the first contraceptives appeared, following the personal involvement of Dr Franc Novak. In 1950, he spent three months on study visits to the United Kingdom and America. While there he became acquainted with the contraceptive methods in use at that time and bought a couple of complete sets of diaphragms, which at that time was the most effective means of protection, at his own expense. In an attempt to interest the Yugoslav authorities in its production and distribution, he took one lot to the Federal Ministry of Industry, another to the Slovenian Minister of Industry Franc Leskošek and the third to the Sava, a tire factory. Both ministries demonstrated their interest, and the management of the Sava factory promised to start with production once the springs from Switzerland and Sweden had been acquired. However, it soon turned out that the rubber processing machines were old and technically inappropriate for that type of production. New ones were purchased, and the production of diaphragms began in Yugoslavia in 1954. The first articles on contraception and its importance emerged in journals shortly afterward. A breakthrough was made by another prominent Yugoslav gynaecologist, Professor Vladimir Bazala, who, after much effort and refusal, managed to publish work on the unreliability of the Knaus-Ogino method in preventing conception in the journal *Medicniski arhiv* (Medical Archive) in 1951. Lectures by Dr Angelina Mojić (1951) and Dr Grujica Žarković (1954) on family planning followed.[74] Although, from 1952 onwards, a certain number of women did receive imported contraceptives – diaphragms and chemical paste from the gynaecological outpatient clinic in Ljubljana – most gynaecologists expressed their doubts about contraception in the early 1950s, considering it a 'depopulation measure'.[75] The supporters of the new methods of protection, such as Dr Franc Novak, claimed that contraceptives 'should be given to all of the women who wanted them'.[76] However, despite the fact that contraception was acknowledged as a prophylactic method at the Third Gynaecological Congress (1956), in practice only certain physicians had the enthusiasm, time and knowledge to recommend women contraceptives as part of their regular duties.[77]

In 1955, the effort and commitment of Yugoslav gynaecologists in promoting contraceptives was given an institutional framework with the establishment of a contraceptive counselling centre at the Central Gynaecological Infirmary in Ljubljana, and shortly thereafter at the clinics in Belgrade, Zagreb, Sarajevo and Priština (1955–1956). The counselling network was expanding, but it was restricted to towns, so couples in rural parts of the country were hardly aware of available contraceptives. In the early years, the counselling centres provided mainly diaphragms and various, unreliable chemical agents to interested women, this was due to the modest choice of contraceptives available.[78] The shortage of such products on the market was partially remedied by obtaining 9 tonnes of EMCO foam, which came in the form of humanitarian aid from the United States (1963).[79] The selection of contraceptives at pharmacies in Yugoslavia became slightly better over time, since in the mid-1960s, domestic factories produced condoms, diaphragms, spermicides, spirals and beginning in 1964, pills. However, the fluctuations in the product quality and periodic shortages of funds as a result of poor distribution forced women to give up using contraceptives. Despite the fact that the decision of the Federal Social Security Council (1963) meant that contraceptives were dispensed under the same conditions as medicines and should have also served as an incentive for the Yugoslav industry to improve quality and distribution, the production of contraceptives was not excessively profitable due to little demand.[80]

In the period between 1958 and 1960, the health services organized lectures, printed brochures and leaflets in an effort to make the public aware of the benefits of contraception. Still, any concrete results were absent. Despite the decisions made at the federal counselling level in 1958, contraception did not become an integral part of the health service.[81] Paradoxically, abortion as a method of birth control, was unwittingly favoured by state institutions in the mid-1960s. The social security branches, especially those in Bosnia and Herzegovina, were ready to cover women's travel expenses to the nearest clinic and associated abortion costs, but not to issue a contraceptive for free, justifying to themselves that it was not a drug. The absence of propaganda material – brochures, leaflets, instructions and educational films – also saved money, but made work difficult for the healthcare institutions working on the popularization of contraception. Despite numerous consultations and discussions organized around the topic, the state authorities practically turned a deaf ear to the huge number of abortions, a burgeoning health problem of the time, and shifted the entire burden of educating the population to the shoulders of few enthusiasts – primarily gynaecologists and members of certain mass organizations.[82] Throughout the entire existence of Yugoslavia, couples learned about family planning through informal channels, and only as an exception at school or through some organized activity.[83] Media was poorly used in the service of education, for example, the Ris factory tried to get a space for advertising condoms on television unsuccessfully for one full year (1967),[84] and the texts on sex and sexuality filling the pages of the Yugoslav press since the mid-1960s bore no educational component.

Paradoxically enough, the progressing sexual revolution was unable to change the rooted prejudices. Gender relations became increasingly free, sex and free love ceased to be a taboo, but partners still continued to avoid the use of medical contraceptives. Women were reluctant to visit gynaecological centres, justifying to themselves that they had neither the time nor the money to buy the cheapest means of protection. The traditional and patriarchal views, poor health culture, resistance of all kinds to modern methods of birth control even by health professionals, but also the feelings of shame, discouraged women from obtaining medical counselling. Many women were not supported by their partners, since men showed very little interest in abortion issues and their prevention, expressing a negative attitude towards the use of modern contraceptives. In those circumstances, it was not surprising that in 1962 only 0.75 per cent of women of reproductive age went to one of the counselling centres.[85] Some doctors thought that the cause of the poor reception to contraceptives could be summed up in one sentence: 'No activity on the part of the health service, nor on the part of the mass organizations was carried out systematically in a persistent and planned way'. The counselling centres, as special service in the administration of contraception, were closing down due to a lack of profitability and women were poorly informed about how to obtain counselling on the issue in other women's care institutions. Because doctors were also overburdened with their existing workload, minimal attention was given to promoting contraception. Additionally, there were no systematic efforts to improve the knowledge of medical workers, and by the mid-1960s, a lot of doctors and nurses working at the Yugoslav hospitals and polyclinics were not even aware of the importance of contraception in maintaining the reproductive health of women.[86] Although it was perceived that both partners should be involved in the use of contraception,[87] the educational campaign focused exclusively on women,[88] which gave the impression that pregnancy, despite the recent social modernization, was still exclusively viewed as an issue that concerned women.

The 1969 Resolution on Family Planning which was supposed to advance the field of family planning one step forward, was still not a guarantee that Yugoslavs would be provided with 'contraceptive services of such a scope and quality to make abortion unnecessary'.[89] By the mid-1970s, the use of contraceptives was still low. The efforts to popularize contraception were insufficient, and the choices in available contraceptives remained modest: there were five types of pills on the market, mostly of a similar hormonal composition, two types of intrauterine devices, and domestic condoms of poor quality. Instead of helping to raise awareness about the harmfulness of abortion, the press reaffirmed superstitions, publishing sensational news articles about the harms of hormonal agents and intrauterine devices.[90] The relative success of the government efforts in the health and educational plan was also evidenced by a survey conducted by the Centre for Demographic Research at the Institute of Social Sciences (1972) on a representative sample of 8,000 women of fertile age. The results obtained showed that 24.58 per cent of women knew about intrauterine devices, 32.43 per cent knew about condoms, 66.68 per cent knew about birth control pills and 77.57 per cent knew about coitus interruptus.[91]

Although the service of contraceptive counselling was free of charge under the Compulsory Health Care Act (1970), the republics set different rates for contraceptives. Thus, in some parts of the country, they were completely free of charge, while in others, women paid a portion of the costs for prescriptions or paid a full price.[92] Experts from different fields, most notably physicians and demographers, conducted numerous studies trying to establish the cause of the poor use of medical contraceptives and the prevalence of abortion. The insufficient awareness of contraceptive options by women, as well as numerous prejudices,[93] caused Yugoslavs to think little about their reproductive health. The educational attainment rate, as well as economic status, were also factors that influenced the acceptance of contraception, for example, couples in Slovenia chose to use modern contraceptives more easily than those in Kosovo.[94] Old habits die hard, thus coitus interruptus remained the preferred method of protection against unintended pregnancy until the breakup of the state. Women entrusted their partners with the responsibility of the unintended pregnancy, mostly out of ignorance, and fearful of the harmful effects of contraceptives,[95] but also fearing that if they took the initiative upon themselves, they would appear to be promiscuous.[96] Furthermore, despite the fact that a large number of Yugoslavs were becoming aware of the harmful effects of abortion, a survey conducted in Novi Sad found that couples continued to view it as a very 'effective' method of family planning.[97]

Conclusion

The deliberate termination of unintended pregnancy was a major social and medical problem that affected demographic trends throughout Yugoslavia (1918–1991). Beginning in the 1920s, Yugoslavs chose to have families with less children, primarily for economic and social reasons. Some of the main causes that led to a decreased desire for offspring were: low living standards, difficult living conditions in the countryside, better healthcare and declining child mortality, changing attitudes towards children and greater commitment to their upbringing and education, rising unemployment, unresolved housing issues, and the workload on women at their jobs and at home. Birth rates had been declining in certain regions since the beginning of the twentieth century, yet there used to be a slight change in the tendency of those trends shortly after a war, when a greater desire for posterity would emerge to neutralize demographic losses.[98]

Abortions, first illegal and then legal, were a simple form of family planning which, despite the recent social modernization, was gaining in popularity even as late as the 1970s and 1980s. Changes in the national family planning policies managed to decriminalize abortion and, through legalization, allowed almost all abortions to be done in gynaecological clinics, under optimal medical conditions.[99] However, bigger improvements were impossible to make. The emancipatory and modernizing role of the state in the field of family planning, just like in many other fields, only went halfway. Although the Federal Assembly Resolution on Family Planning (1969) established the societal obligations to develop the conditions for the acquisition of knowledge and to provide the necessary resources for family planning,[100] the results achieved were modest. Although there was a slight increase in the number of women using gynaecological consulting services, especially during the 1970s, the use of modern contraceptives remained poor and was strongly influenced by shortages in Yugoslav pharmacies.[101] The attempts to introduce sexual education in schools provoked discomfort and resistance, and the introduction into biology curricula of topics such as puberty, sexually transmitted diseases and protection against unintended pregnancy did not produce the desired results. In modernized Yugoslav society, sex and sexuality were to remain a taboo, and those young people who had already started an intimate relationship were unable to obtain adequate knowledge either at school or at home. The number of adolescent pregnancies was increasing year in year out, and abortion remained one of the favoured methods of family planning.[102] However, despite a huge number of abortions, accurate statistics were missing.[103] According to the incomplete data, the number of abortions reached the approximate number of 350,000 in 1980, which averages out to over 900 abortions per 1,000 live births. A particularly high number of abortions were executed in Serbia proper (1,885 abortions per 1,000 live births) and in Vojvodina (1,409 per 1,000 live births).[104] Considering the rate of legal abortions per 1,000 women between the ages of 15 and 44, only the Soviet Union was ahead of Yugoslavia, while all other countries had a lower incidence.[105]

Despite the decline in birth rates, the statements of certain gynaecologists that 'the number of abortions in Serbia was so large that we could actually ask ourselves if we were committing genocide'[106] and the warnings by demographers that some population policy measures should be adopted due to the negative trends,[107] Yugoslav family planning policy was not based on either a pronatalist or an anti-natalist concept. The Yugoslav model of family planning, as a human right, was intended to create a 'socially-active and desired parenthood' that was to be realized 'based on the self-management position of the working people' and thus become 'a basis for a happy life in the family and harmonious socio-economic development'.[108] Family planning, therefore, was an integral part of social child care, with the full involvement of parents in upbringing and the educational issues of their children.[109] The population policy, according to the Yugoslavia Social Development Plan for 1976–1980, was supposed to become 'a part of socio-economic development and contribute on a larger scale to the further humanization of biological reproduction and the affirmation of the right of a person to freely decide on childbirth', while the 'demographic trends according to the needs and specifications of particular regions' were to be affected by creating, among others, more favourable educational, health and social conditions.[110] However, according to the available sources, the ideal family size in Yugoslavia was never specified,[111] nor discussed. Furthermore, despite the significant fluctuations in birth rates in the republics and provinces, the Yugoslav officials dealing with the issue considered different views on family planning or the specification of different principles of population policy to be unacceptable, i.e. that the human rights established by the constitution should not be violated when establishing actual measures of population policy. It was specifically emphasized that the task of society was to consider demographic trends and view them as part of general development in an effort to strike a balance between the level of development and the rate of population growth. Parents were not conditioned in such a way to make decisions about giving or not giving birth in accordance with the demographic and population policies of the republics.[112]

Notes

1 Archive of Yugoslavia (further abbreviated as AJ), 142 / II – S 274; Stanovništvo i zaposlenost u dugoročnom razvoju Jugoslavije.
2 Neda Božinović, *Žensko pitanje u Srbiji u 19. i 20. veku* (Beograd: Devedesetčetvrta, 187); V. Vera Gudac Dodić, 'Divorce in Serbia', *Tokovi istorije* 1–2 (2008): 140–141, 147.
3 AJ, 142 / II – S 274; Stanovništvo i zaposlenost u dugoročnom razvoju Jugoslavije.
4 Ratibor V. Popović, *Agrarna prenaseljenost Jugoslavije* (Belgrade: Geca Кon, 1940), 19–21.
5 Vera Stein Erlich, *Jugoslavenska porodica u transformaciji. Studija u tri stotine sela* (Zagreb: Liber, 1971), 263.
6 Erlich, *Jugoslavenska porodica u transformaciji*, 268 – 270.
7 Popović, *Agrarna prenaseljenost Jugoslavije*, 32.
8 AJ, 142 / II – 417; A. Milojković, G. Žarković, M. Džumhur, 'Historijat liberalizacije pobačaja u Jugoslaviji. Savetovanje o izgradnji društvenih stavova o populacionoj politici u Jugoslaviji' (1973).
9 Pavle Mijović, 'Pobačaj na selu u Crnoj Gori', *Socijalno–medicinski pregled*, oktobar, novembar, decembar (1940): 119.
10 Ivana Dobrivojević Tomić, 'Trajnost i promena. Abortusna kultura, liberalizacija propisa i pokušaji seksualne edukacije stanovništva Jugoslavije (1918–1991)', *Prispevki za novejšo zgodovino* 3 (2019): 118.
11 Milovan Milovanović, 'Letalni namerni pobačaj', *Medicinski pregled* oktobar (1936): 375.

12 Erlich, *Jugoslavenska porodica u transformaciji*, 272.
13 Mihajlo Pražić, 'Sociološki elementi problema pobačaja', *Liječnički vijesnik* 7 (1936): 308.
14 Aleksandar Petrović, *Rakovica: socijalno-zdravstvene i higijenske prilike, t.* 2 (Belgrade: Centralni higijenski zavod, 1939), 28.
15 Aleksandar Petrović, *Pobačaji na selu* (Belgrade: no publisher, 1938), 5–6.
16 Petrović, *Rakovica: socijalno-zdravstvene*, 28.
17 Petrović, *Pobačaji na selu*, 6–7.
18 Momčilo Isić, 'Dete i žena na selu u Srbiji između dva svetska rata', in *Žene i deca 4. Srbija u modernizacijskim procesima XIX i XX veka* (Belgrade: Helsinški odbor, 2006), 152.
19 Predrag Marković, *Beograd i Evropa 1918–1941. Evropski uticaji na proces modernizacije Beograda* (Belgrade: Savremena administracija, 1991), 62.
20 Dobrivojević Tomić, 'Trajnost i promena', 117.
21 Pražić, 'Sociološki elementi problema pobačaja', 308.
22 Željko Dugac, Ingrid Marton, 'Kada žena ženi pomogne-naudi: sankcioniranje ilegalnih pobačaja između 1920-ih i 1940-ih godina', in *Na rubu znanosti: društveno i pravno neprihvatljiva ponašanja kroz povijest*, ed. Suzana Miljan (Hrvatski studij Sveučilišta u Zagrebu, 2009), 223.
23 Gordana Drakić, 'Prekid trudnoće prema Krivičnom zakoniku Kraljevine Jugoslavije i projektima koji su mu prethodili', *Zbornik radova Pravnog fakulteta u Novom Sadu* 3 (2011): 540–541.
24 Žika B. Marković, *Pogled na pitanje pobačaja i antikoncepcionih mera* (Belgrade: Zadružna štamparija, 1934), 3.
25 Dobrivojević Tomić, 'Trajnost i promena', 117.
26 Predrag Marković, 'Seksualnost između privatnog i javnog u 20. Veku', in *Privatni život kod Srba u 20. veku*, ed. Milan Ristović (Belgrade: Clio, 2007), 115.
27 Ustav Federativne Narodne Republike Jugoslavije, Službeni list FNRJ, br 10 (1. 2. 1946).
28 AJ, 142 / II – 279; Neki problemi porodice u savremenom jugoslovenskom društvu.
29 Ivana Dobrivojević Tomić, 'Između nebrige i neznanja. Žene, seksualnost i reproduktivno zdravlje u socijalističkoj Jugoslaviji', *Glasnik Etnografskog insituta SANU* 2 (2019): 310.
30 AJ, 142 / II – 279; Neki problemi porodice u savremenom jugoslovenskom društvu.
31 Dobrivojević Tomić, 'Između nebrige i neznanja', 311–316.
32 AJ, 672 – 323; Angelina Mojić, Olivera Kokić, Priručnik za kontracepciju.
33 Krivični zakonik, *Službeni list*, br. 106/47.
34 Srećko Zanela, 'Abortus artificialis legalis', *Liječnički vijesnik* 11–12 (1950): 393.
35 Velimir Sveško, 'Abortus artificialis legalis', *Liječnički vijesnik* 11–12 (1950): 409.
36 Dobrivojević Tomić, 'Trajnost i promena', 118–119.
37 Ivan Simić, *Soviet Influences on Post-War Yugoslav Gender Policies* (London: Palgrave Macmillan, 2018), 73.
38 According to the estimates of the Slovenian gynaecologist Pavel Lunaček, around 250,000 abortions per year were performed in the period between 1945 and 1951: *Treće redovno zasedanje Veća naroda i Saveznog veća (drugi saziv) 25–27 februara 1951, Stenografske beleške* (Belgrade: Prezidijum Narodne skupštine FNRJ), 87.
39 The term was frequently used in sources, by (pro-abortion) gynaecologists, e.g. Angelina Mojić and Berislav Berić, who believed that more effort should be put in promoting contraception. See for example: AJ, 672–323; Aktuelni problemi rada prvostepenih komisija za prekid trudnoće u AP Vojvodini; AJ, 672–84; Epidemiološko–pravni aspekt problema pobačaja.

40 AJ, 141–33–187; Zaštita matera i dece.
41 AJ, 142/II–623; Dr Franc Novak, Abortus i kontracepcija.
42 Franc Novak (1908–1999) was a prominent Yugoslav and Slovenian gynaecologist and professor at the Faculty of Medicine and a member of the Slovenian Academy of Sciences and Arts. He is the author of a large number of works in the field of gynaecology and one of the first proponents of contraception in socialist Yugoslavia. He was married to Vida Tomšič, a distinguished party worker, a member of the Central Committee of the League of Communists, president of the Women's Antifascist Front and an active member of the Family Planning Council.
43 Ivana Dobrivojević Tomić, 'Za željeno roditeljstvo. Državna politika Jugoslavije u oblasti planiranja porodice 1945–1974', *Istorija 20, veka* 1 (2018): 121; V. i AJ, 142 / II – 417. Milojković et al., 'Historijat liberalizacije pobačaja' (1973).
44 AJ, 672 – 323; Angelina. Mojić, Olivera. Kokić, Priručnik za kontracepciju.
45 See: AJ, 142 / II – 623; Savetovanje o problemima prekida trudnoće i kontracepcije (1963); AJ, 142 / II – 626; Problemi kontracepcije, prekida trudnoće i obrazovno – vaspitnog rada sa područja odnosa među polovima (1965); AJ, 142 / II – 623; Zadaci i društvena briga na polju seksualnog vaspitanja; AJ, 142 / II – 417. G. Žarković, A.M. Džumhur, S.M. Džumhur, Š. Segetlija, M. Maglajić, and A. Softić, Znanje, stavovi i praksa planiranja porodice kod ženskog stanovništva u fertilnoj dobi u Jugoslaviji. Savetovanje o izgradnji društvenih stavova o populacionoj politici u Jugoslaviji (1973); Mirjana Rašević, *Planiranje porodice kao stil života* (Beograd: Insitut društvenih nauka. Centar za demografska Istraživanja 1999), 125–126; Berislav Berić, 'Neki problem planiranja humane reprodukcije u SAP Vojvodini, *Zbornik Matice srpske za društvene nauke* 80 (1986): 93; Rada Drezgić, *'Bela kuga' među 'Srbima'. O naciji, rodu i rađanju na prelazu vekova* (Belgrade: Institut za filozofiju i društvenu teoriju 2010), 43.
46 Dobrivojević Tomić, 'Trajnost i promena', 121–122.
47 AJ, 142 / II – 623; Dr Franc Novak, Abortus i kontracepcija.
48 AJ, 142 / II – 417. Milojković et al., 'Historijat liberalizacije pobačaja' (1973).
49 Vida Tomšič, Da li je legalizacija pobačaja prihvatljivo rešenje, AJ, 142 / II – A 816.
50 Ibid., AJ, 142 / II – A 816.
51 AJ, 672 – 323; Dr Ruža Šegedin, Problemi pobačaja i Uredba za dozvoljavanje prekida trudnoće.
52 AJ, 672 – 323; Dr Angelina Mojić, Ispitivanje posledica dozvoljenih i dovršenih pobačaja.
53 AJ, 672 – 323; Dr Ruža Šegedin, Problemi pobačaja i Uredba za dozvoljavanje prekida trudnoće.
54 'Uredba o uslovima i postupku za dozvoljavanje pobačaja', *Službeni list FNRJ*, 9/60.
55 Dagmar Herzog, *Sexuality in Europe. A Twentieth-Century History* (Cambridge: Cambridge University Press, 2011), 101.
56 Ivana Dobrivojević, 'Planiranje porodice u Jugoslaviji', *Istorija 20. veka*, 2 (2016): 88.
57 *Savetovanje o problemima trudnoće i kontracepcije* (Beograd: Novinsko izdavačka ustanova Beogradske novine, 1963), 24.
58 AJ, 142 / II – 623; Stenografske beleške sa sastanka održanog u konferenciji za društvenu aktivnost žena Jugoslavije u vezi sa pripremom savetovanja.
59 AJ, 672 – 323; Dr Ruža Šegedin, Problemi pobačaja i Uredba za dozvoljavanje prekida trudnoće.
60 AJ, 142 / II – 623; Informacija sa sastanka održanog 27. 5. 1963. sa socijalnim radnicima članovima komisije za prekid trudnoće.

61 Savetovanje o problemima, 32.
62 AJ, 142 / II – 626; Kretanje pobačaja i porođaja u zdravstvenim ustanovama SFR Jugoslavija 1963–1967.
63 Tomić, 'Trajnost i promena', 123.
64 AJ, 142 / II – 626; Problemi kontracepcije, prekida trudnoće i obrazovno – vaspitnog rada sa područja odnosa među polovima (1965).
65 Dobrivojević Tomić, 'Planiranje porodice', 95.
66 AJ, 142 / II – 417; Nevenka Petrić, Društveno – politički aspekt planiranja porodice u Jugoslaviji. Savetovanje o izgradnji društvenih stavova o populacionoj politici u Jugoslaviji (1973).
67 AJ, 142 / II – 342; Rezolucija o planiranju porodice.
68 AJ, 142 / II – A 816; Planiranje porodice u Jugoslaviji.
69 AJ, 142 / II – 417; Petrić, Društveno – politički aspekt planiranja porodice u Jugoslaviji. Savetovanje o izgradnji društvenih stavova o populacionoj politici u Jugoslaviji (1973).
70 AJ, 142 / II – 294. Stav Sekretarijata Saveznog saveta za planiranje porodice povodom zahteva Biskupijske konferencije Katoličke crkve u SFRJ.
71 Opšti zakon o prekidu trudnoće, *Službeni list SFRJ*, 20/69.
72 *Ustav Socijalističke Federativne Republike Jugoslavije* (Belgrade: Službeni list, 1974), 115.
73 AJ, 142 / II – 1173; Stavovi, mišljenja, preporuke.
74 AJ, 142 / II – 417. Milojković et al., 'Historijat liberalizacije pobačaja' (1973).
75 AJ, 142 / II – 417. Franc Novak, Lidija Andolšek, M. Kuštrin, I. Veter, Prikaz razvoja odnosa do celokupne problematike planiranja porodice u medicinskim krugovima. Savetovanje o izgradnji društvenih stavova o populacionoj politici u Jugoslaviji (1973).
76 AJ, 142 / II – 623; Dr Franc Novak, Abortus i kontracepcija.
77 AJ, 142 / II – 417. Franc Novak, Lidija Andolšek, M. Kuštrin, I. Veter, Prikaz razvoja odnosa do celokupne problematike planiranja porodice u medicinskim krugovima. Savetovanje o izgradnji društvenih stavova o populacionoj politici u Jugoslaviji (1973).
78 AJ, 142 / II – 417. Milojković et al., 'Historijat liberalizacije pobačaja' (1973).
79 AJ, 142 / II – 623; Sredstva za kontracepciju.
80 Tomić, 'Trajnost i promena', 127.
81 AJ, 672 – 323; Materijal za savetovanje 'O problemima prekida trudnoće i kontracepcije' (1963).
82 Dobrivojević Tomić, 'Planiranje porodice u Jugoslaviji', 92.
83 AJ, 142 / II – 417; A. Džumhur, Grujica Žarković, S. Džumhur, Upliv različitih metoda komunikacije na korišćenje usluge planiranja porodice u zdravstvenim ustavovama (1973).
84 AJ, 142 / II – 279. Stenografske beleške sa Prve sednice Saveznog zavoda za planiranje porodice (juli 1967).
85 Dobrivojević Tomić, 'Planiranje porodice u Jugoslaviji', 91–92.
86 Savetovanje o problemima, 49.
87 AJ, 672 – 323; Anglelina Mojić, Olivera Kokić, Priručnik za kontracepciju.
88 AJ, 142 / II – 417; Milojković et al., 'Historijat liberalizacije pobačaja' (1973).
89 AJ, 142 / II – 417; Milojković et al., 'Historijat liberalizacije pobačaja' (1973).
90 AJ, 142 / II – A 840; Lidija Andolšek, Aktuelni problemi kontracepcije i ostalih oblika planiranja porodice; AJ, 142 / II – A 803; Pregled proizvodnje i potrošnje kontraceptivnih sredstava (1979).
91 AJ, 142 / II – 417. Žarković et al., *Znanje, stavovi i praksa* (1973).
92 Dobrivojević Tomić, 'Planiranje porodice u Jugoslaviji', 93.
93 Drezgić, *'Bela kuga' među*, 43; Rašević, *Planiranje porodice kao stil života*, 125–126.

94 Dobrivojević Tomić, 'Za željeno roditeljstvo', 129.
95 Berić, 'Neki problem planiranja humane reprodukcije', 93.
96 Branka Bogdan, 'Cold War Entanglements and Abortion Technology: Writing Yugoslavia into the Global History of Vacuum Aspiration, 1964–1974', *Australian Journal of Politics and History* 64, no. 3 (2018): 414.
97 Nila Kapor-Stanulović and Henry P David, 'Former Yugoslavia and Successor States', in *From Abortion to Contraception: A Resource to Public Policies and Reproductive Behaviour in Central and Eastern Europe from 1917 to the Present*, ed. Henry P. David (Westport, CT: Greenwood Press/Greenwood Publishing Group, 1999), 305.
98 Dušan Breznik and Miroslav Rašević, 'Razmatranja o populacionoj politici u Jugoslaviji', *Stanovništvo* 1–2 (1972): 10.
99 AJ, 672 – 193; Razvoj zdravstvene zaštite žena u prvoj dekadi OUN za žene.
100 AJ, 672 – 193; Razvoj zdravstvene zaštite žena u prvoj dekadi OUN za žene.
101 AJ, 142 / II – A 803; Pregled proizvodnje i potrošnje kontraceptivnih sredstava (1979).
102 Dobrivojević Tomić, 'Trajnost i promena', 129.
103 Mirjana Rašević, 'Sadržaj i kvalitet podataka o prekidu trudnoće', *Stanovništvo* 1/4 (1989), 1/2 (1990): 118.
104 AJ, 672 – 193; Razvoj zdravstvene zaštite žena u prvoj dekadi OUN za žene.
105 Rašević, 'Sadržaj i kvalitet', *Stanovništvo*, 117.
106 A. Mirković et al., 'Sadašnje stanje pobačaja u Srbiji', in *VII kongres ginekologa – opstetričara Jugoslavije. Referati i koreferati* (Belgrade: Medicinska knjiga, 1972), 189. See also John F Besemeres, *Socialist Population Politics: The Political Implications of Demographic Trends in the USSR and Eastern Europe* (New York: M. E. Sharpe, 1980), 361.
107 Breznik and Rašević, 'Razmatranja o populacionoj', 7–11.
108 AJ, 142 / II – A 803; Neveka Petrić, Odgovorno roditeljstvo kao ustavno pravo i humanizacija odnosa među polovima u SFRJ (1982).
109 AJ, 142 / II – A 816; Planiranje porodice u Jugoslaviji; AJ, 142 / II – A 808; Uticaj porodičnih struktura i uslova na ulogu žene u razvoju i obrnuto, maj 1979.
110 Nevenka Petrić, 'Pravci razvoja slobodnog roditeljstva u SFRJ', in *Slobodno roditeljstvo – činilac društvene promene* (Belgrade: Insitut za socijalnu politiku, 1979), 11.
111 AJ, 142 / II – A 803; Neveka Petrić, Odgovorno roditeljstvo kao ustavno pravo i humanizacija odnosa među polovima u SFRJ (1982).
112 Dobrivojević Tomić, 'Trajnost i promena', 125–126.

7 Blind Faith or Divine Providence?

Global Catholicism and the Population Bomb

Wannes Dupont

During one of his lectures, Michel Foucault used the image of lepers' banishment from medieval towns to describe authorities' incapacity of dealing with the menace of death in any other way than by cutting loose and casting out the infected parts of the social body. Later, as plague epidemics regularly swept Europe after the initial massacre of the Black Death, those same authorities began to discern a seasonal pattern in recurrent outbreaks. They developed increasingly sophisticated systems of quarantine and continuous surveillance in order to prevent contagion from spreading like wildfire. Born from necessity, these systems of 'close and meticulous observation' were fundamentally different from the crude and fatalistic ostracization of lepers.[1] Far more ambitious, they were aimed at controlling movement, isolating the sick, organizing care for those who might live and the sanitary disposal of the many that perished. As they bolstered both authorities' competence and their capacity for control, Foucault noted how these measures inspired a political dream 'in which the plague is rather the marvellous moment when political power is exercised to the full'.[2] A society's 'threshold of modernity', he later argued in *The History of Sexuality*, was reached when authorities managed to 'bring life and its mechanisms within the realm of explicit calculations', shaping, scripting and administering it with increasing levels of instrumental zeal and managerial precision.[3]

Of course, the powerful metaphor of a threshold belies the fact that this development actually encompassed a long and gradual process of governmental capacity-building. If the political reverie inspired by the plague dated from the late Middle Ages, it was still a pipe dream by the time Thomas Malthus wrote his landmark treatise on the rationality intrinsic to population dynamics in 1798. Even during the late nineteenth and the early twentieth centuries, when sharp declines in European fertility raised the alarm, governments remained reluctant to intervene forcefully, faced with the sheer scale of the administration involved, its financial implications, and, of course, the formidable political, moral and religious objections to such an undertaking. Indeed, for a long time, private pressure groups were far more ambitious than public authorities were in responding to them.[4] In the collective memory, of course, Nazi Germany, with its racist and

DOI: 10.4324/9781003161080-9

genocidal commitment to turning a biopolitical mirage into a grotesque nightmare, stands out as the culmination of biopolitical power in the eager hands of the state.[5] But as a wealth of scholarship has shown, before and after the disastrous totalitarian intermezzo of the interwar years, non-state actors often took the lead, particularly where the ultimate biopolitical chimera of population control on a planetary scale was concerned.

Recent scholarship on global population control has emphasized the importance of private philanthropic organizations' ability after the Second World War to act as a counterweight to the traditional focus in biopolitical analyses on national states and official bureaucracies.[6] With networks spanning the globe, organizations like the Population Council, the Ford Foundation and the International Planned Parenthood Federation (IPPF) were instrumental in encouraging and enabling national policymakers, not rarely in neo-imperial ways. Indeed, the works in question have vastly improved our historical understanding of the triadic connections between governments, intergovernmental agencies, and the growing chorus of non-governmental pressure groups. At the same time, however, while transcending national frameworks, that same scholarship can seem skewed in at least two respects. First of all, much of it tends to be highly American-centred. It rightly reflects the outsized role of both US private organizations and governments in pushing the population control agenda during the second half of the twentieth century, but it also overshadows the roles of other players in the field and the relative weight of non-American interests on policy. Secondly, and perhaps even more importantly, the existing literature on global biopolitics is overwhelmingly concerned with the anti-natalism of transnational organizations, like the ones mentioned earlier, to stem the tide of overpopulation. Paradoxically, that same literature universally recognizes one institution as the resolute, daunting and ubiquitous nemesis of the so-called population establishment while, at the same time, giving it short shrift for the most part. If it is accepted as a matter of course that the Roman Catholic Church was the main restraint on growing attempts to curb population growth worldwide throughout the twentieth century, we still know surprisingly little about the internal coordination of its efforts.[7]

The time seems ripe for an analytical counterbalance to the lopsided focus on US population controllers by zooming in more closely on the transnationally orchestrated Catholic bid to keep them at bay. Many Church historians, after all, have concentrated on doctrinal developments as they were shaped by the encyclicals *Casti Connubii* (1930) and *Humanae Vitae* (1968) in their relation to the reformism of the Second Vatican Council. Others have looked at debates about family planning within a national framework.[8] Historians of gender and sexuality, for their part, have often been more interested in how Catholic debates about birth control have shaped wider cultures of sexual conservatism up until the early 1960s and their liberalization from that point onwards.[9] Indeed, much of this literature focuses more on developments in the Cold War's 'First World' of North

America and Europe than it does on those elsewhere. It also devotes more attention to the regionally central debates about the morality of contraception than to global problems regarding rapid population growth. By contrast, the role of the Catholic Church on debates about reproductive rights in the present has been examined to a far greater extent by more synchronically oriented feminist, gender and sexuality studies. These commonly take the 1994 International Conference on Population and Development in Cairo as a starting point for analyses of an ongoing showdown between a pro-life and pro-choice culture war on the global stage with the Vatican in a leading role.[10] In short, we still know far too little about the outsized role the Church has played on the international stage in this respect, particularly during the first few decades after the Second World War when population management emerged as one of the most contentious global policy issues.

Why is this (still) the case? Why, as historical scholarship has increasingly looked at biopolitics beyond the level of plague-ridden cities and overpopulated states in recent decades, has the oldest and most global biopolitical actor not received closer attention? No doubt, as Matthew Connelly has pertinently observed, this is in large part because the Church 'has been more reluctant' than, for example, the Ford and the Rockefeller Foundations 'to provide meaningful access to its documentary record'.[11] Even so, and although fragmented and indirect, there are sources available for the reconstruction of the Church's persistent campaign against birth and population control. The present essay, based on ongoing research about the influence of religious discourse on global biopolitics, is mostly programmatic in nature. It will limit itself to outlining the contours of the initial Catholic response to the post-war spectre of overpopulation. In doing so, it wants to emphasize the institution's transnational outlook, its early successes in blocking the issue from being placed on the World Health Organization's agenda, and its deployment of dedicated task forces to lobby the international community through the United Nations.

Overpopulation's Emergence

Catholicism's concern with the population question began in earnest in 1909, when the Belgian Church was the first to warn the faithful against the sins of neo-Malthusianism and to issue instructions to priests and confessors on how to fight Malthusianists in response to the country's declining birth rates.[12] France, of course, had been the first nation in Europe to react to falling fertility rates as early as the 1860s, but French anxieties were dominated by the inauspicious rise of German economic and military might. Unlike France's secular and jingoistic anti-Malthusian campaign, Belgium's took on an overwhelmingly religious, anti-socialist, and (therefore) anti-French character. The architect of the Belgian campaign, and the archbishop's right-hand man, was a Jesuit moralist named Arthur Vermeersch. After the First World War, Vermeersch took up a professorship at the pontifical university in Rome, where he soon became the world's most authoritative moral theologian of the interwar period. Vermeersch was a driving force behind the landmark encyclical *Casti Connubii* in 1930, the clearest and most important statement of Catholic doctrine on the matter of conjugal ethics and sexuality in the modern age.[13] *Casti Connubii* strictly condemned any and all 'unnatural' forms of birth control and was a reaction to developments in the secular world such as the liberalizing reforms in Weimar Germany and elsewhere, but it served more particularly as a rebuttal to the growing permissiveness of Protestant denominations. Most notably, the Anglican Lambeth conference of 1929 had voted to grant lay-Christians wide latitude with regard to family planning as long as contraceptives were used in good faith. To Vermeersch and to the Catholic Church more generally, this was an outrage. Procreation, after all, was the primary and inalienable purpose of marriage.

The Great Depression put further pressure on the near-total Catholic ban of contraception during the 1930s, and internal debates concentrated on the extent to which Catholics could resort to periodic abstinence, a 'natural' and therefore licit method of spacing births that had been rendered more workable – if still heavily error-prone – by recent breakthroughs in gynaecology. It took until October of 1951 before a new pope spoke out again on the regulation of births, and his speech to the association of Italian midwives hoped to accommodate lay-Catholics by allowing for a wider use of natural methods of birth control, which Pius XII now sanctioned on the basis of 'serious', but unspecified motives of a 'medical, eugenic, economic and social' kind.[14] However minimal from an outsider's perspective, this concession was of monumental importance for those within, and Church historians have overlooked some of the main reasons that motivated it. They have focused primarily on theological developments regarding personalist conjugal morality, which certainly were important. However, global developments with regard to population management were arguably even more important, and the pope's restrained concession was first and foremost a reaction to the plight of the 'Third World', a term, incidentally, coined by the prominent Catholic demographer Alfred Sauvy in 1952.[15] With the Cold War at its height, a race for geopolitical influence was underway in the unaligned parts of the world. In Asia, the Cold War's hottest battle zone, this race coincided with an unprecedented demographic revolution. South, East and Southeast Asia were experiencing massive population growth, ominously decried as an apocalyptic 'population bomb' with great effect.[16] Whereas the fear of depopulation in Europe had dominated biopolitical discussions on the national and the international levels before the war, those after 1945 oozed with the menace of Asian overpopulation.

There were two main reasons for overpopulation to become a global spectre from the late 1940s onwards. Firstly, even though prophets of doom had already warned against unchecked population growth before the war, it was only during the late 1940s and the early 1950s that reliable and internationally comparable censuses were undertaken in non-Western countries by the newly created Population Commission of the United Nations. Secondly, it was the enormous success of the post-war public health programmes run by the specialized agencies of the UN, most notably the World Health Organization (WHO), which helped to create the threat of overpopulation in the first place. Dramatic decreases in mortality levels were achieved in mere years, driven in no small part by the systematic use of DDT. In Ceylon, for example, over half of the population had been suffering with some mosquito-borne infection in 1945.[17] After two years of DDT dusting and spraying, the incidence of malaria had been reduced by more than 75 per cent. Between 1945 and 1953, the average life expectancy on the island rose from 46 to 60 years.[18] More than anything else, the spectacular drop in infant mortality was swelling human numbers across the world, especially in poor countries. These numbers were nothing if not spectacular, and they almost immediately raised pressing questions of sustainability, especially in developing countries where agricultural output could not keep up with the growing number of new mouths to feed.

In 1949 and 1950, Ceylon repeatedly pressed the newly established World Health Organization to prioritize the issue of population growth.[19] Growing impatient with the Geneva headquarters' inaction on this front, the WHO's Regional Office for Southeast Asia took the initiative to study the matter and possible solutions independently in 1950.[20] That inaction was explained by the certain knowledge in UN circles that the Catholic Church would do everything within its power to block attempts at even broaching the matter within the international community. Old-timers remembered how the Church had successfully nipped any discussion of the problem in the bud at the League of Nations during the interwar years.[21] Though not a member of the United Nations – the Holy See would first acquire limited observer status in 1964 – the Catholic Church was branched out globally like no other organization save for the UN itself. It had rushed to coordinate its transnational network of organizations in the aftermath of the war, keenly aware of how important a role the United Nations would play in times to come. A token association before the war, the *Organisations Internationales Catholiques* (OIC) expanded and professionalized quickly from the late 1940s onwards, with a well-organized office at Fribourg, an international UN-information gathering centre in Geneva, a UNESCO coordination centre in Paris, and a liaison office with Catholic missions worldwide in Rome. The umbrella organization met annually at the Vatican and served to synchronize the work of 31 international Catholic NGOs by 1953, 26 of which held consultative status at various UN bodies, including the WHO. The OIC also created special task forces, and it began to publish its own widely read monthly by 1953.[22] In response to international developments, the organization's Conference of Chairmen called to life a standing committee on childhood and family matters in February of 1951. The committee was to report regularly on population problems 'with the double goal of asserting itself in scientific circles and official international organizations, and to establish ... an effective defence against the nefarious advocacy in favour of birth control'.[23] Though indirectly, Pius XII's speech in October of 1951 contained a tacit acknowledgment of the pressures bearing down on poor parents in the Third World.[24]

Biopolitical Spheres of Influence

Where it came to population management, the cogs of the complex Catholic machine had been set into motion by developments in occupied Japan.[25] The repatriation of many millions and the pronatalist policies of the militarist government since the 1930s were creating a population pressure cooker in a country famous for its scarcity of arable land. Japan's strong indigenous pre-war family planning tradition was revitalized, and parliament passed several very liberal family planning laws by 1948. Since these included wide latitude for medical abortions, and since abortion quickly became far and away the most common form of contraception in Japan, the tiny Catholic community (which consisted mostly of expatriates) raised the alarm with the occupying American forces.[26] The latter officially distanced themselves from birth control initiatives, pointing out that this was a matter for the Japanese to decide for fear of being accused of murderous policies in a post-Shoah world. Behind the scenes, however, influential American officials assisted the Japanese in designing the 1948 abortion legislation. Meanwhile, the Rockefeller Foundation's 1948 mission to the Far East contributed to the growing sense among Catholic observers that, if not the US government, then at least powerful private American foundations were pushing a population control agenda at the expense of the unborn and the underprivileged.[27]

As the Church came to see it during these years, there may well have been two main spheres of influence in an increasingly bipolar world from a geopolitical point of view, but there were at least four such spheres insofar as biopolitical matters were concerned. One of these comprised the English-speaking and Northern-European world dominated by Protestant denominations, which Catholics accused of accommodating a trend towards the wanton liberalization of contraception. The World Council of Churches (WCC) offered a good example of this. The ecumenic umbrella organization of essentially non-Catholic Christian denominations born in 1948 was openly in favour of what it called 'responsible parenthood', which allowed for a wide gamut of contraceptive methods condemned by the Vatican as unnatural.[28] Of course, the WCC was a much broader organization than only American and Western European Protestants, encompassing, as it did, Orthodox and other Christian Churches as well. But, like most Western Protestants, Orthodox Churches did not have an extensive moral theology on problems of sex and procreation. They all recognized the Old Testament imperative that man be fertile and fill the earth, but, as the WCC itself admitted, not much beyond a very general pro-life attitude and certainly little in the way of the huge body of scholarship that had been produced on the problem of conjugal morality by the more legalistically and systematically conceived theological tradition of the Catholic Church.

A second biopolitical bloc the Catholic Church discerned was that of 'godless' communism. In 1936, the previously liberal policies of the Soviet Union with regard to abortion had been reversed. Although the USSR vehemently preached anti-Malthusianism abroad, it often pushed pro-natal policies at home. Even so, the international birth control movement came under sharp attack from communist countries during the 1940s and 1950s as an alleged instrument of Western imperialism intended to keep developing countries poor and easily exploitable. The third bloc was the more heterogeneous one comprised of the Third World countries themselves, and more particularly those of the Islamic world, South, Southeast and the non-communist parts of East Asia as well as the Pacific. The religions that shaped cultural attitudes towards sexuality and reproduction here, including Islam, Hinduism, Buddhism, Taoism, Shintoism and folk religions, all celebrated life and fertility, but once again, none of them shared an extensive and rules-based theological pre-occupation concerning such matters in the manner that Roman Catholicism did. In fact, from Cairo to Tokyo, there were unmistakable signs that these 'Eastern' religions, as they were commonly referred to back then, could be made to accommodate birth control programmes. This was most notably the case in India, where Prime Minister Jawaharlal Nehru entertained strong and warm contacts with the person and the institution which Catholics regarded as the embodiment of the evil of birth control, namely Margaret Sanger and her newly formed International Planned Parenthood Federation (1952). In the course of 1951 and to the horror of the Vatican, India announced that it would launch the world's first state-sponsored family planning programme. Owing to Nehru's close involvement with the international population establishment, the Catholic Church took this initiative as further confirmation that a Western conspiracy was driving global population control politics.

The final biopolitical power bloc was the Catholic world itself, consisting of Western and Central Europe's southern half, the Portuguese, Belgian and French colonies of sub-Saharan Africa and most of Latin America, as well as the Philippines in the Pacific. During the 1950s, it was heartening for the Church to learn that in denominationally mixed countries, like the Netherlands and the US, Catholics out-reproduced Protestants. However, such reassurances were severely tempered by the active repression of the Catholic Church under state socialism in Eastern Europe, especially because the communist pro-life attitude was increasingly suspected of being little more than a rhetorical device in the Soviet Union's battle for global dominance with the West. Indeed, there were clear indications that actual practice in the USSR and its satellites was very much at odds with their humanitarian and anti-imperial rhetoric at the UN. Catholic Church officials, at any rate, had long felt very awkward about finding themselves on the same side of the argument about birth control with socialist countries. The Vatican liked to stress and genuinely saw the Catholic Church as the only unyielding bulwark against what Pope John Paul II would later call a 'culture of death'.[29] The Church's main problem, however, was that the fight over birth control was primarily being waged in that rapidly swelling part of the world where the influence of Catholicism was weakest, i.e. Asia. As Catholic demographers had calculated, a paltry 1 per cent of the world's fastest growing continent was Catholic, which, by implication, also meant that the relative proportion of Catholics in the world was set to wane considerably as the population boom there persisted.[30]

Despite its minority opposition to nearly all forms of contraception and birth control, the Vatican could still rely on its strongest assets for the time being, namely the governments of Catholic European countries, which were still overrepresented and disproportionately powerful within the young UN establishment of the 1950s. Combined with US presidential hopefuls' fear of committing political suicide by bringing down the wrath of the country's powerful episcopate and large Catholic electorate upon themselves, the veto of the Catholic bloc led by continental European countries ground birth control's growing momentum at the WHO to a sudden halt in 1952. When the organization's Executive Board met in January of that year, mere months after calculatedly limited concessions to family planning had been made in Pius XII's speech to Italian midwives, Catholic representatives began drawing a line in the sand. The recent démarche of the WHO Southeast Asia Regional Office mentioned earlier and its tacit endorsement by the Canadian director-general Brock Chisolm, who was well-known to be a birth control enthusiast, were one major stumbling block. Another was that the WHO leadership had unadvisedly sent population expert Abraham Stone, a close collaborator of Margaret Sanger's, to assist the Indian government in running a family planning trial at the latter's request.[31] Even though the trial had strategically been based solely on the use of the rhythm method to obviate Catholic criticism, the Italian delegate aimed a clear shot across birth controllers' bow by insisting that 'family planning was contrary to the beliefs of various nations'.[32]

When the WHO's annual World Health Council met four months later in May, suggestions about the formation of an expert committee made by an unapologetic pro-birth control delegate from Norway were interpreted by Catholics as a further provocation.[33] Belgian and Irish representatives now threatened to withdraw their countries from the WHO altogether. A resolution to effectively ban any and all discussion of population matters by the WHO was jointly submitted by Belgium, Italy and Lebanon, and it began gathering support from a majority of countries who feared that a failure to pacify the unyielding Catholic caucus would put the very survival of the organization at risk. A last minute compromise led to the resolution's withdrawal, but only on the condition formulated by the Belgian delegate that 'there can be no question of our organization becoming the advocate of, still less the means of implementing, certain economic and social theories which are far from receiving universal approval'.[34] The result was that, despite further attempts by India and Ceylon to raise the matter again, most countries henceforth actively shunned the issue and the WHO persistently refused developing nations' requests for technical assistance with regard to family planning throughout the 1950s. Catholics had won a critical battle in a war the Church would only start losing around the turn of the decade.

Fissures Behind the Geneva Front

It would, however, be a misrepresentation to suggest that the Catholic Church spoke with one voice when it came to the issue of family planning, as the cursory discussions in work on global population control often suggest. Many priests and confessors in the West were confronted with the agony of overburdened young mothers and large but poor families on a daily basis. To them and to some higher up in the hierarchy, the problem of Third World overpopulation only added to a sense that the Vatican's near-total ban on contraception was not only impractical but also that it lacked compassion and threatened to alienate even the most conscientious Catholics from the Church. This growing progressive faction had to tread with considerable care, but it interpreted the pope's 1951 speech to Italian midwives with a degree of hope and as an invitation to explore the matter in closer detail. After all, that speech had, deliberately or not, failed to spell out what exactly the 'serious' 'medical, eugenic, economic and social' motives that justified natural family planning methods were exactly.[35] At the Catholic University of Leuven in Belgium, one of the most important Catholic intellectual powerhouses outside Rome, an interdisciplinary group of scholars and moral theologians soon began to build a body of sexological expertise.[36] As the 1950s progressed, this group was increasingly identified as the headquarters of an intra-Church reform movement. Its leader, the Belgian deputy archbishop and later cardinal Leo-Jozef Suenens, used his high-profile opening address to the First World Catholic Health Conference in 1958 to call for Catholic scientists around the world to assist in 'clearing a path' for the conscientious and effective use of morally acceptable forms of natural family planning methods by lay couples.[37] As it had in 1929, the Anglican Church was once again a major influence on Catholic discussions when it rolled out its official doctrine of 'responsible parenthood' at the Lambeth conference of 1958. Stepping up his efforts, Suenens began organizing annual International Catholic Sexological Conferences at Leuven from 1959 onwards and created an Institute for Family and Sexological Sciences.

'The pill' was an important driver of the discussions at Leuven and elsewhere. Catholic physicians in the Low Countries were at the cutting edge of developing a more balanced and (thus) more useful anovulant compound than the pioneering American Enovid. By the early 1960s, the most daring scholars at Leuven were making the controversial case, like the physician John Rock was in the United States, that such a pill could be made to adjust irregular menstrual cycles, thereby acting as a natural and acceptable method of birth regulation. Among them, one theologian went so far as to argue cleverly that the pill was, in fact, the only natural form of family planning according to a scientifically grounded interpretation of Church teachings. In the middle of all this, Suenens became a key organizer of the Second Vatican Council and the leader of a largely Northwest European push for doctrinal moderation on the issue of contraception. In 1963, he gained permission from his close friend, the new reformist Pope John XXIII, to set up a secret Population Studies Group (*Groupe d'études sur la population*). Among the six initial members of the group were the Swiss cleric and Vatican diplomat Henri de Riedmatten, who would become the Catholic Church's point man at the UN when it first acquired official observer status a year later. Another was the Belgian economist Jacques Mertens de Wilmars, who had been on the UN Population Commission since 1951, where he did much to contain the issue of birth control. As the Second Vatican Council progressed, and even after Pope John died later in 1963, the Population Studies Group continued its work and expanded into the famous papal Commissio Pro Studio Populationis, Familiae et Natalitatis whose final report, completed in 1966, advocated for doctrinal relaxation with regard to contraception, and therefore proposed nothing short of a revolution within the Church. However, Pope John's successor, Paul VI, had been closely involved in the debate on global demographics and overpopulation since the early 1950s when he was still Cardinal Montini. As Pro-Secretary of State at the Vatican, he had addressed the 1953 Italian Catholic Social Week conference on population matters in Palermo, warning all participants 'against that modern way of thinking, which is hostile to the ideal of a numerous family'.[38] Later, Montini was keenly aware of the fact that birth control advocates were making serious headway at the UN during the early 1960s, and he was deeply concerned about it. After the USSR loosened its stance on the issue in the middle of the 1950s, the Catholic bloc stood alone in its radical opposition to UN-sponsored birth control programmes. When, despite his Catholicism, American presidential candidate John F. Kennedy indicated in 1959 that he would rely on his personal conscience rather than on Church doctrine for any future decisions about providing family planning assistance abroad, a portentous crack appeared in the Church's formidable dam against population management.[39]

By October 1962, the expanding UN General Assembly came within inches of a resolution in favour of providing technical assistance with regard to problems of overpopulation, despite the Catholic phalanx' staunch resistance, the hard core of which was formed by Argentina, Austria, Belgium, Colombia, France, Ireland, Italy, Lebanon, Liberia,

Luxembourg, Peru, Portugal, Spain and Uruguay, while the United States and the entire communist bloc abstained.[40] Meanwhile, family planning initiatives were flowering in many South and Southeast Asian and Caribbean countries, a growing number of which had begun to collaborate and coordinate through the International Planned Parenthood Federation. By 1964, the director-general of the Food and Agricultural Organization (FAO), the 'life-giving' policies of which the Vatican had long perceived as a positive alternative to 'life-taking' birth control, chose the occasion of the International Eucharistic Conference attended by Paul VI himself to sound the alarm over fast-falling food rates per capita in poor countries. The pope personally addressed the UN General Assembly the following year, urging world leaders 'to multiply bread' rather than 'diminish the number of guests at the banquet of life'.[41] But the spectre of murderous famines finally persuaded US President Johnson to declare his administration in favour of aid to developing nations' population management programmes on Christmas Day 1966. That same year, the UN General Assembly also approved the hard-fought mandate for UN assistance in matters concerning population. The Catholic dam had collapsed. In the summer of 1967, UN secretary-general U Thant announced the creation of a special United Nations Fund for Population Activities.[42]

The Catholic world was now waiting for the pope to speak out on the matter, and much of it was hoping and expecting him to adopt reforms in accordance with his own commission's report. After all, the use of contraceptives among Catholics had long ceased to be an ominous prospect in order to become a social reality. Feeling cornered, Montini began to insulate himself from progressives like Suenens. Hard-line conservatives saw themselves and the Catholic Church as the world's last stand against an all-out attack on life itself. Some radicalized leaders of the minority US Church were an important influence in this regard, but equally, if not more important were unworldly curial officials in Europe, who felt as if the ground was moving beneath their feet. In Eastern Europe, where Catholics were often being persecuted for their beliefs, the purity of Catholic principles was guarded with particular zeal. Horrified by the liberalization of abortion in the mid-1950s, a group of Polish theologians quietly drafted a minority response to the report of the papal Commissio.[43] This reactionary minority report was to form the basis of the encyclical *Humanae Vitae*, which was published in the summer of 1968. Shocking the world with its forbidding tone, this famous document reaffirmed the stern teachings of the Church outlined in *Casti Connubii* 38 years earlier. The key thinker behind the Polish minority report and thus behind Paul VI's fateful encyclical was Cardinal Karol Wojtyła, the future Pope John Paul II, whose intransigence on questions of sex and contraception is legendary. In his 1995 encyclical *Evangelium Vitae*, promulgated in response to the landmark liberal Programme of Action concerning women's reproductive rights recently adopted by the UN's Cairo Conference of Population and

Development, Wojtyła reaffirmed the Church's 'gospel of life' as the antithesis of a 'veritable conspiracy against life' fostered 'at the international level'.[44] The Church, he promised, would continue its crusade against 'an idea of society excessively concerned with efficiency'; against this feverish biopolitical daydream, which, ironically perhaps, was first dreamt as men sought to protect life against a plague of death.

Notes

1 Michel Foucault, Valerio Marchetti and Antonella Salomoni, eds., *Abnormal. Lectures at the Collège De France, 1974–1975*, Lectures at the Collège De France (New York: Picador, 2003), 46.
2 Ibid., 47.
3 Michel Foucault, *The History of Sexuality. Volume I: An Introduction*, trans. Robert Hurley (New York: Pantheon Books, 1978), 143.
4 Matthew Connelly, 'Seeing Beyond the State: The Population Control Movement and the Problem of Sovereignty', *Past & Present* 193, no. 1 (2006): 199–201. This reluctance is well illustrated by the prolonged gap between early alarmist discourse and belated legislative government action in France. See, for example, Alain Becchia, 'Les Milieux Parlementaires Et La Dépopulation De 1900 À 1914', *Communications* 44 (1986): 201–246; Richard Tomlinson, 'The "Disappearance" of France, 1896–1940: French Politics and the Birth Rate', *The Historical Journal* 28, no. 2 (1985): 405–415.
5 The brutality and centrality of Nazi-Germany have often shrouded interwar negative eugenics elsewhere. See, for example, Björn Felder and Paul J. Weindling, eds., *Baltic Eugenics: Bio-Politics, Race and Nation in Interwar Estonia, Latvia and Lithuania, 1918–1940* (Amsterdam and New York: Rodopi, 2013); Marius Turda and Paul J. Weindling, eds., *'Blood and Homeland': Eugenics and Racial Nationalism in Central and Southeast Europe, 1900–1940* (Budapest and New York: CEU Press, 2007).
6 The two most prominent publications, focusing respectively on the interwar and the post-war period, are Alison Bashford, *Global Population: History, Geopolitics, and Life on Earth* (New York: Columbia University Press, 2014); Matthew Connelly, *Fatal Misconception: The Struggle to Control World Population* (Cambridge and London: Harvard University Press, 2008). Others include Chikako Takeshita, *The Global Politics of the Iud* (Cambridge: MIT Press, 2012); Thomas Robertson, *The Malthusian Moment: Global Population Growth and the Birth of American Environmentalism* (New Brunswick: Rutger University Press, 2012); Carole R. McCann, *Figuring the Population Bomb: Gender and Demography in the Mid-Twentieth Century* (Seattle and London: University of Washington Press, 2017); Ian Dowbiggin, *The Sterilization Movement and Global Fertility in the Twentieth Century* (Oxford: Oxford University Press, 2008).
7 Similarly, we also know far too little about the pushback of the Soviet Union and of communism, more generally, against population control. Indeed, the Roman Catholic Church often found itself awkwardly allied with communist countries in their opposition to the international birth control movement.
8 E.g. Kathleen A. Tobin, *The American Religious Debate over Birth Control, 1907–1937* (Jefferson: McFarland, 2001); Leslie Woodcock Tentler, *Catholics and Contraception: An American History* (Ithaca, NY: Cornell University Press, 2004); Martine Sevegrand, *Les Enfants Du Bon Dieu: Les Catholiques Français Et La Procréation Au Xxe Siècle* (Paris: Michel, 1995).

9 For a recent example, see Alana Harris, ed., *The Schism of '68: Catholicism, Contraception and 'Humanae Vitae' in Europe, 1945–1975* (Basingstoke and New York: Palgrave Macmillan, 2018).
10 E.g. Doris Buss and Didi Herman, *Globalizing Family Values: The Christian Right in International Politics* (Minneapolis, MN: University of Minnesota Press, 2003).
11 Connelly, *Fatal Misconception*, 14.
12 Jean Stengers, 'Les Pratiques Anticonceptionnelles Dans Le Mariage Au Xixe Et Au Xxe Siècles: Problèmes Humains Et Attitudes Religieuses', *Belgisch tijdschrift voor filologie en geschiedenis – Revue belge de philologie et d'histoire* 49, no. 2 and 4 (1971): 403–481 and 1119–1174.
13 John T. Noonan, *Contraception: A History of Its Treatment by the Catholic Theologians and Canonists. Enlarged Edition* (Cambridge and London: Harvard University Press, 1986 [1965]), 424–425.
14 Pius XII, *Moral Questions Affecting Married Life: The Apostolate of the Midwife* (New York: Paulist Press, 1951), 15 (§ 36).
15 His 1952 essay was republished as Alfred Sauvy, 'Trois Mondes, Une Planète', *Vingtième siècle. Revue d'histoire* 12, no. October–December (1986): 81–83.
16 The term emerged in the mid-1940s, and became widespread through the various editions of the alarmist pamphlet. Hugh Moore, *The Population Bomb* (New York: Hugh Moore Fund, 1954).
17 On Malaria in Ceylon, see R.H. Gray, 'The Decline of Mortality in Ceylon and the Demographic Effects of Malaria Control', *Population Studies* 28, no. 2 (1974): 205–229.
18 Connelly, *Fatal Misconception*, 116.
19 Richard Symonds and Michael Carder, *The United Nations and the Population Question, 1945–1970* (New York: McGraw-Hill, 1973), 59–60.
20 Ibid., 61.
21 Bashford, *Global Population*, 218; Symonds and Carder, *The United Nations and the Population Question*, chapter 2, 26–27.
22 I.e. *Informations Catholiques Internationales*.
23 'Vœux. Conférence des présidents. Utrecht, 16–18 Février 1951', Map 30: Commission Famille-Enfance 1962–1964 OIC, Fund Pierre de Locht, Archives of the Catholic University of Louvain (UCL), 5.
24 It was, for example, clearly interpreted as such in Louis Janssens, *Morale Et Problèmes Démographiques* (Brussels: Universelle, 1953).
25 On post-war reproductive politics in Japan, see Aiko Takeuchi-Demirci, *Contraceptive Diplomacy: Reproductive Politics and Imperial Ambitions in the United States and Japan* (Stanford, CA: Stanford University Press, 2018); Tiana Norgren, *Abortion before Birth Control: The Politics of Reproduction in Post-War Japan* (Princeton, NJ: Princeton University Press, 2001); Aya Homei, 'Between the West and Asia: "Humanistic" Japanese Family Planning in the Cold War', *East Asian Science, Technology and Society. An International Journal* 10, no. 4 (2016): 445–467.
26 Deborah Oakley, 'American-Japanese Interaction in the Development of Population Policy in Japan, 1945–52', *Population and Development Review* 4, no. 4 (1978): 632.
27 Marshall C. Balfour et al., *Public Health and Demography in the Far East: Report of a Survey Trip, September 13–December 13, 1948* (New York: The Rockefeller Foundation, 1950).
28 See Richard M. Fagley, *The Population Question and Christian Responsibility* (New York: Oxford University Press, 1960).
29 John Paul II, 'Evangelium Vitae', Holy, http://www.vatican.va/content/john-paul-ii/en/encyclicals/documents/hf_jp-ii_enc_25031995_evangelium-vitae.html (accessed 30 April 2021).

30 'La Situation Religieuse Dans Le Monde', *Informations Catholiques internationales* 43 (1955), 18.
31 John Farley, *Brock Chisolm, the World Health Organization, and the Cold War* (Vancouver and Toronto: UBC Press, 2008), chapter 11, 173–184.
32 World Health Organization, 'Executive Board. Ninth Session. Minutes of the Fifteenth Meeting' (1952), 26.
33 WHO, *Offical Records of the World Health Organization. Fifth World Health Assembly. Geneva, 5 to 22 May 1952* (Geneva: World Health Organization, 1952), 204–207, 230–242.
34 Ibid., 242.
35 Pius XII, *Moral Questions Affecting Married Life*, 15 (§36).
36 Wannes Dupont, 'The Case for Contraception: Medicine, Morality and Sexology at the Catholic University of Leuven (1930–1968)', *Histoire, médecine et santé* 13 (2018), 49-65; 'Of Human Love: Catholics Campaigning for Sexual Aggiornamento in Postwar Belgium', in *The Schism of '68. Catholicism, Contraception and 'Humanae Vitae' in Europe, 1945–1975*, ed. Alana Harris (Basingstoke and New York: Palgrave Macmillan, 2018). The following passage is based on the research for these publications.
37 Léon Joseph Suenens, 'Christianisme Et Santé', *Saint-Luc médical – Sint-Lucastijdschrift* 4 (1958): 282.
38 Quoted in Anthony L. Zimmerman, *Overpopulation: A Study of Papal Teachings on the Problem, with Special Reference to Japan* (Washington DC: The Catholic University of America Press, 1957), 305.
39 Symonds and Carder, *The United Nations and the Population Question*, 95.
40 Ibid., 120.
41 Quoted in Robert Blair Kaiser, *The Encyclical That Never Was: The Story of the Commission on Population, Family and Birth, 1964–1966* (London: Sheed and Ward, 1987), 145.
42 Symonds and Carder, *The United Nations and the Population Question*, 149.
43 'Les Fondements De La Doctrine De L'église Concernant Les Principes De La Vie Conjugale. (Un Mémoire Rédigé Par Un Groupe De Théologiens-Moralistes De Cracovie)', *Analecta Cracoviensia* 1, no. 1 (1969), 194-230; Janet E. Smith, 'The Kraków Document', *Nova et Vetera* 10, no. 2 (2012): 361–381.
44 John Paul II, 'Evangelium Vitae'.

Section II

Beyond Procreation: Health, Nutrition and Hygiene

8 Feeding Hungry Bodies

Children's Nutrition as Biopolitics after the Great War

Friederike Kind-Kovács

Introduction

The First World War and the food shortage that ensued required massive intervention on behalf of the starving children of Europe, and especially Central Europe. While the food crisis in the region was largely triggered by the geographic reconfiguration, massive displacement and the economic blockade, the 'extreme undernutrition' was, according to an American nutritionist in post-war Poland, 'due at least as much to poverty and lack of knowledge as the results of the war'.[1] Under the pressure of the war and economic crisis, food production and consumption were becoming essential areas of national and international attention and intervention. The 'starvation conditions' provoked a new 'attention on the vulnerability of infants and young children in periods of nutritional deprivation'.[2] The experience of the First World War triggered in various countries the aspiration that 'it was essential to protect its own [children]', if they were to prevent the decline of the concerned population.[3] In that spirit, many European states responded to children's malnutrition with 'unprecedented programs of mass feeding'. The 'act of eating' was developing into a major public concern, as Dominique Marshall pointed out, with the 'science of nutrition and paediatrics' driving it.[4] At the time, the United States played a crucial role in triggering a new approach towards the use of food in times of war and crisis. With the creation of the Commission for Relief in Belgium (CRB) in 1914, the United States Food Administration in 1917, and the American Relief Administration (ARA) in 1919, the United States responded first to the obvious need to provide food to the population of German-occupied Belgium, then to their allies in Europe with food overseas, and lastly to the starving children in Europe and Russia. Both local governments and international relief organizations came to regard the food consumption of their populations as matters requiring constant governmental and institutional supervision and regulation.[5]

By 1943, a contemporary relief worker to post-First World War Poland was convinced that 'educational programs in nutrition are needed by the people of all countries'.[6] Feeding the starving post-war generation of the

DOI: 10.4324/9781003161080-11

young was becoming, as Corinna Treitel has showcased, 'one of the major biopolitical projects of the twentieth century'.[7] The actual feeding was based on a new academic understanding of nutrition which was spreading across Europe and beyond. Against this backdrop, this chapter engages with the question of how the discovery of new connections between children's appropriate/inappropriate diet and certain childhood diseases were essential in bringing about a new 'scientific' approach to children's nutrition and respective feeding programs. Exploring the new focus on milk as *the* foodstuff that was considered the ideal nutrition for infants offers an insight into a new public interference into children's feeding and thus their very corporality. An analysis of this new international trend shows how food was beginning to be understood and applied to masses of children as 'preventive medicine'. Here, the article investigates the theoretical notion of the biopolitical management of the individual and collective body. Feeding infants and managing the proper nutrition of young children was conceived and propagated as a medical tool to cure the bodies of Hungary's post-war population and the coming generations.

Fearing for the Nation

While various countries in Central and Eastern Europe were collectively affected by the food crisis of the post-war years, the post-imperial condition of Hungary and especially the hungry children of its capital sheds light on the biopolitical function of children's nutrition. Hungary – which had suffered extensively from the social consequences of the aftermath of war and imperial dissolution – drew much attention to its hungry children. The Hungarian physician, Dr Ödön Lévai, observed in 1918 that Hungary's children were particularly suffering from 'the miseries of the war'.[8] He called on the government and the international community to prevent that the war would destroy the child and thereby hinder the regeneration of the Hungarian nation.[9] Lévai drew a parallel between the corporal condition of the starving children in Budapest and the physical and mental constitution of Hungary's entire post-war population. Just weeks before the singing of the Treaty of Trianon the *Hungarian Territorial Integrity League* condemned in a publication, entitled *The American Peace and Hungary* that was prepared for circulation at the Paris Peace Conference in 1919, Hungary's unfolding territorial losses as a 'dissection of Hungary'.[10] The harmed, starving or even dying child body became an icon of post-war suffering that was useful for lobbying in the international humanitarian community for the rescue of the defeated nation's children.

Another publication by this very same league entitled, *The Consequences of the Division of Hungary from the Standpoint of Eugenics*, linked the territorial loss to the declining Hungarian population. Its authors claimed that the division of the country could 'not be justified by ethnographical or racial differences'.[11] While an 'increase of the population', which was 'very much to be desired after this bloody war', was judged not to be imaginable if the territory was to be narrowed down and economical regeneration would be prevented. In that case, the author argues, 'the desire to raise a large family' would be 'greatly reduced if the possibilities of gaining suitable stations of life are diminished by territorial distraction'. The territorial loss, as well as the economic hardships, would thus have an immediate and imminent effect on Hungary's populational evolution: 'No mother will give life to political and economic desperates' and 'the birth-rate [would] … rapidly fall and voluntary "race suicide" would terminate the cruel work of war and of short-sighted, misinformed international politics'.[12] He further contemplated about the future composition and constitution of the Hungarian race if the displaced 'middle and upper class', which he considered 'a very valuable material from a racial point of view' would 'lose its love of life, would not raise enough children and would to a great extent soon become extinct'.[13] He saw a particular danger in the intelligentsia's displacement to Budapest, where the 'conditions for raising children' were judged to be 'not favourable at all'.[14] Fears of a further declining population and the collectively harmed physique of the future generation were ideal ammunition to demand a revision of the territorial losses because this would be, so the rhetoric, the end to the Hungarian nation.[15]

In Hungary, contemporary research articles about child mortality often raised the issue of children's 'degeneration' – the fear that a whole generation might turn out unfit for the tasks of life. Dr Adolf Juba, a Hungarian school doctor, wrote in 1916 an article on 'children's nutrition during the war'.[16] He first looked at the high child mortality rate 'from the family perspective', which was tragic because parents' efforts were rendered 'useless' and their hopes 'destroyed at the grave of the little ones'.[17] But he then looked at the issue 'from the perspective of the nation's future', comparing Hungary's declining population to the growing populations of neighbouring nations that were 'competing' with Hungary. He instanced Russia, whose 'confidence in the future' he fully understood as the natural result of its 'immense growth of population'.[18] Juba followed up this observation by presenting a scenario in which Hungary was invaded by Russian troops – he expected that Russia would 'simply invade us in the coming decades'.[19] He believed that Hungarians must take good care of their infants so that there would be a population in readiness. '[M]ost of the boys born now will then be drafted', and 'the girls will be just about to become mothers'.[20] It was 'the duty of all educated people in the land' to undertake another type of 'war service', one he believed was 'as important from the perspective of the future of our nation as the one the valiant warriors are fulfilling in the plains of Russia and the mountains of the Balkans'. The purpose of this was to raise a healthy, vigorous new generation.[21] This discourse on children's health was part of a larger public debate that was not only about 'the health of the nation and the protection of society but also ultimately about national survival', which, according to Marius Turda, expressed itself in the spreading of eugenic ideas and the emergence of a 'eugenic milieu', which sought for ways to 'counteract the negative effects of war'.[22]

In a similar vein, Herbert Hoover and various American relief workers feared the long-term implications of the war and especially how the lack of food would affect the future generations of Europe. Hoover was convinced of the particular need 'to secure physical, mental and moral health' because 'every child' that was 'delinquent in body, education or character' would be a 'charge upon the community as a whole'. It was clear to him that 'crime is due to undernourishment at some period', which is why the starving children would 'fill ... the jails' if they were not taken care of. Perceiving children as the society's 'army' with which one 'must march to progress', he was convinced of the moral duty to properly feed them.[23]

In 1940, William R Grove, an American relief worker to Poland, recalled the American approach to Central Europe's starving children. 'Those of us who had undertaken the moral responsibility for the aid of the children', he remembered, tried to continuously keep in mind the time 'when the children would grow to manhood or womanhood'.[24] They were aware that if these future citizens 'were not well nourished as children, they would not be able to carry their share of the burdens of life, but would always be handicapped by stunted physical and mental development'.[25] Herbert Hoover himself had come to the conclusion that in Central Europe's 'cities and industrial centres', it had become an impossible undertaking for working men and women 'to obtain the food which is required to maintain their children in such health as to insure growth into strong man- and womanhood'. Furthermore, he had noticed that the high mortality among the region's children was 'so large as to warrant the sympathy and active aid of the entire civilized world', which is why he felt that this destitute 'situation appeals especially to the American people'.[26] Hoover cared especially about the children of Central Europe, where he feared the spreading of Bolshevism as a reaction to increased suffering and social conflicts. He hoped that American food donations would relieve children's suffering while positively 'affecting future social life in Central Europe'.[27]

The compassionate dedication to relieve children's destitution was based on the conviction that 'the suffering of children from cold or hunger always seemed ... to be much worse than the sight of adults in similar distress'.[28] The reason behind this conviction was the American suspicion towards the former enemy. Grove, for instance, acknowledged that he feared 'the possibility that the adult might have had some connection, however remote, with causing the war'.[29] In contrast, he and most American relief workers were fully convinced that the 'children could not by any reasonable stretch of the imagination be so charged' and that they were 'innocent victims'.[30]

Retrospectively, Grove questioned the meaningfulness of war in general: 'It is so fallacious to consider that war is necessary or desirable'.[31]

The Nutritional Study of Malnutrition

Many efforts were made to fight children's malnutrition out of the fear of the material degeneration of Central Europe's population. The mass public efforts to rescue the region's hungry children after the war turned into a transnational enterprise which relied on global actors and local infrastructures and personnel. To target the nutrition of large groups of children, standardized feeding had to be introduced and applied. In Hungary, rapid urbanization and industrialization had been shifting the individual consumption of food from the private to wards the public domain; new forms of public food consumption had been developing that were linked to new styles of industrialized labour. By the time the war broke out, social feeding initiatives like school meals and 'charity meals for the poor, mothers and workers', along with 'propaganda campaigns about dietary habits' based on experimental research in the physiology of nutrition were part of the scene. Public feeding initiatives and public education about nutrition were used to 'fight hunger as an intolerable reality'.[32] Whereas food consumption within the family could hardly be controlled or regulated, feeding in schools most certainly could. Schools and other childcare institutions were 'where the children were and thus where healthcare providers could have guaranteed access to them'.[33] Large-scale intervention on behalf of children's nutrition outside of the home helped to secure both continuous nutrition as well school attendance in the post-war years. Yet, before relief could be provided to the children of Budapest on a daily basis, the relief workers had to apply existing knowledge about children's appropriate nutrition. To that end, more needed to be known about the link between children's malnutrition, their corporal constitution and certain childhood diseases. Post-war relief could both rely on, as well as advance, recent nutritional research.

Throughout post-war Europe, a 'scholarly effort' was made to better 'understand the physiological mechanism of hunger'.[34] The physical destitution and suffering of children made the scientific study of nutrition necessary. The medical profession was considered as 'stand[ing] out' from other professions for its knowledge, experiences with and its fight against 'the many and various adversities of the world war'.[35] While the destructiveness of the war and its aftermath call for increased medical intervention, so did these crises, paradoxically, also 'improve the medical sciences' and medical knowledge.[36] Starvation and food crises turned into 'public health issues', which demanded the intervention of 'new regimes of calculation, intervention and direction'.[37] Nutritional experts and special commissions offered expertise for the professionalization of nutritional science and its application in the post-war climate. In response to conditions of famine, famous nutritionists like Max Rubner, Clemens von Pirquet and

Ralph Kellogg conducted research in Central Europe, thereby gaining new knowledge about the physiological basis of nutrition.[38] This international research was complemented by important experts in the various relief countries. Although less known, much knowledge on nutrition was produced by Hungarian medical doctors, especially children's doctors, as well as nutritionists.

In a 1928 report on the history of artificial infant feeding, produced by the Hungarian Stefánia Association for the Protection of Mothers and Infants, Hungarian paediatrician Dr János Bókay pointed out how intertwined the fields of children's protection and medical as well as nutritional science were. He observed that the early twentieth century had started well in the 'spirit of child protection' and that it could build on the 'well-prepared foundation of science, governmental support and global social philanthropy' that was highly invested in the rescue of mothers and babies.[39] Yet, it had been the repercussions of the First World War which had intensified these efforts because every country that had been dragged into the war, so the report, felt 'that the deep wounds caused by this pandemic of passion could only be repaired by patriotic cooperation'.[40] The early twentieth century, and especially the health and food crisis that was triggered by the international conflict and the imperial dissolution, advanced and promoted the 'full development of infant medicine' and 'a solid-state understanding of the theory of artificial nutrition'.[41] Bokáy was fully convinced that for these scientific and nutritional achievements, 'humanity could be thankful'.[42]

The German nutritionist Max Rubner had developed his concept of ideal 'rational nutrition' in the pre-war period.[43] During the period of the naval blockade, Rubner fiercely criticized the Allied Powers for starving out the former enemy by means of their 'hunger blockade' in the immediate post-war period.[44] The 'discovery of the physiological basis of nutrition' was seen as the clue to restoring the health of Europe's exhausted populations.[45] It paved the way for the 'dream of a rational solution to the problem through the design of minimum and optimum standard diets'.[46] Knowledge about the ideal everyday diet triggered a new approach to the calorie, which 'allowed Americans to see food as an instrument of power'.[47] Yet, relief work in the capitals of Central Europe was hoped to not only be of 'great value' to the respective child population but that the 'results of the scientific observations' on such a large scale would offer new 'knowledge of the essentials, other than calories, of a healthy diet', and 'put to a practical test the recent work done in [Austria] ..., in India, and in America with regard to the nature, prevention and treatment of deficiency diseases'.[48]

Clemens von Pirquet, an Austrian nutritionist, was another central figure in the study of nutritional deficits and the physiological impact of starvation. He was much engaged in the scientific battle against rickets and tuberculosis, which were closely related to nutritional deficiencies. Pirquet had discovered that rickets resulted from the deficiency of vitamin D in the diet and the lack of direct sunlight.[49] In 1920, he invented the Pirquet System of Nutrition, which was meant to combat rickets among children in Vienna. Pirquet's 'NEM' (*Nahrungs Einheit Milch*)-system perfectly reflected the new correlation between science and feeding. The NEM-system was a practical yet scientific instrument to regulate the feeding 'of the individual, the family or the community' in strict accordance with the most recent scientific nutritional knowledge.[50] Pirquet's 'objective' method and measurements were to 'replace the subjective medical examination'.[51] Meanwhile, the 'Nem' – a new nutritional unit – was to offer an alternative to the 'concept of the calorie', that was judged to be 'too abstract and too difficult' for use by 'ordinary people without scientific training'.[52] As mostly 'normal' people were charged with the feeding of children, the new system promised to simply mirror the 'food value of something that can be seen, handled, consumed'.[53] He conducted experiments on children with rickets in a children's charity hospital in the Meidling district of Vienna.[54] Out of the 498 children accepted to his clinics in 1918, 91 per cent were undernourished.[55] He promoted the scientifically based treatment of rickety children with 'air, light, cod-liver oil',[56] and he was convinced that children's proper, regular feeding was the best type of 'preventive medicine'.[57]

During a meeting of the Women's International League Congress in Vienna on 18 July 1921, Pirquet stated that 'the years of undernourishment had given a new lease to tuberculosis', which was 'always rife in the Austrian capital'.[58] He was convinced that a 'good appetite for various kinds of food and satisfaction of this appetite by ample meals' would prevent the germs of tuberculosis from spreading.[59] Pirquet was fully convinced that tuberculosis, 'the great disease of childhood',[60] flourished where there was malnutrition. Moreover, to begin with, it was 'not a certain quality of food' that mattered, but a certain 'quantity': people had to eat the right amount of food.[61] Thus, regardless of where the tuberculosis patient was being treated with sunshine and fresh air, be it at the 'seashore ... mountains ... the desert, or a warm valley', the most essential prescription was that the patient should eat.[62] Pirquet was convinced that he would need to apply feeding principles not to single children or small groups but to the masses if he wanted to obtain 'credible "statistical results"'.[63] In one of his lectures, Michel Foucault once pointed out that '[t]he norm is something that can be applied to both a body one wishes to discipline and a population one wishes to regularize'.[64] Nutritional science needed to become an essential element of the education of the people at large so that every single individual could profit from it.[65]

In the 1920s, the new knowledge of nutritional norms and expected weight ratios produced the idea of a child's 'average body weight'. Pirquet propagated a new understanding of malnutrition, which was previously thought of as simply not having enough nutrition. It was now considered to be something more complex: it represented the lack of certain elements in the diet.[66] Pirquet was fully aware that in 'normal times' there should be 'no general condition of hunger' and that the 'deprivation of food and rest' were 'exceptional conditions of life'.[67] The exceptional conditions prevailing during the latter years of the war and afterwards provided ideal circumstances to test much of the theoretical nutritional knowledge. Children's hospitals, especially those under the control of Pirquet and other nutritionists such as the children's hospital in Vienna, were an ideal space to study the 'nem system in its most perfect expression' because the diet of the children could be controlled by experts. Every single meal was prepared according to quantitative measures, which laid the basis for the strict application of nutritional norms on everyday food consumption.[68] The kitchens in the hospitals, including the 'milk kitchens', turned into laboratories of nutrition sciences, where trained '*Nem Damen*', female nutritional scholars, applied their new nutritional knowledge from training courses.[69] Pirquet's method was applied throughout Central Europe.

The Vienna mission by the Accessory Food Factors Committee was instructed to inquire into the diseases 'attributable to malnutrition' and to 'ascertain, in the case of children, the value of methods of curing deficiency diseases', which had been judged 'effective in experiments on animals'.[70] Dr Elsie Dalyell, who was a member of the child relief mission and had been sent by the Accessory Food Factors Committee to Vienna in 1919, argued that the main objective of the mission had been to identify 'the results ... followed from the extreme scarcity of fats in the diets of the infants of Eastern Europe in the years 1917 to 1919' and to relieve those. She observed that Pirquet's system of exact food measurements in the children's clinic in Vienna had been of maximum use to the international relief workers.[71]

Dr Hariette Chick, assistant in the department of experimental pathology of the Lister Institute of Preventive Medicine in London, and Mrs Dalyell were instructed for their mission to Vienna not only 'to make inquiries as to the prevalence of scurvy, rickets and other disorders attributable to malnutrition and to carefully study the dietaries which have led to such symptoms' but also to assist the food relief organizations 'by acquainting them with the results of recent experimental work on accessory food factors' and by 'ascertain[ing] in the case of children the value of methods of curing deficiency diseases which have been effective by experiments on animals'.[72] An important element in the application of nutrition sciences to children's bodies was the visit to 'children's hospitals, day nurseries, and infant welfare stations to study the incidence of deficiency diseases among children'.[73]

The international relief workers 'hoped that from this investigation in Vienna there would be such an increase in the knowledge of infant feeding', so that 'the problem of securing the normal growth during the first year of life would be brought ... nearer [to a] solution.[74] The experience and statistics collected in Vienna would be of use in every country when dealing with infant nutrition'.[75] Profiting from the experiences gained in Vienna, the relief workers in Budapest and other relief countries used the feeding effort of the ARA, which started on 2 November 1919, to gather important statistical data on the condition of the countries' children.[76] A number of statistical tables identified nutritional and physical deviations from the norm, while statistical comparisons showed the degree of deviation, which, once treatment began, could be used to monitor recovery. Dr Juba also collected the nutrition data of 1,000 pupils over a few years in a metropolitan boy's secondary school in Budapest, which allowed him to draw more general conclusions of the condition of Budapest's children.[77] Yet, beyond such institutional data, the relief effort in Budapest offered the opportunity to collect massive data on the local children and youth. In the fall of 1919, 127,076 school children aged between 6 and 14 years were medically examined. The result was that 73 per cent of the examined children were considered mal- and undernourished.[78] Another table of the monthly report for April 1922 by the American Red Cross, which ran the 'Action for Protecting Mothers and Babies in Hungary', detailed both the feeding situation and the medical condition of 9,689 children in Budapest and the suburbs. The medical table identified 472 cases of rickets (rachitis) as the most widespread medical condition of the examined children. Out of the 2,719 'new cases', either newborns or children who were visited for the first time below the age of 3, 291 were sent to hospital, and 52 died. The scientific examination was directly linked to supplementary feeding of the malnourished children and the medical and nutritional condition of infants that were breastfed, 'mixed fed' and 'artificially fed'. In the month of April, 1,654 babies were able to receive an additional feeding, of which only 1,074 babies between birth and age 1 actually gained weight. Depending on the constitution and weight of the infants, supplementary feeding would be administered to them and their nursing mothers.

Based on the composition of the tables and other reports, one might draw the conclusion that the Red Cross nurses who visited the children in the first months responded to the everyday needs of the mothers and their infants. Because knowledge about the proper feeding of infants was limited, and there was even less experience with the actual use of artificial feeding, much of the food relief strategy mirrors the experimental character of the relief endeavour. Yet, what becomes clear is the fact that the relief organizations considered it valuable to collect data on women's health before birth, the infant's physical constitution and their bodily improvement by means of additional feeding. The statistical data were produced following the individual examination and weighing of the children. Weight charts were meant to trace the weight gain or loss, especially in the first year after birth, on a quarterly basis. The collection of the data went hand in hand with the visual documentation collected by the relief organizations, which was used to prove the children's nutritional needs, document their medical examinations and give readers a glimpse into the everyday realities of the relief effort. Both the statistical data and the visual testimonies called for the immediate nutritional relief of the children. Nutritionists like

Pirquet were worried that malnutrition would lead to a long-term genetic impairment of the concerned population. Once he had concluded his nutritional study on Viennese children, he stated that 'the damage of a year-long malnutrition in childhood' could 'be partially repaired through a long and scientifically guided quantitative diet'. He was also convinced that it was 'unlikely that a human race which was due to malnutrition of small statue would genetically pass this racial feature on'. This would, however, not minimize the need to act on behalf of the concerned children and secure their proper nutrition. Only if undernutrition and malnutrition were fought would there be a chance to balance out the damage of the nutritional deficit.[79] Juba thought that the poor feeding of infants was a major hindrance to Hungary's urgently needed population growth, and this, in turn, was due to a lack of knowledge. So he considered it 'necessary to bring the principles of good nutrition to the people, who, due to superstition and ignorance have caused the premature deaths of many, many children'.[80] Juba cited occasions when infants had been 'fed with all sorts of things ... not meant for them'.[81] On a farm in Szeged, they fed infants 'sugared cabbage, the inner part of bread rolls, pork bacon and who knows what: there was no food they would not have given to such tender stomachs'.[82] Juba was not alone in making this accusation: the author of an article published in June 1918 referred to a host of doctors jointly claiming that the main reason for the high infant and child mortality was that 'the poorer class does not know how to properly feed its children', and that the Hungarian population as a whole 'does not manage the proper artificial feeding of needy and sick children'.[83] Proper and sufficient feeding was considered the best means to remedy this defect.

(Mother's) Milk as Preventive Medicine

Based on new research on nutrition and certain infant diseases, the control of an infant's nutrition became a central element in paediatric medicine. Yet, modern nutrition science was struggling to convince people to implement their recommendations, as 'it is always hard to change the customs and habits of the people – these household laws are older and stronger than acts of parliament'.[84] Yet, international relief organizations succeeded in getting involved in various types of children's feeding programs, which I have discussed elsewhere.[85] Among the various types of child feeding programs, the rescue of infants was a prime objective of the relief organization. Alonzo Taylor and Vernon Kellogg, two of Herbert Hoover's most important nutritionists, even stated in 1917 that 'our diet is built around bread and milk' and that children were in particular need of a continuous supply of this foodstuff, as the insufficiency of milk could have long-lasting effects on the bodily condition of children.[86]

A table entitled the 'Supply of Milk for the Children in Budapest' captured the deficit of available milk supply in the years 1918–1920. While in 1918, the deficit of milk amounted daily to 5,324 litres for the children aged 2–3 years old, it amounted in 1919 to 9,718 litres for 1–2 year-olds, and in 1920 to 9,337 litres for those aged 0–1 years old. In total, according to this table, 24,374 litres were lacking daily in Budapest. Yet, the caption even remarked that 'the real deficit in milk supply was still greater'. The table uncovers the shift of milk relief from toddlers to infants, which was most likely caused by the high infant mortality rate of 20 per cent, which the international relief agencies were trying to remedy in particular. This table was part of a report by Rodolphe de Reding-Biberegg of the International Red Cross Committee in Budapest to the Save the Children International Union, asking for additional assistance in providing food relief to children in Budapest. The high mortality rate of newborns at the time was taken as a reflection of the overall condition of the Hungarian state in the post-war period and was used to call for the rescue of the future of the Hungarian nation.

As the lack of milk was considered to be the major cause of malnutrition in children, relief workers invested much in the import and distribution of cow milk, which they saw as the best way to secure and improve their health. Especially when it came to the children of 'people of poorer classes', who could not afford a proper diet, it was judged to be important to 'continue the use of milk in the diet of the child as long as possible'.[87] They were not alone in this approach to milk: throughout Europe and beyond, much research was invested into the nutritional study of milk. For instance, in 1915, a great effort was made in the United States by the National Dairy Council to study and promote milk as an 'all-around healthy and nutritious food that was particularly good for growing children'.[88] Already in 1905, in the Polish part of the Austro-Hungarian Empire, 'Drop of Milk' stations were installed, where impoverished urban mothers could buy pure cow milk for their babies.[89] In various countries, much propaganda material was created, including plays and films featuring milk, so that everyone got the message that the 'consumption of milk was absolutely necessary for healthy childhood development'.[90] By the mid-1920s, the daily consumption of milk had become 'a basic requirement for healthy child growth and development'.[91] In order to scientifically justify the need of milk kitchens, research was conducted on the connection between certain diseases, infant mortality and the availability/consumption of milk. The two diseases which were considered to have 'taken the greatest toll of the infant population of Vienna were scurvy and rachitis', whose prevalence was judged to be 'due to the lack of milk or unsatisfactory conditions of its supply more than to any other factor'.[92]

The production and distribution of milk in Budapest had been organized on a rationalized basis since the late nineteenth century. In 1883, the Budapest Central Milk Hall (*Budapesti Központi Tejcsarnok Szövetkezet*) was established.[93] In 1906, a Free Milk Association (*Az Ingyen Tej Egyesület*) was founded to provide free milk to local child charities and welfare organizations.[94] In October 1916, the district of Újpest initiated the delivery of 400 litres of milk to the Stefánia Association, but during quality control it was found that the milk had been 30 per cent diluted with water, and there were accusations of 'milk adulteration' (*tejhamisítás*).[95] The Stefánia Association cooperated with the National Uránia Association for the Protection of Women (*Uránia Országos Nővédő Egyesület*) in setting up facilities to ensure the continuous provisioning of milk for children.[96]

In the framework of the 'Milk-Meal Initiative', which began as a result of a private donation at the beginning of 1917, thousands of 'milk-meals' were distributed every day in four Budapest schools on Szentlászló, Egressy, Palota and Váci Streets. These milk-meals went to children between 1 and 4 years old, and especially to children whose fathers had been recruited to fight in the war.[97] Another initiative of about the same time targeted older school children. Children were reported to be arriving at school in the mornings 'with empty stomachs' and even fainting. Of course, this reduced their 'mental receptiveness'.[98] The Hungarian newspaper *Pester Lloyd* collected money to support an enhanced 'breakfast action for school children', which made the continuation of the Milk-Meal Action superfluous.[99] The breakfasts were available in 25 primary schools, especially those in impoverished neighbourhoods, and were extended to 28 kindergartens so that around 2,500 children a day could benefit from it.[100] The breakfasts included 'egg soup' and a bread roll for the schoolchildren, and 200 millilitres of milk with a bread roll for those in kindergarten.[101] Yet again, 'due to financial restrictions', this initiative had to be stopped for older children.[102] Thanks to the *Pester Lloyd* collections, it could continue in kindergartens for a while, but by the fall of 1918, the Central Milk Office was unable to make the required deliveries.[103]

In April 1918, in the building of the Budapest Central Milk Hall, the Uránia Milk Kitchen was opened, being considered the 'most modern' infant milk kitchen for the distribution of pasteurized milk in the city.[104] Public health authorities were to 'require and supervise the pasteurization of all milk supplies for young children', and recommended that all milk for children be boiled in the home.[105] 'Priority rations, particularly of milk, were in almost every instance allocated to children and pregnant women', which could be considered 'an index of the importance attached to the preservation of child health'.[106] Under continuous, daily 'medical rule and control', the milk kitchen provided Budapest's infants and sick children with 'hygienic healing milk'.[107] It also supplied seventeen types of special milk products.[108] The aim was to guarantee that infants from impoverished families below the age of seven could have access to 'suitable and trustworthy' nutrition.[109] A source dated June 1918 speaks of 30,000 litres of milk being distributed every day in exchange for 'milk tickets 1 and 2' (for one- and two-year-olds).

Beyond the immediate control of the milk kitchens, much effort was done to educate mothers about children's proper nutrition. The medical committee of the milk kitchen issued booklets about proper 'infant feeding' (*A csecsemő táplálása*).[110] A report by the US Food Administration on the economic situation in Austria-Hungary in the first half of 1918 makes a point of mentioning the milk kitchens in Hungary: 'Finally, in order to reduce the mortality among children', Hungarian 'children less than two years old ... receive pasteurized milk at the price of ordinary milk, the difference being made up by the Food Office'.[111] If mother's milk was unavailable, pasteurized dairy milk was considered the best means to secure the survival of infants and toddlers. The arrival and distribution of pasteurized dairy milk from the United States to Hungary was visually captured at the time. One image from the opening day of the American child feeding in Hungary in September 1919 (see Figure 8.1) depicted four nurses and a female representative of the better-off-classes, ready to serve Sharps canned milk with bread rolls and some kind of rusk or cookies to Hungary's starving children. While the decoration of this place with the American flag stressed the origin of the food relief items, the official arrangement and presentation of the canned milk and the bread turned these foodstuffs into embodiments of this transatlantic humanitarian endeavour.

In 1921, the ARA initiated a 'Mothers' and Babies' Breakfast Initiative' in Hungary, responding to the special needs of mothers and infants. In the earlier mentioned monthly American Red Cross report, one sheet from April 1922 was dedicated to detailing the 'social work in the country', which identified the distribution of 'supplementary food given to nursing mothers' and of 'food to babies and children' as the main activities of this relief organization in Hungary. This monthly report that, centred in particular on the 'Problems handled by the social office', of which there were apparently 2,962, reports that 1,400 nursing mothers received supplementary food, while 847 portions of food were given to babies or children.[112] In 1921, 4 milk stations for small children distributed a total of 650 milk tins daily.[113] The Budapest Welfare Centre was involved in milk distribution and it supported nursing mothers, giving out around 500 litres of milk through four dispensaries situated in the second, third, sixth and nineteenth districts of the city, as well as at the White Cross and Jewish hospitals.[114]

While most of the food relief was meant for the children, also mothers' supplementary feeding was considered important. Mothers' feeding reflects the importance given to breastfeeding, as it was known by then that nursing mothers needed more caloric intake. Once the mothers' and babies' breakfast initiative was running, the ARA captured in photographs the everyday recruitment and feeding of mothers and babies. Local photographers were accompanying the relief actions through the various steps.

Figure 8.1 American Relief Administration Hungary, Child Feeding Opening Day. American Relief Administration European operational records, Box 859, Folder 2, Hoover Institution Library & Archives.

Visually capturing large groups of breastfeeding and young mothers consuming with their infants and toddlers an American breakfast served to prove the special need of mothers and babies to receive transnational relief.

Centring the visual attention at times on one single mother feeding her child (see Figure 8.3) was even more powerful a means to individualize this

Figure 8.2 Újpest, Industrial Suburb of Budapest, 19 May 1921, a morning at a ARA Breakfast Station. American Relief Administration European operational records, Box 851, Folder J, Hoover Institution Library & Archives.

massive relief action. It enabled, in particular, the female viewer to either identify or solidarize with the depicted mother.

As the breakfast action was dependent on financial and moral support, representatives of the Hungarian political elite, such as Governor Miklós Horthy himself, medical personnel like Prof. János Bókay, as well as local staff of the A.R.A. came to inspect the relief activity. Many visuals (see Figure 8.4) were used to prove and visually capture the close ties between the relief initiative and the country's political elite.

While in these transatlantic relief actions, both cow and canned milk were distributed, the post-war period saw a real revival of breastfeeding. Taylor and Kellogg observed that even if 'the mother's milk contains less than 10 per cent of its energy in the form of protein', it actually contributes to 'the highest intensity of growth in the life of the individual'.[115] Juba and other nutritionists were convinced of the paramount value of breastfeeding. 'Infants' were known to 'thrive best on breast milk', whose use was supported by 'experience[s] based upon instinct, tradition and scientific fact'.[116] He called upon Hungarian mothers to obey the first and most important rule of infant care: to feed their offspring throughout the first six months with 'nothing but mother's milk'.[117] He insisted that there was no better infant food: 'it is always ready, one does not need to warm it up, it is perfectly clean and the wisdom of nature has taken care that its

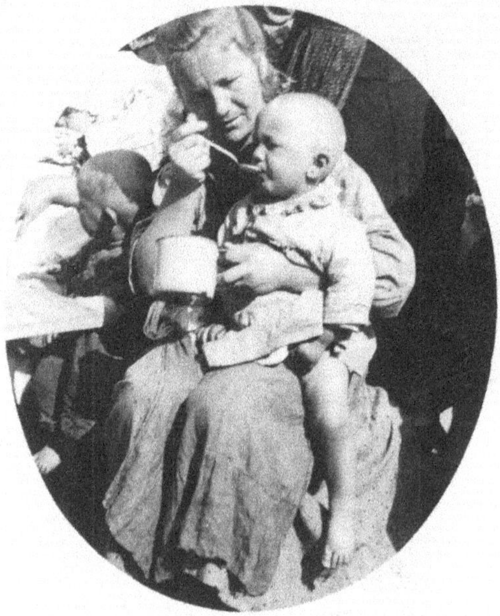

Figure 8.3 Újpest, Industrial Suburb of Budapest, 19 May 1921, A mother feeding her child at a ARA Breakfast Station. American Relief Administration European operational records, Box 851, Folder J, Hoover Institution Library & Archives.

composition is appropriate'.[118] The 'decrease of digestive diseases' in post-war Hungary was considered to be 'mainly due to the fact that in view of the fatal scarcity of fresh milk a far greater proportion of mothers nursed their babies now than in pre-war times, despite their own state of under-nourishment'.[119] Hence, as a scientific article from March 1921 argued, the paradoxical situation arose that 'one of the disadvantages of war', namely children's malnutrition, had 'become the advantage of the next generation', because need triggered the shift towards breastfeeding as well as more child support to parents and mothers.[120]

The scientific discourse of the time on infant nutrition often stressed the advantages of breastfeeding. An article in *Doctors Weekly* (*Orvosi Hetilap*) affirmed that sick infants who were 'often breastfed ... became calmer ... [and] ... slept well', while 'their stool improved, their vomiting ceased and they gained weight without any appearance of disease'.[121] Such science-based recommendations were not confined to mothers in

Figure 8.4 A.R.A. Hungary. Visit of Governor Horthy and Countess Széchényi at an ARA dinner, 14 April 1921. American Relief Administration European operational records, Box 851, Folder J, Hoover Institution Library & Archives.

individual families. Due to the increasing obsession with breastfeeding, Hungary's Welfare Centre urged Budapest's main factories to install 'nursing rooms' on their premises where 'working mothers could place their infants during the day and breastfeed them during breaks'.[122] Dr József Madzsar realized that the 'artificial feeding' of infants was particularly dominant in 'industrial neighbourhoods', where women returned straight to factory work after recuperating from giving birth. To prevent this, women were encouraged to take their newborn infants to work with them and feed them there, a common occurrence among female peasant workers.[123] Once nursing rooms were made available in the factories, 'hundreds of infants' could 'get access to mother's milk, with which their lives [could] be saved'.[124] In 1917, the Stefánia Association (supported by state funds) installed 'breastfeeding shelters for infants' throughout Budapest.[125] However, breastfeeding was not always possible. Because 'no other food [had] so stolidly symbolized natural purity' as milk, cows' milk, as outlined earlier, became an important part of children's diet if mother's milk was not available.[126] Once children survived the first years of their life, their nutritional dependence on mother's milk and milk decreased gradually.[127]

Conclusion: Child Feeding as Transnational Biopolitics

The national effort to feed children can be approached as one of the various biopolitical techniques which Foucault identified as one of the major 'technologies of power'.[128] Providing food to the undernourished child population in Hungary and altering thereby the harmed corporality of Central Europe's child population was often coupled with power mechanism at the time. Identifying the nutritional needs of this population and applying new expertise to their undernourished bodies was only possible within the framework of the international community of nutritionists, child relief workers and local physicians. The new knowledge about child and infant nutrition could be applied to the harmed and fragile physique of the concerned children, who required the material and nutritional intervention on their behalf. The collective body of Hungary and the surrounding region's undernourished children allowed international humanitarian agencies to exercise biopolitical power. The regulation of the collective body of children was utilized as an instrument to alter the 'material' constitution of the concerned societies. In contrast to the health regulations of social 'outliers' during and after the war, such as prostitutes,[129] the interference in the health and corporality of Central Europe's malnourished children mirrored the biopolitical regulation of the societies' social core. As much of the foodstuffs were delivered from abroad and much relief work was implemented by foreign relief workers, we can identify here some asymmetrical power dynamics between the international community of experts and relief workers on the one hand and the child population on the other hand. International food relief, and especially Herbert Hoover as its personal embodiment, were portrayed as the saviours of Central Europe's children. Fellow Americans presented Hoover as 'a modest American whose genius had translated the charity and sympathy and compassion of our people into practical measures to save the lives of these thousands of children'.[130] Through his transatlantic deeds, he could see to it that 'a whole generation he had saved from disease and death ... might lead useful lives'.[131]

The material delivery of food and the implementation of the relief scheme in the target countries eased the creation of economic and social hierarchies between the donor and recipient country and between the individual relief workers and the receiving children. Various international relief workers also drew direct comparisons between the nutritional condition of children in their home countries and in the Central European countries that received relief. An American nutritionist to Poland judged the nutritional condition of a Polish school class to be 'on a much lower level of nutrition than any children [she] ... had ever seen in New York city'.[132] Although nutrition sciences were, in fact, widespread in Central Europe, she stated that the Polish mothers 'had not had the advantage of nutrition education as many mothers of their type had had in New York City for some years'.[133] She judged the international food relief as an important educational tool because 'the Poles will not have had the advantages of increased knowledge of food value the people of Great Britain and the United States are gaining during the war'.[134]

Beyond using child nutrition to apply modern knowledge to the suffering child population, improved nutrition and 'children's welfare work' were also approached as factors 'in the promotion of international friendship and co-operation'.[135] Dr Hilda Clark, a British Quaker and general secretary of the Friend's Relief Mission in Vienna, appreciated the 'extraordinary response that the appeal for help for children had called forth, alike from countries recently belligerent and those ... neutral'.[136] The German feminist Miss. Lida Gustava Heymann argued that relief work on behalf of German children 'had assisted the international ideal' and that 'the children who benefited from this real Samaritanism would, later on, become apostles of humanity and peace'.[137] Jane Addams, the president of the Women's International League of Peace and Freedom, demanded the 'setting up of an international standard of child welfare which should make it impossible for children to starve on one side of a frontier when there was bread to spare on the other'.[138] Hence, children's corporal destitution triggered international cooperation, both among physicians, nutritionists and humanitarian relief workers. A 1919 article titled 'The Food of Europe' called upon the better-offer countries to be aware of the condition of 'the nations of Central Europe', that was 'passing through a moment of extreme difficulty' and 'to which no European worthy of the name can pretend to be indifferent'.[139] The destitution was used to trigger transnational solidarity and philanthropic relief. One time, for instance, under the auspices of the League of the Red Cross Societies, 'eighteen nurses from as many different countries had been sent to London for post-graduate public health training'.[140] Against this backdrop, the nutritional needs in post-war Central Europe could, on the one hand, only be fought with the help of the advanced nutritional sciences, while, on the other hand, they also demanded and enabled further research about the interconnection between diet and physical constitution of children. Consequently, the discourse about and the approach to children's nutritional deprivation in Central Europe mirrors well the contemporary social value of children for the remaking of the post-war populations of the region.

Notes

1 Bertha Holman, 'Experience of an American Dietitian and Nutritionist in Post-War Work in Warsaw, Poland 1922–23', *Bulletin of the Polish Institute of Arts and Sciences in America* 1, no. 4 (July 1943): 801–808, 806.
2 Richard W. B. Ellis, 'Effects of War on Child Health', *The British Medical Journal* 1, no. 4544 (7 February 1948): 239–245, 243.
3 Ellis, 'Effects of War on Child Health', 243.

4 Dominique Marshall, 'Children's Rights and Children's Action in International Relief and Domestic Welfare: The Work of Herbert Hoover Between 1914 and 1950', *The Journal of the History of Childhood and Youth* 1, no. 3 (2008): 351–388, 357.
5 Corinna Treitel, 'Max Rubner and the Biopolitics of Rational Nutrition', *Central European History* 41, no. 1 (2008): 1–25, 4–5.
6 Holman, 'Experience of an American Dietitian', 808.
7 Treitel, 'Max Rubner and the Biopolitics of Rational Nutrition', 11.
8 Ödön Lévai, 'Az elhanyagolt gyermekegészség', *Budapest Hírlap* 38, no. 153 (4 July 1918): 8.
9 Ibid., 8.
10 Albert Apponyi, *The American Peace and Hungary, 1919* (Budapest: Hungarian Territorial Integrity League, 1919), 11.
11 Paris Peace Conference, Hungary, *The Consequences of the Division of Hungary from the Standpoint of Eugenics* (Budapest: Hungarian Territorial Integrity League, 1919), 1.
12 *The Consequences of the Division of Hungary from the Standpoint of Eugenics*, 2.
13 Ibid., 2.
14 Ibid., 2.
15 Ibid., 2.
16 Adolf Juba, 'A gyermek táplálása és a háború', *Néptanítók lapja* 40, no. 4 (27 January 1916): 4–6.
17 Ibid., 4–6.
18 Ibid.
19 Ibid.
20 Ibid.
21 Ibid.
22 Marius Turda, 'The Biology of War: Eugenics in Hungary, 1914–1918', *Austrian History Yearbook* 40 (2009): 238–264, 239, 240.
23 Herbert Hoover, 'Children's Relief and Democracy', *American Relief Administration Bulletin* Series 2, no. 15 (1 August 1921): 1–2, here 1.
24 William R. Grove, *War's Aftermath* (New York: House of Field, 1940), 169.
25 Grove, *War's Aftermath*, 169.
26 Inauguration of the ARA Children's Fund, Letter by Herbert Hoover to Colonel Grove. Grove, *War's Aftermath* (New York: House of Field, 1940), 171.
27 Herbert Hoover, 'Children's Relief and Democracy', *American Relief Administration Bulletin* Series 2, no. 15 (1 August 1921): 1.
28 Grove, *War's Aftermath*, 169.
29 Ibid., 169.
30 Ibid., 169.
31 Grove, *War's Aftermath*, 171.
32 Barona Vilar, 'International Organisations and the Development of a Physiology of Nutrition during the 1930s', *Food & History* 6 (2008): 133–166, 131.
33 Richard A. Meckel, *Urban Schools and the Protection and Promotion of Child Health, 1870–1930* (Rutgers: Rutgers University Press, 2013), 1.
34 Bruno Cabanes, *The Great War and the Origins of Humanitarianism, 1918–1924* (Cambridge: Cambridge University Press, 2014), 228.
35 Clemens Pirquet, 'Einleitung', in *Volksgesundheit im Krieg*, ed. Clemens von Pirquet (Yale/New Haven, CT: Yale University Press, 1926), 1–13, 1.
36 Pirquet, 'Einleitung', 13.
37 David Nally, '"That Coming Storm": The Irish Poor Law, Colonial Biopolitics, and the Great Famine', *Annals of the Association of American Geographers* 98, no. 3 (2008): 714–741, here 717.

38 Vilar, 'International Organizations', 130.
39 János Bókay, *A Csecsemők mesterséges táplálásának története* [History of the Artificial Nutrition of Infants] (Budapest: Országos Stefánia Szövetség, 1928), 8.
40 Ibid., 8.
41 Ibid.
42 Ibid.
43 Treitel, 'Max Rubner and the Biopolitics of Rational Nutrition', 11.
44 Paul Weindling, 'From Sentiment to Science – Children's Relief Organizations and the Problem of Malnutrition in Interwar Europe', *Disasters: The Journal of Disaster Studies and Management* 18, no. 3 (1994): 203–212, 204.
45 Vilar, 'International Organizations', 130.
46 Ibid., 129.
47 Nick Cullather, 'The Foreign Policy of the Calorie', *American Historical Review* 112, no. 2 (2007): 337–365, 339.
48 'The Food of Europe', *The British Medical Journal* 2, no. 3072 (15 November 1919): 640–641, 641.
49 Clemens Pirquet, *An Outline of the Pirquet System of Nutrition* (Philadelphia, PA: W.B. Saunders, 1922), 45.
50 'The "Nem" System of Nutrition', *The British Medical Journal* 2, no. 3122 (30 October 1920): 666–667, 666.
51 Gusztáv Riegler, 'Egészségtan' [Hygiene], *Budapest Orvosi Ujság* 19, no. 13 (31 March 1921): 196.
52 'The "Nem" System of Nutrition', 666–667, 666.
53 Ibid., 666–667, 666.
54 Walter Gratze, *Terrors of the Table: The Curious History of Nutrition* (Oxford: Oxford University Press, 2005).
55 Clemens Pirquet, 'Ernährungszustand der Kinder in Österreich Während des Krieges und der Nachkriegszeit', in *Volksgesundheit im Krieg*, ed. Clemens von Pirquet (Yale/New Haven, CT: Yale University Press, 1926), 151–179, 155.
56 Pirquet, *An Outline of the Pirquet System*, 45.
57 Ibid., 59.
58 'Child Welfare Work in Vienna', *The British Medical Journal* 2, no. 3163 (13 August 1921): 244–245, 244.
59 Pirquet, *An Outline of the Pirquet System*, 46.
60 Ibid., 59.
61 Ibid., 47.
62 Ibid., 46.
63 Cabanes, *The Great War and the Origins of Humanitarianism*, 225.
64 Michel Foucault, '17 March 1976', in *Society Must Be Defended: Lectures at the Collège de France*, eds. Mauro Bertani and Alessandro Fontana (New York: Picador, 2003), 252.
65 Cabanes, *The Great War and the Origins of Humanitarianism*, 225.
66 Ibid., 225.
67 Pirquet, *An Outline of the Pirquet System of Nutrition*, 18.
68 'The "Nem" System of Nutrition', 667.
69 Ibid., 667.
70 'Deficiency Diseases in Vienna', *The British Medical Journal* 1, no. 3092 (3 April 1920), 477–478.
71 'Child Welfare Work in Vienna', 244.
72 'The Food of Europe', 640–641, 640.
73 Ibid., 640.
74 'Child Welfare Work in Vienna', 244–245, 244.

75 Ibid., 244–245, 244.
76 Johann v. Bókay and Adolf Juba, 'Ernährungszustand der Kinder in Ungarn', in *Volksgesundheit im Krieg*, ed. Clemens von Pirquet (Yale/New Haven, CT: Yale University Press, 1926), 180–224, 191.
77 Bókay and Juba, 'Ernährungszustand der Kinder in Ungarn', 191.
78 Ibid., 192.
79 Pirquet, 'Ernährungszustand der Kinder', 179.
80 Juba, 'A gyermek táplálása és a háború', 4–6.
81 Ibid., 4–6.
82 Ibid., 4–6.
83 'A csecsemők és gyermekek tejjel való ellátása' [The milk supply for infants and children], *Budapesti Hírlap* 38, no. 141 (15 June 1918): 7.
84 Charles McNeil, 'An Address on Tuberculosis in Early Childhood', *The British Medical Journal* 2, no. 3588 (12 October 1929): 655–658, 657.
85 Friederike Kind-Kovács, 'The Great War, the Child's Body and the "American Red Cross"', *European Review of History* 23 (2016): 1–2, 33–62.
86 Alonzo Taylor and Vernon Kellogg, *The Food Problem* (New York: Macmillan 1917), 157 and 78.
87 Ibid., 120.
88 Meckel, *Urban Schools and the Protection and Promotion of Child Health*, 185.
89 Sylwia Markowska-Kuźma, 'From "Drop of Milk" to "Bureaus for Mothers": Infant Care and Visions of Medical Motherhood in the Early 20th Century Polish Part of the Habsburg Empire', in *Medicine Within and Between the Habsburg and Ottoman Empires, 18th–19th Centuries*, ed. Teodora Daniela Sechel (Bochum: Winkler, 2011), 131–147, 138.
90 Meckel, *Urban Schools and the Protection and Promotion of Child Health*, 185.
91 Ibid.
92 'Child Welfare Work in Vienna', 244–245, 244.
93 It was renamed in 1915/16 into 'Budapesti Központi Általános Tejcsarnok'.
94 Susan Zimmermann and Gerhard Melinz, *Gyermeksorsok És Gyermekvédelem: Budapest a Monarchia idején* (Budapest: Fővárosi Szabó Ervin Könyvtár, 1996), 53.
95 'Újpest városát tejhamisítással vádolják', *Népszava* 45, no. 38 (7 February 1917): 11.
96 Lajos Keller, *Országos Stefánia Szövetség 10 Éves Működése, 1915. Június 13–1925. December 31* (Budapest: Egyesült Könyvnyomda, 1926), 9.
97 Ibid., 117.
98 Ibid.
99 Ibid.
100 Ibid.
101 Ibid., 118.
102 Ibid., 117.
103 Ibid., 118.
104 'Áprilisban kinyílik a tej konyha', *Az Újság* 16, no. 74 (28 March 1918): 7.
105 McNeil, 'An Address on Tuberculosis', 655–658, 657.
106 Ellis, 'Effects of War on Child Health', 239–245, 243.
107 'Egyesületi hírek', *Budapesti Hírlap* 36, no. 280 (8 October 1916): 15.
108 'A csecsemők és gyermekek tejjel való ellátása', 7.
109 'Áprilisban kinyilik a tej konyha', 7.
110 Az Uránia Tejkonyha orvosi bizottsága, *A csecsemő táplálása* (Budapest: Az Országos Stefánia Szövetség kiadványa, 1918).

111 'Public Kitchens: Hungary', in *Economic Situation: Austria-Hungary during the First Half of 1918*, 1–24, 21. United States Food Administration Records 1909–1957, Alphabetical File, Austria Hungary, Reel Box 95.1 to Box 95.14., Folder 7. HIAS, Stanford.
112 'Monthly Report. Problems handled by the social office'. Amerikan [sic] Red Cross for Protecting Mothers and Babies in Hungary, April 30. 1922, NARA Washington, Commission to Hungary. Child Welfare. 954.621/08.
113 'Cablegram by Childfund to Mr. Gay. Budapest February 2, 1921'. ARA, European Unit. London Office. Cable and Telegram File. Hungary-'Yellow' Budapest to London 1920 August–1922 February. Box 36, Folder 2, R57. HIA, Stanford.
114 Hugó Csergő, *A Budapesti Nyomor Vöröskönyve* (Budapest: Népjóléti Központ, 1919), 102.
115 Taylor and Kellogg, *The Food Problem*, 113.
116 A. B. Schwartz, 'The Use of Lactic Acid Milk in Infant Feeding', *The American Journal of Nursing* 26, no. 12 (December 1926): 927–932, 927.
117 Juba, 'A gyermek táplálása és a háború', 4–6.
118 Ibid., 4–6.
119 'Child Welfare Work in Vienna', 244–245, 244.
120 'Egészségtan', 195.
121 Sándor Szana and Béla Totis, 'Hiányosan táplált szopós csecsemők', *Orvosi Hetilap* 63, no. 26 (29 June 1919): 285.
122 'A Népjóléti Központ a gyári szoptatószobák érdekében', *Népszava* 45, no. 199 (11 August 1917): 10.
123 József Madzsar, *Mit akar a Stefánia-Szövetség?* (Budapest: Pfeiffer, 1916), 11.
124 'A Népjóléti Központ a gyári szoptatószobák érdekében', 10.
125 'A Stefánia-Palota Ára', *Az Est* 8, no. 213 (26 August 1917): 5.
126 Kenda Smith-Howard, *Pure and Modern Milk: An Environmental History Since 1900* (Oxford: Oxford University Press, 2014), 4.
127 Taylor and Kellogg, *The Food Problem*, 119.
128 Foucault, '17 March 1976', 241.
129 Nancy Wingfield, 'The Enemy Within: Regulating Prostitution and Controlling Venereal Disease in Cisleithanian Austria During the Great War', *Central European History* 46, no. 3 (2013): 568–598, 598.
130 Hoover Overseas and War Service Organizations. 1914–1924. Addresses Delivered at the Reunion Dinner. Washington: 3 March 1929, 12.
131 Ibid.
132 Holman, 'Experience of an American Dietitian', 806.
133 Ibid., 807.
134 Ibid.
135 'Child Welfare Work in Vienna', 244–245, 244.
136 'Child Welfare Work in Vienna', 244–245.
137 Ibid., 245.
138 Ibid.
139 'The Food of Europe', 640–641, 640.
140 'Child Welfare Work in Vienna', 245.

9 Disinfection Trains

Fighting Lice on Polish Railways, 1918–1920

Łukasz Mieszkowski

The Polish economic historian Michał Kopczyński,[1] when citing the examples of the Roman Empire, the Inca kingdom, fascist Italy and Nazi Germany, noted that 'until the mid-twentieth century, the existence of a distinctive road network was not so much a sign of economic development as a measure of the degree of despotism'.[2] In this context, Russia under the rule of Tsar Nicholas II presented itself as the exception that confirmed the rule. The country was connected to the western part of the continent by only a few macadam roads, continually hardened with layers of crushed stone or brick, but which nevertheless remained impassable for most of the year and were so muddy that a writer and journalist familiar with the region poetically referred to them as 'murky rivers' through which 'dirty silver' flowed.[3]

The network of railway lines – or 'iron roads' as they were described at the time – was also very sparse. This was in part due to the vastness of the area covered by the network, but the principal reason was Russian military doctrine, which required a strip of 'railway desert' to be maintained on the western borders of the empire in order to prevent invading armies from quickly encroaching into native Russian territory. Prior to 1918, only six lines branched off from the huge arc of the line connecting Vilnius in the north with L'viv in the south.[4] Communication was further complicated by the fact that Russian railways used a wider gauge than in Central Europe and thus required different rolling stock. As a result, Russia had the least developed railway network in Europe after Turkey and Greece; in the occupied Polish territories, the average length of railway line per 100 km^2 was less than 3 km, whereas in the Prussian-occupied Polish territories, by comparison, this figure stood at more than 10 km![5]

Paradoxically, in the battles of the fought on the borderlands of the Russian Empire during the First World War, railways were of crucial importance, and despite the huge overall damage done to infrastructure, railways would assume even greater importance in the conflicts to follow. Given the vastness of the terrain, and the fact that a system of macadam roads usable by modern vehicles was virtually non-existent, trains remained the fastest,

DOI: 10.4324/9781003161080-12

most reliable, and indeed the only way to transport troops, civilians, and goods over long distances. Each railway line became worth its weight in gold; even the smallest railway junction took on the importance of a fortress, and trains from the deep hinterland would force their way onto the front lines, the most spectacular example being armoured trains. The railway was likewise a key element of another silent war that was waged at the margins of the noisier wars but which was equally bloody. And in this conflict, as in those other wars, the railways served both sides.

Epidemic typhus, also known at the time as typhus fever, is a bacterial infectious disease. In the Kingdom of Poland and Galicia, it was endemic, and during the combined German and Austro-Hungarian offensive of 1915, as a result of the Russian army's retreat and the refugee crisis, the biggest pandemic in the history of this disease broke out on two continents – Europe and Asia. The pandemic could not be contained until the end of the Russian Civil War. By the middle of 1919, more than 320,000 cases had been recorded in Poland alone, and nearly 20,000 people lost their lives.[6] Apart from the skin rash and petechiae, the symptoms of the disease were similar to those of the flu – high fever, headaches and disorders of the heart and nervous system. At a time when the Spanish flu pandemic was raging throughout the world,[7] the two diseases were often mistaken for each other. What distinguished typhus was the much higher mortality rate and the manner of infection. Only a decade or so earlier, it had been considered an airborne disease, although cases were often associated with vagabonds, seasonal workers and migrants. It was not until 1914, at the Pasteur Institute's branch in Algiers, that scientists discovered that the disease was spread by lice, specifically their faeces, which the human host would scratch into the flesh where the louse had drawn blood.[8] This was of huge importance to how the disease was understood. The science of hygiene and its new branch – parasitology – offered a convincing interpretation of typhus and the role of the disease in public health policy. The fight against lice became a clear and distinct goal: it was based on specific measures that brought palpable effects and were not devoid of symbolic meaning; on mass vaccination, the washing and disinfection of clothing, the cutting of hair and the washing of bodies. However, above all, it was based on an attempt to control the flow of that part of the population, which, due to the appalling sanitary conditions that prevailed, was a hotbed of louse infestation and typhus – soldiers, travellers and refugees, who were constantly on the move.

Railways, being the primary means of transportation, played a crucial role in this fight. Under normal conditions, this would have consisted in controlling the movement of people by creating a sanitary cordon between areas where the epidemic was present and those where it was not. The cordon was simply a demarcated, closed border that could only be crossed at designated points, usually railway stations, where the examination, delousing, and compulsory quarantine of travellers would take place.[9] Despite continual efforts, for the duration of the Polish–Ukrainian–Russian war, it proved impossible to establish an effective sanitary cordon in the borderlands of Central and Eastern Europe. The constantly changing front, the inadequacy of the administration and sanitary infrastructure, and the waves of troops and civilians on the move meant that trains departing for the interior of the country, whether passenger, military or (especially) sanitary, became plague trains.[10]

Although parasites were the singular cause of the epidemic, there were multiple reasons why they could not be eradicated. Those who were in charge of organizing the war against the epidemic knew that they had to wage it on many fronts. Since the stationary defences at railway stations proved ineffective, it was necessary to seize the initiative and, using the railways, take the fight to the epicentre of the disease – the war-torn borderlands.

The equivalent of the armoured train in the fight against lice, and therefore against typhus, was the bathing and disinfection train.[11] These two types of trains, thanks to the use of railway lines, were more mobile and more efficient than horse-drawn artillery batteries and field hygiene units, both in terms of firepower and the healing effect of hot water.

The first to take advantage of them was the Swiss army, which wanted to improve the hygiene of thousands of reservists mobilized to protect the borders of neutral Switzerland,[12] but they were most fully and widely deployed in the East.[13] Due to the scarcity of sanitary infrastructure and the fact that the hostilities mainly involved manoeuvre warfare, bathing and disinfection trains were used by the armies of Germany, Russia, Austria–Hungary and other countries of the region. In all likelihood, the first Polish units of this type were modelled on those of the partitioning powers.

When, on 15 March 1919, the chief medical officer of the Polish Army informed the Supreme Army Command about the need to create two bathing and disinfection trains in order to 'decontaminate the troops at the front',[14] reality had already pre-empted his plans. According to the account of the deputy head of the L'viv branch of the Armoured Train Construction Directorate, at the end of February 1919, despite the Ukrainian siege of the city, the shelling of the station and workshops, and the growing demand for rolling stock, it was possible to complete the construction of the first bathing train; its name, which derives from the Poltva [Polish: Pełtew] river that flows through L'viv, evokes the gurgling and splashing of running water.[15]

It is likely that the composition of the Pełtew did not differ much from that of the proposed trains referred to in the chief medical officer's letter; in their original form, they were to consist of nine cars, each serving a different purpose. Although in subsequent years, the configuration of the echelons changed according to need, the basic elements remained the same. A preserved and very detailed description (together with technical drawings) of bathing and disinfection train no. 5, built between June and August

1920 in L'viv, almost certainly in the local railway workshops, gives us insight into the operating principles of these complicated and technically advanced structures,[16] which were able, at least in theory, to provide people living on the eastern borders of the country with services and even luxuries that most had not previously enjoyed.

Of the two functions implied by the name of these trains, the more important one was disinfection. Although bad for human health and conducive to parasites, dirt did not kill directly, whereas lice and typhus did. For this reason, located just behind the locomotive at the front of the train was its most important element: the disinfector car, where lice and nits would be removed from clothing. Best suited to this task was a refrigerated freight car with insulated double walls used for transporting perishable food, but in this case, its purpose was to keep the temperature high rather than low. A separate door in the side wall of the car led to two chambers lined with iron sheeting covered with anti-corrosion paint to protect against moisture. Affixed to the ceiling were rows of hooks for hanging disinfected clothing, while the floor, protected by a thin layer of concrete and a wooden grate, had iron coils placed upon it. These were connected via rubber tubes to the steam boiler pulling the locomotive. In one of the chambers, the coils were perforated to allow hot steam to burst through the holes. This was where the so-called wet disinfection of underwear and outer clothing would take place. Shoes, belts, other leather items and especially valuable furs, which could easily be destroyed in a steam room, were disinfected in a second chamber, the so-called dry chamber. There, the coils had no holes; the steam flowing through the tubes did not escape but only heated the air.[17] Where such chambers were sealed and properly fitted, a temperature of over 170°C could be obtained. According to parasitologists, for the procedure to be effective – that is, for the heat to kill the lice and their eggs – the temperature inside the disinfector could not fall below 100°C. Of course, the colder it was, the longer the clothes had to remain inside the chamber, and this period could never be shorter than two hours.[18]

Behind the disinfection car began the most impressive part of the train – three long, refitted ex-passenger cars, of third or fourth class, connected by gangways in the front walls topped by bellows; like the disinfector car, they were heated centrally by hot steam fed from the locomotive. In the first passenger car was an undressing room and barber shop, in the second were showers and in the third was a dressing room. The direction of movement was one-way, such that the bathers – soldiers, civilians, refugees or prisoners of war – having handed in their outer clothing for disinfection and their underwear for replacement, and having had a haircut and a wash and sometimes having undergone disinfection that involved kerosene, grey mercury ointment or other chemicals being rubbed into the scalp, underarms and groin, did not return to the dirty, louse-infested undressing room, but instead proceeded to the 'uninfected' dressing room. There, after receiving a new and previously prepared change of underwear, they waited for their clothes to come out of the disinfection chambers.

The heart of the bathing area was the shower. Beneath the ceiling of the car, from which benches and other obstructions had been removed, were 28 to 30 shower heads set in two rows along the axis of the car. Water was supplied to them from a tank on the roof with a capacity of three to four thousand litres; the water was heated by steam from the locomotive. The floor, which sloped gently towards the drain in the middle of the car, was lined with sheet metal or concrete and covered with a grating. At the end of the car was a partition separating the towel-drying room from a small room used by the plumber responsible for the showers. His main task (apart from looking after the whole installation) was simply to ensure the flow of water – each shower head had a valve, but it was locked and not meant to be used by individual bathers. Ostensibly, the bathers' comfort was to be ensured by a thermometer affixed to the main pipe running from the tank; it was equipped with an electric bell that would sound if the water temperature was too high. However, the way in which bathing and disinfection trains operated in practice, as described below, would suggest that the bell did not sound too often.

The locomotive, as is evident from the descriptions above, was not just a source of propulsion. While some structures had their own furnaces, the shower room and especially the disinfector, could not function properly without the heat produced by the locomotive, although in all likelihood, the water was heated, and the installations filled with hot steam only when the train was stationary. The amount of water used restricted the range of the train and its disinfection and bathing capacity much more than the stock of coal; even big locomotives with a larger supply of coal in the tender and water in the water tank found it difficult to meet the demand. To remedy this, the composition of the train included – according to drawings, right at the front, perhaps in order to protect the engine as in armoured trains – a huge, 200-hectolitre cistern or tank carried on a platform car, connected to the steam boiler by rubber hoses. The other cars and locomotive were supplied thanks to a steam pump installed in the cistern, and in the absence of functioning water towers and cranes, the cistern could also be filled directly from a river or pond via a hose.

However, the cistern, the heating and propulsion unit, and the bathing, disinfection and haircutting section did not even account for half of the train in its final, most developed form. Behind the passenger cars, connected by covered passages woven with iron pipes and rubber hoses supplying steam and water, was a string of smaller passenger and freight cars that were essential to the proper functioning of the whole system.

Of key importance was what shall be referred to as the 'underwear' section, which, as will later become apparent, sometimes disrupted the overall functioning of the train. It consisted of a laundry room and two storage areas for clean and dirty underwear located in separate freight cars. Two additional, four-axle, third-class passenger cars housed a drying room together with an ironing room as well as a sewing room with living quarters for the seamstresses.

Added to this was the commandant's residential car, also containing his office, at least two residential cars for male and female crew members, a kitchen car with a pantry, a fitter and lathe operator workshop, a canteen and tearoom and finally, a wood repository for the 'steam room'. All of these, at least in theory, were centrally heated and had lighting powered from the 'power supply',[19] as well as lots of items and equipment: irons, sewing machines, tools, samovars, dishes and underwear. A complete bathing and disinfection train was meant to consist of 17 cars[20] and be almost 150 meters in length. Being a mosaic of various types of rolling stock, it was undoubtedly an interesting and impressive sight.

In the early spring of 1919, commanders estimated the crew of a train to be equivalent to 19 full-time positions,[21] but the Supreme Army Command decided that this was far too few given the tasks it was expected to perform.[22] Eighteen months later, the crew had grown to thirty-four people: seventeen women, including a cook, kitchen maid, barmaid, five seamstresses, six washerwomen, a manageress and her two assistants, and seventeen men: a commanding officer, two NCOs, two qualified plumbers to service the installations, shower room and disinfector, a qualified stoker, a barber and ten privates unable to serve on the front line who were used to provide escort and manpower.

Two and a half months after the demand for bathing and disinfection trains was reported, the Sanitary Department of the Ministry of Military Affairs decided to allocate, to military district HQs, various railway medical units – hospital trains providing medical care to the sick and wounded as well as other trains and special sanitary units that allowed the sick and wounded to be transported and evacuated.[23] Two military districts, Warsaw and L'viv, were assigned three bathing and disinfection trains, numbered 1, 2 and 3; the second of these, operating in eastern Galicia, was the aforementioned Pełtew. The name was so catchy that it remained in unofficial use for many years until the train was taken out of service. Little is known about the construction of the other two trains. Correspondence between the general staff and the Polish Military Liquidation Commission in Vienna shows that Poland was trying to obtain three bathing trains under the division of assets of the now defunct Austro-Hungarian monarchy.[24] The documentation is incomplete, but it is possible that at least one of the first three trains came from abroad. If not, then domestic railway factories and workshops were able to build bathing and disinfection trains at the rapid rate of one train every month and a half. Whether they were built properly is another matter that will be discussed later.

The urgency was understandable since the initially postulated number of two trains proved completely inadequate given the swelling ranks of the army, the escalation of hostilities, and the catastrophic impact of the epidemic between the autumn of 1918 and spring of 1919. On the basis of the preserved documents, it is impossible to reconstruct the exact timeframe within which subsequent units were constructed, but it is at least possible to determine their number. There were certainly 12 units at minimum, probably a few more. This calculation is corroborated by the 14 bathing and disinfection trains mobilized by the Polish Army on 1 September 1939. However, any discrepancy in the actual number of such units would not be big enough to give a false picture of the size and scale of their operations.

According to the quartermaster of the Polish army, a well-commanded and fully staffed and stocked train should have been able to wash between 500 and 800 people each day, disinfect their outer clothing, and give them a clean change of underwear.[25] These numbers sound impressive – at the time, the largest, most modern stationary bathing facilities were designed to have a daily capacity of between 480 and 600 people.[26] Given this capacity – considering that in early September 1920, the condition of the 'bayonets and sabres', i.e. the number of soldiers directly involved in the fighting, amounted on the Polish side to around 150,000 men[27] – ten trains, cooperating with bathhouses, disinfection chambers and mobile 'epidemic columns' (usually horse-drawn carriages), which performed the same functions in areas distant from railway lines, were theoretically able to provide each front line soldier with a regulation bath, a clean uniform, and a change of underwear every two weeks, thus greatly diminishing the threat of louse infestation and typhus. As one can imagine, in practice, the situation was rather different.

In early June 1920, a week before the start of the Polish Army's retreat from Kiev, behind the railway station in Volochysk [in Polish: Wołoczyska], a small town located halfway between Ternopil [in Polish: Tarnopol] and Khmelnytskyi [in Polish: Płoskirów] in western Ukraine, a high-ranking Polish official responsible for combating the epidemic, and a liaison officer from the French military mission who was accompanying him, came across bathing and disinfection train no. 1 standing in a siding. A brief inspection (its brevity can be inferred from the official's schedule) revealed that the train, which had been assigned to the POW camp and army training camp in Volochysk, was in terrible condition. Most importantly, the disinfector was not working. A portable disinfector borrowed from an army unit had been installed in the car, but it did not even have a thermometer, so it was impossible to tell whether any disinfection carried out would be effective.

The commissar and the accompanying officers found only a few rank-and-file soldiers in the bathing area. As the POW camp had been closed down, the only people using the train were the recruits at the army training camp, although, as the report summarizing the inspection noted,[28] attendance was 'very low'. It is not difficult to see why. The showers only had cold water, and the bathers were not given any cleaning products or offered a haircut. While the underwear they handed in before bathing was indeed disinfected, albeit in a low-temperature chamber, it was not washed due to a lack of soap. They had to put their dirty underwear back on, which was so dirty that its condition was noted in the report.

When 'summoned to explain himself', the train's commandant, a medical officer cadet, reported as follows: he did not cut the bathers' hair because he was not in possession of good clippers. He had on several occasions requested one from the Central Sanitary Depot, but to no avail. Nor did he wash any underwear because although the train had a laundry, there were no women willing to work there. None of them wanted to undertake this work, which was hard and dangerous due to the threat of typhus, for the daily rate of six marks set by the army commissariat. Even if he managed to hire some washerwomen, there was not a single piece of soap on the entire train, and because he was unfamiliar with the local chain of command, he did not know whom to contact about it. He did have at his disposal a sewing room equipped with several sewing machines operated by three seamstresses, but unfortunately, for several weeks, he had not been able to repair any uniforms or underwear due to the lack of thread.[29]

The visiting officers decided that the commandant was to blame for the sorry state of the train since he had been insufficiently energetic in ensuring its proper functioning and was not fully aware of duties that were incumbent upon him. The report was silent about what action was taken against the commandant; the person formally in charge of the train, the sanitary chief of the staging district HQ, was notified about the condition of the unit. It was also decided that in order to repair the disinfection chamber, the train had to return to Warsaw as soon as possible – as soon as a locomotive arrived to collect it. The hairdressing crisis was solved straight away by the visiting officers. One of the privates was taken to Płoskirow, where he was given clippers[30] from the depot of the chief commissariat.

A modern researcher or reader might draw a different conclusion from the content of the inspection report, however, the poor condition of the train and the ineffectiveness of the actions taken by its crew were as much due to 'objective' problems, above all connected with supply, as they were to the incompetent and apathetic commandant. The officers carrying out the inspection noticed these problems and even took steps to resolve them,[31] as in the case of soap, but they did not treat them as mitigating circumstances.

What primarily aroused the officers' interest and indignation was that standards among the personnel had not been maintained. The chronic lack of working equipment, cleaning products, thread, fuel and decent wages for the crew was not seen as anything unusual. The source documents confirm that other units faced similar and even more mundane problems. When, in February 1920, Minsk had completely exhausted its coal reserves, and the only fuel available was wet wood, unsuitable for firing disinfectors, bathing and disinfection train no. 3 had to suspend its operations until the arrival of a consignment of coal.[32] At around the same time, in Podolia, train no. 4, which serviced Russian White Guards coming over to the Polish side, withdrew from the place where it had been stationed – the town of Gródek – because it lacked water to fill the steam engine.[33]

In fairness, and in defence of the good name of the cadet commandant mentioned in the source documents, it should be noted that the regulations in force did not make his job any easier. Unlike hospital trains,[34] which employed dozens of crew members charged with transporting, feeding and clothing hundreds of patients, bathing and disinfection trains were relatively small units. Therefore, their commandants did not – which turned out to be a serious error – have the right to possess their own cash registers, keep their own accounts or issue travel documents; in other words, they could not send people out to get provisions, equipment and sanitary materials. In practice, they had to rely on the goodwill of the quartermasters in the areas in which they were currently located and on the availability of stock in the quartermasters' warehouses. The effectiveness of a train depended not only on its technical condition and equipment but also on the morale of its crew, which was seriously undermined by the lack of cigarettes, clean underwear and soap and by the monotonous food. Although many of the region's inhabitants could only dream of having a comparable diet, crews complained about the unchanging food – lunches always consisting of the same ingredients cooked together (groats, peas, tinned meat) and breakfasts and dinners invariably accompanied by a slightly sweetened, but very bitter lupin coffee.[35]

But these were just the norms; what was abnormal was a commander unable to cope with them. Indeed, the examples of other sanitary units and facilities show that under similar conditions, with the same technical, supply, and transport problems, the condition of hospitals, sick rooms, staging points or epidemic columns could be diametrically different – from genuine centres for combating disease and providing medical assistance, through malingerers' hideouts and cold and hungry places of enforced isolation, to horrific dying rooms; and it largely depended on the competence, organizational skills and goodwill of the commanders. It is for this reason that the case of bathing and disinfection train no. 1 should be treated as an exception rather than the rule. A short excerpt from its history, which serves as an excellent pretext to reveal the complexity and scale of the problems its crew faced, still does not answer the question of whether the campaign to combat the epidemic, which, after all, was conducted across a much longer timeframe and by more units, was actually effective.

The answer to this lies hidden behind two facts. First, the woefully poor supply of uniforms and underwear and the terrible level of louse infestation persisted in the ranks of the Polish Army until the end of the war. Large-scale purchases of uniforms and underwear,[36] and the bathing and disinfection campaign described above, brought only short-term effects, which were effectively nullified by the dramatic twists and turns of the situation on the front – a quick march eastwards followed by an even faster retreat and counter-offensive. As a result – similarly to 1919 when they were attacking the Ukrainians in Volhynia and the Bolsheviks in Lithuania – in 1920, the Polish soldiers defended Warsaw in bare feet and in louse-infested uniforms that were full of holes[37] and hung off their naked bodies due to the absence of underwear which was not – as one of the peasant recruits[38] indecorously put it – 'farted into thin air'. Second, despite the measures taken, the army failed to defend itself successfully against the impact of the epidemic. The situation was most dramatic in 1919 when typhus no longer appeared only in the spring and autumn. In June alone, it infected more than 2,000 soldiers (the real number could be several times higher).[39] Throughout the year, tens of thousands of people fell ill, and at least several thousand died.[40]

In 1920 the situation improved. The campaign to combat the epidemic, pursued with desperate determination, brought some limited effects. It consisted of a multitude of individual measures – repeated attempts to organize a cordon, mass washing, shaving and delousing (in which the trains discussed here played an important role), and a pioneering, not very effective, but nonetheless large-scale campaign to vaccinate people against typhus.[41] As a result of these measures, the wave of infection within the army subsided, although the epidemic did not disappear completely. It continued to ravage the civilian population, especially in the countryside, and its tragic epilogue occurred after peace was signed, during the repatriation of hundreds of thousands of war refugees from the East.

The conclusions that can be drawn on the basis of the above findings, being the result of an imperfect interpretation of incomplete sources, may relate not just to the typhus-combating activities of bathing and disinfection trains but also to the entire campaign against the epidemic. Its effects were certainly disappointing – the plague could not be suppressed, and tens of thousands of people lost their lives. In the absence of personnel, disinfection, laundry and bathing equipment, clean underwear, fuel, medicines and crucially, a culture of hygiene – including a widespread lack of understanding among those at whom the campaign was directed as to why hygiene was important – louse infestation maintained a permanent presence in the Central European borderlands. Because manoeuvre warfare was the rule, and soldiers and civilians were in constant and close contact – in rural cottages, small-town lodgings, railway stations and trains – just a few hours after washing and changing their uniform, soldiers were at risk of catching fresh lice, and with them a potentially fatal disease.

On the other hand, without a wide range of measures, the plague would have in all likelihood taken many more lives. The hopeless struggles of 1918–1920, the trials and errors and the organizational and logistical failures prepared the ground for an effective plan of action and for suppression of the epidemic, which finally took place two years later, obviously in the much more favourable conditions of peace, relative stability and closed borders.

The phenomenon of bathing and disinfection trains also conceals something rather disturbing, which demands at least an attempt at explanation. The trains were designed to improve the general health of the people who used them and to keep the disease at bay, but in practice, as shown above, their effect was quite the opposite. Users had to undress in unheated carriages and rinse themselves in cold water due to the lack of soap, while their clothes and underwear – disinfected too quickly and at too low a temperature – were returned to them still louse-infested and dirty but now wet. All this usually took place in the harsh conditions of the Eastern European autumn or spring, not to mention winter. As a result, bathing offered no protection against typhus, but it did significantly increase the chances of catching a cold, or the flu, which was raging at that time. In many cases, the health of the unfortunate users of bathing and disinfection trains would have been better had the trains not been in service at all.

But despite this, the trains had to operate. In a political crisis, physical dirt, as well as a metaphorical and invisible impurity, became the focus of public attention – symbols of both the tangible material deficiencies and the moral or ethical dilemmas afflicting the community.[42] It is no accident that point no. 1 of the first joint order to be issued by the Ministries of Public Health and Internal Affairs called upon all inhabitants of the Polish state to 'comprehensively and thoroughly cleanse themselves, as well as their apartments, appliances, clothes and linens, of dirt and vermin'.[43] These words were an instruction but also an entreaty and an example of wishful thinking. The campaign to combat the epidemic, which absorbed a lot – and yet always too little – time, money and effort in war-ravaged and disease-infected Poland, was also the frontline in the battle to overcome the threats hanging over the safety and cohesion of the national state-building project: radical political ideas and national minorities. The former was embodied in the figures of Bolshevik invaders emerging from the steppes of 'big, dark, and half-wild Russia', the latter in the 'dirty, sloppy Jewish masses' and Christian Orthodox inhabitants of the eastern borderlands.[44] As Katherina Kreuder-Sonnen notes, in Polish medical and sanitary discourse, all these groups were quickly associated with the spread of the typhus epidemic.[45]

This 'comprehensive and thorough cleansing' had to start somewhere. In a daily reality collapsing under the weight of shortages, the introduction of a coherent and complete system, such as that postulated in the theoretical operating principles of bathing and disinfection trains, was impossible. It became the norm to select individual elements of that system more or less at random, without paying attention to its glaring and sometimes dangerous shortcomings – such as a cold shower in the middle of winter – which undermined its whole purpose.[46]

Visits to hairdressing and bathing cars were not only unhealthy but also unpleasant and painful. Blunt clippers used by an untrained hand caused wounds, ointments and disinfectants irritated and stung the skin, and for many the act of publicly exposing or losing hair or stubble was humiliating or contrary to religious beliefs. Because the vigorous execution of sanitary procedures required discipline, and the procedures themselves concerned exposed areas of the body that were sensitive for every human being, they shifted from the sphere of hygiene to the sphere of social discipline, in other words, to the main protagonist of this volume – biopolitics. Activities carried out on trains, as well as in public bathhouses, sanitary columns or quarantine stations, quickly degenerated into acts of violence, both symbolic and physical.

At that time and place, arbitrary force was the most common method of governance. With the weakening, and then complete collapse, of the monopoly on violence exercised by the states of the *ancien régime*, violence came within reach of most of the players in the political landscape. Contrary to the propagandist claims made by both sides, its 'red' version was by no means a response to the 'white' version and vice versa. The construction of revolutionary states and nationalist states was a symmetrical process; in both cases, the pretenders assumed power not just by brute force[47] but also by whipping up a cyclone of terror and brutalizing successive areas of public life. They tried to regain the monopoly on coercion that wielding power entailed, and it was no different in the sphere of hygiene and epidemiology – the sanitary procedures detailed above seem to be the perfect means of enforcing obedience.

Several months earlier, at the other end of the world, Chinese volunteers from the Chinese Labour Corps departing for Europe underwent a procedure similar to that practised on Polish bathing and disinfection trains. The volunteers were stripped naked, shaved completely bald, including having their traditional Manchurian braids cut, and then bathed, or rather immersed, in a bathtub filled with cold water mixed with disinfectant. This was meant to transform the dirty and epidemiologically dangerous 'coolies' into members of the human race. The procedure, which British overseers armed with clubs dubbed the 'sausage machine', helps us to visualize the brutality with which it was enforced. In order to understand what those who were subjected to it thought, one can look to another example, which was not very far removed geographically or temporally.[48]

Created and equipped by the American Red Cross, the Inter-Allied Typhus Train, or the 'Great White Train' as it came to be known, operated on railway lines in Siberia between February 1919 and May 1920, carrying out the same mission as the Polish bathing and disinfection trains. It differed from them in one respect – the composition also included an ambulance car and a pharmacy. The crew, which, apart from the technical staff, consisted of both American and Russian medical personnel – doctors, nurses and field surgeons – could thereby directly fight the symptoms of typhus and not just the lice that heralded its arrival. During one year of its operation across a gigantic area stretching from Vladivostok on the Pacific coast to Omsk, now on the border with Kazakhstan, the train provided medical assistance, clothing, as well as delousing, bathing, and shaving facilities to over a million people. Despite this, one of the members of the crew, a doctor, noted with bitterness in his journal that help had to be imposed on the Russians by force. Although huge numbers of soldiers and civilians passed through the showers and disinfection cars, many were simply forced to do so, and the sanitary procedures they found so alien, combined with the sense of superiority and patronizing attitude shown by the staff, were repaid with 'a deep, dark, wholehearted resentment'.[49]

During my archive research, I did not come across any reports or documents that would reveal what the Polish users of bathing and disinfection trains felt and thought, but the examples cited above – the Russian certainly more than the Chinese – may prove helpful in attempting to draw a final conclusion about the course and effectiveness of the fight against typhus, and not just on the railways. Since the attitude of Polish sanitary personnel to Jews and Ruthenians was often similar[50] to that of their British and American counterparts towards the Russians and Chinese, and the actions of both the civil and military administrations were characterized by increasing brutality, it must be assumed that at least some of the people who underwent disinfection and bathing procedures did so under duress. Aside from the chronic shortages of supplies and qualified personnel, the coercive, violent aspect of sanitary measures aimed at combating typhus was, therefore, another factor that had a major impact on their effectiveness.

Notes

1 This chapter was translated by Jasper Tilbury.

2 Michał Kopczyński, 'O kolei po kolei. Fascynujące dzieje pociągów, Pomocnik Historyczny', *Polityka* 6 (2015): 27.

3 Joseph Roth, *Listy z Polski* (Kraków, Budapest and Syracuse: Austeria, 2018), 30.

4 Ibid.

5 Ireneusz Bujniewicz, 'Kolejnictwo w przygotowaniach obronnych Polski w latach 1935–1939', in *Wojskowe Teki Archiwalne. Kolejnictwo w polskich przygotowaniach obronnych i kampanii wrześniowej*, vol. I, ed. Centralne Archiwum Wojskowe Instytut Polski i Muzeum im. gen. Sikorskiego (Warsaw: Centralne Archiwum Wojskowe, 2011), 10.

6 CAW, I.301.17.20, Zwalczanie tyfusu plamistego i masowe oczyszczanie ludności.

7 For more on the Spanish flu epidemic in Poland, see Łukasz Mieszkowski, 'A *Foreign Lady:* The Polish Episode in the Influenza Pandemic of 1918', URL: http://dx.doi.org/10.12775/APH.2016.113.08 (accessed 6 February 2020).

8 Paul Weindling, *Epidemics and Genocide in Eastern Europe 1890–1945* (Oxford and New York: Oxford University Press, 2000), 14–15.

9 Agnieszka Młódzik, 'Występowanie i zwalczanie duru plamistego na ziemiach litewsko-białoruskich w latach 1904–1920', *Archiwum historii i filozofii medycyny* 76, no. 1 (2013): 20.

10 The Sanitary Headquarters of the Supreme Army Command produced countless reports describing the typhus and louse-infested trains that travelled around the country in the years 1919–1920. See CAW I.301.19, vol. 9, Raport czynności za miesiąc kwiecień; Ibid., Telegram, CAW I.301.19, vol. 18, Transport chorych żołnierzy.

11 According to modern nomenclature, this term is incorrect. The eradication of harmful (from the human perspective) parasitic insects such as flies, mosquitoes, fleas, lice, bedbugs and cockroaches, as well as their eggs and larvae, is called *disinsectisation*. Disinfection is a procedure to remove microorganisms and their spores from objects and surfaces.
12 https://www.drehscheibe-online.de/foren/read.php?17,6339279 (accessed 13 October 2018).
13 I have not come across any cases of bathing trains being used by the Allied armies on the Western Front. The stationary nature of trench warfare made it possible to set up permanent bathhouses in close proximity to the front lines.
14 CAW I.301.19., vol. 1, Do Dowództwa Okręgu Generalnego.
15 The author of the account was an engineer by the name of Marie Adą (*sic*) – probably Adam Marie; his boss was Captain Kazimierz Bartel, whose success as head of the Armoured Train Construction Division brought him a promotion to the post of Minister of Railways and was the beginning of a political career that culminated in his appointment as prime minister on five occasions. CAW I.400.3195/92.
16 CAW I.301.19., vol. 82, Opis techniczny wojskowego pociągu dezynynfekc. kąpielowego.
17 Ibid.
18 CAW I.301.19., vol. 143. W sprawie urządzeń dezynfekcyjnych za pomocą pary i gorącego powietrza, w których parę sprowadza się z lokomotyw, a specjalnie urządzony wagon towarowy zastępuje komorę dezynfekcyjną.
19 Ibid.
20 CAW I.301.19., vol. 92, Do Naczelnego Dowództwa Szefostwa Sanitarnego.
21 CAW I.301.19., vol. 1, Do Naczelnego Dowództwa.
22 CAW I.301.19., vol. 87, Do Ministerstwa Spraw Wojskowych Oddział IV Kolejowy.
23 CAW I.301.19., vol. 3, Rozkaz nr 36.
24 CAW I.305.5., vol. 15, Do Sztabu generalnego Wojsk Polskich, Oddział III w Warszawie.
25 CAW I.301.19., vol. 82, Opis techniczny.
26 Elżbieta Więckowska, *Walka z ostrymi chorobami zakaźnymi w Polsce 1918–1924* (Wrocław: Akademia Medyczna we Wrocławiu, 1999), 191.
27 Precisely 134,057 soldiers of the Polish Army and 16,332 soldiers of the Ukrainian and Russian White Guards. Overall, the army numbered approximately 943,976 men. Lech Wyszczelski, *Wojna o polskie kresy 1918–1921* (Warsaw: Bellona, 2011), 385–386.
28 CAW I.301.19., vol. 143, Raport kpt. D-ra J. Przedborskiego z podróży inspekcyjnej na terenie D.O.W. Płoskirów odbytej łącznie z zastępcą Nacz. Nad. Kom. do spraw walki z epid. i ofic. łącznikowym misji wojsk. francuskiej mjr. D-r Roudouly, pp. 2–3.
29 Despite the fact that three months earlier the Polish Purchasing Mission had bought 500 million metres of thread in Paris. CAW I.301.19., vol. 90, Polska Misja Zakupowa w Paryżu, Raport Tygodniowy za czas od 7-go do 13-go Marca 1920 r., 8.
30 Ibid., 3.
31 It turned out that there was no soap for the soldiers in the entire district. There was none in the military hospital in Płoskirow nor, most importantly, in the army's central sanitary depot. This was due to changes in the regulations – the supply of soap was to be the responsibility of the army commissariat and not, hitherto, the job of the sanitary services. Yet the former was not up to the task. In the end, the Chief Commissariat handed over 200 kilograms of soap to the army from its own reserves. The cost of a patient's standard daily

meals in a military hospital was approximately 17 marks; for bathing and a change of underwear in the garrison, an officer paid 5 marks; and for half a kilo of soap on the free market, traders demanded 75 marks! Ibid., 4–8.

32 CAW I.301.19., vol. 84., Do sekcji kwaterunkowej.

33 CAW I.301.19., vol. 87, Tarnopol Szt. 1124 9.312.

34 Operating under the name of 'sanitary trains', they were used to transport sick and wounded soldiers from the front to facilities in the hinterland. They sometimes had cars adapted to carry out minor or major surgical procedures. Epidemic trains were used to transport people ill with infectious diseases.

35 CAW I.301.19., vol. 96, Zeznanie szereg. Józefa /kucharza/.

36 The Polish Army purchased over half a million uniforms and items of underwear during the war from the huge amount of supplies left in Europe by the American Expeditionary Corps. See Bolek Rosiński, 'Douhgboy w Wojsku Polskim 1918–1921', *Szabla i koń* 2, no. 5 (2012): 35.

37 Aleksander Smoliński, 'Początkowe dzieje barwy i symboliki strzelców podhalańskich oraz ich związki z kulturą ludową Podhala – lata 1918–1920: przyczynek do badań mundurologicznych i kostiumologicznych', *Czasy Nowożytne* 14 (2003): 126.

38 Jochen Boehler, *Wojna Domowa Nowe Spojrzenie na Odrodzenie Polski* (Krakow: Znak, 2018), 187–189.

39 Czesław Jeśman, *Choroby zakaźne w Wojsku Polskim w latach 1918–1939 jako zagadnienie epidemiologiczne i profilaktyczno-lecznicze* (Łódź: Wojskowa Akademia Medyczna, 1997), 57.

40 Ibid. The official figures mention 15,591 cases and 995 deaths, but these are estimates and are certainly understated.

41 Ibid., 64.

42 Włodzimierz Karol Pessel, *Antropologia nieczystości. Studia z kultury sanitarnej Warszawy* (Warsaw: Trio, 2010), 78.

43 Elżbieta Więckowska, 'Centralny Komitet do Walki z Durem Plamistym (1 sierpień 1919 – 5 marca 1920)', *Przegląd Epidemiologiczny* 52, no. 1–2 (1998): 206.

44 Katherina Kreuder-Sonnen, 'Epidemiological State-building in Interwar Poland: Discourses and Paper Technologies', *Science in Context* 32, no. 1 (2019): 47–48.

45 Ibid.

46 Pessel, *Antropologia nieczystości*, 78.

47 Jochen Boehler, Generals and Warlords, 'Revolutionaries and Nation-State Builders: The First World War and Its Aftermath in Central and Eastern Europe', in *Legacies of Violence. Eastern Europe's First World War*, eds. Jochen Böhler, Włodzimierz Borodziej and Joachim von Puttkamer (München: De Gruyter, 2014), 60–63.

48 Daryk, Coolie Labour Corps. 1. Haircutting; 2 Cleaning, from the *South China Morning Post* archives, URL: http://multimedia.scmp.com/ww1-china/ (accessed 20 February 2020).

49 Julia F. Irwin, 'The Great White Train: Typhus, Sanitation, and U.S. International Development during the Russian Civil War', *Endeavour* 36, no. 3 (2012): 95.

50 Aneta Prymaka-Oniszk, *Bieżeństwo 1915. Zapomniani uchodźcy* (Wołowiec: Czarne, 2016).

10 The Intricacies of Communist Biopolitics

Control of Disease and Epidemics in the Polish Countryside after 1945

Ewelina Szpak

Soon after the end of the Second World War,[1] discussions were taking place in the Polish Ministry of Health about the shape of the new healthcare system.[2] During the most chaotic period (1944–1947), which saw major epidemics take hold throughout Poland, officials realistically considered adopting a healthcare model based on the British system of the 1930s. The prevailing view was that healthcare should be introduced gradually to take account of the country's economic situation. It was to be based on sickness insurance, with coverage being gradually extended, and would involve the successive takeover of health institutions (health centres, delivery rooms, etc.) by local government.

However, this seemingly settled position changed with the adoption of a new, Stalinist course of state policy. In mid-1947, a bill drafted by a team led by the Deputy Minister (and later Minister) of Health, Jerzy Sztachelski, was passed into law. Under this legislation, the new system of healthcare was to be fully based on the Soviet model; the health service itself was to be free, comprehensive, and universal. Among other things, this meant abandoning the idea of a gradual roll-out of medical services; instead, everyone was to receive full healthcare coverage at the same time. The newly created system was centralized, bureaucratic, and subject to the powerful influence of the communist party.[3] Social and charitable organizations, which had hitherto enjoyed autonomy in the area of healthcare, as well as private healthcare services and those provided by social insurers, were taken over by the state. All aspects of healthcare thus came under total state control. They were an important element of the new, centrally controlled, socialist social policy, which included elements of Foucauldian biopolitics and biopower.

As the future post-war system of healthcare was being debated in the ministries, a profound social change was taking place in the Polish countryside. The liquidation of large, landed estates and the creation of new farms (the agrarian reform) thoroughly transformed the existing social structure in rural areas, causing, among other things, mass population movements. The scale of Poland's post-war destruction, as well as poverty and the outbreaks of typhus, scarlet fever, diphtheria, tuberculosis and venereal disease

DOI: 10.4324/9781003161080-13

that accompanied it, affected the health of rural inhabitants too. With the increasing mobility of the peasant population, the problem became all the more acute, especially as habits related to hygiene and disease prevention left much to be desired. Furthermore, rural inhabitants' access to healthcare, which was conditioned by the pre-war (and even more so by the post-war) situation, remained very limited. As shown by rural diaries from the 1930s and 1940s and by accounts from the early 1950s, the need for contact with healthcare facilities was also limited, as peasants often mentioned. Despite the presence of ad hoc 'anti-epidemic columns', which from time to time reached epidemic-stricken rural settlements and regions, in many such places (especially in south-eastern Poland), it was still common for people to self-medicate, seek the advice of local quacks and faith healers and refuse to cooperate with the employees of 'anti-epidemic columns'.[4]

That orders issued by the employees of 'anti-epidemic columns' were often ignored was an effect of low health awareness among the peasant population. This resulted not so much from what the propaganda of the time termed the 'civilizational backwardness' of the Polish countryside as from the consequences of the entire health policy towards rural areas (biopolitics) hitherto pursued by the Polish state, and therefore also by the pre-war state.

For although, even prior to the First World War, each of the three partitioning powers[5] implemented its own system of rural healthcare, its availability to the average peasant was often highly debatable. During the interwar period, which saw the standardization of social policy and the dismantling of the institutional and organizational legacy of the partition era, the rural healthcare system was mainly based on so-called sickness funds (and, from the 1930s, on 'social insurers'), which mainly covered wealthy farmers and their employees on account of the high costs involved. A programme to create district health centres, introduced in the Polish provinces from the 1930s, did little to remedy the situation. The same could be said of 'health cooperatives', that is, grassroots rural healthcare institutions financed from peasant contributions, of which around only eight were established.[6]

At the dawn of the People's Republic of Poland, grassroots interest in healthcare seemed to be on the back burner. The countryside, for centuries accustomed to taking health matters into its own hands, likewise did not seem to notice when, in 1948, it was excluded from the newly introduced system of free, comprehensive, and supposedly universal healthcare.[7] In public discourse, this exclusion was put down to ideology (and to the promotion of a 'modern', socialist, collectivized and nationalized countryside). In reality, however, the reasons for excluding peasant farmers from free healthcare were more prosaic and had to do with the need to adapt the system to the economic possibilities of the post-war state. The healthcare model being implemented at the time did not allow for immediate coverage of the whole Polish population. Since rural inhabitants accounted for almost 70 per cent of the national population at the end of the 1940s,[8] their partial exclusion from the full range of benefits was a common-sense political strategy. The economic and – from 1948 – also ideological justification for this strategy was expressed in the slogan of the struggle for the socialist reconstruction of the countryside, in which 'the health service should play an active role, providing care in areas with collectivized agriculture above all others .... Creating appropriate sanitary conditions on collective farms is, in the present era of struggle for the socialization of the countryside, not only important in terms of health, but also has political significance'.[9]

The two groups excluded from the context of the aforementioned struggle were children of individual farmers under the age of 14 and peasant women who were pregnant or in childbirth.[10] This is because their protection fell within one of the social policy priorities of the post-war socialist state, i.e. care for mothers and children.[11]

This peculiar game of power through the medium of 'healthcare' is an interesting example of biopolitics, that is, the application in practice by the nascent totalitarian state of elements of biopower, the purpose of which, as Michel Foucault emphasized, is to 'to ensure, sustain, and multiply life'[12] in a given population. Biopower, which realizes itself through medicalization in the broad sense, and which expresses itself through the creation of new institutions as well as new social practices and mental habits, 'normalizes' society by promoting 'the practice of caring for oneself and others, making live, and letting die'.[13] As Piotr Kępski points out, 'biopower usually employs the discourse of security understood in the broad sense (protection, prevention)'.[14] In the social policy discourse of the People's Republic, the concepts of 'security' and 'care' provided by the state were of particular importance. Universal healthcare, generally accessible thanks to new institutions, combined with an extensive package of other social benefits, was to be one of the fundamental achievements of the socialist state, reflective of its caring attitude towards society.

This article attempts to show how communist biopolitics, as defined above, was implemented in practice in the Polish countryside after 1945, which tools were used, and which actors involved. In the countryside's new and dynamically changing post-war social and cultural environment, what was the role played by the diverse group of newly established healthcare institutions and their often sudden incursion into rural life?

My starting point, therefore, is the question of the social relations and reactions that resulted from the health policy implemented over successive decades. How did rural inhabitants respond to plans – both consulted and imposed – to protect and sustain their lives and well-being? To what extent was the state's offer perceived in terms of coercion and oppression, and to what extent was it genuinely desired? Was it achievable in practice, or it just another projection of a utopian, socialist reality?

In my analysis of biopolitics in the countryside, I focus on three main actors involved in the changes and transformations taking place. Firstly, tracing the reactions that emerge from the source materials, I focus on the rural population itself, which was heterogeneous in terms of gender, material (and cultural) status, geography and generational affiliation.

Secondly, and in parallel, I investigate two other groups of actors. The first comprises representatives of central government policy (both decision-makers in Warsaw and people in local health departments responsible for implementing programmes at the district and municipal level), while the second is an intermediate group situated between government and society – principally the doctors and medical staff employed in rural health institutions.

Medicalization of the Social and Cultural Environment

Immediately after the war, when the new healthcare system was being established in the countryside, there was initial support for the idea of reviving the pre-war health cooperatives, and indeed, in the face of rampant epidemics, they received a degree of public funding. However, when the decision was taken to introduce a healthcare system following the Soviet model, the role of health cooperatives diminished. They were forced to dissolve and to have their assets transferred to state institutions, namely, health centres and first aid stations run by doctors and feldshers (medical or surgical practitioners without full professional qualifications).

First aid stations were created mainly in the early 1950s and the process was very chaotic. Although in line with ideological assumptions, these institutions were to be established first of all in areas where agriculture was collectivized (farming cooperatives – RSP) or nationalized (state collective farms – PGR), regardless of criticism from the central authorities and given the lack of suitable real estate, health centres were usually located in the larger and wealthier villages which had more or less adequate infrastructure.

In fact, until the late 1960s, it was extremely rare for a health centre to be built from scratch. They were usually located in adapted buildings that were not fully functional and where the sanitary conditions were less than optimal. The problems most frequently mentioned by health centre staff were insufficient heating, dampness, poor window insulation, and limited access to hot water (especially running water). In the first post-war decade, these institutions and other in-patient healthcare facilities were usually located in the manors and palaces of the former gentry or in larger houses, some of which were leased from local landlords. Other abandoned, dilapidated, and unused spaces were sometimes adapted to accommodate health centres (the former parish building in the village of Siedliszcze being one example).

Interestingly, many of the centres, although ordained by the central government, were built with the enormous dedication and involvement of local communities, which carried out the renovation and construction work as part of so-called 'social actions and deeds'.[15] However, such engagement in the creation of rural health facilities was not necessarily reflected in their subsequent use. This was witnessed first-hand by Dr Aleksander Bałasz, who came up with the idea of establishing a delivery room for pregnant women in Siedliszcze and who was principally responsible for organizing it. Despite being a modern facility, the delivery room stood empty for several weeks after its opening.[16]

Many of the health centres created in this way likewise had to wait weeks before welcoming their first patients. And even when patients did show up, their visits were few and far between. As the source materials from the south-eastern regions of Poland show, this problem was especially pronounced in the case of health centres located in premises let by local village residents. In 1958, in the district of Lubartów (eastern Poland), one of the centres was accommodated inside 'rented premises comprising two rooms, one designated as a surgery and the other as a waiting room. The centre is separated from the landlord's apartment by a door that does not shut properly'.[17]

Rickety doors and less-than-soundproof walls, especially when a patient was diagnosed with a 'shameful disease' (in rural areas, this included not just venereal diseases but also tuberculosis, which was extremely common at the time), could often have far-reaching social consequences, determining an individual's status and causing them to become indefinitely stigmatized within their local community. Having been diagnosed with a venereal disease, the 19-year-old heroine of a radio reportage from 1968 learned just how painful the consequences of a lack of doctor–patient privacy could be:

> [At the clinic] the nurse told my mum [about the disease], at which point the doctor shouted at the nurse, telling her that I was, after all, an adult and that my mother shouldn't have been told. People were no doubt curious and put their ears to the door to find out what all the fuss was about. Mum kicked me out of the house. To this day, I still have the marks on my forehead where she hit me. Two scars. I didn't go home for two weeks ... the only person who came to visit me in hospital was my sister. Every day I am reminded about what happened ... When people see me, they say: ooh, look, here comes the clap! They call me the worst possible names. The whole town does it. It's as if I'd been with a hundred men, but I only had one. It's difficult to live here now.[18]

This rather extreme example of the brutal encroachment of institutions into the privacy of individuals – an extremely sensitive area because it carried the risk of social rejection – revealed first and foremost the destructive power and influence that new institutions could have on the fabric of social relations in the countryside. As in the case of the young woman described above, a diagnosis made public, even if unintentionally, could wreak havoc not only within close family relationships but also within the broader social context.

Some members of the rural population were, of course, aware of these potential consequences. As doctors at the time testified, in the 1940s and 1950s, health centres, like local hospitals and delivery rooms, were regarded by many as a last resort. Rather than visit such places, people would self-medicate, ignore less troublesome ailments or, at least up until the 1960s, rely on the services of various local practitioners of 'folk' (i.e. unscientific) medicine, such as 'sorcerers', 'bone setters', 'blacksmiths' and 'shepherds'.[19] People would usually only visit a doctor when all the aforementioned 'traditional methods' had failed and the patient's condition had become acute.

What is interesting, however, is that in such cases, many villagers would avoid their local health centre and go directly to a doctor in the nearest town. As Ministry of Health documents reveal, in 1955, more than half of the rural population seeking medical consultation visited health facilities in towns and cities rather than local ones, as the former offered a greater chance of anonymity.[20]

People's reluctance to visit rural health centres was a huge problem for the central authorities. On the one hand, it exposed the ineffectiveness of the system, and on the other hand, it meant that the health of rural inhabitants was clearly beyond the state's control. However, poor attendance was not solely due to the ignorance of peasants or their distrust of local institutions. The very uneven distribution of healthcare facilities in the 1940s and 1950s meant that in some regions, there were simply too few of them or they were located too far away from the villages they were meant to serve. In the late 1950s and early 1960s, the number of rural inhabitants per local health centre (i.e. per doctor) often exceeded 20,000 or even 30,000 in the more neglected regions – for instance, around the cities of Olsztyn and Cracow (the accepted norm at the time was 4,000 to 5,000). Fewer health centres also meant greater distances; it was not uncommon for peasants to travel 30 or 40 km in order to visit their nearest centre.[21] Given that the principal mode of transportation in the countryside in the 1950s and 1960s was the horse-drawn cart and that local roads were often impassable during the spring thaw and in periods of heavy snow or rain, the situation often became quite dramatic. Even if a health centre (or a first aid station staffed by a doctor or feldsher) was 10 or 15 km away, reaching it in such conditions entailed not only huge effort but also considerable cost (not all farmers had horses, carts, etc.).

Considering the circumstances of rural health centres described above (long distances, poor infrastructure, low attendance, staff shortages) and the generally distrustful attitude of peasants towards state institutions in the 1950s,[22] it is quite obvious that in the first decade of the People's Republic the Ministry of Health and other central government institutions had little or very limited knowledge of the actual health situation in rural areas. Most of the figures analyzed at the Ministry of Health were based on reports from field trips undertaken by ministry officials and reports prepared from the 1950s onwards by local health department representatives in collaboration with local health facilities.

In the latter's records, irrespective of the region (province), an oft-repeated mantra was the lack of medical staff or their high turnover.[23] As the data analyzed in Warsaw showed, the majority of village health centres were staffed by feldshers, who, as graduates of two- or three-year college courses, often had superficial medical knowledge and were unaware of the latest advances in medicine, and whose treatment methods were frequently disapproved of by physicians. In 1955, one sanitary station director summarized the problems with feldshers as follows:

> At one point the ministry sought to resolve its staffing problems and set up feldsher colleges. These young people are victims of their own profession. Indeed, the health service bears much of the blame for not training them properly. The feldsher is a loose cannon. Weekly consultations are a fiction, and there is a great deal of bitterness on their part. What next? For two years they were told that they were going to be doctors. Yesterday we heard that they treat every runny nose with penicillin.[24]

Although the skills of feldshers varied across the country (many of them went on to pursue full medical degrees in the academies of the day), as a rule, their position and social status in the countryside were somewhat different to that of physicians. Both in their treatment methods and, above all, in the way they communicated with patients, feldshers were often closer to rural patients than doctors were. Indeed, especially in the 1960s and 1970s, when the problem of local medical staff was somewhat less acute and the provinces became increasingly 'saturated' with medical academy graduates, acrimonious personal disputes between feldshers and physicians working in the same health centre (or region) were quite frequent. These tensions usually revolved around status and competence issues, and in any conflict, it was important for the opposing parties to win the support of the local community and local decision-makers.[25]

However, during the 1940s and 1950s – the most difficult period in terms of the availability of medical staff and the scale of the epidemiological threat – the presence of feldshers in the Polish provinces, regardless of how skilled they were, was vital. Feldshers sometimes offered the only chance of saving a life – for instance, that of a mother in labour or someone with a serious disease – or at least of establishing the cause of death. In my opinion, it is this last issue which exposes the problems of communist biopolitics in relation to the countryside most strikingly. Although the data collected in registers compiled for the Ministry of Health showed that in terms of morbidity and death from infectious diseases, the figures for rural and urban areas were quite similar, a closer analysis of the statistics concerning the causes of all deaths in the countryside revealed significant gaps. Indeed, this was confirmed by the medics who worked there: 'The sick mostly die and no one visits the doctor. Judging from the death certificate form, the cause of death is established by some sort of "corpse inspector", recalled one doctor in the 1960s, adding: Who is this? The village elder? The head of the local village council? ... I have no idea. In any case, these "corpse inspectors" don't seem to harbour the same objections a doctor would. In this respect, our public administration is hardly demanding'.[26]

The absence of physicians in the countryside in the 1940s and 1950s was not solely due to wartime losses or a lack of interest in 'field work'. The causes of the problems lay much deeper, also stemming from the ambivalent and sometimes ignorant attitude of local authorities to health issues and to the challenges faced by people who worked in the local (provincial) health service. As for example, reports from the Gdansk province in 1949 show, there were 'numerous misunderstandings between the managers of health centres and the municipal authorities, who want to make the centres completely subordinate to them and require the managers to perform various duties which have nothing to do with the activities of the centre'.[27] The situation in many areas remained tense well into the following decade,[28] which made the presence of trainee feldshers in the countryside all the more justified. However, this did not mean that they, too, did not encounter incomprehension on the part of the local authorities.

The lack of understanding that local decision-makers showed towards the activities, initiative, and often enormous effort of doctors, nurses, and more active feldshers often left them feeling very frustrated. An interesting example of this is a story about how mass vaccinations were organized at the time, as recalled by one of the nurses involved: 'On one occasion, when I arrived at a village and asked to see the premises where the vaccinations were to take place the following day, the village elder led me to the hen house. He didn't understand what I meant. He had been expecting a vet to come by in order to vaccinate the chickens'.[29]

Being a consequence of such difficulties and organizational problems, the disappointing results of mass vaccinations and the poor attendance of rural inhabitants at health centres – seen from the vantage point of the central government – revealed the low effectiveness of the medicalization effort begun in 1948. Medicalization was understood not only as the saturation of rural areas with health institutions and the dissemination of basic medical knowledge in everyday practice but also as the gradual creation of new everyday habits and ways of 'managing' one's own body and physicality.

Poor attendance at rural health centres became a subject of increasing debate at the Ministry of Health in the early 1950s. At the central level, officials began to realize that existing health policy in regard to rural areas was proving to be a failure. An analysis of the statistics shows that rural areas remained beyond the control of the health authorities at least until 1952/53, and it was not until 1954/1955 that a division into rural and urban areas was introduced into healthcare reporting for the first time.[30] In 1956, during a meeting at the Ministry of Health, it was admitted that 'the development of the health service in the first decade has not kept pace with the development of the countryside, particularly with the development of collectivized agriculture – which is manifested, among others, in the often haphazard location of rural health facilities, and in too much emphasis being placed on their quantity, while neglecting the quality of the services provided.'[31]

Building the Foundations of Biopolitics

In the early 1950s, the central authorities knew the health situation in rural areas was beyond the full control of the state. This, combined with the infectious disease epidemics that were raging across the country at that time (polio, diphtheria, tuberculosis), made it obvious that the state had to intensify its efforts aimed at taking control of this aspect of life in the Polish countryside. The collection of biological data required major improvement.

During the interwar period and before it, records were kept of the number of births and deaths in the countryside, but more specific data concerning, for instance, morbidity, mortality and the causes of death among the rural population remained largely unavailable. After 1945, if only due to the enormous scale of the epidemic outbreaks, the collection of such data became increasingly necessary, and this was to be carried out with the aid of both stationary facilities (health centres, delivery rooms) and mobile ones. Among the latter, a special role was played by ambulances, reactivated after the war, which was *de facto* travelling institutions that performed basic diagnostic tests (screening, X-rays) and provided basic medical and dental services.

Ambulances had their origins in the interwar period,[32] but at that time, they were somewhat experimental (participating in campaigns to combat tuberculosis); it was only after the Second World War that they were introduced on a larger scale and began to enjoy interest among the rural population. As they were able to reach the more remote regions, these 'institutions' gradually became another tool for collecting data about the health of the rural population, and the diagnoses made by ambulance staff often influenced the subsequent treatment of patients.[33]

In the 1950s, a similar role, albeit on a smaller and more local scale, was played by student camps, which were *de facto* student internships that usually took place in the summer holidays. They were organized by, among others, the medical universities in Lublin, Szczecin and Łódź. Participants were tasked with performing diagnoses and administering first aid, observing the hygiene practices of rural residents, and collecting materials for scientific papers on sanitary and hygiene conditions in the Polish countryside in particular.[34] On several occasions, student groups were also stationed in housing estates affiliated to collective farms, but this was not the rule. The results of the research conducted by the Lublin team show that the attitude of rural residents towards such initiatives was positive; however, as one participant of a camp near Lublin in 1958 noted, 'there was much resistance among that section of the population that was to participate in the research, especially men who were healthy or who had no particular ailments'.[35]

Despite the activities of the above-mentioned institutions from the late 1940s onwards, data collection encountered many problems. However, the process of acquiring knowledge about the health of the rural population improved significantly after 1952 when it came to be coordinated principally by the Institute of Rural Medicine, an institution established by a team of doctors and scientists led by Dr Witold Chodźko, a physician, community worker, and the first minister of public health in the interwar period. The institute Chodźko created (which in 1955 assumed the name of the Institute of Occupational Medicine and Rural Hygiene) became directly subordinate to the minister of health and social welfare; it thus gained independence and legal personality, *de facto* determining rural health policy over the decades to follow. From the outset, the Lublin-based institute pursued activities aimed at 'recognizing the specific health needs of the rural population' and proposed ways to address them.[36] The staff included specialists in general hygiene, food hygiene and sanitary education, as well as physicians specializing in the treatment of zoonoses and diseases related to farm work. From the 1960s, the institute carried out research on the introduction of the hitherto non-existent category of rural occupational diseases, becoming the most important expert institution in the area of rural health.[37] It supported all kinds of informational and educational activities related to the promotion of hygiene and health culture in the countryside, such as health weeks, White Sundays,[38] etc.

Knowledge Transmission: Strategies of Reaching the 'Masses' and Public Reactions

As an expert institution, the Institute of Rural Medicine also coordinated work carried out under the rural hygiene programme, which was launched in 1958 in the Poznań province by a group of public-spirited doctors and hygienists who, in cooperation with local health departments, began to establish rural hygiene committees.[39] This initiative was quickly picked up by the hygienists at the Lublin institute, who gradually rolled it out across the whole country. As a social movement, however, hygienization developed somewhat unevenly, with the best results being achieved in the Poznań, Cracow, Lublin and Olsztyn provinces. The pace and intensity of the work did not only differ between regions but often also within a single province or district. Several factors played an important role in this regard: the attitude of the local community, the available infrastructure, and also the presence of the supporters, leaders, and driving forces behind the programme. Of considerable importance, too, was the attitude of local authorities. The latter was supported by the State Sanitary Inspectorate established in 1954[40] (a sort of sanitary police able to impose criminal sanctions for failure to follow guidelines) and the Act on the Maintenance of Order and Cleanliness in Towns, Cities and Housing Estates, implemented after 1959, which promoted the idea of establishing rural hygiene committees at the provincial and district level. Involved in the work of the committees were local organizations such as the Rural Housewives' Association and the Union of Rural Youth.

Diverse activities were carried out under the hygienization programme. They included the establishment of health schools and a return to the idea of competitions, propagated in the 1930s, as well as support for the creation, construction, and renovation of state and cooperative health centres and other institutions supporting sanitary education (including rural hygiene centres, bathhouses and bathing areas). In order for the programme to be successful, however, the involvement of a local activist, community worker, or physician was essential. Health schools in particular – which taught 'habits, customs, and behaviours in the field of medicine and hygiene and addressed issues related to personal hygiene, food hygiene, physical and mental development, family planning, first aid, the principles of communal hygiene, and occupational health and safety'[41] – evoked a range of attitudes among rural residents. Organized in the autumn and winter, health schools usually took the form of lectures, talks, and training sessions given by specialists representing various medical and para-medical professions (doctors, dentists, nurses, hygiene instructors and feldshers).

While in some villages, such meetings were treated as cultural events, accompanied by food and fun,[42] which relieved the tedium of the late autumn evenings, in other villages, they were met with indifference.[43] In her memoirs, one nurse described her attempts to organize a meeting for peasant women on the subject of contraception:

> I gave a little talk about planned pregnancy, among other things. I showed them all the contraceptives and explained how they were used in practice. The participants patiently listened to what I said, but when I asked them if they would know how to use the contraceptives and whether they intended to use them, they replied: 'Madam, that's not how things are done in the countryside! We don't use the rhythm method around here. When a man wants it, you have to give it to him. There's no time to use other methods'.[44]

Interestingly, although hygiene education was often conducted without age restrictions, in the 1950s in particular, rural customs and cultural norms influenced (at least to some degree) the gender and age composition of audiences. As another nurse recalled, the attendance of young girls at the talks was not well received: 'Unfortunately, the older women are not very pleased that girls as young as sixteen are coming to listen to lectures about human development or construction. At times they stare menacingly at the younger ones, as if to say: how dare you attend this course! In their view, young people should only learn about things after they get married'.[45]

Cultural norms and customs, as well as generational differences in world-views, became increasingly apparent, at once revealing the scale of rural resistance to change and the unwillingness to accept new knowledge and social practices. Indeed, this did not only apply to activities that were part of the rural hygiene programme. Attitudes of active resistance or passive detachment surfaced at various times and in various places, beginning in the late 1940s and early 1950s, and were usually associated with the entry of new institutions (health centres, delivery rooms, rural hygiene centres), knowledge or new practices into the countryside.

Tensions reached their apex during visits to health centres. These were often obligatory for rural residents employed in the collectivized or nationalized agricultural sector, for pregnant women and mothers of small children, and also for all people (including the uninsured) who were exposed to infectious diseases. And although the greatest escalation of tensions was in the 1950s, many health-related frictions and antagonisms between rural patients and health centre staff were also present in later decades due to the slow roll-out of in-patient healthcare facilities in the countryside.

A careful analysis of several of these conflict situations reveals that both sides used a variety of defensive strategies and pushed the boundaries in different ways. The accounts of doctors and nurses who carried out home visits during a polio epidemic say a lot about the attitude of rural residents towards the dissemination of biological knowledge and orders from above. One of them recalled:

> After going around the whole village, I went back to the house [where a mother had not wanted to talk to the doctor – E. Sz.]. Although I was received coldly and distrustfully, she allowed me to enter ... I decided to go to the room where the children were lying. And that is when things erupted: 'You are not allowed to go near the children,' shouted the mother, 'they are frightened of you! I know because I checked by pouring wax onto water through the twigs of my broomstick, and you know what I saw? A woman made of wax with a thermometer in her hand!' ... I didn't know what to say. I began to feign interest in her story and continued the conversation in a similar vein ... that I would like to see her pour wax onto water and learn how to do it myself ... my ostensibly good intentions were taken seriously and the woman not only agreed to demonstrate how to break spells and remove curses, but also allowed me to approach the sick children and even to call an ambulance. As it turned out, the children were suffering from Heine-Medina disease [polio] in the pre-paralytic phase.[46]

Other doctors, too, used similar strategies to convince reluctant parents to protect their children from polio, diphtheria, and other diseases. In another example, a doctor is driven to despair by her own failure to mobilize a community for vaccination:

> I resort to lying. I tell a patient I know well, in confidence, that the vaccine is in short supply and that there is not enough to go around. I tell her that she should inform her sister and her next-door neighbour, but no one else. The outcome? People are falling over themselves to get the vaccine as if they were trying to buy lemons in the city. After all, every neighbour has another neighbour – why would they not want to impress them with secrets from the health centre? ... I tell them that there is a medicine that will prevent their children from becoming paralysed. I say that a plane has arrived with that medicine, and that if they don't show up tomorrow, the medicine will have to be returned and sent to another province. What happened next is difficult to describe. Two of us were performing the vaccinations, each in a different village ... Children were handed to us through the window. People queued from dawn. Some children were brought in from other areas where vaccines were available, but where there had been no propaganda.[47]

In 1966, the journal *Medycyna Wiejska* [rural medicine] published the recollections of another doctor, who also mentioned the problem of communication:

> You have to know how to talk to country people. They are prickly and easily offended. You can't lecture them in a condescending way. You have to be able to admit they are right and at the same time show the error of their thinking. There is an art to it, and like all the arts, it can be learned. You have to respect the person, not their uniform or their position. You have to try to understand them, to understand their point of view. Once you have gained the confidence of country people, there is a lot you can do with them ...[48]

Verbal persuasion or some form of negotiation with recalcitrant patients was not, however, always sufficient. There were also occasions when, out of concern for their patients' health (or wishing to follow the medical knowledge available to them at the time), doctors resorted to more violent strategies. Elements of symbolic violence are clearly present in the account of another doctor from the 1970s:

> Sometimes it would drive us crazy. We tried various arguments, which included referring them to the priest. On one occasion a mother did not want to send her child to hospital. It was the middle of the night, pitch black, with just an oil lamp for illumination. I stood there and said: 'Woman, this is a small child; it will die, and that innocent little

> soul is going to be wailing and rattling its chains under your window at midnight'. 'Doctor... No! Please, No!', replied the horrified woman. She was practically kissing my hands. In the end she agreed to hand over the child. But cajoling and persuading someone like that is tedious and difficult. Not everyone does it, especially after being on call for several hours.[49]

Nevertheless, the methods used by doctors, the main implementers of biopolitics at the time, to break rural resistance or to win the trust of rural patients took into account, to some degree, the needs and cultural boundaries (differences) of Polish society. In some cases, however, respect for a patient's wishes or cultural differences could be trumped by the doctor's attitude resulting from his medical knowledge and education. In such cases, the doctor would, in accordance with the Hippocratic Oath, prioritize the life and health of the patient regardless of the latter's beliefs. And although the beliefs of rural residents and the way they perceived many phenomena related to health and hygiene underwent a degree of transformation due to medicalization and the impact of the rural hygiene programme, in many areas, they remained resistant to new knowledge and change at least until the end of the 1970s. Judging from the complaints made by doctors at the time, the areas most resistant to change included: self-medication, the arbitrary use of medicines found in first-aid kits or the improper dosing of medicines, the persistence of many common names of diseases (e.g. croup[50] or whooping cough[51]) and, finally, the persistence of beliefs about the point at which an illness can be ascertained as a fact and what constitutes a disease as such.

As can be seen, rural doctors, who were the creators of the new biopolitics (through the Institute of Rural Medicine in Lublin) but who also implemented it in practice together with local medical staff, were the most active participants in the process of medicalization, the pace of which was determined on the one hand by the administrative, institutional, and economic support of the state, and on the other by the attitude of rural society itself. The central authorities supported and controlled the rural health policy created by specialists and regulated its direction and scope primarily by means of ordinances and legislation. This could be seen in the ordinances on sanitation and public order (e.g. the establishment in 1954 of the State Sanitary Inspectorate, whose purpose was to support the activities of the Lublin Institute), in the legislation that gradually allowed farm owners to receive free hospital and sanatorium treatment (e.g. the right to sanatorium treatment for tuberculosis, which was free from 1959 onwards), and finally in the extension of the full package of free health services (hospital treatment, free prescriptions, etc.) to the rural population.

However, for economic reasons and contrary to their own propaganda, the central authorities would often also support or accept a state of affairs that was inadequate from the point of view of academic medical knowledge and expertise. One example was their attitude towards the problem of rural births. Just after the war, given the enormous scale of the phenomenon of *babkarstwo*[52] as well as the abortion 'epidemic', proactive administrative measures were undertaken to track down and punish people unlawfully engaged in delivering babies or performing abortions.[53] In the 1940s and 1950s, eradicating non-professional midwifery was not easy for other reasons too: staff shortages, the reluctance of medical personnel to work in rural areas, and the influence of local loyalties and social ties. As the materials from field inspections carried out during this period show, local authorities, faced with insufficient staff numbers and a lack of suitable premises that could serve as delivery rooms, often turned a blind eye to the activities of unqualified midwives. In 1948, the author of one report described the phenomenon as follows: 'currently, the issue of unqualified rural midwives, whose activities in the municipalities have apparently been "legalised" by the tax administration because taxes are being collected from them, is continuing to take its toll. The authorities have a number of qualified midwives at their disposal, but they cannot be sent to work in the municipalities on account of the competition from unqualified rural midwives. The matter has even gone to court, but the midwife concerned was allowed to go free'.[54]

Although the eradication of non-professional midwifery and quackery was one of the priorities of rural policy (biopolitics), certain inconsistencies appeared at the administrative level. These were exposed by one of the doctors interviewed for a 1963 radio reportage who described the disastrous consequences of the activities of one local quack: 'We do not know exactly how many quack-doctors are operating in Poland today ... what we know for sure is that a few of them at least are officially paying taxes. They are classified as "artisan bone setters", and the tax office is perfectly happy with that'.[55]

However, the medical community itself, to a certain extent and often solely for financial gain, also collaborated with the shrinking (or increasingly secretive) 'quack underground'. Physicians would sometimes make characteristic modifications to their illegal private practices, as is shown by the case of the doctor cited below, which was by no means an isolated case:

> Dr Trześniewski took a completely different approach to people. He set up residence in the most distant village between Lipniaki and Szczuchnia and pretended to be a quack-doctor. He did not admit to having a medical degree, and offered rational treatments, albeit modified by quackery. The prescribed concoctions were to be mixed half-and-half with holy water and drunk three times a day with a wooden spoon. Powders had to be dissolved in pure water collected from a forest spring at full moon. To restore someone's vitality, a hen had to be slaughtered at midnight, cooked all day in a clay pot, and then fed to the sick person after sunset. News of the good doctor quickly spread,

> and within a few months he was treating half the province. However, the local militia got wind of the situation and the complaints started, so the quack-doctor came out of hiding, revealed who he was, and promptly disappeared.[56]

Another example of collaboration with the quack underground is the mechanism developed by the local community of the Podkarpacie region, described in the late 1970s by Stanisław Nowak, an ethnographer at the Jagiellonian University's Institute of Ethnography:

> Nowadays, the fact that people rely on quack doctors is kept secret ... the card on which the quack writes the patient's name and the remedies to be used is brought to the patient's home by an intermediary ... the card then has to be given to a genuine doctor so that he can rewrite it as a medical prescription. One hundred zlotys must be handed to the intermediary, and another hundred to the manager of the health centre in Czarny Dunajec, otherwise the doctor will not issue the prescription. The quack does not use herbal remedies, only products that are available in the pharmacy.[57]

Summary: The Negotiable Nature of Biopolitics in the People's Republic of Poland

Communist biopolitics in relation to the countryside was not an entirely new phenomenon. Its origins could be traced back to the 1930s, specifically to the activities of Marcin Kacprzak, Witold Chodźko, the Rockefeller Foundation, and others. In the 1950s, doctors, hygienists, and community workers – from 1952 integrated under the aegis of the Institute of Rural Medicine in Lublin – took inspiration from this earlier body of work.

Despite the establishment of a healthcare system based on the Soviet model and the 'ideological' exclusion of private farm owners, after 1953, and especially after 1956, when collectivization was abandoned, there was a concerted effort to expand the scope of healthcare and to exert greater biological control over rural society. This was manifested in the faster pace of medicalization (healthcare institutions, immunization, collection of population data) and hygienization.

In practice, the people mainly involved in performing this work were doctors and members of the medical community (nurses, feldshers, health centre personnel, ambulance workers), who cooperated to varying degrees with the central and local authorities. Decisions relating to biopolitics and the guidelines for its practical implementation were taken at the central level (committee meetings at the Ministry of Health) with the full participation of experts. The inconsistencies and difficulties in implementing central government decisions at the local level were usually related to the budgetary constraints of local decision-makers (municipalities) and/or their low awareness of health issues. This was reflected in the fact that the challenges of healthcare in rural areas were often belittled or ignored.

On the other hand, as the brief analysis above shows, although the people most actively involved in creating and implementing biopolitics in communist Poland were government officials and members of the medical community, rural residents also developed a degree of agency for themselves. Like many representatives of the local authorities, they often remained inconsistent in their attitude towards medicalization and hygienization, which were carried out with varying impetus across the regions. Having played an active role in building and establishing local institutions, such as delivery rooms or health centres, rural residents often maintained a distance towards them and were reluctant to use their services. The characteristic tensions and frictions that arose within health centres, first aid stations, or rural hospital rooms showed that peasants remained highly reactive to biopolitics implemented from above. Immunization and the hospitalization of births in the name of concern for the life and prospects of future generations were conditioned and explained by the fight against epidemics. However, it was not always an argument that persuaded rural residents to immediately change their own habits and beliefs concerning cleanliness and dirt (hygiene) or the essence and definition of disease. Their distrust meant that the healthcare professionals who encountered them often had to adopt certain negotiating strategies that involved improvisation or the use of different communication methods and language, which sometimes verged on symbolic violence or intimidation.

The negotiable and inconsistent nature of biopolitics in the People's Republic is also evidenced by the fairly persistent acceptance of folk medicine as an alternative to science-based medicine. This was expressed in a legislatively sanctioned tolerance for the activities of 'corpse inspectors', 'bone setters', poorly educated feldshers and 'legally' operating faith healers such as Clive Harris or Anatoly Kashpirovsky, who were extremely famous in Poland in the 1980s.

Notes

1 This research was financed by the National Science Center in Poland pursuant to Decision no DEC-2012/04/S/HS3/00316 and no DEC-2018/29/B/HS3/01243. This chapter was translated by Jasper Tilbury.
2 Zbigniew Jastrzebowski, *Spory o model lecznictwa. Opieka zdrowotna w koncepcjach polskiej polityki społecznej w XIX i XX wieku (do końca 1948 r.)* (Łodź: Akademia Medyczna w Łodzi, 1994), 267.
3 Ibid.
4 See, for example, Irena Brzozowska, Halina Stefańska and Stanisław Rybicki, eds., *Wspomnienia pielęgniarek* (Warsaw: Państwowy Zakład Wydawnictw Lekarskich, 1962), 664. I also write about the problems in fighting epidemics just after the war in: Ewelina Szpak, 'Epidemie chorób infectnych w

powojennej Polsce jako problem społeczny', in *Od powietrza, głodu, ognia i wojny ... Klęski elementarne na przestrzeni wieków*, eds. Tomasz. Głowiński and Elżbieta Kościk (Wrocław: Gajt, 2013), 299.

5 Russia, Germany and Austria-Hungary - trans.

6 By 1939, barely 300 health centres had been established in the countryside, and the estimated number of health cooperatives in 1938 was only 8. It would therefore be more accurate to speak of an experiment of sorts than common practice.

7 Barbara Fogt, *Ośrodek Reumatologiczny w kontekście zmian zachodzących w ochronie zdrowia w latach 1952–2005*, doctoral dissertation, supervised by Prof Michał Musielak, Wielkopolska Digital Library.

8 In 1946, rural residents accounted for 68.2 per cent of the total population. *Mały Rocznik Statystyczny 1974* (Warsaw: Główny Urząd Statystyczny, 1975), 15.

9 *Zdrowie Publiczne* 1 (1953), quoted in M. Jarosz and S. Kosiński, 'Geneza i zmiany strukturalne wiejskiej służby zdrowia', in *Stare i nowe struktury społeczne w Polsce, vol. 2, Wieś*, eds. Irena Machaj and Józef Styk (Lublin: Uniwersytet Marii Skłodowskiej Curie (UMCS), 1993): 169.

10 Janusz Indulski, ed., *Organizacja ochrony zdrowia* (Warsaw: Wydawnictwo Lekarskie, 1984), 316.

11 Of course, an important role was played here by the desire to increase the birth rate of the nascent state.

12 Thomas Lemke, 'Analityka biopolityki. Rozważania o przeszłości i teraźniejszości spornego pojęcia', *Praktyka Teoretyczna* 2–3 (2011): 18; M. Foucault, *Narodziny biopolityki* (Warsaw: Wydawnicstwo Naukowe PWN, 2011), 22, 42; Lech W. Zacher, Biowładza i biopolityka (refleksje, przykłady, predykcje), *Wiedza – władza* (Lublin: Wydawnictwo KUL, 2009), 95.

13 Lech W. Zacher, *op. cit.*, p. 6.

14 Piotr Kępski, 'Liberalizm a biopolityka – pomiędzy dyskursem wolności i bezpieczeństwa', *Górnośląskie Studia Socjologiczne, Seria Nowa* 8 (2017): 95.

15 In the People's Republic, 'social actions and deeds' (*akcje i czyny społeczne*) was the name given to unpaid work performed for the common good, usually on days off – trans.

16 *Pamiętniki lekarzy*, Selection and Introduction by Jan Borkowski (Kraków: Orion, 1987), 36.

17 State Archives in Lublin, PGRN, catalogue no. 23, fol. 19.

18 Polish Radio Archives, catalogue no. B-6762a, *O chorobach wenerycznych*, ed. B. Markowska, 1968.

19 Blacksmiths, for instance, would use their metal tools to extract teeth, while shepherds, with their knowledge of treating animal fractures, would set broken bones – trans.

20 Central Archives of Modern Records (AAN), Ministry of Health, catalogue no. 1/27, *Analiza sieci i działalności zakładów służby zdrowia w okresie 1950-1955*, fol. 274.

21 Central Archives of Modern Records (AAN), Ministry of Health, catalogue no. 1/41. *Protokoły z narady aktywu służby zdrowia odbytej dnia 26 marca 1959 r. w Sali Prezydium Wojewódzkiej Rady Narodowej w Opolu*, fol. 393.

22 In this regard, the intensive and brutal collectivisation implemented at the time was also significant.

23 For instance, Central Archives of Modern Records (AAN), Ministry of Health catalogue no. 1/14 *Sprawozdanie z działalności służby zdrowia woj. olsztyńskiego za rok 1953*, fol. 55; *Sprawozdanie z działalności służby zdrowia woj. opolskiego za rok 1953*, fol. 106.

24 Central Archives of Modern Records (AAN), Ministry of Health, catalogue no. 1/24, *Sprawozdanie z narady aktywu województwa poznańskiego*, fol. 192.
25 One example of an interesting case and a conflict lasting several years between a rural doctor and a feldsher took place in a village in Western Pomerania, State Archives in Szczecin, catalogue no. 2482, *Analiza skarg i 4 wniosków 1972–73*, fol. 13.
26 *Pamiętniki lekarzy*, 737.
27 Central Archives of Modern Records (AAN), Ministry of Health, catalogue no. 56, *Akta kontrolne 1949*, fol. 150.
28 Central Archives of Modern Records (AAN), Ministry of Health, catalogue no. 1/13, *Protokół nr 54/53. Kolegium Ministerstwa Zdrowia z dn. 8 grudnia 1953*, fol. 255.
29 Brzozowska et. al., *Wspomnienia pielęgniarek*, 668.
30 Central Archives of Modern Records (AAN), Ministry of Health, catalogue no. 1/27, *Analiza sieci i działalności zakładów służby zdrowia w okresie.*
31 Central Archives of Modern Records (AAN), Ministry of Health, catalogue no. 1/25, *Ocena stanu zdrowia na wsi na podstawie analizy wykonania Uchwały Kolegium dot. wsi w latach 1954-1955*, fol. 181.
32 Marcin Kacprzak, 'Gruźlica na wsi', *Warszawskie Czasopismo Lekarskie* 45–47 (1938): 20–21.
33 Brzozowska et. al., *Wspomnienia pielęgniarek*, 689; Kacprzak, 'Gruźlica na wsi', 20–21.
34 Stanisław Grzycki et al., eds., *Stan zdrowotny i higiena wsi lubelskiej. Materiały z obozów naukowo-społecznych 1954–1960* (Lublin: Wydawnictwo Lubelskie, 1964).
35 Grzycki et al., *Stan zdrowotny i higiena*, 82.
36 The institute's website: http://www.imw.lublin.pl/index.php/en/o-instytucie/historia (accessed 12 February 2019).
37 The institute published both academic and popular-science papers on rural diseases and issues related to sanitation and hygiene; from the 1960s it was authorised to educate cadres of specialists in rural medicine, and from 1966 it published a newsletter called *Medycyna Wiejska* (Rural Medicine).
38 White Sundays were local events, often organized in villages, during which teams of doctors and nurses would perform check-ups (usually of children), offer advice, and provide referrals for specialist medical examinations (according to many doctors, White Sundays were somewhat propagandistic in nature).
39 Stanisław Kosiński and Stanisław Tokarski, *Ochrona zdrowia ludności wiejskiej (ze szczególnym uwzględnieniem Lubelszczyzny)* (Łodź: Państwowe Wydawnictwo Naukowe, 1987), 71.
40 Decree of 14 August 1954 on the State Sanitary Inspectorate, *Journal of Laws* (Dz. U.) 1954, no. 37, item 160.
41 Zbigniew Wojdyła, 'Rady Zdrowia a postęp wsi. O programie szkoły zdrowia II stopnia', *Medycyna Wiejska* 4 (1969): 285.
42 Oral account – doctor – anaesthesiologist, Lublin province (2013).
43 Brzozowska et. al., *Wspomnienia pielęgniarek*, 572.
44 Ibid., 572.
45 Polish Radio Archives, reportage, catalogue no. C-5040, *Wsi spokojna, wsi wesoła. Pan wychodzi panie doktorze?*, ed. Krystyna Usarek,1963.
46 Brzozowska et. al., *Wspomnienia pielęgniarek*, 672.
47 Maria Bajorkowa, 'W oczach lekarza wiejskiego. Konfrontacje', *Medycyna wiejska* 1 (1966): 62.
48 Ibid., 61.

49 Polish Radio Archives, catalogue no. C-10420, *T-11 – zgłoś się*, ed. Piotr Komorowski, 1971.
50 The common name of diphtheria.
51 The common name of pertussis.
52 Non-professional midwifery practised by elderly women in the countryside – trans.
53 Another step towards securing care for mothers and children (in both rural and urban areas) was the policy of hospitalization of births implemented after 1956. This initially led to the creation of local delivery rooms in rural areas and, in subsequent decades, to an increasing number of births in district hospitals.
54 Central Archives of Modern Records (AAN), MZ, catalogue no. 49, vol. 2, *Sprawozdanie z podróży inspekcyjnej dr S. Kochańskiej na teren woj. Rzeszowskiego, w dn. 15–20 czerwca 1948*, fol. 353.
55 Polish Radio Archives, catalogue no. C-5040, *Wsi spokojna, wsi wesoła. Pan wychodzi panie doktorze?*, ed. Krystyna Usarek (1963).
56 'Nowe zawody, Pamiętniki', selected and compiled by Bronisław Gołębiowski and Zdzisław Grzelak, foreword by Józef Chałasiński, in *Młode Pokolenie Wsi Polski Ludowej*, vol. 7 (Warsaw: Ludowa Spółdzielnia Wydawnicza, 1969), 144.
57 AIEiAK UJ, catalogue no. 158, S. Nowak, *Terapia ludowa w Czarnym Dunajcu ze szczególnym uwzględnienie osoby leczącego*, 1977, fol. 79.

11 State Socialist Biopolitics

Four Stages of Human Development in Post-War Czechoslovakia

Jakub Rákosník and Radka Šustrová

Introduction

The origin of the concept of 'biopolitics' dates from before the First World War when, in 1911, on the pages of a modernist magazine called *The New Age*, an article was published with that title.[1] Biopolitics meant, on the one hand, the orientation of state power towards the growth in population numbers and, on the other hand, care for managing the quality of the population in the interest of state needs.[2] The later use of this concept by Michel Foucault does not contradict this definition; when concluding his lectures given in 1978–9 entitled *The Birth of Biopolitics*, he stated: 'biopolitics, by which I mean the attempt, starting from the eighteenth century, to rationalize the problems posed to governmental practice by phenomena characteristic of a set of living beings forming a population: health, hygiene, birth rate, life expectancy, race'.[3]

Foucault's successors who oriented their research towards social policy, such as Jacques Donzelot, saw in the biopolitical dimension the 'proliferation of political technologies that invested the body, health, modes of subsistence and lodging'.[4] Such a perspective opens the door to applying the concept of biopolitics to state socialist dictatorships as well, although Foucault himself did not do so and, in *The Birth of Biopolitics,* drew a clear dividing line between the liberal model of the state on the one hand and fascist/communist governance through a political party on the other.[5] Apparently, for that reason, the association between biopolitics and state socialism is not considered a matter of course in historiography, and we do not find more frequent mentions of it until the new millennium.[6] In this chapter, we would like to point out the usefulness of a biopolitical perspective for comprehending how the conditions of existence for the population in state socialist Czechoslovakia were controlled, as well as for comprehending the forms of new practices that were not specific to the Soviet bloc and can be grasped rather as characteristics of modern governmentality.[7]

It is in this sense that the historian Sergei Prozorov also notes that the biopolitical orders in capitalist Europe and the Soviet Union are similar. Despite their clear deviations from each other in terms of socioeconomic

DOI: 10.4324/9781003161080-14

conditions and their ideological antagonism, each adopted the same system of values, in his opinion. Prozorov argues that the Soviet type of society actually 'provide[d] ample historical evidence of both the positive and negative aspects of biopolitics, its power to "make live" and to "let die"'.[8] While at the macro level of state ideology and socioeconomic development, Soviet socialism rejected Western capitalism and liberal democracy, at the micro level of biopolitical practices and disciplines, what functioned was the continuity of governance techniques that were more or less similar to those used in the West. In European historiography, of course, there is still essentially less interest in the countries of the former Soviet bloc than in those of the capitalist West.

The distinction between the biopolitics of race, typical of national socialism, and the biopolitics of class struggle, particular to the period of Stalinism, is a partially functional one, but not absolutely. In that context, Prozorov emphasizes that while 'Foucault was certainly correct about the use of Western biopolitical technologies, including racist ones, by the Stalinist and the post-Stalinist regime, he was wrong to interpret it in terms of the inherently racist character of socialist biopolitics'.[9] In the Czech lands, the principle of ethnicity and/or race began to play a more pronounced role in the construction of social protection during the authoritarian order of the short-lived Second Czech-Slovak Republic at the turn of 1938 and 1939 and then in Nazi-occupied Bohemia and Moravia in the following years. In that context, the question arises to what degree that racial construction persisted during the post-war years at the level of policy promulgated by the state and applied to the Czechoslovak population.

We consider the project to transform human beings into the form of a 'New Soviet Man' or 'New Socialist Personality', a project that came out of the humanist tradition and projected itself as a Western prototype, to be the central feature of communist biopolitics.[10] This bombastic project, adapted in parallel by the countries of the socialist bloc, created the assumptions behind the modelling of the ideally typical socialist individual through socialist child-rearing, corrections or re-education, if necessary. The perspective of biopolitics, therefore, entails studying the evolution and transformation of modern power practices and different forms of control. In the context of a state socialist dictatorship, we are interested above all in the practice of maximizing human potential in the context of economic efficiency while simultaneously minimizing individual capacity for political and sociocultural resistance.[11]

For the purposes of this chapter, biopolitics, as described above, is still too broadly drawn. Beginning with Foucault's lectures from 1975–6, we are endeavouring here to differentiate between biopower and disciplinary power:

> Unlike discipline, which is addressed to bodies, the new non-disciplinary power is applied not to man as body but … to man-as-species. …

> The new technology that is being established is addressed to a multiplicity of men ... a global mass that is affected by overall processes characteristic of birth, death, production, illness, and so on. ... After the anatomo-politics of the human body established in the course of the eighteenth century, we have, at the end of that century, the emergence of something that is no longer an anatomo-politics of the human body, but what I would call a "biopolitics" of the human race.[12]

Foucault clarifies that the core of these new approaches was the control and direction of birth rates. Some authors, therefore, consider the welfare state a typical historical example of this kind of power through which modern populations are controlled.[13] We will adhere to the connection between biopolitics and the welfare state in this study as well.

In its own way, state socialism carried out William Beveridge's maxim of a social (welfare) state serving people 'from the cradle to the grave'.[14] In this chapter, our aim will be to analyze the biopolitical approaches through which that maxim was fulfilled under the conditions of state socialism. We will argue that the concept of a state socialist biopolitics is justified, as it provides an instrument for describing the formation of the New Socialist man during the different phases of human development. In order to meet this goal, our piece is structured in five parts. The first is dedicated to the more general subject of biopolitical governance, i.e. the population and its formation according to the ideas of socialism. Next, we concentrate on the four phases of human development: on the child as an ideal object of socialist child-rearing, on parenthood during socialism, on the phase of life that is economically productive (socialist working people) and on the socialist senior citizen. We are aware that Foucault's duality of biopolitics and disciplinary power has the character of a Weberian ideal type, and for that reason when applying both of these concepts to historical material, they will inevitably overlap.

Becoming Socialist: Population in Post-War Czechoslovakia

Despite the attempt at homogenization, the project of socialist society was extensively permeated by class criteria and by racial criteria. At first glance, this may be surprising. In both cases, basic changes had occurred even before 1948, and we can see the power practices of the biopolitical transformation of society as the organic continuations of those previous tendencies. Rationing, wartime and post-war inflation, and above all, the post-war nationalization and land reforms left a deep mark on the social stratification of society, which became far more egalitarian than it had been between the wars. The ethnic purges and racial policies that began during the war (in relation to Jewish, Romany and Sinti people) and that continued after the defeat of Nazism (in relation to non-Slavs, especially ethnic Germans) emphasized the importance of ethnicity. For that reason, too, we have developed elsewhere the concept of 'socialist eugenics' (neo-eugenics), where we question the continuity and raptures of racial biopolitics after the Second World War.[15]

The biopolitics of race in the Czech lands appears most clearly during the period of the Second Czech-Slovak Republic and the Nazi Protectorate of Bohemia and Moravia. After the Munich Agreement was concluded in September 1938, the systematic intensification of the segregation of communities of different nationalities took place, as did the separation of ethnicities and nationalities according to 'objective' features established by experts on populations and races. At that time, the Czech-Slovak authorities themselves applied ethnic/racial criteria and began categorizing the distinct ethnicities of Czechs, Germans, Slovaks and Jews, as well as creating the relevant institutional background for these divisions. Jewish people were considered an absolutely alien element in society and were meant to receive completely specific treatment. The Romany population at that time was also more significantly ostracized and, when categorized as 'asocial' or 'work-shy' persons, was excluded from the Czech national unity. These measures against Jewish and Romany people unequivocally had domestic roots. They were designed and implemented before the announcement of the Nazi Protectorate of Bohemia and Moravia in mid-March 1939, and during the Nazi occupation, they became even more radicalized. What was typical at the time was the pressure put on the non-Jewish Czech population to absorb the racial language of this new social order when interacting with the administrative bodies of the Nazi Protectorate, which managed to distinguish between Jews and non-Jews, as well as the pressure exerted on the non-Jewish Czech population to absorb the national impulses that either Czechified or Germanized the reality around them. The most discontinuous feature, with respect to both interwar and post-war practice, was the racial construction of legislated social policy executed by the public administration with respect to legal norm-setting and the application of that policy in practice in the Protectorate.[16]

Those who were active after the liberation of Czechoslovakia between 1945 and 1948 considered the country's post-war synthesis of democracy and socialism to have its origins in the 'national revolution' of 1945, and they included a harsh racial motif in their own legislation at the time, in an altered form. This was especially about the form of privileges for citizens of 'Slavic origin', which would continue to be displayed through the ethnic determination of full-fledged citizenship.[17] The exclusionary tendency in this post-war concept of Czechoslovakia's population appeared first during the 'wild' expulsion and then in the organized expulsion of German people and in the rejection of German-speaking Jewish people.[18] After the war, Czechoslovakia was greatly interested in its own 'biological regeneration', which was meant to aid the country with recovering from the Nazi occupation and was directly associated with a 'national threat'. In that atmosphere, a vision of Czechoslovak population policy reform that involved an explicitly eugenic motivation found room for application. It is surprising how matter-of-fact Czechoslovak experts were when emphasizing the necessity of 'eugenic considerations' (*eugenický zřetel*) after the Second World War. However, they also acknowledged that there must be a new, more comprehensive view of the individual and of society that would also pay attention to the opinions of social sciences such as psychology or sociology.[19] Among the strong supporters of eugenics in the daily post-war interactions between doctors and patients was František Pachner, a gynaecologist and obstetrician from Brno who had spent the occupation in hiding because his Jewish origin meant he was at risk of deportation. His concept of eugenics as sociomedical prevention was meant to demonstrate the advantages and opportunities afforded by that perspective for making deeper observations about the Czechoslovak population.[20] Czechoslovak eugenicists were responded to by high state officials, e.g. at the Healthcare Ministry, but the implementation of eugenics as a practice was made impossible around the year 1949 by the primacy of the Soviet doctrine of Lysenkoism, which dominated genetic research in the Soviet Union and subsequently in Soviet bloc countries. By the 1960s, eugenics had been completely replaced by the phrase 'population quality', which made it possible to follow sociocultural aspects of the condition and development of Czechoslovak society.

While it was broadly communicated in Czechoslovakia that population policy was understood as a method of selection, the enforcement of that policy in legal norm-setting was limited. Eugenics was meant to generally address the sociocultural causes of crime, illegitimacy and poverty, but because of the strong homogenization, in terms of nationality, of Czechoslovak society after the war, the Roma were almost exclusively the only distinct group to end up at the centre of such attention. Stalinist Czechoslovakia sought ways to actively address the issue of Roma through mass mobilizations, attempts at paternalistic intervention in child-rearing, and the care given to the Romany population, but this resulted above all in a claim to emancipation being made by the Roma themselves.[21] As Matěj Spurný states, the Communist Party of Czechoslovakia (*Komunistická strana Československa* – KSČ) had long resisted using bureaucratic methods of repression, identifying them with the 'capitalist oppression of the Gypsies' that up until then had chiefly come from local actors subordinated to Local National Committees, the lowest state administration bodies.[22] Of course, a harsh assimilation policy predominated towards the Czechoslovak Roma from the mid-1950s and culminated in the absolute prohibition against living on the road.[23] The demand for the 'complete fusion of the Gypsies with the rest of the population' meant that staffers at the Ministry of Education and Culture were supposed to chiefly emphasize 'what unites us' in their work with the Romany population.[24]

During late state socialism, the state may have facilitated expert debate on eugenic prognoses and formats for influencing the gene pool of the

Czechoslovak population, but combining these ideas with their application in practice was difficult to achieve and was almost exclusively the initiative of the local actors interested in what were called the 'gypsy commissions' at the Local National Committees. The socialist state did not dictate racial policy in its legislation. It is more accurate to speak of the state creating the room to manoeuvre, in which popular antisemitism and antigypsyist racism could be applied. After the completion of the ethnic post-war purges, the state held to class-based definitions, not racial ones; something that can be considered a consequence of the distinct ethnic homogenization of society, which during Stalinism was meant to also become homogenous in terms of social categories.

In contrast to the criterion of race, which had just been implicitly in play, the class principle, according to which the population was to be restructured into a socialist one, was announced in an absolutely open manner. The declared aim of state socialism was the creation of a classless society. Later, in the 1960s, it became evident that even a socialist society had to involve a complex and inevitably stratified social system. Sociologists spoke of the existence of groups that were not, of course, in antagonistic relationships with each other, as had been the case in a bourgeois, class-based society.[25] During the building phase of socialism, which is considered the period between 1945 and 1960, an entire series of measures to achieve a classless society were used. We can generalize them into three groups, although frequently they mutually overlapped in practice: (1) Adjustments to property relations (across-the-board nationalizing, expropriating individuals, land reforms, collectivization); (2) Regulation of consumption by the economically active population (differentiated allocations, wage policy) and (3) Regulation of consumption by the economically inactive population (social security). With regard to the subject of this chapter, the following paragraphs will pay attention above all to the third area because it is chiefly here that we are able to find biopolitics implemented through the instruments of the welfare state. According to the ideas of the Communist Party of Czechoslovakia, the system of social security was meant to consistently 'respect the aspect of class and thereby contribute to suppressing what remains of the capitalist sector'.[26]

The approach involving class was displayed most visibly in the pension system, to which attention is paid below. Healthcare, which had come under the absolute control of the state by the close of the 1950s, was, of course, not spared this either (see the section on socialist labourers). Class membership also influenced access to education. The deeply below-average educational levels of the children from families where the parents had been manual laborers during the interwar period were, after 1948, balanced by privileging such people while simultaneously discriminating against the progeny of previously better-situated families, above all such families where the authorities did not assume the parents were inclined positively towards the 'people's democracy', or rather, the socialist regime.[27] Changes are also apparent in Czechoslovakia during those 40 years of the existence of state socialism. The landmark symbolizing these changes is the year 1968. Before then, the biopolitical change in the population had been emphasized predominantly in the direction of a more balanced structure among those who were attaining an education, but during late socialism, the measures undertaken by those in power were exclusively limited to disciplining inconvenient, non-conforming individuals, or rather, families. That is also why the Charter 77 documents published up until 1989 so frequently and periodically attacked discrimination against young people's access to education on the basis of their parents' political positions.[28]

Taking Foucault's distinction between the biopolitics of race and the biopolitics of class, it is possible to observe a clear development throughout the state socialist dictatorship. Because of child-rearing norms and moral norms under socialism, biopolitics continued to involve racial traits, especially during late socialism, when biopolitics acquired a chiefly disciplinary function. Class criteria, by contrast, inevitably lost importance along with the disappearance of what remained of capitalist production structures, as society was meant to evolve features that were non-antagonistic – at least according to the acclamations of officials. However, class criteria remained an essential element of the communist welfare state and society even in the 1960s. Karel Pinc, one of only a few experts on social security at the time with a well-founded grasp of theory, made the following eloquent statement in his 1962 book: 'Socialist humanism does not close its eyes to class struggle. It sides with the forces of progress, i.e., the working class. Class struggle also enters into the social security sphere ... To quite a broad extent, our social security today has yet to be permeated by aspects of class, it must also fulfil its class function.'[29]

In the late socialism of the 1970s and 1980s, criteria other than class membership took on importance. When, at the beginning of the 1990s, Johan De Deken analyzed the functioning of social security in socialist Czechoslovakia, he accurately reported what the criteria for guaranteeing the population's rights to social security had previously been: 'the condition for being included in the social security system was not performance as such, but rather a combination of physical presence in the workplace and loyalty (or at least the absence of any evident disagreement) toward the party and the state'.[30]

The Socialist Child

Both the social welfare policy guaranteed by the state and the institutional infrastructure for children's development and upbringing organically proceeded from the interwar debates about the benefits of such an infrastructure and policy for children and youth from the standpoint of the accessibility of healthcare and hygiene, or rather, the question of the appropriateness of collective child-rearing in institutions during socialism.

Thanks to an extensive institutional system, the child became the all-but-ideal object of education and re-education by the socialist state. Emphasis was placed above all on the complexity of the instruments for shaping the individual to conform to the ideal of socialist man. The child's entire personality, with all of its human attributes (memory, rationality, imagination, emotion, will and bodily functions), was to be activated and literally 'exposed to the stimulating work' of crucial processes and values such as labour, productivity, science, technology, economics, philosophy, morality, literature, art, etc.[31]

The basic ambition of the state in this field was formulated by the Act on Education, adopted in December 1960. According to that legislation, the institutional mission of socialism was

> to bring up the youth and the workers, in the spirit of the scientific world view, into citizens who are educated, able to acquire knowledge of contemporary science and technology, and prepared for socially useful work, into able-bodied people finding a joyful satisfaction in the collective and in working for the whole, imbued with ideas of socialist patriotism and internationalism – into conscious citizens of the Czechoslovak Socialist Republic, enthusiastic builders of communism.[32]

At this juncture, we will restrict ourselves just to the aspects of care for younger children that were meant to aid in the reproduction of socialist man. In addition to crèches and nursery schools, we will be specifically interested in children's homes as a kind of residential caregiving.

What had been the stubborn enforcement of the collective upbringing of children during the 1950s was transformed during late socialism in association with the announcement that such caregiving in institutions had been overestimated as a tactic and was not producing anywhere near the kinds of results that would contribute to reducing the causes of negative phenomena in society, such as parents being unable to care for their children due to long-term illness, or having been sentenced to prison, or failing to manage their children's upbringing or the disharmony in families that was increasing. Children's collective facilities were a component of the class-oriented biopolitics of state socialist Czechoslovakia, aiming to create convenient, equal conditions for the employment of salaried women and to facilitate the state's contribution to children's socialist upbringing, as well as the state's contribution to the subsequent phases of each individual's life.

Czechoslovakia, in the post-war period, administered crèches for children between the ages of three months and three years, in addition to the children's healthcare facilities set up at Institutes of National Health (*Ústavy národního zdraví*) or otherwise under the Health Ministry, which was the second pillar of these children's collective facilities. Their continual construction beginning in the interwar period, continuing during the Nazi Protectorate and then into Czechoslovakia's post-war phases, chiefly addressed the problem of employment growing among women and of how to combine their care for their families with the activities generating income that these mothers were now performing. Caregiving involving both prevention and treatment in a uniform fashion was set up in 1951.[33] In the interests of 'the development of the new generation', the state set up, among other things, caregiving facilities for children and their mothers, including maternity hospitals, infants' institutions, children's homes for toddlers up to the age of three, crèches with both daytime and night-time operations, and counselling centres for children and women. While the health and social infrastructure of caring for children and their mothers improved the accessibility of healthcare, the crèches remained a problematic part of the system. Critical voices were repeatedly raised asking whether crèches did not unnecessarily allow women's attention to wander away from their motherly obligations and whether they had a good influence on child development. In this regard, the absolutely resolute statement by Czech doctor Emilie Lukášová in the second half of the 1940s is eloquent: 'Medical professionals, for this reason, cannot be supporters of the concept of crèches'.[34] Comprehension of the influence, in psychosocial terms, of children's crèches continues to be gradually transformed into the subject of complex negotiations among the various actors, including experts, parents and societies, especially the Czechoslovak Union of Women, the central institution for the labour and political mobilization of women after the Second World War.

We can observe a change in childcare concepts starting in the 1960s when crèches became an intermediary option between the child-rearing that took place only within the family or in institutions. In the cases of both half-orphans and orphans, crèches were considered especially useful. The number of crèches decidedly did not decline; on the contrary, during the 1970s, it was assumed there would be another radical increase in nursery school places for children between 3 and 5 years of age, which was meant to compensate for the employment of women 40-years-old and older and the resulting lack of grandmothers available to help care for children in the home. Care in the crèches in combination with care in the family was considered appropriate in the years that followed, as well as 'characteristic for the socialist establishment', which is why abandoning crèches was not desirable. In 1974, sociological research into the role and utility of common crèches from a child development perspective demonstrated that the most appropriate approach was the combination of collective facilities and the environment of the family.[35] According to different findings, children's co-educational collectives and game-playing would also positively shape their abilities to establish future relationships as men and women.[36]

Similar to the transformation of the crèches, the boarding-school child-raising format of the children's homes, as shaped by state socialist biopolitics, was also transformed in terms of function – instead of providing social security, they were to chiefly fulfil educational, re-educational and therapeutic tasks.[37] In essence, the development of such institutions from what had previously been social welfare institutions into child-rearing educational institutions of socialism consisted of implementing 'a child-rearing process conditioned by the aims, principles and forms of socialist pedagogy'.[38] The early phase of a child's stay in such a place concentrated on 're-education in social habits, attitudes and relationships' and on eliminating emotional disorders.[39] Opinions about the merits of this institutionalized, isolated life were replaced over time by a concept emphasizing the greatest amount of contact possible between the institution and the 'outside world'. Around the mid-1970s, the Czechoslovak education ministry admitted it had overestimated boarding-school child-rearing and underestimated the prevention of the social problems that could happen at a certain phase in the development of socialist society. At that time, the authorities at the state level absolutely changed their strategy, emphasizing the family as irreplaceable and designating adoptive and foster families as the most appropriate approach. This change was evidenced by the new law on foster care adopted in 1973.[40] Foster families were meant to be allocated to all abandoned, half-orphaned or orphaned children and those who had relatives but lived 'outside of the family'. All of them needed the 'society's help', experts agreed.[41] The children in the collective facilities who were most numerous were those whose parents, for the broadest possible range of reasons, demonstrated no interest in their care.

In 1970, the biggest proportion of children in that category was from families of Romany origin, a total of 54.1 per cent of the children aged 3 to 6.[42] The population of Roma was more weighed down by poverty, and their behaviour was perceived far more frequently as 'asocial' or 'deviant' and therefore as failing to conform to the norms of socialism, and this contributed to the fact that a disproportionately large part of the children in children's homes were Romany. To comprehend the context of the day, the guileless statements of the social workers for the District National Committee in Ostrava-Zábřeh (northern Moravia), in their 1970 report on the *cikánská* (gypsy) question and its solution, speak volumes when they write that 'such measures should not be seen as discrimination, but as a necessity demanded by the current state of the gypsy children's upbringing'.[43] The state authorities gave the label of 'social orphaning' to this modern phenomenon. The children came most frequently from families that were broken, disturbed, and incomplete, or they were the children of separated or unmarried mothers who were unable to take care of their children or unwilling to do so alone. Those assigned to the children's homes were there under a kind of placement that was not meant to disrupt the legal ties between the biological family and the child – on the contrary, the children's home was tasked with maintaining those contacts and returning children to their homes of origin after the families' affairs had stabilized.

It was typical that the local national committees played a key role with respect to the population of Romany people, and these decision-making power structures were delegated what was called 'work with the gypsy population' in the field.[44] The child-rearing efforts of the social workers used by the lowest level of the administration were allegedly meant to arrange for establishing the most appropriate strategies and for that child-raising work to be as effective as possible. Assigning children from Romany families to nursery schools and involving them more in extracurricular activities was meant to create conditions for them to acquire Czech as the language of instruction and to eliminate the shortcomings caused by the child-rearing they had received in their families, which was seen as 'incorrect'. These child-focused and youth-focused institutions were then loosely succeeded by institutions that took up these individuals at the phase of their lives when it was desirable to direct them towards the proper philosophy of parenthood.

The Socialist Parent

The creation of the New Socialist Man was a fundamental aim of communist transformation.[45] The argumentation in a Soviet textbook on the family and marriage by Lev Zalkind, translated into Czech in 1953 (which then became, for Czechoslovak state socialism, part of the literature that was normative), was straightforward about child–parent relationships in this regard. The transformation of ownership relations is said to transform class structures towards a greater degree of equality, producing the desired behavioural models which parents would then transfer to the new generation of their offspring. In addition, the children would be formed further by facilities for preschools and schools that were all part of a planned structure.[46] The key prerequisite for this project's success, in contemporary eyes, was that children who were healthy would be led to establish their own families with 'healthy' relationships. We can distinguish, at a general level, three basic biopolitical strategies applied to achieve these aims: (1) Counselling (sexual counselling, partner counselling, premarital counselling, marriage counselling, maternity counselling, contraceptive counselling, etc.); (2) Completing the process of medicalizing midwifery in the form of the hegemony of institutionalized births and (3) Defensive strategies to prevent the birth of undesirable individuals or of infants being born into inappropriate conditions (abortions, sterilizations).

This counselling served a distinctly controlling, preventative, and later also a remedying function. The staffers were agents operating as the long arm of the party and the state, entering into direct contact with an expectant couple or mother to instil them, as subjects, with the most appropriate behavioural models corresponding to the morality of the times.[47] The category at the centre was impeccability in moral terms. It was according to such criteria that counselling centre staffers awarded approvals of applications for loans to newlyweds that literally stated they had been approved 'because of their current lifestyle and health status'.[48] While in the 1940s and 1950s, we can encounter counselling centres that were 'eugenic' still, (basically due to their fulfilling the function of premarital counselling) and where the staffers, during their direct interactions with clients, floated the issue of 'population quality' with respect to the betrothed couple and their medical conditions, as of the 1960s this counselling had developed into a form of family planning, a systemic tool for it. It is possible to designate its ethos as having been the opinion that 'in marriage, a non-productive orientation' means the institution is not functioning correctly. For that reason, the authorities had to target interventions that were seen as necessary.[49] The marriage counselling network was built chiefly during the 1970s and not finished until the mid-1980s. These counselling centres during late socialism provided both awareness-raising and social services, in the sense of fixing broken marriages and family relationships, most frequently pointing in the direction of keeping families together.

The question as to what extent the health of an individual should be the subject of the attention and control, medically speaking, of public authorities naturally predated such counselling. In its modern form, the medicalization of midwifery had been in process since the Enlightenment. During the twentieth century, a breaking point in that development arrived during the second half of the 1940s when the state began, with all of its vigour, to claim control over the population's reproduction. The occupying authorities in the Nazi Protectorate of Bohemia and Moravia supported midwifery and maintained the practice of home births for reasons that served their own purposes, but Czechoslovakia in the post-war period primarily preferred to provide such care in institutions of the medical profession.[50] The nationalization and unification of healthcare took effect as of the spring of 1948.[51] This aided in decreasing the effort it took to find clientele and facilitated better inspection of the health status and living conditions of the Czechoslovak population. A distinct effect of this was not just healthcare professionalization. In class terms, when it came to the medical care provided to the population, conditions were levelled in a marked way and corresponded with the distribution of Institutes of National Health and the district-level establishment of the midwife's job.[52] The system was subsequently completed by instituting the provision of preventive care and treatment in a uniform fashion, which began to be developed as of December 1951.[53]

Abortion and sterilization were the third biopolitical strategy of Czechoslovak socialism and a rich literature exists on both today.[54] Abortions were legalized relatively early in Czechoslovakia compared to other European states in 1957.[55] In the debates held publicly prior to the law being promulgated, arguments may have been made about the individual right of a woman to decide about her own motherhood, but the rationale for the legislation unequivocally privileged the collective interest of the nation in healthy, numerous offspring. Abortion was controlled by the authorities, therefore. Commissions that decided whether to permit abortions were established at some hospitals, and their members included, in addition to the director of the healthcare institution and two specialists, a public representative appointed by the District National Committee. The public representative was meant to be 'a woman with experience of life who has a serious, trusted reputation'.[56] The commission was meant to ensure that the abortion would be in accordance with the interest of the public, not done out of frivolity on the part of the woman seeking it, or because she failed to grasp life's purpose or for any other cause that contradicted the morals and principles of socialism. Despite the strong criticism aimed at these commissions during their entire existence (1957–1986), their closure was only seriously discussed when technological advances facilitated what was called mini-suction during the early phase of pregnancy and when the commission's process created so much delay that opportunities for the technique to be used were missed. The commission's procedure was, for the abortion-seeking women, quite humiliating, and specialists considered convening the commissions to be a waste of time since more than 90 per cent of the applications were always approved. Despite that fact, there were surprisingly few voices calling for the commissions to be closed. An eloquent example was the respected gynaecologist and paediatrician Miroslav Vojta who, in 1968, at a conference on abortions, harshly criticized the commissions for the reasons mentioned above on the one hand, while on the other hand recommending that they be kept in place without making any deeper changes to them. In his opinion, as deterrence instruments, they worked well to make sure women did not apply for abortion lightly. At the same time, he considered it desirable for abortion decisions not to remain exclusively in the hands of just one person (the attending physician).[57]

At first glance, it may seem surprising that even during the period of pro-natal policy in the 1970s, there were no attempts made to limit abortions in a more pronounced way in the interest of boosting growth in the population, as occurred in communist Romania.[58] In addition to the political pragmatism of Czechoslovakia's leaders during the era of normalization, apparently, domestic experts' influence played a role here, as demographers indicated unwaveringly that it would be delusional to believe abortion restrictions would actually boost growth in the population.[59]

The applied approach of biopolitical policy that was more controversial and done in the interest of population quality was sterilization. Until the beginning of the 1970s, sterilizations had only been performed quite rarely. In 1972, new regulations on sterilization took effect.[60] The Czech Parliament has enacted a law that compensates women who were unlawfully sterilized, on which lawmakers have reported 'the unacceptably eugenic nature of this practice, which aimed at limiting the number of children born in some groups of the population perceived by the regime at the time as problematic, inadaptable or undesirable, whether that was the population of Romany people, persons living with mental or other disabilities, or persons with a larger number of children'.[61]

The problem was not the regulations on sterilization, as they assumed the procedure would be sought on the basis of consent that was informed and voluntary, but in practice, medical professionals were supported by National Committee social workers to apply the regulations too loosely or even to perform the procedure unlawfully. The historical interpretation remains open with regard to this practice today. On the one hand, the binding documents themselves were consistently ethnically neutral as regulations; it was during their implementation in practice that considerations of race weighed so heavily, as it was mainly Romany women who were sterilized. On the other hand, from primary sources, it is apparent that the central administrative authorities, for example, the Ministry of Finance, did not comprehend the compensation in material terms that was to be offered to the sterilized women as some kind of comfort, as intended originally, but as an incentive, a 'stimulus' that could effectively motivate compliance by those in economically weak households.[62] From our current study of primary sources, however, we are convinced that this has more to with an *inventive* manipulation of the existing legal regulations by some components of the lower level of the state administration – healthcare workers, social workers and ordinary citizens sharing prejudices that were racist – not about a concept dictating policy on race from the top down.[63]

Socialist Labourers

Compared to the situations prior to 1945, there was an apparent change in the conceptualization of the population in the post-war period. Civil society was replaced by 'the working people'; the citizen was replaced by 'the worker'. The 1960 constitution under socialism opens significantly, with the words 'We, the working people of Czechoslovakia, declare ...', announcing the holder of power to be the 'working people', and in many places speaking of a 'society of working people'.[64] The society described here was meant to be distinctly homogenous, both in terms of property and values.[65] There was an assumed monism, not a pluralism, of values, as Article 16 of the constitution declared Marxism–Leninism to be the 'scientific world view'. For civil law relationships in society, the civil code defined the individual and his or her status, following the constitution. The civil code established that 'the satisfaction of the material and cultural needs of citizens is provided above all by remuneration for work according to its amount, quality and social significance' and furthermore that 'according to the opportunities of society, distributions free of charge are also provided with a view to the social importance of the need'.[66] Since state socialism, unlike the liberal order, lacked the market that in liberalism, according to Foucault, becomes 'the site of truth', a far broader field was opened up for the authorities to directly intervene with their power to shape the population into the desired form.[67] When we review the broad palette of state socialist tools for forming the society of working people, this is apparently the most complicated point for adhering to Foucault's ideally typical distinction between biopolitics and discipline (disciplinary labour technology), as they are intertwined in practice so strongly.

During the first months after the Communist Party of Czechoslovakia assumed power in February 1948, it was not apparent in which direction things would develop. At first, their attempts were concentrated on enacting, as fast as possible, the promises of the Košice Government Program of April 1945, according to which there was to have been built a new, post-war republic, and much of which remained still unfulfilled even three years after the war. At the same time, the communists had not yet begun any radical reconstruction of society. By the beginning of 1949, at the very latest, however, the 'general line of building socialism' began to be ever more obvious and was subsequently also confirmed by the 9th Communist Party Congress in May of that same year.[68] For clarity regarding the broad palette of the measures that can be more or less subsumed under the category of biopolitics, we are breaking it down into three thematic spheres: (1) Homogenization of the population of working people; (2) Control over their health status and (3) Command over the time of working people.

No social stratum was spared during the formation of this 'society of working people'. In addition to individuals who were inconvenient or non-conformist, politically speaking, another object of this formation was persons who were self-employed. In the economy based on rationing that lasted from the war until 1953, this was rather easy. At least, in the beginning, indirect instruments of discrimination, in economic terms, were more often used. Over time, especially during the forced collectivization from 1949 to 1953, repression through criminal law grew in importance.[69] Doing away with the condition of the independent peasantry and forcing such persons into association with villages was the most visible change. Other actions, while accompanied by spectacular propaganda about the building of socialism, yielded leaner results from a long-term perspective.

In that regard, the famous 1951 action of moving 77,500 bureaucrats into manufacturing, the aim of which was to transfer that number of employees of the state into industrial labour, is instructive. Approximately 20 per cent of those who were singled out for transfer to the Kladno steelworks in central Bohemia, for example, managed to return to their former workplaces (the bureaucracies of ministries, predominantly) through personal connections and favouritism (*protekce*). The transfer into manufacturing, in other cases, frequently meant just placing the affected party in the administration of the enterprise.[70] The inverse direction consisted of cadres from the working class being promoted to higher positions in clerical or intellectual jobs. According to the estimates of Jiří Maňák, however, by the mid-1950s, when most of the process of creating a new intelligentsia attached to the communist party had been realized, this may have involved roughly 100,000–120,000 persons.[71] While that may not be an absolutely negligible number, it is evident that given the population of the state as a whole, these actions had a limited effect, certainly a smaller one than what the elites in power had associated with these approaches.[72]

This fact is confirmed to us by the comprehensive sociological survey undertaken by the collective led by Pavel Machonin, which in 1969 contained this assessment:

> Despite the many years of a cadre policy preferring working class origins, no essential reversal has happened on average in society in the relationship between those doing physical and intellectual labour as far as their location on the vertical scale of social differentiation goes ... At the same time, however, in comparison with the erstwhile capitalist order, the proportion of workers and people of working class origin, or from manual occupations originally, is apparently considerably higher especially in the area of management and in terms of income.[73]

For that reason, the researchers spoke just of a 'certain "democratization" of the social order, [aiming] toward compensating for class differences'.[74] Miroslav Petrusek, who also worked on that survey, clarified its findings in the *Sociologický časopis* [Czech Sociological Review] in 1969: Income levelling does not cause, not even partially, any corresponding levelling in the consumption and lifestyle sphere. What has been demonstrated, therefore, is the existence of a society with incomes that have been levelled, relatively, but that is not itself culturally uniform.[75] These levelling trends continued even during late socialism, albeit not in so spectacular a form as during the building phase. This has been confirmed to us by the findings of sociologists verifying that the greatest degree of equality in consumption and remuneration was recorded in the year 1990.[76]

An extensive economic growth strategy, taken over from the Soviet Union, was based on building new production capacities and on employment growing quickly. For the Czechoslovak economy, which was already fairly developed, what would have been more appropriate would have been an intensification strategy for its sector of technology because that economy did not have available to it the same amount of labour force as rural Russia had to offer during the era of industrialization under Stalin. Employment rates reveal this trend. While in 1948 there was 67 per cent of inhabitants of productive age employed, by 1970 there were already 79.8 per cent of them employed, and in 1987 a percentage point more. The main source of this new labour force was women who had been homemakers. The proportion of women among those employed between 1950 and 1980 grew from 36.5 to 45.2 per cent, so almost nine-tenths of women of productive age were employed.[77] Another source was those transferred from agriculture into industry and, within the framework of assimilatory approaches, the involvement of the Romany population in the production system during socialism.

To fulfil these aims, biopolitics created different ways of hierarchizing the population in state socialism. In order that allocations would become more efficient in terms of the workforce, in 1956, three categories of employment were introduced, to which we will return in the section on pensioners during socialism. In relation to the female workforce, the legal order during socialism was based consistently on the equality principle, including remuneration, but the reality differed from the declared principles. While, in comparison to many Western countries, Czechoslovakia made significant progress in the emancipation of women during the building phase of socialism, there was no improvement in the feminization of less prestigious jobs and the gender pay gap.[78] During the 1960s, satisfying noises were made about discrimination in wages based on gender principles, but when the communist dictatorship fell in 1989, Czechoslovakia reported some of the Eastern bloc's worst results in that regard.[79]

When it came to including the population of Romany people into production relationships during socialism, from 1948 to 1989, the categorizations were created in a specific way so as to justify the authorities' definitions of different groups to be handled in various ways. At the close of the 1950s, when the Communist Party of Czechoslovakia resorted to its program of consistently sedentarizing people living on the road, the population of Romany people was divided into three groups: Gypsies (*Cikáni*) who were settled (employed persons with permanent residence 'not requiring care'); Gypsies who were semi-itinerant, the most numerous group (persons frequently changing their residences and their workplaces whom bureaucrats identified as of a 'culturally low level'); Gypsies who lived only on the road (migrating, making dishonest livings, 'uncultured'). From that rationalization resulted in their subsequent categorization into three groups according to the amount of their assimilation, based on which their biopolitical control demanded differentiated strategies. With a certain degree of simplification, this rationality is approximated by Nina Pavelčíková in the following words: 'If, for members of Category I and II, what applied were the rules for using methods that were more about mild persuasion (naturally with the exception of the forced relocations of members of the second group), for the "inadaptables" (according to the criteria of officialdom) the regime was above all one of punishment that was severe'.[80]

Access by the families of labourers and by the labourers themselves to medical care was opened up and was a chief instrument of legitimization for state socialism. Even before February 1948, tendencies towards the gradual nationalization of healthcare had been obvious, at the latest from the moment in 1947 when Institutes of National Health were administratively created as components of the state. In the beginning, these were just in charge of counselling and preventive care. As of 1952, they covered, in each district, all facilities that were medical. This achieved the aim of their centralization and statization.[81] At the same time, 1948 saw the adoption of benefits for labourers in need of sick time.[82] Right after the war, the Communist Party of Czechoslovakia had embarked upon gaining monopoly control of the power of the state basically by demanding health insurance for the population, for all strata. However, after 1948, it abandoned that claim in silence. This kind of protection for the population in the social (welfare) system began to be exploited for the aim of building socialism, as benefits were cancelled in order to deteriorate the position, specifically of the self-employed who were sick.[83] There were conditions to caring, free of charge, for everybody's health, irrespective of the principles of universalism. Even after the building phase at its most radical was through, class principles persisted, as the clientele's hierarchization in the health institutions run by the state testifies. At the beginning of the 1960s, the operating rules divided clients into four groups: (1) acute status requiring immediate aid, where delay would be dangerous and could cause even more severe disease; (2) industrial labourers in plants of preferred production,[84] mothers with children up to the age of six and pregnant women; (3) all other family members of insured persons, the insured persons themselves and their peers and (4) persons who are uninsured.[85] In the biopolitical sense, it is characteristic of state socialism that healthcare for industrial labourers in plants of preferred production was provided to them from that position of privilege with respect to the rest of the population. Especially in late socialism, access by cadres to facilities for the nomenclature where ordinary people would never have been privileged with such superior treatment was increasingly negatively perceived. During the 1989 Velvet Revolution, therefore, it was frequently possible to see signs being held at demonstrations or graffiti reading '*SANOPS dětem*', where the acronym stood for 'hospitals for leaders of the party' and the call was for such facilities to serve all children.

All of the above notwithstanding, the achievements of Czechoslovakia in those first decades in the field of healthcare for the population were a significant success of state socialism. The documentation of the development of life expectancy evidences this fact well. In the year 1937, in the Czech lands, the average life expectancy was 58.5 years, while in Slovakia, it was just 53.3 years, although the gap gradually narrowed between these parts of the republic.[86] By the beginning of the 1960s, average life expectancy had increased to 70 years, with child and infant mortality declines explaining most of the rise. The mid-1960s, however, saw the end of that trend, and average life expectancy in Czechoslovakia declined in European terms until the year 1989 (from 11th in 1964 to 21st in 1989).[87] In healthcare, the problem during socialism was that when its capacity development had depended on the extensive growth of hospitals and the enforcement of mandatory preventative programs (check-ups, vaccinations), the results had been relatively satisfactory. Once its development depended on expensive new technologies, the centrally planned economy failed to generate that investment and the limits of its resources surfaced as usual.

After the Second World War, there is no doubt that the expansion of leisure time also contributed to improving the quality of life. This was achieved by adjusting the holidays recognized by the state, expanding the right to vacation for working people, and above all, by shortening the required time for work. Holidays had a minimal role, dropping to seven days from 10 in 1951.[88] Since 1945 the length of leave had been the standard two weeks. Some categories were entitled to an extra week (miners, adolescents, persons aged 50 and over, employees with 5 or more years on the job). Companies gave an extra 2 weeks to workers with 15 or more years on the job. The categorization of the health of the population in terms of risk is revealed by these rules, as is an attempt to motivate working people not to switch trades, which the centrally planned economy experienced as disruptive to the system.[89] The 1965 Code of Labour proceeded from a rationale that was similar.[90] The 48-hour work week of 6 workdays was gradually shortened, which expanded free Saturday time. The definitive introduction of the 2-day weekend was not until the year 1968.[91]

Distribution was not equal with respect to leisure time for men and women; childcare and housework implied immeasurably less leisure time in practice for women, as had been repeatedly shown by sociological surveys since the 1960s, and as of 1989, no change of any fundamental kind had occurred there yet.[92] Leisure time was also limited in its scope by other structural factors. Commuting was important and had become very widespread; during the 1960s, a third of the workforce was doing so. The communist party leadership considered this desirable for rapprochement between residents of rural and urban areas on the one hand, but on the other hand, it lengthened the workday. Commuting was considered desirable by experts if it lasted 30 minutes, but the average commute was 45 minutes, i.e. 90 minutes round-trip.[93] In addition, considering the conditions of economic scarcity, considerable free time went into tracking things down that were unavailable. The famous 1969 analysis by Radovan Richta of socialist society, entitled *Civilization at the Crossroads*, found that these actual limits to leisure and self-realization had led him to a cheerless conclusion. Despite its gains for society, the socialist system was slipping back into a situation where the content of the lives of a large part of the working people was bounded by 'the limits of the simple reproduction of the labour force', which was 'wasting an incalculable amount of the socially beneficial talents and creative forces of these individuals'.[94]

In the beginning, at least, the communists had taken quite ambitious approaches to free time for working people. Communist child-rearing was comprehended as delivering education in how to spend free time as an integral component of socialism. The capitalist contradiction between labour and leisure time that had been typical was now meant to be erased by this humanism in the socialist spirit.[95] Activities of collective leisure were organized that controlled individual lives most visibly, whether that was recreation organized by trade unions, clubs for racing, or the hobby groups of socialist organizations. The age of building socialism, in this case, was distinctly different from the late socialism of the 1970s and 1980s, as the collectivist forms of leisure organized as spectacle – embodied, for example, in the famous 1955 film *Anděl na horách* [Angel in the Mountains] about recreation during socialism – transitioned into a 'privatized citizenship' based on certain consumer needs being satisfied and ensuring peace and quiet in the workplace.[96] Conformism and a formal loyalty manifested towards the regime, as expressed so unforgettably by Václav Havel in his parable of the greengrocer who hangs propaganda posters in his display window so as to be 'left in peace', became crucial instruments for stabilizing the system, while the ambition of biopolitics to create a New Socialist Man fell into oblivion.[97]

The Socialist Senior Citizen

In biopower's customary definition, the cohorts that are the oldest in a population participate in pension systems and retirement planning.[98] This undoubtedly also applied to the control of the population during state socialism. For the aims of this chapter, we consider the most important subjects to be: (1) the aiming of these kinds of measures at the population's structure in order to transform it and (2) care for the elderly being exploited, along with gerontological knowledge, for direct discipline or for directing the forms of individual behaviour.

After February 1948, the communist party's creation of a universalist pension system was an important instrument for legitimizing its monopolization of power. The new political regime, termed the 'Third Republic', which had been established after the liberation in May 1945, had announced it would build up such insurance per its program promise so as to include the population as a whole.[99] Before then, Bismarckian principles (wage-related pensions) had been the basis in Czechoslovakia of an otherwise solid system, but it excluded the self-employed, who were the biggest segment of the economically active population. According to the 1930 census, which was relatively reliable and last taken in the inter-war period, 44 per cent of the active population was self-employed, while just 41 per cent were employees.[100] The limited pluralistic system in the years 1945 to 1948 and the conflicting interests among the companies offering such insurance, the different cohorts in the population, and the political parties themselves, delayed the enactment of any fast pension reform in a universalist vein. The bill in the cabinet was not debated until the eve of the February 1948 political crisis. Approval there was again blocked by the conflict between communists and non-communists. The crisis concluded with the communists emerging as the political victors, and in an effort to legitimize their position, they embarked on a legislative whirlwind; based on the Košice Government Program issued on 5 April 1945, the parliament passed reforms in rapid succession in the subsequent months. Thus, it was that on 15 April 1948, the Act on National Insurance saw the light of day, creating coverage for 95 per cent of the population through an insurance system that was unified.[101]

Changing, to some extent, the population's structure is one of the impacts insurance systems have on social stratification. The heavy-handed levelling of pensions and wages during the Nazi occupation period and then in the post-war Third Republic was a tendency that was typical.[102] When the class being harmed by this levelling was the upper one, whose interests had been served by the Austrian legacy of the Bismarckian logic behind wage-related pensions, the communists encouraged equality and increases to the lower-range and mid-range pensions. However, the centrally planned economy of the early 1950s experienced these egalitarian pensions as conflicting with other needs; thus began the communist party's push in the opposite direction against levelling efforts in order to aid with the allocation of the workforce, according to the central plan. In the historiography, the opinion presents itself, and we agree with it that Bismarckian merit principles were partly introduced by the state socialist social security system *sui generis*.[103] The idea of 'according to what you have done for society (in the opinion of its rulers), according to what you were, you shall receive' merely replaced the merit-based insurance of the old, pre-war times. Instead of market-based principles as the site of truth, contribution to building the socialist system became the credit-determining criterion.[104]

The alpha and omega of assessing and classifying different groups and individuals and measuring them was political power relations and people's societal work (societal interests). '"Allocations" emerged in economics and politics, a system that, in all contexts that were human, "gave" individuals things, "permitted" them to do things and "provided" for them', as was aptly, albeit critically, declared by an eminent expert on the law and social security towards the end of the 1960s.[105]

The adoption by Czechoslovakia of the categories, in 1956, from the Soviet system's three types of work resulted in the re-stratification of senior citizens and workers. Because that categorization had first been introduced for massive industrialization when resources had been lacking in the Soviet Union at the time, it had been impossible to sufficiently secure senior citizens as a whole. Thus, the rewards went to employees in professions important in terms of building a socialist economy.[106] Categories I and II included occupations that were preferred, while category III included employees representing the remaining 60 per cent of the workforce. Most noticeably, the age of retirement and the amount of the pensions were what made the categories different. This category system demonstrated its own excessive inequality a few years after its introduction. Categorization reform was shelved, though, as 'restrictions [could not] be implemented in the near future for political reasons'.[107] Even in the 1970s and 1980s, no decision was made by the government and the party to intervene more vigorously in the system of the three categories, so it was not abolished until the fall of communism.

The aspect of health, when classifying into these categories, was emphasized, as was the importance, in the official documents, of a profession to society. There is a completely different interpretation possible for this strategy, however. Because hygienic, technical and technological conditions were, to a large extent, predetermined by the state, including the consequences to health and the level of occupational safety, any compensation for the damage that emerged or was expected for health had to be provided from society-wide sources. Companies had limited possibilities vis-à-vis these factors to affect, in any fundamental way, health protection in the workplace, so the categories of jobs that were preferred suited them as a system. Dangerous, harmful, or obsolete technological operations could be kept running without major protests by trade unions or workers, and hazard pay, in part, would be paid by the state. Also, any damages, existing or future, from long-term performance would be postponed payment-wise until the pension for the risky work took effect. The category I and II preferences made it possible to channel into such industries, through material motivation, their workforce.[108]

The social security system, as a tool, was used to punish or reward individuals from the oldest cohorts of the population. Cases can be found in Czechoslovakia, even after the expulsion in 1945–1946 of the vast majority of the German population, in which older citizens of German nationality were typically targeted. The Czechoslovak government granted German nationals a special maintenance allowance for anti-fascists and elderly Germans in particular, but the central authorities in Prague had to report in July 1947 the 'disregarding' by lower-level authorities of that regulation. Aid conditions in some cases were met, but the aid was never awarded, or the decisions kept being postponed.[109] The consequence was difficult economic situations for these individuals, many of which remained unresolved. The experience from Liberec (northern Bohemia), the former centre of the Sudeten German borderland, shows that applications for pensions in the social security system, in the case of Czech–German marriages and incapacitated citizens, lacked local, significant social support. This often involved informal reviews of morality and national reliability. This practice, which lived on after the war, assessed an applicant's political credibility and reputation and could have come from the experience of such practices in social policy during the Nazi occupation of Czech lands own thorough verifications, as well as being a response to the recent German domination.[110] The argument in 1949 was required, still, that these were not citizens who had 'behaved toward the Czech nation with enmity'.[111]

The alleged enemies of the people's democratic regime were most visibly punished through pension reductions, an approach taken by the Communist Party of Czechoslovakia in 1953.[112] This was carried out in concert with the controversial monetary reform announced in May of that year, which actually liquidated the population's savings – affecting, of course, the population strata that were wealthier. As was eloquently expressed by the *Gazette* of the State Pension Office with respect to the intention of both measures in its June issue of that year:

> The monetary reform has set its blade against the class enemy and speculators and has thus deepened the effects of Government Decree No.

> 22/1953, Coll. By devaluing the assets of the former representatives of the bourgeois economic and political oppression, their privileged position has been further dismantled, and those who did not trust the government and who were hostile to the people's democratic order have been punished by devaluing savings not deposited in state-owned financial institutions.[113]

There was no appearance, later on, of such an openly discriminatory procedure, although in *ad hoc* cases, the door was left open by the laws on social security for them to be used that way. The 1958 Act on Social Security Changes allowed, for example, for individuals' pensions to be reduced if, before entering that employment relationship, they had done business and employed foreign labour.[114] In the decades that followed, the persecution of the bourgeoisie lost its justification. On the contrary, there was a problem with the fact that, due to having been insured for just a short time, formerly self-employed persons usually had very low pensions. The aspect of class no longer appeared in the discourse, which differentiated groups and individuals into income categories for pension insurance depending on *when* they had been awarded a pension. It was not until the Act on Social Security underwent a major amendment in 1968 that the level of legislative consequences saw the removal of this suppression of capitalist elements, old political opponents and other 'former people'.[115]

Functioning as an instrument of an opposite, positive preference was also possible for pensions. The case that was most visible was that of the 'personal pensions' (*osobní důchody*), as they were termed. These were awarded to activists in the communist movement who were considered deserving as of February 1948 – without any legal basis. Their introduction as part of the 1956 reform was austerely limited to this provision: 'Particularly deserving workers in the fields of economy, science, culture, administration and other areas of public activity or their survivors may be granted a personal pension'.[116] This affair was explicitly elitist. It has been stated that for the entire period from 1957 to 1990 when they were cancelled without compensation, personal pensions had been awarded to just 20 or 30,000 persons.[117] Political preferences remained relevant to social security in state socialism throughout its whole existence. There was a discretionary basis upon which the elite was given, by the government, its reward, while the administration's lowest levels made sure the 'ordinary deserving communists' were taken care of.

Conclusion

Although biopolitics as conceived by Foucault is an issue primarily of technology, of controlling human bodies through a set of techniques, we can never detach it from a definite set of starting points in terms of values. After all, for Foucault, the 'efficiency' he speaks of, which governmentality in the modern period has been formed in order to maximize, is not only a category of economic management, as it appears at first glance, but is just as much a category of morality, where the 'common good' and its achievement by the actions of government is represented. Our analysis concludes that the analytical category of 'socialist biopolitics' is useful for three reasons.

In the first place, the regimes of socialism were just a variant of industrial modern society, as the sociologist Peter Wagner says, an aspect of 'organized modernity', as a phenomenon, in the short twentieth century.[118] The different forms of organized modernity ranged from the social market economy of the European social model to the American New Deal, to different forms of fascist dictatorships and state socialism, and they arose in response to the systemic crisis of the 'limited liberal modernity' of the nineteenth century. The interest of such regimes was in shaping their populations – structures, birth rate, health, etc. – according to (ideological) claims that were normative of the 'common good'. Nevertheless, it depended on how that was defined (although what almost exclusively interested Foucault was formed, which we have described here as 'social market'). Biopolitics is an issue purely, still, of technology at this point, i.e. of controlling human bodies and the method for doing so. The different demands, ideologically, of these political regimes, required the use of sets of techniques that varied, and we find it therefore useful, as has already been said, to add an adjective to the biopolitical concept – *socialist* – so the normative objective is specified for which these techniques were used.

In the second place, while the liberal regimes addressed by Foucault aimed above all to form a highly disciplined population in the sense of Bentham's Panopticon that allowed, by its very existence, for effective governance at low cost, the aims towards which the socialist dictatorships were heading were more ambitious. The creation of a highly egalitarian 'society of workers' was meant to accompany the formation of the New Socialist Man. The catalogue of biopolitical techniques differs between liberal regimes and those of state socialism in spite of their many similarities, therefore, and commonalities would be difficult to find west of the Iron Curtain, or not in such acute, explicit forms, at least.

In the third place, the allocation of power was different under the regimes of state socialism because the dictatorship had its own power structure. Clearly, the centrally coordinated, directive decision-making processes facilitated the measures that needed to be upheld. We are drawing attention at the same time to the fact that, on the other hand, the agendas chosen for delegation to the lower structures of public power probably promoted a radicalization in the degree of this oppression. An analytical category that is separate from the biopolitics of liberal regimes is required, despite the many superficial similarities, so we find 'socialist biopolitics' more useful to work with, as it not only allows us to capture similarities among forms of control over human bodies and populations throughout modernity, but it also adequately emphasizes the fundamental differences flowing from these various ideological bases and from the objectives at which the biopolitical techniques are specifically targeted.

In this chapter, we have considered the class principle and the ethnic/racial principle to have been the central categories in the Czechoslovak conditions after the war with respect to socialist biopolitics. The biopolitical and disciplinary procedures that were brought to life by the communist party in order to create and direct a levelled 'society of workers' were of a diverse range, above all in the building phase of socialism during the 1950s. The authorities in Czechoslovakia declared in 1960 that the establishment of socialism had been successful, so the class criterion for categorizing different groups and the differentiated distribution of obligations and rights among the population then receded. With the criterion of race, it was different. The discriminatory, racist elements that we have pointed out did demonstrably exist in the period under review but were not a central pillar as they had been under the Nazi occupation with respect to the welfare state. We assess them as having been a consequence of the claim that the socialist norm of 'correct' behaviour by individual subjects in terms of their life strategy and work ethic had to be fulfilled. We agree with Sergei Prozorov, therefore, that as a category, race was secondary from the standpoint of state socialist biopolitics. It aided the identification of an individual who was deviating from the established norm, where external manifestations were more often the cause of that identification than was the individual's origin in and of itself. Actions by the authorities at the administratively lower levels were conditioned much more on a racial basis and were much more spontaneous, originating from a popular racism that the daily practices under the National Socialism had significantly supported. Therefore, when the agenda became decentralized, that enabled even more pronounced procedures of repression with respect to the issue of the population of Roma.

We have attempted to demonstrate the usefulness of the analytical category of 'socialist biopolitics' through extensive empirical material wherein the human individual's life cycle and its main phases were the organizing principle: childhood, adult parenthood, the economically active adult and old age. The agents of state socialist biopolitics attempted to maximize the effectiveness, in terms of the economy and the population, of the measures promulgated by the state and, by means of a comprehensive patronage system, endeavoured to minimize not just political resistance but also, above all the Czechoslovak population's resistance in sociocultural terms to the idea of the New Socialist Man. The effects of these measures and their long-term impact on individuals and on the population were considerably uneven.

Notes

1 This study was conducted as part of the 'Creativity and Adaptability as Conditions of the Success of Europe in an Interrelated World' project, supported

by EU Structural Funds received by the Faculty of Arts of Charles University. Sincere gratitude goes to Christiane Brenner for her careful reading and comments.

2 Marius Turda, *Modernism and Eugenics* (Basingstoke: Palgrave, 2010), 112. This article was translated from Czech by Gwendolyn Albert.

3 Michel Foucault, *The Birth of Biopolitics* (Basingstoke: Palgrave, 2008), 317. For the development of this concept, see Alberto Spektorowski – Liza Ireni-Saban, *Politics of Eugenics: Productionism, Population, and National Welfare* (London: Routledge, 2013), 92–95, 182.

4 Jacques Donzelot, *The Policing of Families* (New York: Pantheon, 1997), 6.

5 Foucault, *The Birth of Biopolitics*, 190–191.

6 E.g. Sergei Prozorov, 'Living Ideas and Dead Bodies. The Biopolitics of Stalinism', *Global, Local, Political* 38, no. 3 (2013): 208–227; Barbara Klich-Kluczewska, 'Biopolitics and (Non-)Modernity. Population Micro-Policy, Expert Knowledge and Family in Late-Communist Poland', *Acta Poloniae Historic* 115 (2017): 151–174; Radka Dudová, 'Interrupce v socialistickém Československu z foucaultovské perspektivy', *Gender, rovné příležitosti, výzkum* 10, no. 1 (2009): 25–36.

7 Compare Stephen J. Collier, *Post-Soviet Social: Neoliberalism, Social Modernity, Biopolitics* (Princeton, NJ: Princeton University Press 2011), 6, 39–52.

8 Sergei Prozorov, 'Foucault and Soviet Biopolitics', *History of the Human Sciences* 27, no. 5 (2014): 7.

9 Ibid., 17.

10 Compare Peter Fritzsche and Jochen Hellbeck, 'The New Man in Stalinist Russia and Nazi Germany', in *Beyond Totalitarianism: Stalinism and Nazism Compared*, eds. Michael Geyer and Sheila Fitzpatrick (Cambridge: CUP, 2008), 302–342. In the Czech-language literature, the most recent work is Denisa Nečasová, *Nový socialistický člověk: Československo 1948–1956* (Brno: Host, 2018).

11 See also Gwendolyn Albert and Marek Szilvasi, 'Intersectional Discrimination of Romani Women Forcibly Sterilized in the Former Czechoslovakia and Czech Republic', *Health and Human Rights Journal* 19, no. 2 (2017): 24.

12 Michel Foucault, *Society Must Be Defended* (New York: Picador, 2003), 242–243.

13 Mikael Baaz, Mona Lilja and Stellan Vinthagen, *Researching Resistance and Social Change: A Critical Approach to Theory and Practice* (London: Rowman and Littlefield Int. Ltd., 2018), 53.

14 See the authoritative *Oxford Handbook of the Welfare State* from 2010, where the term 'communist welfare state' is used in several passages (Franz Xaver Kaufmann and Linda Cook). In fact, two years earlier, Tomasz Inglot published his in-depth comparative study in which he wrote about welfare states in East Central Europe between 1919 and 2004 as being separate from the divergent political regimes that existed during this period. If we adopt the most frequently used 'qualitative' definition ('The essence of the welfare state is government-protected minimum standards of income, nutrition, health and safety, education, and housing assured to every citizen as a social right, not as charity'.), then the category can be used across Europe regardless of the particular political regimes. See Francis Castles, Stephan Leibfried, Jane Lewis, Herbert Obinger and Christopher Pierson, *Oxford Handbook of the Welfare State* (Oxford: Oxford University Press, 2010); Tomas Inglot, *Welfare States in East Central Europe 1919–2004* (Cambridge: Cambridge University Press, 2008); Harold Wilensky, 'Social Policy: Is There a Crisis of the Welfare State?', in *Handbook of Public Policy*, eds. Guy Peters and Jon Pierre(London: Sage, 2006), 201.

15 Radka Šustrová and Jakub Rákosník, 'Everyday Eugenics: Expert Thought and Social Practice in Czechoslovakia after 1945', manuscript.

16 Radka Šustrová, *Zastřené počátky sociálního státu. Nacionalismus a sociální politika v Protektorátu Čechy a Morava* (Praha: Argo – Masarykův ústav a Archiv AV ČR, 2020).

17 See Jakub Rákosník, Matěj Spurný and Jiří Štaif, *Milníky moderních českých dějin: Krize konsensu a legitimity v letech 1848–1989* (Praha: Argo, 2018), 182–195.

18 Benjamin Frommer, *National Cleansing: Retribution against Nazi Collaborators in Postwar Czechoslovakia* (Cambridge: 2005); Kateřina Čapková, 'Národně nespolehliví?!: Německy hovořící Židé v Polsku a Československu bezprostředně po druhé světové válce', *Soudobé dějiny* 22, no. 1–2 (2015): 80–101.

19 Národní archiv v Praze, fond Státní úřad plánovací I, karton 228, 12th Conference on Preventive Medicine (April 1947).

20 František Pachner, *Otázka potomstva – otázkou národního bytí: (problémy populační s hlediska lékařského)* (Brno: Svaz československé péče o mládež, 1946).

21 Compare Celia Donert, '"The struggle for the soul of the Gypsy": Marginality and Mass Mobilization in Stalinist Czechoslovakia', *Social History* 33, no. 2 (May 2008): 123–144.

22 Matěj Spurný, *Nejsou jako my: česká společnost a menšiny v pohraničí* (Praha: Antikomplex, 2011), 283. See also Celia Donert, *The Rights of the Roma: The Struggle for Citizenship in Post-war Czechoslovakia* (Oxford: Oxford University Press, 2017).

23 Ibid., 273, 281.

24 Nina Pavelčíková, *Romové v českých zemích v letech 1945–1989* (Praha: Úřad dokumentace a vyšetřování zločinů komunismu, 2004), 79.

25 Pavel Machonin, *Sociální struktura socialistické společnosti* (Praha: Svoboda, 1966).

26 Všeodborový archiv Českomoravské konfederace odborových svazů, fond: Národní pojištění, sign. 194–197, k. 75: Nárokový systém důchodového zabezpečení – uplatnění hlediska zásluhového a hlediska sociálního.

27 Jan Doležal and Zdeněk Ullrich, *Výzkum abiturientů českých středních škol v zemí České a Moravskoslezské ve škol. roce 1933/34* (Praha: Státní úřad statistický, 1936), 198, 201.

28 Vilém Prečan, ed., *Charta 77 (1977–1989): Od morální k demokratické revoluci* (Bratislava: Scheinfeld, 1990), 359–362.

29 Karel Pinc, *Společenská spotřeba obyvatelstva v ekonomice socialismu* (Praha: NPL, 1962), 69.

30 Johann De Deken, 'Sociální politika a politika solidarity', *Sociologický časopis* 28, no. 3 (1992): 355.

31 Miroslav Cipro, *Výchova k socialism* (Praha: SPN, 1976), 56.

32 Zákon č. 186/1960 Sb. o soustavě výchovy a vzdělávání (školský zákon) (15. prosinec 1960), preamble.

33 Zákon č. 103/1951 Sb. o jednotné preventivní a léčebné péči (27. prosinec 1951).

34 Emílie Lukášová, 'O jeslích', *Péče o mládež*, 26, no. 3 (1947): 79.

35 Z. Kuncová, J. Pavlásková, V. Kořínková, 'Jesle ve světle výzkumu', *Populační zprávy* 4, no. 2–3 (1974): 35.

36 Libuše Ivanovová, 'K realizaci nového pojetí předškolní výchovy', *Populační zprávy* 9, no. 1–2 (1979): 62.

37 Jiřina Taxová, *Výchovné problémy dětských domovů* (Praha: SPN, 1967): 42.

38 *Koncepce dětských domovů (Ideový záměr Ministerstva školství ČSR)* (Praha: SPN, 1970), 8.
39 Ibid., 3.
40 Zákon č. 50/1973 Sb., o pěstounské péči (4. květen 1973).
41 *Koncepce dětských domovů*, 10.
42 Ibid., 4.
43 Archiv města Ostravy, f. Obvodní národní výbor Ostrava-Zábřeh, karton 36, inv. č. 93: Rozbor činnosti oddělení péče o děti za rok 1970 z hlediska sociální a právní péče, s. 8.
44 Marie Kallmünzerová, Jiří Vyšín, Karel Lebeda, Marta Brtníková, Marta Zelenková, *Práce s cikánských obyvatelstvem* (Praha: Organizační odbor Ministerstva práce a sociálních věcí ČSR, 1976), 6.
45 In accordance with the current approach taken by Denisa Nečasová, we comprehend the concept of the 'New Socialist Man' as a culturally and socially constructed discursive figure representing a positive vision of the future, the promise of solving the problems of the day, or an anchoring in a predetermined security that was attractive and fulfilling for a part of the society of that time. Nečasová, *Nový socialistický člověk*, 13.
46 Lev Zalkind, *Zdravé manželství a zdravá rodina* (Praha: Státní zdravotnické nakladatelství, 1953).
47 Facilitated by the nationalization of medical counselling work as per Act No. 49/1947, Coll. (11 April 1947).
48 Act No. 56/1948, Coll., § 2.
49 Jindřich Cibulec, *Láska, partnerství a manželství* (Praha: Práce, 1974), 124–127.
50 Šustrová, *Zastřené počátky*.
51 Zákon č. 49/1947 Sb. o poradenské zdravotní péči (11. duben 1947).
52 Zákon č. 248/1948 Sb. o okrskových porodních asistentkách a o úpravě oprávnění k výkonu pomocné praxe porodnické (17. listopad 1948).
53 Zákon č. 103/1951 Sb. o jednotné preventivní a léčebné péči (27. prosinec 1951).
54 Radka Dudová, *Interrupce v České republice: Zápas o ženská těla* (Praha: Sociologický ústav AV ČR, 2012); Věra Sokolová, 'Planned Parenthood behind the Curtain: Population Policy and Sterilization of Romani Women in Communist Czechoslovakia, 1972–1989', *Anthropology of East Europe Review* 23, no. 1 (2005): 79–98; Gwendolyn Albert and Marek Szilvasi, 'Intersectional Discrimination of Romani Women Forcibly Sterilized in the Former Czechoslovakia and Czech Republic', *Health and Human Rights Journal* 19, no. 2 (2017): 23–34; Sarah Marks, 'The Romani Minority, Coercive Sterilization, and Languages of Denial in the Czech Lands', *History Workshop Journal* 84 (2017): 128–148; *Telo i duša: násilné sterilizácie a d'alšie útoky na reprodukčnú slobodu Rómov na Slovensku* (Bratislava: Centrum pre reprodukčné práva – Poradňa pre občianske a ľudské práva, 2003).
55 Zákon č. 68/1957 Sb. o umělém přerušení těhotenství (30. prosinec 1957).
56 Senta Radvanová, Jiří Nezkusil, Oto Novotný, 'Pro zdraví žen', *Literární noviny* 6, no. 27 (6 July 1957).
57 Miroslav Vojta, 'Náměty na zlepšení činnosti interrupčních komisí', *Zprávy Státní populační komise* 7, no. 2 (1968): 17–20.
58 Compare Katherine Verdery, *National Ideology under Socialism: Identity and Cultural Politics in Ceausescu's Romania* (Berkeley, CA: University of California Press, 1995); Gail Kligman, *The Politics of Duplicity: Controlling Reproduction in Ceausescu's Romania* (Berkeley, CA: University of California Press, 1998).
59 Libor Stloukal, 'Vývoj potratovosti v ČSR mezi lety 1980 a 1987', *Demografie* 31, no. 4 (1989): 309.

60 Směrnice MZd ČSR o provádění sterilizace ze dne 17. 12. 1971; Věstník MZd ČSR, ročník XX, částka 1–2, 29. února 1972.
61 Tisk 603, https://www.psp.cz/sqw/text/tiskt.sqw?O=8&CT=603&CT1=0 (accessed 21 May 2020).
62 Národní archiv v Praze, fond Ministerstvo práce a sociálních věci ČSR 1969–1990, karton 206: Poskytování stimulačního příspěvku při sterilizaci.
63 Jakub Rákosník and Radka Šustrová, *Rodina v zájmu státu: Populační růst a instituce manželství v českých zemích 1918–1989* (Praha: Nakladatelství Lidové noviny, 2016), 182–185; Radka Šustrová and Jakub Rákosník, 'Everyday Eugenics: Expert Thought and Social Practice in Czechoslovakia after 1945', manuscript.
64 Ústavní zákon č. 100/1960 Sb., Ústava Československé socialistické republiky (11.7.1960), Article 2.
65 Compare Josef Pokstefl, *Der soziale Wandel in der ČSSR und sein Reflex auf das politische und Verfassungssystem* (Marburg: J. G. Herder Institut, 1984), 20.
66 Zákon č. 40/1964 Sb., Občanský zákoník (5. červen 1964), Article III.
67 Foucault, *Birth of Biopolitics*, 30: 'This site of truth is not in the heads of economists, of course, but is the market'.
68 Karel Kaplan, *Útváření generální linie výstavby socialismu v Československu* (Praha: Academia, 1966).
69 Karel Jech, *Kolektivizace a vyhánění sedláků z půdy* (Praha: Vyšehrad, 2008).
70 Peter Heumos, 'K sociálněhistorickému výzkumu komunistických režimů', *Soudobé dějiny* 15 (2008): 698.
71 Jiří Maňák, 'Orientace KSČ na vytvoření socialistické intelligence', in *Bolševismus, komunismus a radikální socialismus v Československu*, eds. Zdeněk Kárník and Michal Kopeček, Volume II (Praha: Dokořán, 2004), 153.
72 Pavel Machonin et. al., *Československá společnost: Sociologická analýza sociální stratifikace* (Bratislava: Epocha, 1969), 95–111.
73 Ibid., 107.
74 Ibid., 390.
75 Miroslav Petrusek, 'Sociální stratifikace československé společnosti (shrnutí výsledků empirického šetření)', *Sociologický časopis* 5, no. 6 (1969): 578.
76 Milan Tuček, *Zpráva o vývoji sociální struktury české a slovenské společnosti 1945–1990* (Praha: Sociologický ústav AV ČR, 1996), 33.
77 Ibid., 16.
78 Compare Alena Wagnerová, *Die Frau im Sozialismus: Beispiel ČSSR* (Hamburg: Hoffmann und Campe, 1974).
79 Jiří Večerník, *Občan a tržní ekonomika – Příjmy, nerovnost a politické postoje v české společnosti* (Praha: Nakladatelství Lidové noviny, 1998), 60–65.
80 Pavelčíková, *Romové v českých zemích*, 88–89.
81 Vládní nařízení č. 219/1948 Sb. o ústavech národního zdraví (7. 9. 1948) a zákon č. 103/1951 Sb. o jednotné preventivní a léčebné péči (27. prosinec 1951).
82 Zákon č. 99/1948 Sb. o národním pojištění (15. květen 1948).
83 Národní archiv v Praze, fond Klement Gottwald, sv. 90: Sociálně politický program KSČ.
84 This was not exclusively about an argument related to the need to provide for production. Privileged access to treatment was expressly guaranteed in the Regulations on Treatment to shock workers, to those who showed improvement, and to manual labourers in important manufacturing sectors. See Jiří Chýský, *Národní pojištění: Přehled a výklad nejdůležitějších ustanovení* (Praha: Orbis, 1952), 49.
85 Pinc, *Společenská spotřeba*, 60.

86 Cited in Alena Šubrtová, *Dějiny populačního myšlení v českých zemích* (Praha: Česká demografická společnost, 2006), 165.
87 Alena Šubrtová, *Dějiny populačního myšlení*, 196; Hana Švejdová and Igor Michal, 'Životní prostředí a délka života', *Vesmír* 73, no. 7 (1994), https://vesmir.cz/cz/casopis/archiv-casopisu/1994/cislo-7/zivotni-prostredi-delka-zivota.html (3 September 2021).
88 Zákon č. 93/1951 Sb. o státním svátku, o dnech pracovního klidu a o památných a významných dnech (6. prosinec 1951).
89 Zákon č. 82/1947 Sb. o přechodné úpravě placené dovolené na zotavenou (4. červen 1947).
90 Zákon č. 65/1965 Sb., Zákoník práce (30. červen 1965).
91 Vyhláška Státní plánovací komise č. 62/1966 Sb. (5. Srpen 1966) a vyhláška Ministerstva práce a sociálních věcí č. 63/1968 Sb. (10. červen 1968).
92 Hana Havelková, '(De)centralizovaná genderová politika: Role Státní populační komise', *Vyvlastněný hlas: Proměny genderové kultury české společnosti 1948–1989*, eds. Libora Indruch-Oatsová and Hana Havelková (Praha: Slon, 2015), 40.
93 Václav Lamser, 'Pohyb obyvatelstva mezi venkovem a městem', *Demografie* 2 (1960): 138.
94 Radovan Richta, *Civilizace na rozcestí: Společenské a lidské souvislosti vědeckotechnické revoluce* (Praha: Svoboda, 1969), 105. Published in English in 1969 and 2018.
95 Milan Bartoš, *Zájmová činnost ve volném čase jako součást formování socialistického způsobu života* (Praha: Univerzita Karlova, 1987), 27.
96 Pauline Bren, *The Greengrocer and His TV: The Culture of Communism after the 1968 Prague Spring* (Ithaca, NY: Cornell University Press, 2010).
97 See Václav Havel, *The Power of the Powerless* (London: Routledge, 2010).
98 Compare Beatriz da Costa and Kavita Philip, *Tactical Biopolitics: Art, Activism, and Technoscience* (Cambridge: MIT, 2008), 111.
99 Included in Košický vládní program.
100 Václav Průcha, *Hospodářské a sociální dějiny Československa 1918–1992*, Vol. I (Brno: Doplněk, 2004), 368.
101 Zákon č. 99/1948 Sb. o národním pojištění (15. květen 1948).
102 Jakub Rákosník, *Sovětizace sociálního státu: Lidově demokratický režim a sociální práva občanů v Československu 1945–1960* (Praha: Filozofická fakulta UK, 2010), 246–248.
103 Tomasz Inglot, *Welfare States in East Central Europe 1919–2004* (Cambridge: Cambridge University Press, 2008), 26.
104 Igor Tomeš, 'Úvahy o sociální politice – III. Sociální politika v sociálním zabezpečení', *Sociální zabezpečení* 17, no. 8–9 (1968): 13.
105 Ibid., 12.
106 Ramesh Mishra, 'Convergence Theory and Social Change: The Development of Welfare in Britain and the Soviet Union', *Comparative Studies in Society and History* 18 (1976): 30, 36–39; Gaston Rimlinger, *Welfare Policy and Industrialization in Europe, America, and Russia* (New York: J. Wiley and Sons, 1971), 274–275.
107 Všeodborový archiv Českomoravské konfederace odborových svazů (VOA ČMKOS), fond Národní pojištění, karton 75, archivní jednotka 195: Nárokový systém důchodového zabezpečení zaměstnanců.
108 *Důvodová zpráva k vládnímu návrhu zákona o zrušení pracovních kategorií*, FS ČSFR 1990–1992, Tisk č. 1400.
109 Státní okresní archiv Liberec (SOkA Liberec), fond Okresní národní výbor Liberec, karton 290: Ministerstvo vnitra Zemskému národní výboru v Praze, 4. červenec 1947.

110 See Šustrová, *Zastřené počátky*.
111 SOkA Liberec, fond Okresní národní výbor Liberec, karton 290: Místní národní výbor v Lázních Kundraticích Jednotnému národnímu výboru v Liberci, 2. září 1949.
112 Nařízení 22/1953 Sb., o úpravě důchodů z důchodového zabezpečení a zaopatření osob nepřátelských lidově demokratickému zřízení.
113 Valter Vergeiner, 'Peněžní reforma a důchodové zabezpečení', *Důchodové zabezpečení* 11, no. 6 (1953), 1.
114 Zákon č. 41/1958 Sb. o některých změnách v sociálním zabezpečení (23. červenec 1958).
115 Zákon č. 161/1968 Sb. o zvláštním přídavku k dávkám, o změnách v důchodovém zabezpečení účastníků odboje a o některých dalších změnách v sociálním zabezpečení (22. prosinec 1968).
116 Zákon č. 55/1956 Sb. o sociálním zabezpečení.
117 Inglot, *Welfare States in East Central Europe*, 138. According to official statistics, from 1948 to 1983 an average of 2,500 personal pensions were paid out annually. Compare *Historická statistická ročenka ČSSR* (Praha: Státní nakladatelství technické literatury 1985), 416.
118 Peter Wagner, *A Sociology of Modernity: Liberty and Discipline* (London: Routledge, 1994), 55–71.

12 Imperial Biopolitics

Famine in Russia and the Soviet Union, 1891–1947

Immo Rebitschek

The term 'biopolitics' describes rationales for governing life and death in a society. Most historiographical analyses trace these rationales in a framework of national population control. The 'societal body' of a race/nation was the reference value and the object on whose behalf, life was fostered or 'disallowed'.[1] This reading reflects the experiences of most national states in the first half of twentieth-century Europe, where nationality and citizenship became intertwined as political privileges[2] and where certain 'bio-policies' were used to preserve those privileges. The case of Tsarist Russia and the Soviet Union, however, suggests a different angle. Both were multi-ethnic empires with a diverse societal body. The key to governing these states was not to mobilize a major national narrative but to manage national/ethnic differences in a wider supra-national framework.[3] This paper argues that biopolitics provided one of those managing techniques. Assuming that imperial rule is the pattern of an unequal relationship between the centre and its multi-ethnic peripheries,[4] 'imperial biopolitics' therefore refers to the principles of governing life and death that aim to preserve the imperial body, that is, to maintain control over heterogeneous and dependent societies. Imperial biopolitics thus was about fostering or disallowing life to the benefit of imperial stability and/or control and not about securing a single national body. The modern empire was managing the biological needs and bodies of its different subjects in a concerted and institutionalized manner, treating them according their estate-based role in society.

This chapter will follow this assumption by examining hunger relief policies in Russian and Soviet history. The question of how and why famines occur should not be limited to the realm of state policies. The classical definition of famine as an 'acute and widespread lack of *access* to food' already implies the multicausality of this phenomenon.[5] Still, the question of how states responded to such crises is an essentially biopolitical matter. Famine always brought up life into the 'sphere of political techniques'.[6] From a very simplistic viewpoint, aid could either be provided or withheld, making famine relief policy an instrument to either 'let live' or 'induce death'.[7] Furthermore, over the course of wars and revolutions, famine is the common biopolitical denominator in Russian history. Both late tsarist

DOI: 10.4324/9781003161080-15

Russia and the Soviet Union experienced at least four disastrous famines over the course of a half-century.[8] The origins of these crises were quite different from one another, but the political responses tell us about both changes and continuities in imperial biopolitics.

The chapter will examine the changing purposes and priorities of famine relief policy in the aforementioned cases – against the backdrop of imperial claims and challenges. The underlying question is: how and why did the Russian and Soviet states offer or deny hunger relief when famine was imminent in multi-ethnic territories? How did the political centre communicate about policing non-Russian bodies in the midst of these crises and to what end? How did the late Russian and the early Soviet empire operate and evolve as biopolitical regimes? The following approach deals with the central motivations and strategies/premises for dealing with crises in multi-ethnic contexts. It is not an inquiry as to how these strategies were implemented and dealt with by local elites and intermediaries. The sole focus of this article will be on the provision of direct aid and loans – in cash or in kind – by the hands of the state. By focusing on food provision, it singles out a policy tool that had an immediate effect on the chances of biological survival, excluding other anti-scarcity tools (such as price adjustments, prohibition). It thereby also excludes the debate on larger economic rationales. How, why and to whom did the Tsarist and Soviet authorities provide or deny food/money in the midst of a subsistence crisis?

Food provisioning played an essential role for Foucault's reasoning about population management, and yet the geographer David Nally is one of the few to treat famine in the context of biopolitical techniques.[9] Nally views the 'biopower' of food provisioning in the light of socio-economic transformation – from a 'moral economy of hunger' to a market-oriented political economy. He analyzes the colonial powers' means to destroy (indigenous) non-market safety nets and to efface 'customary entitlements' as an expression of biopolitical engineering. British famine control in its colonies was left to market dynamics that helped to categorize and distinguish those conforming to the new liberal order ('the population') from those rejecting it ('the people').[10] Nally's take on biopolitics emphasizes the use of strategies to dismantle anti-scarcity structures while using state power to safeguard private market dynamics in order to counter the threat of hunger. Although market interest played a significant role in imperial Russia's governing of peripheral agricultures, here the spectre of famine called for state intervention – even after the zemstvo reforms.[11] The following article thus will draw the focus on the strategy of monopolizing and controlling anti-scarcity structures (through the provision of cash/food) in order to underline how the Russian and especially the Soviet state were managing scarcity for the sake of imperial political control.

Andrey Makarychev and Alexandra Yatsyk used the term 'imperial biopolitics' to describe a Russian foreign policy toolkit that includes spreading socially conservative agendas and 'de-bordering' visa policies in neighbouring countries.[12] In historical research, the realms of the Soviet Union play little or no role as far as questions of population management are concerned. While Russian imperial hygiene and disease control attracted considerable attention in terms of medical progress and the development of a professional infrastructure,[13] only a handful of authors have examined either the biopolitical narratives of post-Soviet Eurasianism or the theoretical biopolitical rationalities behind the Stalinist transformation.[14] The practical implications, the question of how the citizens' biology was actually governed by Soviet authorities and the larger rationales of population management remain uncharted territory for historiography – if we exclude the orchestrated acts of mass violence like the infamous 'mass operations' of the late 1930s as biopolitics.[15] Peter Holquist's account on Russian and Soviet 'population policies' emphasized strategies to operate the 'social body' through military statistics. It pointed out important continuities as both the Tsarist and the Soviet states attempted to catalogue and reverse a diverse population profile.[16] Dan Healey analyzed the Gulag as 'a criminally reduced version' of a larger Stalinist biopolitical regime that mobilized scarce resources and favoured industrial output over individual health: 'Soviet planners had other priorities'.[17] The focus on famine can help to contextualize these priorities in an imperial, non-national framework.

In contrast to this desideratum, famine and hunger play a dominant role in historical research about Russia and the Soviet Union. The famine of 1891 is a neuralgic point in the history of the autocracy and of the battle for interpretation of the peasant question.[18] The great famines of the 1920s and 1930s serve as evidence for either structural failure, institutional confusion and/or the reckless and, to some extent, genocidal design of Soviet domestic policies.[19] Plenty of studies have demonstrated how hunger became the biological consequence of war communism and Stalinist state-building, yet apart from the meteorological and climatic aspects, no one attempted to view these catastrophes in a shared context of relief policy – let alone biopolitics.[20]

Although these crises resulted from highly different sets of conditions, sometimes from criminal neglection and intent, it is worthwhile asking about the common logics of relief policy. A state's rationale for policing life becomes particularly visible in its attempt to shield people from death. This is especially true when there is sufficient evidence to claim that the state had facilitated the deadly threat in the first place.

In the first part, the chapter will show how the imperial government in Tatarstan in 1891 and in Georgia in 1907/08 provided grain/seeds with no regard to ethnic considerations. Famine relief policy was supposed to help maintaining socio-economic and political control – through preserving life. Part two will illustrate how, in 1921, the Bolsheviks turned to a more 'instrumentalist' view, acknowledging hunger as both a mighty incentive and a possible threat to their political project. Consequently, the Bolsheviks used the distribution of hunger aid for creating loyalty and breaking resistance. Ethnic considerations did not play a decisive role in the Bolsheviks' decision-making either for the Volga Valley or for Ukraine. Whether to allow or to prevent people from starving was dependent on military and budgetary considerations. This approach determined how the Soviet leadership dealt with hunger crises in the future.

Stalin pushed this approach to the extreme by not only 'instrumentalizing' but 'weaponizing' famine relief. Between 1931 and 1933/34, in Ukraine, the North Caucasus or Kazakhstan, millions of people were starved to death. Part three will examine how the regime not only created famine but withheld and distributed relief only after the main economic and political goals were considered fulfilled: breaking the peasants' resistance to the Kolkhoz order, maintaining supply for cities and heavy industry, and cleansing the countryside from any possible opposition. This perceived opposition partially and temporarily assumed national shapes, unleashing genocidal practices, especially in Ukraine, but the primary objective of famine relief policy was to enforce state socialism and maintain political control. This outlook will show how the Soviet government adjusted its rationales from 'weaponizing' back to 'instrumentalizing' relief when in 1946/47, it hesitantly organized hunger aid in the former war zones of Ukraine, Moldavia and even the Soviet Occupation Zone in Eastern Germany. Here again, the leadership sought to maintain control over the populace by providing relief primarily for those parts of the population that helped to maintain the social and economic model of the USSR – regardless of their national background.

By including my findings about famine relief in Imperial Russia, this article suggests a reinterpretation of existing narratives for the Soviet Union as well. The goal is not to find a common causal pattern for these catastrophes. By focusing on relief practices, I would like to point out, on the one hand, the different biopolitical approaches of the Russian and Soviet leadership towards their populace. As the autocracy strove to maintain order through preserving life, the new rulers in the Kremlin saw and used the opportunity to enforce their will through 'inducing death'. On the other hand, this chapter will emphasize the continuity of the concern by both St. Petersburg and Moscow to preserve the 'body of the empire' with little to no regard for the ethnic or national affiliation of their subjects. Furthermore, it places the 'nation' as a referential point for biopolitical strategies in a broader perspective.

'Tsar Hunger': Hunger in the Russian Empire, 1891–1907

There is no direct line from crop failure to famine. The lack of access to food results from a conjunction of factors such as meteorological conditions, institutional communication or market dynamics, although not every phase with deficient access to food is defined or remembered as 'famine'.[21] In the history of the late Russian empire, several droughts led to devastating subsistence crises; this was most acute in 1891/2 but also in the years between

1905 and 1907.[22] The 'Great Famine' of 1891 left a deep mark in cultural memory, causing between 300,000 and 500,000 excess deaths.[23] The latter rarely received attention and appears like background noise for the revolution of 1905 (also because the excess death rate remained considerably low).[24] Still, both catastrophes challenged the imperial administration to invest millions of roubles and plenty of goods in order to maintain stability and control in vast and (although different) multi-ethnic territories.[25]

In the 1890s, crop failures hit especially the 'central and southern producer' regions (covering most of the central black earth area, the Volga valley, Ukraine and even the Ural area), whereas the second crisis period between 1905 and 1908 had devastating consequences primarily for the central producer region, although the southern producer regions were affected as well.[26]

During both crises, the non-orthodox population segments were in a particularly vulnerable position. In the late nineteenth century, 97 per cent of Tatars in the lower Volga area were former state peasants. The agrarian reforms of the 1860s increased economic pressure on this group. Most Tatars ended up with the smallest and worst lots, while only a fraction of farmers were considered 'independent', which contributed to further social and economic polarization in Tatar agriculture.[27] Soviet historians have pointed out how Tatar peasants had worse prospects, less financial or other reserves and were, in general, more vulnerable to crop failures.[28] In recent historiography, famine is mentioned as the major factor for the massive rural exodus when thousands of families were leaving Russia for the Ottoman Empire.[29] Already contemporary observers had knowledge about the economic hardships and the vulnerability of the Tatar peasants.[30]

The ethnic dimensions of hunger are hard to quantify as the central famine relief system did not differentiate religious/ethnic backgrounds among the starving peasantries. What becomes clear is that those who were involved in famine relief at the local level (mostly privateers, land captains and zemstvo officials) perceived the Tatars as a particular risk group that relied heavily and immediately on gratuitous relief (charity). Local authorities and private fundraisers organized in trustee bodies (*popechitel'stva*) were voicing concerns or at least pointing at the devastating situation of the Tatars, whose settlements were often too remote from soup kitchens and bakeries.[31] Experts like Yuri Nechaev-Mal'tsov from the Special Committee on Famine Relief were sent to Kazan to give an assessment about charity work and local needs among the populace. They, too, made it clear that Tatars were the first and sometimes the only ones to suffer from crop failures, which made not just them but non-Russians, in general, a clear indicator for structural problems in rural areas: 'The multi-ethnic composition (*raznoplemennyj sostav*) of the population, with either of those nationalities being predominant in some settlements and villages, describes their economic and sanitary situation, and places with a Tatar population are staggeringly impoverished'.[32] There was extensive knowledge about minorities being exposed to special hardships and its potential social effects.

The imperial system of famine relief did not utilize this dependence. On the contrary, ethnicity was simply a non-factor in the communication of the higher echelons of the imperial administration. Neither Mal'tsev nor others were making deductions or recommendations to tackle this issue in particular. Throughout the famine of 1892, the prime objective of the central government was to raise the living standards for the peasantry in general. In St Petersburg, neither charity organizations, the ministerial departments, nor the press differentiated among the 'peasantry' throughout the famine of 1892. Grain loans were given out without regard for ethnic/religious background.[33] The entire relief system was designed to 'secure the national provision' for the 'rural dwellers' [*sel'skikh obyvatelej*] and the 'local residents'.[34] Rural dwellers referred to the members of the pre-reform peasant estate that included sedentary *inorodtsy* (but excluded the Jews, who fell under the category of local residents).[35] Estate and geography determined the legal framework for relief and thus its communication. The Russian food and charity legislation did not differentiate along ethnic division lines but considered the administrative prerogatives of estate-based institutions, reflecting the concerns of financial control and logistics.

Even when individual officials in the administration were bringing up ethnicity as a particular subject for the discussion, the Tatar issue quickly became a 'peasant issue'. In one instance, General Mikhail Annenkov, head of the public works program, and his subordinate, Aleksandr Terekhov, were asked to give an assessment of the logistical situation for transporting seed loans down the Volga river. Terekhov and Annenkov both argued to exclude Tatars from such loans because only a small fraction of them owned horses, and therefore these loans would be a 'waste of state funds'.[36] Neither Anennkov's nor Terekhov's suggestions, much less the wording, were considered. Rather, members of the provincial administration, the zemstva, the Ministry of Internal Affairs (MVD) and the charity committees agreed to re-evaluate the exact need for seed loans but also to organize horses and cattle for the 'peasants without horses'.[37] At no point in this entire communication did the officials use the words 'Tatar' or *inorodtsy*. The zemstvo assembly even suggested that horse owners could pay back their loans by working the lands of their horseless neighbours, referring to the territories inhabited mostly by the Tatars.[38] The officials involved rejected any ethnicized reading of this crisis and addressed the needs of a peasant population instead. The empire did act on behalf of all its subjects. This did not mean that ethnicity was not a determining factor for economic success/survival. On the contrary, the famine exposed infrastructural weaknesses and economic burdens affecting particularly non-Russian rural dwellers.[39] Still, the notion of ethnicity could not and did not correspond with relief policies. While local activists and officials perpetuated knowledge of the Tatars' situation, the central system of famine relief did neither utilize nor acknowledge an ethnic dimension to this crisis. It saved thousands of lives, but it also prevented any significant debate on the relation between ethnicity and poverty.

It was not until 1905 that this connection became gradually visible to the imperial administration. In the aftermath of the revolution, new group identities began to rise and to merge within the framework of political upheaval.[40] Ethnic and social categories became intertwined in the waves of protest that shook the imperial periphery – like in the Caucasus. Here, repeated droughts and crop failures led to a severe subsistence crisis in the southern mountain regions in 1907/08, further escalating the tensions between Armenian and Azeri groups over Nagorno-Karabakh.[41] Duma delegates and revolutionaries alike spread the word about how hunger had fuelled national hatred and that it was up to the imperial government to provide help to the 'suffering sons of our common motherland, Russia'.[42]

At the central level, in the Food Commission [*prodovol'stennaia kommissiia*] of the Duma, none of the members showed a particular awareness for the ethnic complexity of the situation in the Caucasus. Government officials (from the ministries of finance, interior and trade) were concerned about the economic effects of interventionist relief policies (such as cutting grain prices); and about the political risks of sharing detailed information about the Caucasus with Duma delegates (and their non-elected experts). In turn, the Duma delegates (especially those from the region) suspected the central government of deliberately protracting payments and loans for political reasons.[43] Especially in the Duma, leftist and liberal delegates furiously attacked the MVD for creating 'hunger orgies' to suppress rural resistance.[44] This debate reflected the political frontlines of 'revolution' versus 'reaction' but only rarely were there national or ethnic considerations attached to it – even by delegates from the region.[45] The 'food commission' as the entire parliament itself was engaged in debates over money and over how the 'peasantry' as a whole was being under pressure by the autocracy.

More importantly, the interior ministry did arrange famine relief for the Caucasus. Contrary to what the leftist Duma factions were claiming, the imperial government did not weaponize famine relief for political purposes. Over the years 1906/07, more than 11 million roubles in grain loans had been transferred to the southern Caucasus provinces, followed by another 1.2 million roubles in support funds for the 'victims of the Armenian–Tatar conflict'.[46] Although the ministry delayed many of those payments, it could not afford to put pressure on the population by blocking relief. The ultimate goal of the central government was to maintain the imperial architecture by easing interethnic conflict. Thus, in order to maintain political control over the region, relief funds had to be distributed equally. The activities of the governor general for the Caucasus, Illarion Vorontsov-Dashkov provide a vivid example for this premise. The general enjoyed a wide reputation for his unusual approach to de-escalate and moderate interethnic tensions. He invited Tatar and Armenian representatives to a 'Caucasus meeting', called to 'put an end to this terrible mutual conflict'.[47] This approach also determined his actions in solving the hunger crises. He did not hold back grain and charitable funds but managed to distribute them even in the remote mountain areas. By including local elites 'from each nationality', he tried to facilitate the relief operation.[48] Although Vorontsov-Dashkov and the Caucasian Duma delegates were constantly debating the amount of money needed for the region, they agreed on the fact that the task at hand had no ethnic/religious premises. While in 1892, hunger was treated as a 'peasant issue', famine in multi-ethnic territories after 1905 was perceived as a challenge to imperial stability. In both cases, the perception of ethnic difference was limited to the local level, while the central relief strategy was to address a peasant issue. The continuous premise in both instances was: the imperial body could only survive by preserving life in all its parts.

Relief in the Name of the Revolution – Hunger in the Russian Civil War

The Bolsheviks were facing a similar challenge. Over the course of the First World War and various revolutions, the breakdown of central authority had accelerated national movements all over the empire. From the Finnish provinces to those of the far east, every region featured a different set of conditions for national self-determination or other patterns of separatism.[49] The new leaders in Petrograd (and then Moscow) quickly adjusted their internationalist agenda to a more tactical approach. For the sake of the revolution (in one country), the Red Army had to preserve the empire at all costs. Eventually, the Bolsheviks' key to success was to combine brute (para)military violence with social concessions – as national and social demands became inextricably intertwined.[50] In this framework, preserving the imperial body through famine relief was a matter of military, then political and economic control – ethnic division lines notwithstanding.

In most parts of the Volga basin, in southern Ukraine and the Urals, the politics of war communism and droughts had brought agriculture to its knees. Famine had spread over a vast and multi-ethnic territory where the Bolsheviks were trying to confirm their dominion.[51] Already in 1920, Moscow received warnings about an imminent subsistence crisis in the Volga territories. *Pravda* was continuously featuring reports about growing food shortages in the province. The party leaders did not suppress those stories but rather framed the coverage in the context of a class struggle. In this reading, hunger was just another enemy to defeat on the 'bloodless front'[52] between red and white and their alleged international conspirators. Workers and peasants fought shoulder to shoulder with the Red Army on the battlefield of hunger.[53] Just like in pre-revolutionary Russia, ethnicity was a non-factor in this narrative. This battle was about the survival of the working masses, facing a 'national calamity' (*vsenarodnoe bedstvie*).[54] Central and local authorities were informed about how ethnic differences in the rural economy played out during social crises. The first published working report of the Central Commission for the Relief of the Starving (Pomgol) in 1922 addressed the particular hardships most non-Russians went through during the crisis. In Crimea, famine had hit the settlements of the Tatars, who were relying on tobacco and grape farming especially hard, and thus the 'Tatar population ended up in a singularly grave situation'.[55] In the Bashkir SSR, 'all were in immediate of state support, since in good times people also rarely engaged in agriculture'.[56] The Pomgol administration had a sense for structural economic weaknesses within certain ethnic communities, but the dividing line of survival and abandonment was between the revolutionary masses and its enemies (who were still looming).[57]

At first, the politics of War Communism also dictated the procedures of famine relief. Until the spring of 1921, the Central Executive Committee (VTsIK) organized help by calling for more forced requisitioning and militarized sowing campaigns, which helped little to ward off, and maybe even aggravated, the crisis.[58] The Bolsheviks prioritized the enforcement of their agrarian visions over systematic relief measures. It was only with the introduction of the New Economic Policy (NEP) that the government agreed to establish an institutional framework for relief purposes. In the summer of 1921, the All-Russian Famine Relief Committee came into being. This committee was a short-lived bipartisan project where 'bourgeois' experts and politicians from all strata and backgrounds came together to organize charity campaigns. During its short existence, the committee became increasingly popular, in part because it declared that hunger relief was a chance to ease tensions and bridge political trenches: 'The matter of help must be to unite all. It must stand under the peaceful sign of the Red Cross'.[59] This approach ran counter to Lenin's priorities, who considered any cooperation with 'bourgeois' elements to be 'playing with fire'.[60] After 37 days, he decided to close down the committee and have most of the leading figures arrested.[61] Famine relief was, after all, a matter of class struggle. Rather than the experts from the olden days, it was the 'Soviet Power' that was expected to conquer this challenge and thus to safeguard the revolution – for the sake of workers and especially peasants. After years of violent and reckless expropriation, it seemed only plausible that famine relief was a chance to 'prove to the peasantry the value of the proletarian state'.[62] To the Bolshevik leaders, holding control both over the operation and over the narrative was vital, if not more important, than its actual success.

From the summer of 1921 onwards, the relief practices mirrored the inefficiencies and struggles of early (Soviet) state-building. The new leaders in Moscow had to build up (and finance) an imperial administrative infrastructure while establishing guidelines for relief. The RSFSR leadership reacted to the famine by providing tax exemptions and organizing grain shipments for the famine-stricken territories. The strategy was to relieve starving areas and place the tax burden (*prodnalog*) on less affected provinces. This schematic approach was based on great miscalculations (using inaccurate pre-war population census data), thus aggravating the situation in many areas where the crop deficit was not evenly distributed or where the numbers were entirely wrong.[63] The Russian government evaluated the needs of its territories based on demographic data and according to a tight budget plan (as the national grain reserves were nearly exhausted). Officially, only provinces with at least 50 per cent food deficit were considered emergency cases. Although in Astrakhan, the demand for grain exceeded the supply by more than 200 per cent, the Tatar Autonomous Soviet Socialist Republic (on paper) faced only a deficit of 30 per cent. Thus, the population of the TASSR could 'manage with their own means' until the next harvest.[64] At the very same time, in January 1922, only 5 per cent of the population in Astrakhan were considered 'starving', compared to 93.7 per cent of nearly three million people in the Tatar Republic who received plenty of food funds in 1921/22.[65] 'Starving provinces' like the TASSR, Samara, or Ufa could have a low food deficit and still be eligible for funds. The Moscow government confined itself to balance the surplus and deficits taxwise, while Pomgol bore the responsibility of distributing food and organizing other charitable funds.[66] The distribution system was widely inefficient and contradictory, but the regime's priorities were to create somewhat of an equilibrium between different territories – regardless of their ethnic or political composition. Under close supervision, the Bolsheviks allowed certain ethno-political initiatives (such as fundraising for the Kalmyks by the Mongolian government),[67] yet there was no preferential or particular treatment for ethnically homogenous or diverse territories within the famine zone. The equilibrium was a budget-oriented scheme that included emergency food deliveries to 'successful' provinces (those with a small deficit) – either for providing relief to refugees from 'hungry' provinces or for their 'own' population.[68] Achieving financial balance between relief and tax income was the prime objective, no matter how contradictory and inaccurate the procedure. The local organs had to figure out the details.

Provincial Pomgol commissions had to oversee and coordinate all relief efforts (charity work, food distribution) with leaders from the executive committees and Regional Economic Soviets (*Sovnarkhozy*).[69] Although the role of Pomgol in these conflicts is yet to be explored, and the rationale of a class war could and often did translate into interethnic violence, there was no sign of officials systematically instrumentalizing food funds on ethnic grounds.[70] It rather seems that the logic of War Communism still dictated Pomgol's mode of operation. The notion of class was the divisive factor. According to Charles Edmondson, 'political considerations inevitably weighed heavily in the distribution of food and the admission to the public kitchens', as in some cases, relief authorities excluded livestock owners from public feeding.[71] No less than the All-Russian Extraordinary Commission (VChK or Cheka) was also closely observing both the work of Pomgol and the activities of the peasants that the Cheka considered to be hostile elements ('Kulaks').[72] Because hunger had broken the peasants' resistance to expropriations, it made them even more dependent on state relief. From summer/autumn 1921 onwards, Pomgol was a symbol both for the armistice with, and the dependence of, the peasantry. For the leaders in Moscow, the biopolitical task was to frame the narrative of the crisis and to balance supply and demand between republics and provinces. On a local level, Pomgol and the Cheka had to make sure that this catastrophe did not jeopardize Soviet power in the countryside.

These premises also applied for Ukraine. Some researchers and publicists have tried make the case that Moscow was using the famine as a 'weapon' against Ukrainians in 1921/22. Accordingly, the Bolsheviks were squeezing grain out of the Ukrainian peasantry, not just to save Russian lives but in order 'to subdue a hostile nation'.[73] This notion has been rejected in recent years.[74] As a matter of fact, the Ukrainian cases underline how the premises of famine relief were dictated by budgetary and political concerns. Although wide parts of south-eastern Ukraine experienced serious crop deficits in spring 1921,[75] the main focus of the TsIK and TsKPomgol was on the Volga Valley, excluding Ukraine from the list of 'starving provinces'.[76] The Moscow government was well aware of the dreadful situation in these areas. In districts like Nikolaev, up to 80 per cent of the people were suffering from malnutrition and hunger induced diseases.[77] Still, provinces categorized as 'doing well' (*blagopoluchnye*) or 'partially starving' (like Voronezh) were obliged to provide food funds and tax-in-kind for the 'north', i.e. Russia.[78] Ukraine suffered from the same inconsistent administrative strategy as other provinces. Moscow pushed for grain deliveries from provinces in dire need of relief and Ukraine was (on paper) the greatest producer region, although most of their crop prognoses were overblown.[79]

The Bolshevik leadership had political reservations about the Ukrainian Soviet Republic as well. The Ukrainian countryside had been a stronghold for various peasant movements that challenged the Bolsheviks well into 1921, a borderland with multiple national loyalties and demands.[80] There is reason to assume that Moscow's mistrust aggravated the situation in many ways – by being adamant about Ukrainian grain deliveries and by downplaying the situation and blocking the American Relief Administration (ARA) from entering. ARA officials were met with resistance by Moscow when it came to establishing contacts in Ukraine.[81] Ukrainian party leaders were torn between fulfilling the task to supply grain for the Russian heartland and coping with the devastation in their own lands. In early August 1921, the Ukrainian politburo acknowledged that it was 'necessary to discern a call to fight hunger in Russia and to fight crop failure in Ukraine'. Thus, provincial and local funds had to be used.[82] In January 1922, party head Kristian Rakovskii criticized the RSFSR government for their excessive demands while asking Lenin to allow food funds for Ukraine, and only then did direct famine aid from Moscow reach Ukraine.[83]

Moscow's mistrust of the Ukrainian conditions exacerbated an already problematic situation. Still, the Bolshevik approach did not exclude these territories from relief entirely but turned it into a regional/republican operation that was highly dependent on international help.[84] Just like in other territories afflicted by famine, there was no programmatic approach against certain population segments. The alleged equilibrium of producer and receiver in these crises was a statistical pipe dream but not an ethnopolitical strategy, as tens of thousands of Russian children were also evacuated into the 'safe zone' of Ukraine.[85] In transition to the NEP, the imperial famine relief plan was guided by budgetary and political concerns that eventually had to save the proletarian state for the sake of the 'working masses'. Providing relief to the peasantry was a means to create stability and keep political control over a heterogeneous and exhausted Soviet populace.

Weaponizing Famine Relief under Stalin – Hunger between 1929 and 1933

Between 1928/29 and 1934, millions of people in Soviet Ukraine, the Don Area, the Northern Caucasus, and Kazakhstan died of starvation. The famine in these areas was designed, utilized and partly weaponized by a Soviet leadership that blocked relief funds and sealed off cities and country borders with military force. There are debates as to whether the notion of genocide can be applied to these events and if so, to what extent.[86] Most Western historians acknowledge the genocidal practices of the starvation of millions of Kazakh nomads and Ukrainian peasants but deny an overall genocidal strategy.[87] This chapter does not engage in this controversy, however, the strategy and mechanics of famine relief support the latter notion. Stalin did not only utilize but weaponize the famine and the question of relief. Unlike in the time of the NEP, Stalinist biopolitics meant to withdraw help in order to maintain and enforce their agricultural visions. At the same time, the logics of annihilation were not determined by ethnopolitics but by a calculus to destroy rural opposition against what the Bolsheviks claimed to be the 'socialist transformation' of the countryside.[88]

Both the famine in European Russia and in Central Asia must be seen in the context of the massive and violent agrarian policies of the Bolshevik leadership and its first Five Year Plan. From 1929 on, Ukraine, the Don and the Northern Caucasus area experienced waves of forced collectivization that led to the arrest and deportation of hundreds of thousands of peasant families, the destruction of rural infrastructure, unrest and the annihilation of livestock. The central government pressured a shattered rural economy to fulfil unrealistic grain-requisition plans in order to feed the cities and to support the country's drive towards industrialization.[89] In Kazakhstan, this process went hand in hand with the attempt to forcefully sedentarize its nomadic population. The plan was to create a collective agrarian economy from scratch while colonizing the Kazakh deserts. In reality, nomads lost their livelihood, their livestock, and their very own relief networks and they lost out in the distribution of arable land, making them most vulnerable to subsistence crises.[90] The timing and the socio-economic conditions in the famine varied from one another. In Ukraine, the crisis lasted between 1929 and 1933, and in Kazakhstan between 1932 and 1934.[91] Still, in both cases, the violent collectivization drive enabled, if not created, the condition of mass starvation, which in turn was used to break resistance against the campaign. Robert Kindler coined the phrase accordingly as 'Sovietization through hunger'.[92]

This circumstance defined also how Soviet central authorities communicated about famine and relief. Unlike in the decade before, the supply conditions in rural Ukraine were not up to debate in the newspapers. The propaganda outlets avoided any reference to 'hunger'. Even death registers remained silent about the actual cause of death in countless cases.[93] Instead, the official focus was placed on the struggle against the Kulaks and the allegedly hostile class elements that were sabotaging the efforts of collectivization. Stalin personally banned the word itself from official correspondence.[94] As recent findings in Stalin's personal archive suggest, the dictator saw every obstacle on the road to collectivized agriculture, every hint of resistance, and even hunger itself as evidence of counterrevolutionary activities.[95] Regional and local party leaders willingly confirmed and perpetuated this view.[96] The biological reality of Soviet citizens was subordinate to the success or demise of the campaign. A similar logic applied in Kazakhstan, although hunger and especially famine refugees played a significant role as obstacles to the sedentarization campaign there. Officially, the refugee crisis was framed as part of an 'intensifying class war' with 'bandits' who spread rumours about famine,[97] while internally, the political police (*Ob"edinennoe gosudarstvennoe politicheskoe upravlenie*, OGPU) and the party were well aware of the situation of the nomads. Even after Moscow adjusted its collectivization policies in the autumn of 1932, the newly appointed party leader in Alma-Ata, Levon Mirzoyan reprimanded and sometimes fired, party cadres who had sent him 'teary telegrams' about starving people.[98] Soviet party leaders discouraged, sometimes even obstructed communication referring to the famine while the secret police gathered detailed information about it. In top-down communication, famine was less a biological issue to address than a threat to campaign plans.

This prioritization also determined how authorities handled the question of relief. In the Ukrainian countryside, there were no systematic relief efforts between 1928 and May 1933. During the summer of 1928, despite a crop failure, Moscow demanded massive amounts of grain from Ukraine. This was the last time the Soviet Ukrainian government organized systematic relief through a State Commission for Aid to the Victims of Corp Failure. Even then, food aid was limited to 'the poorest peasants' and those who were willing to join the collective farms, excluding anyone who allegedly opposed Soviet policies in the countryside.[99] In the following years, the central leadership only selectively granted regional and local requests for food assistance.[100] In general, it weaponized the hunger situation directly by blocking relief and closing the borders in affected provinces. In both cases, starvation was a means to punish and bring to heel the peasantry that opposed any attempt to collectivize the rural economy. In November 1932, the Central Committee made the notorious 'blacklists' into official policy. As part of the 'struggle with Kulak influence' regional party cells were mandated to list collective farms (later entire villages) that failed to fulfil grain delivery plans and isolate them from any possibility to trade or receive goods. Blacklisted farms were stripped of their goods, the peasants and officials often purged and arrested.[101] Over the course of weeks, the list of sanctions and the number of farms, cooperatives and even entire villages on those lists grew.[102] The basic principle was to starve any possible opposition to campaign plans or deviant behaviour in the realm of collective agriculture. In practice, 'the blacklist became a universal weapon aimed at all rural residents'.[103]

The central authorities denied food and general relief on the grounds of a political campaign to subdue the rural population, to enforce the Kolkhoz system, and to annihilate potential resistance. In May 1933, when the Ukrainian party leaders finally approached and requested food funds for Ukrainian territories, their arguments were based on the need to continue the 'fight with saboteurs'.[104] Even after millions of people had perished, 'food aid' was not classified as a humanitarian act but framed rather as another instrument in the struggle for collectivization. The Central Committee promised two million of grain to Kazakhstan 'already' in September 1932. Here too, food aid was not seen as relief from, but another step towards strengthening nomad agriculture and enforcing the 'correct party line of gradual sedentarization'.[105] It is doubtful that these numbers could cover what was needed due to the fact that nobody in the central administration could even give a rough estimate of how many people were starving at the time.[106] Moreover, Stalin and Molotov continued to pressure Almaty for grain deliveries and encouraged local authorities to apply repressive means. For example, Ukraine, the Kuban area, and the Kazakh districts were blacklisted throughout the autumn 1932.[107] Between 1929 and 1934, the distribution of foodstuff in the Soviet Union was a tactical decision about rural control.

Undeniably these techniques, the closing of borders, the violent expulsion of nomads into the desert and the mass arrest by the hands of the OGPU resulted in the deaths of millions of peasants. The campaign for collectivization went hand in hand with another campaign to eradicate what party leaders in Moscow framed as nationalist opposition – be it Ukrainian peasants, Cossacks or nomads. Both campaigns fuelled each other and targeted the rural population, which were viewed as a 'social base' for nationalism.[108] However, in terms of food provision, the dividing line between survival and death was not between Russians and non-Russians. Apart from the fact that the famine also spread across RSFSR territories, the line was drawn between those who carried the new (collectivized) order and those who could not, or did not want to, fit into it and thus were destined to sabotage it. Biopolitics was thus just another weapon in the war on the peasantry – from the Dnepr to the Kazakh steppe. It was not by accident but rather by design that the Soviet regime ordered food aid to the important urban/industrial sectors, even at the peak of the crisis. In 1933, the urban population of the Donbas received higher bread rations than the inhabitants of Moscow or Leningrad.[109] Barbara Falk has shown how the Bolsheviks prioritized urban areas during the famine, allocating special foodstuffs for industrial workers. In 1932/33, the ethnic composition of a city had no significance whatsoever to the hierarchy of food supply.[110]

This by no means implies that the Soviet government in Moscow was capable of orchestrating a precise campaign against peasants while saving workers and city dwellers. Rather, this was the framework of priorities in which local authorities were encouraged to manage death and survival. The urban population was lacking food as well and even central orders to organize relief were often ignored or protracted since acts of relief had generally little priority.[111] Stalinist imperial biopolitics was not about allowing life but inducing death – not only for the sake of control but for the socialist transformation of the Soviet empire. The countryside was its main target and with it the social and national peculiarities of Ukrainian, Cossack or Nomad agriculture.

Outlook and Conclusion: Famine Relief in Late Stalinism

The hunger catastrophes of the first Five Year Plan were the first and last examples of weaponized famine relief in the Soviet Union. Hunger continued to be a deadly threat to Soviet citizens, but in the following decade, the political leadership conceived of it as an issue of its own and developed systematic strategies to fight hunger and famine in their own country and even in the realms of Soviet influence. In 1936/37, the Soviet state built up grain stocks to maintain the food supply for the population in times of crisis.[112] The war of extermination waged by Nazi Germany introduced famine as a genocidal military strategy, while the war effort itself caused many excess deaths all over the Soviet Union.[113] The leadership reacted with a tight and wide-ranging rationing system.[114] When the consequences of the German invasion in 1946/47 again caused the breakdown of the grain supply in wide parts of Eastern Europe, the Kremlin reacted to the situation with relief policies that extended even into the Soviet Occupation Zone, which prevented the German population from starvation.[115]

In some cases, inadequate relief policies contributed to the spread of famine in the first place. In post-war times especially, political and strategic prerogatives at the central and local levels hindered effective help.[116] However, it is the question of priority that ties these catastrophes to the longue durée of imperial biopolitics. In late Stalinist Russia, food aid was tied to political priorities and prerogatives:

The rationing system during the Second World War established a clear cut 'provisioning hierarchy' that favoured urban workers (who were essential to the arms industry) over rural inhabitants.[117] In 1946/47, the Soviet state lent grain and organized charity structures for the starving regions in Ukraine, Moldova and Belarus, even allowing foreign organizations (United Nations Relief and Rehabilitation Administration – UNRRA) to provide help.[118] At the same time, the political leadership was preparing the country for a future war with the West. Food shortages directly affected international prestige. The state kept filling up grain reserves while denying any confirmation about the country's grave situation, rejecting international assistance until 1947. By any circumstance, the Soviet Union must not appear weak.[119] More importantly, food aid was again tied to social and political status. The provisioning hierarchy for workers in production was still intact.[120] In the countryside, only Kolkhozniks and local activists were eligible for food funds. The Soviet leadership made it clear 'to private owners (*edinolichniki*), that there is salvation only in the Kolkhozy'.[121] In conjunction with the legal and police force, famine relief was a means to (re)establish the Kolkhoz-system in the former occupied territories. This included the closing of borders in famine districts.[122] One could argue that the Soviet Occupation Administration in Germany (SVAG) applied a similar provisioning hierarchy to East Germany. 'Red cities' like Dresden had a strong working-class base and thus received more funds from the authorities at the expense of the rural population.[123] Post-war famine relief prioritized urban and industrial workers, political supporters, functional elites and Kolkhoz members over individual peasants – but without actively facilitating the death of the latter.

As we have seen, the Russian and Soviet governments distributed food aid to their starving populace as imperial subjects. Their national and ethnic backgrounds contributed to, but ultimately did not determine, their entitlement to relief. Sometimes they were not even visible in official documentation before 1917.[124] Tsars and party secretaries assumed responsibility over the biological fate of their subjects in order to maintain control over the periphery. On the one hand, the Soviet leaders perverted this responsibility to political ends. The Bolsheviks gradually introduced conditions and priorities to this form of entitlement. Although aid was tied to a political calculus already after 1917, it was Stalin who turned the biological need of his citizens into a tool of radical political transformation. Lenin and his peers dictated conditions for survival to save the revolutionary state; Stalin induced and facilitated death to transform it. In that regard, war and post-war strategies of relief were rather a retreat to pre-Stalinist strategies, as Stalin refrained from weaponized relief strategies. On the other hand, to the rulers in St Petersburg and Moscow, the body of the empire transcended fantasies of ethnic homogeneity. In order to save (or transform) the empire, autocrats and party leaders alike governed life and death based on the criteria of political value and social category (estate, class). Imperial biopolitics intended to preserve the body in its ethnic diversity.

It is important to state that biopolitics should not be understood as a coherent imperial strategy. Again, Stalin's first Five Year Plan marked the point when the premise of social homogeneity did not transcend but threatened to extinguish this diversity. The Russian Empire accepted and moderated national heterogeneity in order to safeguard an imperial power architecture. The Soviet empire only accepted (and sometimes created) the notion of nationality in exchange for political and social uniformity. The trajectories of biopolitics for the national composition were, by default, fundamentally different. The continuity established the conviction to govern life and death beyond the framework of nationality, which in turn raises the question of whether nations themselves should be considered a referential point for biopolitics.

Notes

1 Michel Foucault, 'Right of Death and Power over Life', in *Biopolitics. A Reader*, eds. Timothy C. Campbell and Adam Sitze (Durham: Duke University Press, 2013), 43. See e.g. Rhiannon Noel Welch, *Vital Subjects: Race and Biopolitics in Italy, 1860–1920* (Liverpool: Liverpool University Press, 2016). I am very grateful to Michel Abeßer and Robert Kindler for their comments on this chapter.
2 Giorgio Agamben, 'Biopolitics and the Rights of Man', in Sitze, *Biopolitics*, 153.
3 Ulrike von Hirschhausen and Jörn Leonhard, 'Zwischen Historisierung und Globalisierung. Titel, Themen und Trends der neueren Empire-Forschung', *Neue Politische Literatur* 56 (2011): 401.
4 Alexei Miller and Alfred J. Rieber (Hg.), *Imperial Rule* (Budapest and New York: CEU Press, 2004), 1.
5 For a discussion on famine and its terminology, see esp. Bas Dianda, *Political Routes to Starvation: Why Does Famine Kill?* (Wilmington: Vernon Press, 2019), 2–6.
6 Foucault, 'Right of Death', 46.
7 Inspired by Foucault's reference to biopolitical 'power to foster life or disallow it'. Ibid., 43.
8 Viktor V. Kondrashin, *Golod 1932–1933 godov. Tragediia rossijskoi derevni* (Moskva: ROSSPĖN, 2008), 318–332; Alfred Eisfeld, Guido Hausmann, and Dietmar Neutatz, eds., *Hungersnöte in Russland und der Sowjetunion, 1891–1947. Regionale, ethnische und konfessionelle Aspekte* (Essen: Klartext, 2017).
9 For Foucault on the issue of food scarcity see Michel Foucault, *Sicherheit, Territorium, Bevölkerung: Vorlesung am Collège de France 1977–1978* (Frankfurt a.M.: Suhrkamp, 2004), 52; David Nally, 'The Biopolitics of Food Provisioning', *Transactions of the Institute of British Geographers New Series* 36, no. 1 (2011): 38.
10 Nally, 'Biopolitics of Food', 43; see especially his take on the British famine policy in mid-nineteenth-century Ireland and the use of the Irish Poor Laws in order to 'regenerate Irish society'. David Nally, '"That Coming Storm": The Irish Poor Law, Colonial Biopolitics, and the Great Famine', *Annals of the Association of American Geographers* 98, no. 3 (2008): 714–741.

11 For the Russian system of famine relief, see esp. Robbins, *Famine in Russia*, 14–30.

12 Andrey Makarychev and Alexandra Yatsyk, 'Imperial Biopolitics and Its Disavowals', *Region* 7, no. 1 (2018): 3–22.

13 Charlotte Henze, *Disease, Health Care and Government in Late Imperial Russia: Life and Death on the Volga, 1823–1914* (London: Routledge, 2011); Nancy M. Frieden, 'The Politics of Zemstvo Medicine', in *The Zemstvo in Russia: An Experiment in Local Self-government*, eds. Terence Emmons and Wayne S. Vucinich (Cambridge: Cambridge University Press, 1982), 315–342.

14 Sergei Prozorow, *The Biopolitics of Stalinism: Ideology and Life in Soviet Socialism* (Edinburgh: Edinburgh University Press, 2016), 4.

15 David Hoffmann analyzed Soviet reproductive and health policies, placing the Soviet example in the modern European context of 'social intervention based on scientific norms', yet unlike in the US or parts of Europe, the Soviet government 'did not seek to limit the production of those deemed unfit'. David L. Hoffmann, *Cultivating the Masses: Modern State Practices and Soviet Socialism, 1914–1939* (Ithaca, NY and London: Cornell University Press, 2011), 140. John Davis' account on disease control in Russia and the Soviet Union laid the focus rather on medical innovation and the history of knowledge. John P Davis, *Russia in the Time of Cholera: Disease under Romanovs and Soviets* (London and New York: I. B. Tauris & Company Limited, 2018).

16 Peter Holquist, 'To Count, to Extract, and to Exterminate: Population Statistics and Population Politics in Late Imperial and Soviet Russia', in *A State of Nations: Empire and Nation-Making in the Age of Lenin and Stalin*, eds. Ronald Grigor Suny and Terry Martin (Oxford: Oxford University Press), 111–144.

17 Dan Healey, 'Lives in the Balance: Weak and Disabled Prisoners and the Biopolitics of the Gulag', in *The Soviet Gulag: Evidence, Interpretation, and Comparison*, ed. Michael David-Fox (Pittsburgh, PA: University of Pittsburgh Press, 2016), 86. See also a more extensive study on the Gulag as a system of exploitation that created a 'population of sick and emaciated prisoners' in Golfo Alexopoulos, *Illness and Inhumanity in Stalin's Gulag* (New Haven, CT and London: Yale University Press, 2017), 233.

18 Richard G Robbins, Jr., *Famine in Russia 1891–1892: The Imperial Government Responds to a Crisis* (New York and London: Columbia University Press, 1975); James Y Simms, Jr., 'The Impact of the Russian Famine of 1891–92: A New Perspective' (PhD diss., University of Michigan, 1976).

19 Altpeter et al., 'Hungersnöte in Russland', 13–19. For the most recent debates on the famines in the 1930s see the thematic issue in *Contemporary European History* 27 (3); Viktor Kondrashin 'Golod 1932–1933 gg. v sovremennoi rossiiskoi I zarubezhnoi istoriografii: vzgliad iz Rossii', in *Sovremennaia rossiisko-ukrainskaia istoriografiia goloda 1923–1933 gg. v SSSR*, ed. Viktor Kondrashin (Moskva: ROSSPEN, 2011), 8–57. R.W. Davies and Stephen G. Wheatcroft, *The Industrialization of Soviet Russia, 5. The Years of Hunger: Soviet Agriculture, 1931–1933* (New York: Palgrave Macmillan, 2009), 440–441.

20 Nikolai M. Dronin and Edward G. Bellinger, *Climate Dependence and Food Problems in Russia 1900–1990. The Interaction of Climate and Agricultural Policy and Their Effect on Food Problems* (Budapest and New York: CEU Press 2005); for a brief overview, see also: R.W. Davies and Stephen G. Wheatcroft, *The Years of Hunger: Soviet Agriculture, 1931–1933: The Industrialisation of Soviet Russia 5* (London: Palgrave Macmillan, 2009), 400–442. For the aspect of relief in 1921/22, see also Bertrand M. Patenaude, *The Big Show in Bololand: The American Relief Expedition to Soviet Russia in the Famine of 1921* (Stanford, CA: Stanford University Press, 2002).

21 See esp. the argument made by Amartya Sen, *Poverty and Famines: An Essay on Entitlement and Deprivation* (Oxford: Clarendon Press, 1982). For the communication about famine, see esp. Robert Kindler, 'Famines and Political Communication in Stalinism: Possibilities and Limits of the Sayable', *Jahrbücher für Geschichte Osteuropas* 62, no. 2 (2014): 255–272.

22 Arcadius Kahan, *The Tsar Hunger in the Land of the Tsars.*, ed. by Roger Weiss (London and Chicago: University of Chicago Press, 1989), 111–113; Robbins, *Famine in Russia*, 1–13.

23 For the varying calculations, see Stephen G. Wheatcroft, 'The 1891–92 Famine in Russia: Towards a More Detailed Analysis of Its Scale and Demographic Significance', in *Economy and Society in Russia and the Soviet Union, 1860–1930: Essays for Olga Crisp*, eds. Linda Harriet Edmondson and Peter Waldron (London: MacMillan 1992), 44–64.

24 Dronin and Bellinger, *Climate Dependence*, 60–64.

25 Over the course of 1891/92 the Russian government spent an estimated 150 million roubles on grain and seeds for over 11 million people. In 1906 alone, the Ministry of Interior granted nutrition credits for over 100 million roubles. Richard G. Robbins Jr., 'Russia's System of Food Supply Relief on the Eve of the Famine of 1891–92', *Agricultural History* 45, no. 4 (1951): 259–269. For the crisis in 1906, see the debate of the Duma 'food commission': *Gosudarstvennaia duma Sessiia II. Stenograficheskii otchet. Zasedanie tridtsat' sedmoe. 11 maia 1907* (Sankt-Peterburg: Gosudarstvennaia Tipografiia, 1907), 458.

26 Stephen G. Wheatcroft, 'Crises and the Condition of the Peasantry in Late Imperial Russia', in *Peasant Economy, Culture, and Politics of European Russia, 1800–1921*, eds. Esther Kingston-Mann and Timothy Mixter (Princeton, NJ: Princeton University Press, 1991),138–141; see also Robbins, *Famine in Russia*, 5.

27 Farida G. Zajnullina, *Tatarskaja derevnia Kazanskoi gubernii: sotsial'no-ekonomicheskaia i etnokul'turnaia transformatsiia (1861-1917 gg.). Avtoreferat* (Kazan: AN RT, 2008), 16.

28 See Rustem M. Mullagaliev, *Social'no-ekonomičeskaja žizn'tatar'skoj krest'janskoj obščiny Kazanskoj gubernii v poreformennyj period (60-90-e gg. XIX v.). Avtoreferat* (Kazan: AN RT, 2011) 7–8.

29 I.K. Zagidullin, *Tatarskoe natsional'noe dvizhenie* v 1860–1905 gg (Kazan: Tatarskoe knizhnoe izdatel'stvo. 2014), 286–297; N.A. Khalikov, *Promysly i remesla Tatar povolž'a i urala (seredina XIX – načalo XX v.)* (Kazan: Akademii Nauk RT, 1998), 73.

30 Konstantin Lavrskij, *Tatarskaja bednota. Ekonomicheskii ocherk dvukh tatarskikh dereven Kazanskoi gubernii* (Kazan: Tipografia Gubernskogo pravlenia, 1894), 33–34. Lavrskii conducted his field work and finalized his book in the 1880s but only managed to publish it in 1894.

31 RGIA, f. 1204, op. 1, d. 62, l. 36; I. K. Zagidullin, ed., *Istoria Kazani v dokumentakh* i materialakh XIX vek. Naselenie konfessii blagotvoritel'nost. Kniga 2 (Kazan: Tatarskoe knizhnoe izdatel'stvo, 2011), 649. The philanthropist Fanny Gangardt collected donations from St. Petersburg and Kazan and set up food kitchens and bakeries in the most affected districts, Laishevsk and Mamadysh, referring to the Tatars as a particularly impoverished group. RGIA, f. 1204, op. 1, d. 196, l. 158–164.

32 RGIA, f. 1005, op. 2, d. 32, l. 170–171.

33 Vremennik tsentral'nogo statisticheskogo komiteta Ministerstva vnutrennykh del: *Statisticheskie dannye po vydache ssud po obsemenenie i prodovol'stvie naseleniiu, postradavshemu ot neurozhaia v 1891–1892 gg.* (Sankt-Peterburg: MVD, 1984).

34 Nikolaus I (Hg.) (1892): Svod zakonov Rossijskoj Imperii. Izdanija 1892 goda. Poveleniem Gosudarja Imperatora Nikolaja Pervogo. Tom trinadzatyj. Ustavy o narodnom prodovol'stvii, obshchestvennom prizrenii i vrachebnye (Sankt-Peterburg: Izdanie Kodif. Otdela pri Gos. Soveta,1892), 1–2.
35 Entsiklopedicheskii slovar F.A. Brokgausa i I. A. Efrona. Tom XXIX. Sakhar – Sem Mudretsov (Sankt-Peterburg: Semenevskaia Tipolitografiia, 1900), 375–376.
36 Aleksandr Terekhov's report to General Annenkov, 15.1.92, in: RGIA, f. 1287, op. 4, d. 2125, l. 197–197ob.
37 Bulletin of the provincial meeting for hunger relief in Kazan, 28.2.92, in: RGIA, f. 1287, op. 4, d. 2125, l. 331.
38 RGIA, f. 1287, op. 4, d. 2125, l. 197ob, l. 330–333.
39 See e.g. Zajnullina, *Tatarskaja derevnja Kazanskoj gubernii*, 14–15.
40 Charles Steinwedel, *Threads of Empire: Loyalty and Tsarist Authority in Bashkira, 1552–1917* (Bloomington: Indiana University Press, 2016), 182.
41 In the shadow of urban revolts and the interethnic conflicts the hunger situation in the Southern Caucasus has received no attention from historiography so far. See e.g. the contemporary report by Simon M. Zavarian, *Ekonomicheskie uslovii Karabaga i golod 1906–1907 g.* (Sankt-Peterburg: Izd. Armianskogo Kulturnogo Sojuza v Baku, 1907).
42 RGIA, f. 1319, op.1, d. 24, l. 12ob.
43 Protocols of the food and budget commission of the 3rd State Duma, 11.12. 1907, in RGIA, f. 1278, op. 2, d. 3157, l. 217. It was especially Zemstvo officials and members of the Free Economic Society that were accusing the autocracy of weaponizing famine relief against revolting peasants. See 'Report of the Chair of the Famine Relief Committee of the Free Economic Society to the 1st State Duma, 9.5.06', in RGIA, f. 1482, op. 1, d. 7a, l. 20.
44 *Gosudarstvennaia duma Sessiia II. 11 Maia 1907*, 458.
45 At the Duma session in March 1907, Konstantin Kaklyugin, a delegate from the Don Host, gave the famine situation in the Don area an ethnic notion, reporting the 'unprecedented phenomenon of a starving Cossak'. People were begging at the train stations, but more importantly, he complained that 'we don't have any zemstvo, we have rural distribution committees composed of officials that are completely alien to the people, alien to their needs'. Kaklyugin criticized the non-Cossak control over the Cossak people, which is why he also demanded an 'organizational plan' that allowed 'self-help' and local 'initiative' (*samodeiatel'nost*). *Gosudarstvennaia duma Sessiia II.* 7 March 1907, 203–204.
46 RGIA, f. 1278, op.1, d. 821, l. 72.
47 GARF, f. 5881, op. 2, d. 234, l. 34. cit. in I. Ismail-Zade, *I. I. Vorontsov-Dashkov. Administrator, reformator* (Sankt Peterburg: Nestor-Istoriia, 2008), 76.
48 Report by Vorontsov-Dashkov to Aleksei Ermolov, 8.10.07, in RGIA, f. 1319, op.1, d. 24, l. 38–39.
49 See e.g. Ivan Sablin, *The Rise and Fall of Russia's Far Eastern Republic, 1905–1922: Nationalisms, Imperialisms, and Regionalisms in and after the Russian Empire* (Milton: Routledge, 2019).
50 Jeremy Smith, *Red Nations: The Nationalities Experience in and after the USSR* (Cambridge: Cambridge University Press, 2013), 17–18; Laura Engelstein, *Russia in Flames: War, Revolution, Civil War. 1914–1921* (New York: Oxford University Press, 2018), 629–631.
51 Engelstein, *Russia in Flames*, 622; Ian Barnes, *Restless Empire: A Historical Atlas of Russia* (Cambridge, MA and London: The Belknap Press of Harvard University Press, 2015), 121. Dronin and Bellinger, *Climate Dependence*, 89–108.
52 Pravda, 17.11.1920, 2.

53 Itogi bor'by s golodom v 1921-22g. Sbornik statei i otchetov (Moskva, Ts. K. Pomgol, 1922).
54 Biulleten Tsentral'noi Komissii pomoshchi golodajushchim VTsIK (Moskva: Tipografia M.S.N.Kh., 1921), 3.
55 Itogy bor'by s golodom, 220.
56 Ibid., 194.
57 In Crimea, Pomgol redistributed food funds for the Red Army whenever 'saboteurs (vrediteli) appeared'. Ibid., 223.
58 Viktor D. Topolyanskii, *Vserossiiskii komitet pomoshchi golodaiushchim* (Moskva: Mezhdunarodnyi Fond Demokratiia, 2014), 5; Charles Milton Edmondson, *Soviet Famine Relief Measures, 1921–1923* (PhD diss., Michigan University, 1979), 66–67.
59 'Informatsia gazety "pomoshch"', 20.7.1921, in Topolyanskii, *Vserossiiskii komitet pomoshchi golodaiushchim*, 18.
60 'Note from Lenin to Stalin, 26.8.21', in Topolyanskii, *Vserossiiskii komitet pomoshchi golodaiushchim*, 57.
61 Viktor D. Topoljanskii, 'Vvedenie', in Topolyanskii, *Vserossiiskii komitet pomoshchi golodaiushchim*, 7.
62 Itogy bor'by s golodom, 4.
63 Edmondson, *Soviet Famine Relief*, 136; Igor Narskij, 'Die multiethnische Bevölkerung des Ural in der Hungersnot von 1921//22', in Altpeter et al., *Hungersnöte in Russland*, 82.
64 Pravda, 12.10.1921, 1.
65 Itogy bor'by s golodom, 460–461.
66 'The government made no attempt to formulate a nationwide criterion for determining a person's eligibility for public feeding'. Ibid., 148.
67 Dittmar Schorkowitz, ed., *'… Daß die inorodcy niemand rettet und das Heil bei ihnen selbst liegt …'. Quellen und Beiträge zur historischen Ethnologie von Burjaten und Kalmüken* (Wiesbaden: Harrassowitz, 2018), 510–513.
68 Biulleten Tsentral'noi Komissii, 14, 20.
69 Ibid., 11.
70 Recent literature indicates that the hunger situation could translate into ethnic conflicts. In the Bashkir region, the famine aggravated tensions between Bashkir peasants and Russian settlers. On the other hand, these were mostly cases of vigilante justice among single population segments. See Narskij, *Die multiethnische Bevölkerung*, 84–87; Even in areas notorious for recent pogroms, hunger did not trigger violence between Jews, Germans and Ukrainians: Maryna E. Kozyreva, 'Hungersnot und Hungerhilfe in der Südukraine in den Jahren 1921 bis 1923. Ukrainer, Deutsche und Juden im Vergleich', in Altpeter et al., *Hungersnöte in Russland*, 82.
71 Edmondson, *Soviet Famine Relief*, 148–149.
72 Engelstein, *Russia in Flames*, 562–563; see also e.g. the Cheka reports Doc. No. 263/ No. 53, 6/7.8.1921, in Alexis Berelovich, ed., *Sovetskaya derevenya glazami VChK – OGPU*. Tom 1. 1918–1922. Dokumenty i materialy (Moskva: ROSSPEN, 1998), 480–481.
73 Veryha, Wasyl, *A Case Study of Genocide in the Ukrainian Famine of 1921–1923: Famine as a Weapon* (Lewiston: Edwin Mellen Press, 2007), 297.
74 Anne Applebaum, *Red Famine: Stalin's War on Ukraine* (London: Penguin, 2018), 67.
75 Ibid., 61.
76 Biulleten Tsentral'noi Komissii, 15.
77 Kozyreva, 'Hungersnot und Hungerhilfe', 260.
78 Ol'ha M. Movchan, ed., *Golod 1921–1923 rokiv v ukraini. Zbirnyk dokumentiv I materialiv* (Kiev: Naukova Dumka, 1993), l, 28, 34.

79 According to a central Pomgol report, 'Ukraine' was supposed to support three 'starving provinces' at the same time (Tsarytsyn, Saratov, Urals). *Biulleten Tsentral'noi Komissii*, 27. Party leader Kristian Rakovskii reported how the 1921 harvest did not even meet 50 per cent of the expectations. See Movchan, ed., Golod 1921–1923, 80.
80 Terry Martin, *The Affirmative Action Empire: Nations and Nationalism in the Soviet Union, 1923–1939* (Ithaca, NY and London: Cornel University Press, 2001), 35; Engelstein, *Russia in Flames*, 573.
81 Harold H. Fisher, *The Famine in Soviet Russia 1919–1923: The Operations of the American Relief Administration* (New York: MacMillan, 1927). 261.
82 Movchan, ed., Golod 1921–1923, 31.
83 Ibid., 75–84.
84 Ibid., 31.
85 Edmondson, *Soviet Famine Relief*, 148–149; Biulleten Tsentral'noi Komissii, 24.
86 Most recent arguments in favour of that hypothesis were made by Applebaum, *Red Famine*; David R. Marples, *Holodomor: Causes of the 1932–1933 Famine in Ukraine* (Saskatoon: Sask. Heritage Press, 2011).
87 See esp. the article for the Roundtable on Soviet Famines' in *Contemporary European History* 27, no. 3 (2018), 432-481. See also a summary on the Russian and Ukrainian debate in 2011 by Viktor Kondrashin 'Golod 1932–1933', 8–57.
88 Lynne Viola, *Peasant Rebels under Stalin: Collectivization and the Culture of Peasant Resistance* (New York and Oxford: OUP, 1999), 235.
89 Applebaum, *Red Famine*, 249–254.
90 Robert Kindler, *Stalins Nomaden. Herrschaft und Hunger in Kasachstan* (Hamburg: Hamburger Edition, 2014), 135–160.
91 Kindler, *Stalins Nomaden*, 232.
92 Ibid., 12.
93 Kindler, 'Famines and Political', 255–272; Diana Boyko u.a., ed. 'Holodomor: The Great Famine in Ukraine 1932–1933 (Warsaw and Kiev: Instytut Pamięci Narodowej, 2009), 41.
94 Applebaum, *Red Famine*, 251.
95 J. Arch Getty: 'New Sources and Old Narratives', in *Contemporary European History* 27, no. 3 (2018): 451.
96 'All sorts of talk about "hunger" in Ukraine needs to be flat out rejected'. 'First Secretary of KP USSR, S. V. Kosior to Stalin, 26.4.1932', in *Holodomor 1932–1933 rokiv v Ukraini. Dokumenty i materialy*, ed. Ruslan Pyrih (Kiev: Kievo-Mohylants'ka adademia, 2007), 128.
97 Sarah Cameron, *The Hungry Steppe: Famine, Violence, and the Making of Soviet Kazakhstan* (Ithaca, NY: Cornell University Press, 2018), 147; see also page 149. Cit. In APRK f. 141, op. 17, d. 465, l. 150 (Letter to Kazkraikom VKP[b] Roshal from the head of the SOU PP OGPU, April 1930).
98 Ibid., 162. Cit. in APRK f. 141, op. 1, d. 5827, ll. 44–47, in LMK, 4.
99 George Liber, *Total Wars and the Making of Modern Ukraine (Toronto: University of Toronto Press, 2016)*, 141.
100 Davies and Wheatcroft, *The Years of Hunger*, 424–426.
101 'Resolution of the Politburo, 18.11.1932', in *Holodomor 1932-1933 rokiv*, 392.
102 Applebaum, *Red Famine*, 196–200.
103 Heorhii Papakin, 'Blacklists as an Instrument of the Famine-Genocide of 1932–1933' in Ukraine' in Key Articles on the Holodomor Translated from Ukrainian into English, trans. Marta Olynyk, in https://holodomor.ca/wp-content/uploads/2016/05/Papakin.pdf, 6.

104 'S. Kosior and V. Chubar to I. Stalin, 29.5.1933', in *Holodomor 1932–1933 rokiv*, 852.
105 'Resolution of the Politburo, 17.9.1932', in Tragedia sovetskoi derevni. Kollektivizatsia i rakulachivanie. Dokumenty i materialy. Konets 1930–1933 (Moskva: ROSSPEN, 2000), 483–484.
106 Kindler, *Stalins Nomaden*, 238.
107 Cameron, *The Hungry Steppe*, 159.
108 Liber, *Total Wars*, 148; Plokhy, *The Gates of Europe: A History of Ukraine* (London: Penguin Books, 2015), 252. The central committee paraphrased their agricultural strategy for Kazakhstan as: 'struggle against the Baj, the struggle with rightist deviants (nationalism in this regard) and left deviations'. 'Resolution of the Politburo, 17.9.1932', 483.
109 Tanja Penter, 'From a Local *Erfahrungsgeschichte* of Holodomor to a Global History of Famines', *Contemporary European History* 27, no. 3 (2018): 446.
110 Barbara Falk, *Sowjetische Städte in der Hungersnot 1932/33. Staatliche Ernährungspolitik und städtisches Alltagsleben* (Köln: Böhlau, 2005), 309–310.
111 Cameron, *The Hungry Steppe*, 159.
112 Michael Ellman 'The 1947 Soviet Famine and the Entitlement Approach to Famines', *Cambridge Journal of Economics* 24, no. 2 (2000): 617.
113 See e.g. Jörg Ganzenmüller, *Das belagerte Leningrad. Die Stadt in den Strategien von Angreifern und Verteidigern* (Paderborn: Ferdinand Schöningh, 2005).
114 Wendy Z. Goldman and Donald A. Filtzer, eds., *Hunger and War: Food Provisioning in the Soviet Union during World War II* (Bloomington, IN: Indiana University Press, 2015).
115 Filip Salevskii, *The Soviet Occupation of Germany Hunger, Mass Violence, and the Struggle for Peace, 1945–1947* (Cambridge, NY: Cambridge University Press, 2013), 87–103.
116 Ellman, 'The 1947 Soviet Famine', 622.
117 Wendy Z. Goldman, 'Not by Bread Alone: Food, Workers, and the State' in *Hunger and war*, eds. Goldman and Filtzer, 56.
118 Ellman, 'The 1947 Soviet Famine', 619.
119 Klaus Gestwa, 'Von der Katastrophe zum Kommunismus. Die Hungersnot 1946/47 und "Stalins Großartiger Plan der Umgestaltung der Natur"', in Eisfeld et al., *Hungersnöte in Russland*, 192–193; Nicholas Ganson, *The Soviet Famine of 1946-47 in Global and Historical Perspective* (Basingstoke: Palgrave Macmillan, 2009), 96–104.
120 Gestwa, ‚Von der Katastrophe zum Kommunismus', 194.
121 Veniamin F. Zima, *Golod v SSSR 1946–1947 godov. Proiskhozhdenie i posledstviia* (Moskva: Izdat. Centr Inst. Rossijskoj Istorii, 1996), 140.
122 Gestwa, 'Von der Katastrophe zum Kommunismus', 199–204.
123 Salevskii, *The Soviet Occupation of Germany*, 102.
124 See Immo Rebitschek, 'Hungry and Different – "Otherness" in Imperial Famine Relief: 1891–92' in Kati Parppei and Bulat Rakhimzyanov, eds., *Images of Otherness in Russia, 1400–1917: At the Crossroads of History and Politics* (forthcoming 2023).

13 Fearing the Nation, Fearing for the Nation and Fearing Other Nations

Compulsory Vaccination in Twentieth-Century Germany

Malte Thießen

It is one of the dreams of modernity: to protect an entire nation through disease prevention. Vaccination is a small sting for man but a giant leap for mankind, one could say. Programs like the campaigns against smallpox in the nineteenth century not only fostered the establishment of concepts of public health but invented the 'politics of prevention'.[1] Besides that, vaccinations are an effective and cheap measure to improve public health. They do not just foster the immunity of the individual but of society as a whole.

This is where the problem begins: vaccination programs are more effective the more individuals become immunized. In public health, this concept is called 'herd immunity' or 'community immunity'. Herd immunity means that about 95 per cent of a community must be vaccinated in order to contain or eradicate diseases. Although the numbers varied during the twentieth century, herd immunity was seen as a precondition to public health from the very beginning.[2] Compulsory vaccination played a major role in guaranteeing this success. In nineteenth-century Europe, most states introduced such measures against smallpox, which resulted in the first mass vaccination. While many European states abolished compulsory vaccination at the beginning of the twentieth century,[3] Germany kept its 'compulsory vaccination act' until the 1980s.[4]

This chapter will present a brief history of compulsory vaccination throughout twentieth-century Germany. In doing so, I compare concepts and practices of biopolitics in five different systems: in imperial Germany, in the first German democracy, the Weimar Republic, in Nazi Germany and lastly in both German states after 1945, during the Cold War. Fearing the nation, fearing for the nation, and fearing other nations, I will argue, were concepts intended to improve participation in vaccination programs. Moreover, they evoked fundamental debates on the relationship between the individual and the community, the state and the family, between fears *for* the nation and fears *of* the nation: in Imperial Germany and the Weimar Republic, compulsory vaccination fanned fears of the nation as an authoritarian 'preventive state'. Fearing the nation corresponded to the idea of the state as an authority that had to take care not just of the 'people's body' (*Volkskörper*) but of the body of every individual. During the 1930s,

DOI: 10.4324/9781003161080-16

vaccination campaigns more and more appealed to the reason and solidarity of the people: from that point forward, fears for the nation and the common good shaped the propaganda. The history of compulsory vaccination thus reveals concepts of prevention on the one hand and concepts of society on the other.

Fearing the Nation: Imperial Germany and Weimar Republic

In the nineteenth century, England was said to be the 'mother country' of vaccination. Due to the success of earlier immunization programs, England introduced a strict vaccination law. Since 1867, all parents were required to have their children vaccinated against smallpox in the first three months of life.[5] Thus, England was a kind of 'role model' for Germany, which introduced compulsory vaccination in 1874.[6] The *Reichsimpfgesetz*, a national compulsory vaccination act, ordered all German children to be vaccinated against smallpox. From this point forward, the immunization of children was mandatory and parents could be punished if they refused to comply. At the end of the nineteenth century, Germany had great hopes for vaccination. A contemporary account pointed out that the value of vaccination exceeded that of purely medical progress. In fact, before the introduction of the vaccination program, up to 70,000 Germans died of smallpox every year.[7]

During these times, fears for the nation and high hopes of health improvement went together. Compulsory vaccination seemed to guarantee a strong army, an increasing economy and a growing population. In the *Reichstag*, Wilhelm Löwe of the National Liberal Party approved the introduction of compulsory vaccination: 'We are talking here about preserving an incalculable number of workers and working days, which enhance the individual's quality of life and contribute greatly to the development of society and the state. ... Therefore, the state has a duty to restrict the freedom of the individual in order to protect the general public'.[8] In this respect, the introduction of a compulsory vaccination program was a negotiation of the modern state's duties and a form of 'nation-building'.

At the beginning of the twentieth century, European countries parted ways and followed different trajectories regarding compulsory vaccination. Criticism against vaccination emerged everywhere. In 1907, a 'conscience clause' was introduced in England stipulating that no children could be immunized against the will of their parents.[9] Thereafter, critics in Germany referred to a liberalization in England whereby the government relied on voluntary participation and thus believed in the maturity of its citizens. During a debate in the *Reichstag* in 1911, a member of the Catholic party Zentrum even referred to the conscience clause as a manifestation of 'ideas about personal freedom' and as a 'concept of civilized nations'. Germans, therefore, should 'also be on the cutting-edge' and give up compulsory vaccination.[10]

In addition to these debates in parliament, England became a point of reference for organizations like the Anti-Vaccination League, an organization which facilitated cooperation between anti-vaccinationists in Germany and England who spoke out against what they called 'state brutality'. In view of such exchange relations, Martin Kirchner, one of the most committed advocates of compulsory vaccination and a member of the National Health Office (*Reichsgesundheitsamt*), spoke sourly of England as the 'Eldorado of the vaccination opponents'.[11] Defenders of compulsory vaccination rejected liberalization as an attempt, as the lawyer Melchior Stenglein put it, 'to bring the state into an undignified position ... to tolerate disobedience and defiance'. In Stenglein's opinion, compulsion was a requirement and 'without its presence the existence of the state was left without any solid basis'.[12] In this view, the introduction of voluntary vaccination or 'individual health protection' was interpreted as surrendering the state's power. Julius Götting, a parliamentary member of the National Liberal Party (*Nationalliberale Partei*), warned against any concessions to critics as a surrender of the state to the people: 'It would be a perforation, the first vibration of the solid bulwark'.[13]

These arguments fit our traditional image of Imperial Germany. In this perspective, biopolitics was not just a demonstration of the state's power. Fearing the nation, one could say, was seen as the glue that kept society together: The duty of the citizen to obey the vaccination act was even understood to be the 'physical education of the cultural man'.[14] Keeping this in mind, it is even more surprising that compulsory vaccination was kept in place after 1918. Despite the high priority attributed to fundamental rights in the Weimar constitution, children were still immunized by force and parents still went to prison if they refused. In 1926, members of the National Health Office, the Ministry of the Interior and the Ministry of Defence formed a state commission to work on the 'introduction of a conscience clause like in England'.[15] In this commission, English experiences with vaccination were translated in different ways. The opponents of forced vaccination referred to English statistics that proved a decline of smallpox, even though the vaccination was voluntary. Compulsory vaccination, hence, was a 'brutality beyond reason' and had to be abolished. Furthermore, the advocates of compulsory vaccination quoted English reports – in this case, reports that highlighted the 'great dangers of vaccination withdrawals' and the 'tragedies of vast smallpox epidemics'. In contradiction to English public health policies, hygienist Hans Reichenbach stated, 'we want to put aside the individual behind the general public'. During the debate in the commission, compulsory vaccination again represented different concepts of the state. In England – so the argument of advocates of compulsory vaccination went – the voluntary nature fits 'the psychology of the British people'. But in Germany, compulsory vaccination was a typical German commitment to state intervention – to protect the *Volkskörper*.[16] In the heated debate, once again, it became obvious that it was never just about medical issues. In the end, the debate revolved around the fundamental question of what was more important: the needs and fears of the individual or the duty of the state to protect the community.

In the Democratic Republic of Weimar, just like in Imperial Germany, compulsory vaccination still demonstrated the power of the state. In other words, fearing the nation was still seen as the foundation both of public health and of state power. How can we explain these continuities from monarchy to democracy? At first glance, it is just one more example of well-known continuities in the administration after 1918. Another reason is more intriguing: The new democracy was (in) a precarious state from the beginning.[17] In this context, compulsory vaccination served as a demonstration of the benefits of the welfare state – the improvement of public health – as well as of the power of the state to rule its citizens. In this respect, compulsory vaccination mirrored the general trend towards authoritarian state interventions in Germany's first democracy.[18] That is why the number of forced vaccinations increased even more in the Weimar Republic compared to Imperial Germany, as Alfred Grotjahn of the Social Democrats (*Sozialdemokratische Partei*) criticized in the aforementioned state commission of 1926.[19] Grotjahn was right. The number of forced vaccinations increased during the 1920s, especially in the case of parents walking in line with anti-vaccinationists. For public authorities, anti-vaccination protests did not just threaten public health in particular but the state and its institutions in general.[20]

Fearing for the Nation: The Third Reich

The 'Third Reich' is known as the most barbarous example of biopolitics: a 'dictatorship of health' that invented measures like compulsory sterilization and the 'euthanasia' or 'mercy killing' of hundreds of thousands of patients.[21] Disease control became an important issue in Nazi Germany too. It was not just seen as an important weapon for the *Wehrmacht*, the German army. Disease control was even developed into a tool for spatial planning, as Paul Weindling and others have shown.[22] Against this background, it is surprising that compulsory vaccination came under fire after 1933.

First of all, anti-vaccinationists saw their chance to establish themselves as a pressure group for questions of public health. The magazine *Gesundheitspost* of the Imperial League of German Anti-vaccinationist associations [Reichsbund Deutscher Impfgegner Vereine] celebrated the Nazi's seizure of power as a turning point in vaccination policy. Nazi leaders like Rudolf Heß and Heinrich Himmler joined the critics. Julius Streicher, publisher of the notorious anti-Semitic newspaper *Der Stürmer*, co-founded the magazine *Deutsche Volksgesundheit aus Blut und Boden* and declared '[v]accinations are a racial defilement' in the first issue.[23] Critics of compulsory vaccination were not just found in the *Gesundheitspost* and the *Deutsche Volksgesundheit*, but in the ministries also. Just one year after Hitler came to power, a state commission discussed the introduction of a conscience clause following the liberal vaccination acts in England and 'according to the English model'.[24] At the end of the discussion, plans for the conscience clause were abandoned. The English principle of voluntariness was 'so absolutely liberal and personal', declared the chairman of the commission, that it was not acceptable for Nazi Germany. Here, the concern was not so much for liberalism and individualism but rather for the welfare of all people. Compulsory vaccination thus stood for the principle: 'common good comes before personal gain', as the commission stated. In this respect, this principle shaped both the concepts of vaccination and the German model of society – the *Volksgemeinschaft* or people's community. But the most important aspect was that compulsory vaccination was seen as a precondition of an effective warfare, as a deputy of the German army explained in the state commission of 1934.

At first glance, the history of vaccination perfectly fits the picture of Nazi Germany and authoritarian public health. However, a second glance reveals surprising developments. In the mid-1930s, the *Reichsgesundheitsamt* declared a flexible approach to compulsory vaccination against smallpox: 'if a doctor here and there does not vaccinate every child, the vaccination act is not in danger, but the implementation of vaccinations is much easier. ... The popularity of the health laws, which must appear to be absolutely desirable especially in the National Socialist state, is, however, better served if unnecessary unrest in the implementation of the laws is avoided among the population'.[25] In 1940, the Ministry of the Interior put this flexible approach in an official decree and called for an 'understanding of the people's fears' of vaccination.[26] In consequence, vaccinations against smallpox from that point forward could be delayed and even suspended.

Another development in the Third Reich is also surprising: the Nazis were the first to introduce a voluntary immunization campaign. In the late 1930s, a new vaccination against diphtheria was implemented as a voluntary measure. How can we explain this kind of liberalization in a political system otherwise known as a dictatorship of health? First of all, the growing power of pharmaceutical companies comes into play. Companies like the Behringwerke in Marburg or the Anhaltisches Serum-Institut Dresden (ASID) did not just invent new vaccines but also introduced new concepts and practices of promotion. Advertisements in newspapers, radio programmes, leaflets, brochures, and even theatrical plays now promoted immunization against diphtheria. From the late 1930s onwards, Germans could also watch immunity on the big screen. Cinemas showed films about vaccination which were rated as 'educational' by state authorities due to the clarity of their depictions of the diseases to be prevented.[27]

For example, in 1942, the mayor of Munich, Karl Fiehler, praised a film about vaccination against diphtheria for depicting the danger to the German nation by showing a child suffering from diphtheria. This was precisely the crucial aspect of the increasing power of companies and their films, brochures, and commercials: it gave a face to people's fears – quite literally.

Images of sick and dying children made a more convincing argument than any laws and threats of legal punishment. Advertisements made fearing for the nation popular: they linked threats to the nation with threats to individuals. The success of this concept quickly became clear to politicians and experts of public health, as a report by Walter Bieber of the Ministry of the Interior stated a few years later: Although the question of compulsory vaccination against diphtheria 'has been asked several times' since the 1930s, Bieber emphasized, voluntariness was a recipe for success. Since the propaganda succeeded in getting 'up to 99 per cent of the children ... to appear at the vaccination appointments, compulsory measures were unnecessary. Bieber concluded assuredly: 'So why use coercion if it works voluntarily?'[28] In other words, the more vaccination became voluntary, the more anxieties increased, which ultimately persuaded the German population to participate. This is why Nazi Germany can be held accountable for changes made to the societal conception of immunity, from fears *of* the nation to fears *for* the nation – and ultimately for oneself'.

Fearing Other Nations: The Federal Republic and the GDR

Biopolitics in East and West Germany are well known when it comes to mirroring Cold War politics. Following the studies of Sigrid Stöckel, Ulla Walter, Jeanette Madarasz and many others, East Germany established a totalitarian public health system to control all Germans from birth until death. In this view, the prevention state is best exemplified by the GDR.[29] Many studies have shown that, on the other side of the Iron Curtain, the West experienced a liberalization of public health and the birth of the 'preventive self' – an individualistic approach to healthcare.[30] At first glance, this description also applies to vaccination. In West Germany, all immunization programs became voluntary – with the exception of vaccination against smallpox. In the East, after a few years of voluntariness, almost all immunization became compulsory during the 1950s and 1960s: vaccination acts ordered mass vaccinations against diphtheria, poliomyelitis, tetanus, pertussis and many more.

At this point, I will turn to biopolitics during the Cold War. In East Germany, healthcare and prevention immediately became the basis for the transformation of human beings towards a 'new socialist personality' and a 'new Germany'. In this perspective, prevention was not just a measure for healthcare, but a founding myth for the state. The saying 'socialism is the best prophylaxis' – and vice versa – became popular everywhere from the late 1940s onward.[31] This entanglement of prevention and social order transformed immunization into a test for socialism. From this point, forward herd immunity was seen as proof of the success of socialism.

The Cold War enforced such entanglements of vaccination and social order. From the 1960s on, the GDR continued to criticize the West for its regressive vaccination program. In this view, the higher herd immunity in the East proved to be an example of a better society, as compulsory vaccination against poliomyelitis clearly shows. Given the lack of polio vaccines in West Germany at the beginning of the 1960s, the East German Ministry of Health offered the West a kind of development aid. In a decree announced in 1961, West Germans who were visiting the GDR could be 'immunized before re-entering the epidemic areas'.[32] Epidemic areas here referred to the West. The future head of the GDR, Willi Stoph, even sent a telegram to West German Chancellor Konrad Adenauer in 1961 with an attractive offer: the shockingly high number of polio cases in the Federal Republic resulted in the GDR promise to make 'three million doses of vaccine available immediately', since the GDR was itself 'free from the dangerous disease', as the telegram to Adenauer stressed.[33]

The fact that this offer was turned down by Adenauer immediately found great resonance in Western media and was met with criticism by West Germans, who blamed the chancellor for downplaying common threats. A disappointed German citizen found it 'completely incomprehensible' that federal ministries 'refuse[d] the GDR's offer of help ... even ignore[d] it. Isn't the health of countless people sacrificed to political resentment?'[34] A letter to the editor of the newspaper *Bonner Generalanzeiger* put it even more sharply: 'People fall ill and die because our authorities are apparently not prepared for this case, because they reject an effective remedy for obvious political reasons and prefer to let people die. Who is playing with people's lives for political reasons?'[35] In a letter to the West German Ministry of Health, a paediatrician summarized the lag in polio vaccinations as an 'inexcusable embarrassment of the West German health system'.[36]

Vaccinations thus opened a field where the West and the East fought for a better model of society. It is ironic that this competition was even strengthened by transnational cooperation. During the Cold War, the World Health Organization (WHO) especially served as a forum for sharing experiences and, therefore, as an agency of competition.[37] The WHO not only coordinated international vaccination programs, especially in Africa and Asia, but it also promoted an international exchange of experiences, even across the Iron Curtain. One famous example for the success – and the tension between East and West – of transnational vaccination campaigns is the Smallpox Eradication Programme (SEP) from the 1960s and 1970s.[38] International cooperation often leads to confrontation. The WHO constantly circulated reports about public health in Europe beginning in the late 1950s and thus fulfilled a kind of messenger role and authentication function for socialist success stories. In 1960, the East German State Academy for Social Hygiene (*Staatliche Akademie für Sozialhygiene*) set up a special Committee for the Scientific and Practical Evaluation of WHO Activities in the GDR. The committee's objective was clearly defined, it was to make WHO members 'more familiar with the successes of the GDR in the field of health care'.[39] It is hardly surprising that vaccination programmes served this objective particularly well. Vaccination programmes were a core objective of the WHO, thus, their circulars demonstrated the successes of the GDR from a quasi-neutral perspective. East Germany even supplied the WHO with extensive reports and statistics about vaccination campaigns, which were intended to prove the success of socialism. One of the reasons why all vaccinations became compulsory in East Germany is that if vaccinations demonstrated the making of a new society and the success of socialism, the programmes had to be successful at all costs.

Beginning in the 1970s, the demand for herd immunity could no longer be enforced, even in the East. In the GDR, one reason for this centred around the criticism of compulsory vaccination. Parents demanded increasing participation in questions of health and freedom of choice. In this view, the concept of compulsory vaccination and *fearing the nation* stood in opposition to concepts of a new socialist personality and eventually became old-fashioned.[40]

Another reason for the liberalization of biopolitics corresponded to a kind of fatigue and reluctance to be vaccinated that was evident throughout Europe. Ironically, the success of vaccinations reduced the fear of disease and, therefore, the interest in immunity. This can be characterized as the 'prevention paradox'. In 1972, a brochure from the East German ministry of health articulated this prevention paradox as a joke:

An old man is spreading white powder at the famous Alexanderplatz in East Berlin.

A YOUNG MAN COMES BY: 'What are you doing?'

THE OLD MAN ANSWERS: 'I am spreading white powder against lions and elephants.'

THE YOUNG MAN WONDERS: 'But there are no lions and elephants anywhere.'

THE OLD MAN ANSWERS: 'Of course not, because I have been spreading white powder for years.'[41]

This joke indicates a fundamental change in East Germany's vaccination program, namely the transition from the compulsion to persuasion. Even though the compulsory acts against smallpox, diphtheria, poliomyelitis, tuberculosis, measles, mumps and rubella officially were never abandoned, the ministry of health now tried to persuade rather than force the German population: advertisements, brochures and leaflets, were meant to convince people of voluntary vaccination. In this view, East and West resembled each other to an increasing degree. Vaccination programs in East Germany used Western concepts and even copied Western advertising techniques.[42]

The exchanges between East and West became even more important after the late 1970s: a lack of vaccines in East Germany, especially a lack of the new triple or quadruple vaccines, endangered the concept of herd immunity. Due to a lack of resources, state companies were no longer able to deliver the required quantities (nor quality) of vaccines. In the 1980s, the lack of vaccines against measles led to a higher disease rate than in the period before the introduction of compulsory vaccination. Worse still, more than half of those affected had previously been vaccinated – a clear sign of the poor quality of the vaccines.[43] The solution to this problem was a masterpiece of Marxist dialectic. On the one hand, the East German ministry of health officially claimed supremacy of socialism in its competition with the West, on the other hand, East Germany secretly imported vaccines from Western companies like Pasteur, SmithKline and even from its greatest enemy, the West-German Behringwerke. Another solution to these limitations of biopolitics was ignorance: although many doctors criticized the lack of vaccines and reported angry discussions with frightened parents, the ministry of health continuously promoted success stories of vaccination coverage of up to 99 per cent.

Before I conclude, I will take a brief look at West Germany. Here, compulsory vaccination against smallpox was highly controversial from the 1950s on, especially with reference to *Grundgesetz*, the new constitution. Despite – or maybe because of – fierce debates on the relationship between state intervention and fundamental rights, the Federal Health Office stood for a rather authoritarian means of vaccination and rejected the priority of fundamental rights. As stated in 1957: 'Even if one makes far-reaching concessions to the personal freedom and self-determination of the citizen, it must be pointed out that personal freedom has a limit where vital interests of the general public prevail'.[44]

A few years later, those concepts changed fundamentally. In an interview with German television in 1966, President of the Federal Health Office Werner Anders pleaded for an end to compulsory vaccination: 'What would happen if compulsory vaccination was abandoned in Germany? In my opinion, it is a question of the maturity of the population. Perhaps the development in general can already be identified that we can overcome vaccine fatigue by a meaningful education of the population rather than by coercion'.[45] The change in biopolitics since the late 1950s is all the more surprising if you put Anders' sentences into context. Since 1958, several West German cities saw the return of smallpox. For example, tourists and businessmen brought smallpox to the cities of Heidelberg (1958), Ansbach (1961), Düsseldorf (1961), Monschau (near the City of Aachen) (1962), Hannover (1967 and again in 1972) and Meschede (1970). The 'comeback of the plagues', as one magazine stated in 1962,[46] raised fears about other nations, especially those in Africa and Asia. Fears about other nations spread in newspapers, brochures, broadcasts and commercials. In 1958, the Süddeutscher Rundfunk (a broadcasting service for Baden-Württemberg) reminded its listeners of the importance of vaccination in the age of globalization: 'In Africa and India, smallpox occurs in large numbers every year. It can be transmitted at any time by people who come to Europe from there. And if practically everyone [in West Germany] had not been vaccinated, the disease would be spreading like wildfire in our country too'.[47] The Hessian department of the interior summed up this developing dangerous situation

Figure 13.1 The Federal Republic of Germany in the crosshairs of global threats. Bundesarchiv Koblenz, B 142/44, Brochure, 'Den Kopf in den Sand stecken' (Burying your head in the sand), 1956.

in a particularly vivid way in one of its brochures: a coloured smallpox sufferer, an African child, stood out in the middle of the picture as a 'danger', while from the edges of the picture several train, ship and airplane connections from Africa, America and Asia aimed at the danger area: the Federal Republic of Germany (Figure 13.1). 'Our modern means of transportation, which shrink worldwide distances dramatically, can bring us this disease back any time in a few days, even hours. The most effective weapon against this is the smallpox vaccination'.[48]

Fears about other nations were very effective. After a long period of disinterest, smallpox was suddenly present again and so was the popularity of vaccinations. Experts literally reported a run on health offices to get immunized against smallpox. Against this backdrop, compulsory measures seemed more and more unnecessary. The greater the fear, experts stated, the less coercion was needed. Despite the official continuity of compulsory vaccination against smallpox – the compulsory vaccination act was suspended in West Germany in the late 1970s – the West, like the East, changed from coercion to persuasion. In the West, persuasion was flanked by advertising campaigns that linked global threats to everyday life: migration, trade and tourism were painted as everyday threats to everyone. The preventive self, one could say, was born out of the fear of other nations in times of globalization.

Conclusion

The history of compulsory vaccination is not just a history of public health but a history of social orders. Compulsory vaccination raised questions about the power of the state and the needs of the individual, on the relationship between the individual and the common good, and on the maturity of the people and the practices of participation. Moreover, the concept of herd immunity shed light on the state of society; it was understood as an indicator for a common sense of duty and responsibility. By comparing five different political systems, the history of compulsory vaccination offers new insights on concepts of society in general. The Third Reich, for example, was not only a health dictatorship. Due to the rise of pharmaceutical companies, it was a system that successfully promoted participation – at least more than its democratic predecessor, the Weimar Republic. East Germany after 1945, as a second example, was also more than a totalitarian health system. The interplay of compulsion and persuasion, of socialist propaganda and flexible practices in everyday life, reveals more similarities to West Germany than one would assume.

Last but not least, the history of compulsory vaccination reveals continuities that still exist until today. In recent years, German secretaries of health again plead for the introduction of compulsory vaccination, especially against measles, but also against diphtheria and polio. It is evident when examining German news since 2013 that history is repeating itself around the topic of introducing compulsory vaccinations against measles. Again, one can read about a strong state fighting not just vaccination fatigue but the defiance of the people.[49] The history of compulsory vaccination, therefore, makes us immune to the simplified success stories of the modern age. It also questions narratives of a continuous liberalization of public health. It draws our attention to the tense and ambivalent relationship between the state and its citizens, between safety and freedom, and between us and the big, wide world.

Notes

1 Martin Woollacott, 'The Politics of Prevention', in *The Politics of Risk Society*, ed. Jane Franklin (Oxford: Polity Press, 1998), 120–123; Dorothy Porter and Roy Porter, 'The Politics of Prevention: Anti-Vaccinationism and Public Health in Nineteenth-century England', *Medical History* 32 (1988): 231–251.

2 Andrew W. Artenstein, ed., *Vaccines: A Biography* (New York: Springer, 2010).

3 Nadja Durbach, *Bodily Matters: The Anti-Vaccination Movement in England, 1853–1907* (Durham: Duke University Press, 2005); Karen L. Walloch, *'A Hot Bed of the Anti-vaccine Heresy': Opposition to Compulsory Vaccination in Boston and Cambridge, 1890–1905* (PhD diss., University of Wisconsin-Madison, 2007); James K. Colgrove, *The State of Immunity: The Politics of Vaccination in Twentieth-Century America* (Berkeley, CA: University of California Press, 2006).

4 Malte Thießen, 'Risk as a Resource: On the Interplay between Risks, Vaccinations and Welfare States in Nineteenth- and Twentieth-Century Germany', *Historical Social Research* 41 (2016): 70–90.

5 Naomi Williams, 'The Implementation of Compulsory Health Legislation: Infant Smallpox Vaccination in England and Wales, 1840–1890', *Journal of Historical Geography* 20 (1994): 396–412.

6 Ernest P. Hennock, 'Vaccination Policy against Smallpox, 1835–1914: A Comparison of England with Prussia and Imperial Germany', *Social History of Medicine* 11 (1998): 49–71.
7 Andreas-Holger Maehle, 'Präventivmedizin als wissenschaftliches und gesellschaftliches Problem: Der Streit über das Reichsimpfgesetz von 1874', *Medizin, Gesellschaft und Geschichte* 9 (1990): 127–148.
8 Protokolle Deutscher Reichstag, 18.02.1874, 104.
9 Durbach, *Bodily Matters.*
10 Protokolle Deutscher Reichstag, 30.01.1911, 4276.
11 Protokolle Deutscher Reichstag, 28.04.1914, 8307.
12 Melchior Stenglein, *Die strafrechtlichen Nebengesetze des deutschen Reiches* (Berlin: Otto Liebmann, 1903).
13 Protokolle Deutscher Reichstag, 28.04.1914, 8315.
14 Jakob Laurenz-Sonderegger, *Gesundheit ist Lebensglück. Gedanken des Volksgesundheitslehrers für Schule und Haus* (Berlin: Springer, 1930).
15 *Über die Einfügung einer Gewissensklausel in das Reichsimpfgesetz. Bericht über Sitzung des Landesgesundheitsrats vom 19. Oktober 1925* (Berlin: Richard Schoetz, 1926).
16 *Über die Einfügung*, 39, 43, 62, 85, 94–95.
17 Ursula Büttner, *Weimar. Die überforderte Republik* (Stuttgart: Klett-Cotta, 2008).
18 Andreas Wirsching, *Die Weimarer Republik. Politik und Gesellschaft* (München: Oldenbourg, 2008), 24.
19 *Über die Einfügung*, 94–95.
20 Malte Thießen, *Immunisierte Gesellschaft. Impfen in Deutschland im 19. und 20. Jahrhundert* (Göttingen: Vandenhoeck & Ruprecht, 2017), 118–123.
21 Paul Weindling, *Health, Race, and German Politics between National Unification and Nazism, 1870–1945* (Cambridge: Cambridge University Press, 1989); Michael Burleigh, *Death and Deliverance: Euthanasia in Germany c.1900–1945* (Cambridge: Cambridge University Press, 1994); Gisela Bock, 'Nazi Sterilization and Reproductive Policies', in *Deadly Medicine: Creating the Master Race*, eds. Dieter Kuntz and Susan Bachrach (Chapel Hill: University of North Carolina Press, 2004), 61–87.
22 Paul Weindling, *Epidemics and Genocide in Eastern Europe, 1890–1945* (Oxford: Oxford University Press, 2000).
23 Thießen, *Immunisierte Gesellschaft*, 144–145.
24 *Beratung einer beabsichtigten reichgesetzlichen Aenderung des Impfgesetzes vom 8. April 1874 durch Einfügung einer Gewissensklausel nach englischem Muster* (Berlin: Richard Schoetz, 1934).
25 Bundesarchiv Berlin, R 1501/3647, Letter of Reichsgesundheitsamt to the Ministry of the Interior, 12.11.1935.
26 *Öffentlicher Gesundheitsdienst* 6 (1940/41), 218.
27 Thießen, *Immunisierte Gesellschaft*, 134–145.
28 Walter Bieber, 'Seuchenbekämpfung im Kriege', *Der Öffentliche Gesundheitsdienst* 6 (1940/41): 65–70, fn. 69.
29 Jens-Uwe Niehoff and Thorsten Röding, 'Steuerung und Regulierung von Prävention in der Deutschen Demokratischen Republik', in *Prävention und Prophylaxe. Theorie und Praxis eines gesundheitspolitischen Grundmotivs in zwei deutschen Staaten*, eds. Thomas Elkeles, Jens-Uwe Niehoff and Frank Schneider (Berlin: WZB/edition sigma, 1991), 159–167; Udo Schagen, 'Aufbau einer neuen Versorgungsstruktur: Gesundheitsschutz als Leitkonzept. Historische Grundlagen für das Präventionskonzept der Sowjetischen

Besatzungszone und der frühen DDR', in *Prävention im 20. Jahrhundert. Historische Grundlagen und aktuelle Entwicklungen in Deutschland*, eds. Sigrid Stöckel and Ulla Walter (Weinheim: Juventa, 2002), 165–177.

30 Martin Lengwiler and Jeanette Madarász, 'Präventionsgeschichte als Kulturgeschichte der Gesundheitspolitik', in *Das präventive Selbst. Eine Kulturgeschichte moderner Gesundheitspolitik*, eds. Martin Lengwiler and Jeanette Madarász (Bielefeld: Transcript, 2010), 11–28.

31 Thießen, *Immunisierte Gesellschaft*, 303–307.

32 Bundesarchiv Berlin, DQ 1/12279, Circular of the East German Ministry of Health, 18.07.1961.

33 Bundesarchiv Koblenz, B 142/55, Report for Secretary of State, 01.07.1961.

34 Bundesarchiv Koblenz, B 142/55, Letter to Ministry of Health, 17.11.1961.

35 Bonner General-Anzeiger, Zone gegen Kinderlähmung immun?, 03.08.1961.

36 Bundesarchiv Koblenz, B 142/1897, Letter of a paediatrician from Karlsruhe to Ministry of Health, 20.01.1962.

37 Kelley Lee, *The World Health Organization (WHO)* (London: Routledge, 2009); Thomas Zimmer, *Welt ohne Krankheit. Geschichte der internationalen Gesundheitspolitik 1940–1970* (Göttingen: Wallstein, 2017), 128–166.

38 Erez Manela, 'A Pox on Your Narrative: Writing Disease Control into Cold War History', *Diplomatic History* 34 (2010): 299–323.

39 Bundesarchiv Berlin, DQ 1/2438, Resolution 'WHO-Komitee der DDR', 09.11.1960.

40 Thießen, *Immunisierte Gesellschaft*, 342–349.

41 Dolf Künzel, *Muss das viele Impfen sein?* (Berlin/Ost: VEB Verlag Volk und Gesundheit, 1972), 10.

42 Henning Tümmers has pointed out the same for the case of prevention campaigns against AIDS/HIV in the 1980s: East Germany even copied the famous West German slogan 'Gib AIDS keine Chance' (Don't give AIDS a chance.). Henning Tümmers, 'Gib AIDS keine Chance. Eine Präventionsbotschaft in zwei deutschen Staaten', *Zeithistorische Forschungen* 10 (2013): 491–501.

43 BAB, DQ 1/13093, East German Ministry of Health, Annual Report 1984.

44 Bundesarchiv Koblenz, B 189/14107, Report of the Bundesgesundheitsamt, 1957, 34.

45 Bundesarchiv Koblenz, B 189/14107, Letter of Anders to Federal Ministry of Health on Interview, 05.08.1966.

46 Welt, Die unbekannte Kontaktperson – ein Gespenst geht um, 04.02.1970; Welt am Sonntag, Pocken – die Strafe Gottes in der Geschichte, 08.02.1970.

47 Behring-Archiv Marburg, 09-15/1612, Script of a broadcast of Süddeutscher Rundfunk, 11.05.1958.

48 Bundesarchiv Koblenz, B 142/44, Brochure, 'Den Kopf in den Sand stecken' (Burying your head in the sand), 1956.

49 Daniel Bahr; 'Impfpflicht hatte bei Pocken Erfolg', *Frankfurter Allgemeine Sonntagszeitung*, 21 July 2013; 'Wie sinnvoll ist ein Impfzwang?', *Süddeutsche Zeitung*, 24 February 2015; 'Gröhe droht mit Impfzwang', *Frankfurter Allgemeine Zeitung*, 12 April 2015.

Contributors

Natalia Aleksiun is a Professor of Modern Jewish History at Touro College, Graduate School of Jewish Studies, New York. She specializes in the history of modern Eastern European Jewry and has written extensively on the history of the Jewish intelligentsia in East Central Europe and the history of medicine and of the Holocaust.

Herwig Czech is a Professor of the History of Medicine at the Medical University of Vienna and co-director of the project 'Brain Research at Institutes of the Kaiser Wilhelm Society in the Context of National Socialist Crimes'. He has published widely on medicine, race hygiene and biopolitics under National Socialism.

Corina Doboş is a Researcher at the University of Bucharest and P.I. of the project 'Crafting Demographic Knowledge in the 20th Century: Population and Development in an Eastern European Periphery' (DEMOECRO). Her research focuses on biopolitics, the history of science, twentieth-century population theories and policies and expert knowledge formation.

Ivana Dobrivojević Tomić is a Research Fellow at the Institute of Contemporary History in Belgrade. Her research interests include the political and social history of interwar Yugoslavia and ordinary life under communism. She is currently writing *Between Ideology and Pop Culture: The Life of Youth in Socialist Yugoslavia (1945–1965)*.

Wannes Dupont is an Assistant Professor of Humanities (History) at Yale-NUS College. His research concerns the history of sexuality and homosexuality, contraception and the intersections of biopolitics and religion. He is currently writing a comparative history of homosexuality in Western Europe and conducting research on the globalization of sexuality.

Agata Ignaciuk is an Assistant Professor at the Department of the History of Science, University of Granada, Spain. Between 2017 and 2019, she was a Marie Skłodowska Curie Actions COFUND Research Fellow at the University of Warsaw's Institute of Ethnology and Cultural Anthropology in Poland. Her research focuses on the history of reproductive health and rights in Catholic countries from a comparative and transnational perspective.

Friederike Kind-Kovács is a Senior Researcher at the Hannah Arendt Institute for Totalitarianism Studies at TU Dresden and a Senior Lecturer at Regensburg University. She is the author of *Budapest's Children: Humanitarian Relief in the Aftermath of the Great War* (2021).

Barbara Klich-Kluczewska is an Associate Professor at the Department of History at the Jagiellonian University in Cracow. Her research focuses on the history of Polish post-war society from a cultural perspective, particularly the history of family and private life. She published *Taboo, Family and Communism in Poland, 1956–1989* (2021).

Łukasz Mieszkowski is a PhD candidate at the Institute of History of the Polish Academy of Sciences with his dissertation, 'Dragons and Lice: The Plague in Poland 1918–1922'. Mieszkowski is an active visual artist. He designed the new museum building and commemoration for the victims of the Sobibór death facility.

Joachim von Puttkamer is Director of the Imre Kertész Kolleg, Jena at the Friedrich Schiller University of Jena. His research focuses on nationalism and statehood in modern Central and Eastern Europe. He is co-editor of *The Routledge History Handbook of Central and Eastern Europe in the Twentieth Century.*

Jakub Rákosník teaches modern social and economic history at Charles University in Prague. He has published widely on the history of social politics in Czechoslovakia in the twentieth century. He is co-editor of *War Employment and Social Policies in the Protectorate of Bohemia and Moravia 1939–1945* (Prague 2018).

Immo Rebitschek is an Assistant Professor at the Department for Eastern European History at the Friedrich Schiller University, Jena. He has published widely on the history of the Soviet procuracy in Stalinist Russia and is currently focusing his research on the history of famine relief in the late Russian Empire.

Radka Šustrová is an Assistant Professor at the Department of Economic and Social History at Charles University, Prague. Her research focuses on family policy, social policy and nationalism in twentieth-century Czechoslovakia. She is co-editor of *War Employment and Social Policies in the Protectorate of Bohemia and Moravia 1939–1945* (Prague 2018).

Ewelina Szpak is an Associate Professor at the Institute of History Polish Academy of Sciences. She specializes in the social and cultural history of the Polish People's Republic, the history of mentalities and the social history of medicine. She has published on the socio-cultural changes of the Polish countryside under communism. Her current project focuses on the social perception of cancer in post-war Poland.

Malte Thießen is a Professor of Modern and Contemporary History at the University of Münster. His research interests span the history of health, healthcare, vaccination, memory culture and the politics of history of National Socialism and the social and cultural history of the nineteenth and twentieth centuries.

Index

For Product Safety Concerns and Information please contact our EU representative GPSR@taylorandfrancis.com
Taylor & Francis Verlag GmbH, Kaufingerstraße 24, 80331 München, Germany

www.ingramcontent.com/pod-product-compliance
Ingram Content Group UK Ltd.
Pitfield, Milton Keynes, MK11 3LW, UK
UKHW020143200926
475702UK00005B/885
* 9 7 8 0 3 6 7 7 5 1 2 3 4 *